D0546414

# Re-Centering

*Syracuse Studies on Peace and Conflict Resolution*
Louis Kriesberg, *Series Editor*

# Re-Centering

## Culture and Knowledge
## in Conflict Resolution Practice

*Edited by* Mary Adams Trujillo, S.Y. Bowland,
Linda James Myers, Phillip M. Richards, *and* Beth Roy

Through the Auspices of the Practitioners Research
and Scholarship Institute (PRASI)

SYRACUSE UNIVERSITY PRESS

With gratitude to the William and Flora Hewlett Foundation
and to the JAMS Foundation for their support.

For a listing of books published and distributed by Syracuse University Press,
visit our Web site at SyracuseUniversityPress.syr.edu.

ISBN-13: 978-0-8156-3187-3 (cl.)
ISBN-13: 978-0-8156-3162-0 (pbk.)

**Library of Congress Cataloging-in-Publication Data**

Re-centering culture and knowledge in conflict resolution practice / edited by
Mary Adams Trujillo . . . [et al.]. — 1st ed.
p. cm. — (Syracuse studies on peace and conflict resolution)
Includes bibliographical references and index.
ISBN 978-0-8156-3187-3 (cloth : alk. paper) — ISBN 978-0-8156-3162-0
(pbk. : alk. paper)   1. Conflict management — Cross-cultural studies.
I. Trujillo, Mary Adams.
HM716.R43 2008
303.6'9—dc22                                              2008007923

*Manufactured in the United States of America*

# Contents

# Figure and Tables

# Preface

*Introducing PRASI*

On a chilly February morning in Chicago, in a warm and hospitable Hyde Park graystone, S. Y. Bowland, Linda James Myers, Phillip M. Richards, Beth Roy, and Mary Adams Trujillo gathered to create this volume. Our roads to the meeting were varied, reflecting diverse relationships with writing, conflict resolution, research, and activism.

That we met in common purpose, however, was abundantly clear. The Chicago discussion culminated five years of work by the Practitioners Research and Scholarship Institute. PRASI, as the Institute is informally known, began in 2000 as a response to troubled experiences involving issues of race and diversity in the conflict resolution world.

Conflict resolution is a field that strives for openness to varying points of view. Resolving conflicts and making decisions collaboratively depend on a willingness to hear all sides and weigh all perspectives. Yet many practitioners and students have a different experience of the field as it applies to themselves. A sizeable number of people of color feel largely invisible in the accepted training modalities and literature, perceiving their experience and insights to lie outside the boundaries of what is defined as pertinent knowledge. Just as in many other arenas of American life, so too in the world of conflict resolution a monocultural dynamic has set in, the domination of a narrowly construed understanding of both practice and theory.

At PRASI's inception, what that meant in practice was an interlocking set of difficulties. More people of color were being hired to teach in university-based conflict resolution programs, in part to promote diversity among the student bodies. But they experienced the frustration of confronting a poverty of materials that related to the lives and experiences of the students. Moreover, many of the new recruits, although experienced as informal peacemakers in their home communities, were new to the structures of postgraduate degree programs. The rules and structures of the university alienated them, suggesting that they were not welcome but instead must prove themselves on someone else's terms and in ways that distorted their own wisdom and intellect.

Meanwhile, other practitioners were debating basic assumptions: that a third-party intervener could and should be neutral; that power imbalances among disputants rooted in social structures of inequality could be righted through collaborative process; that conflict interveners could and should mediate process not content, suggesting an absence of power relationship between "professional" and clients; that "empowerment" was a conflict intervener's to endow. Concerned not only with what they perceived to be increasing exclusion of practitioners and scholars of color, but also with an absence of critical dialogue about questions of social justice, these practitioners and scholars sought a deepening of perspectives at the center of the pool of shared knowledge. A rich alliance was suggested between white conflict resolvers discomfited by the assumptions of the "insiders," and those whose consignment to the "outside" gave them a clearer view "inside" the field.

With support from a rapidly growing circle of practitioners and academics of all races, and with substantial funding by the Flora and William Hewlett Foundation, PRASI was born to address issues such as these.

PROCESS AND PROGRESS

The founders had learned through their own organizational experience one important lesson: if you want to create an institution reflecting diversity along cultural, racial, intellectual, and many other lines, you need to start out with a group of founders who are just that diverse. Slowly, over the course of many conversations and many meetings, a network grew, multiracial, enthusiastic, talented, and knowledgeable. A common perception was quickly blown: "Where are the people of color in the field? Why aren't they joining our ranks?" many white practitioners had been asking for years. PRASI drew dozens of experienced mediators and arbitrators and educators and peacemakers, attracted not only to the ideas the Institute represented but even more to the opportunity to network with others of like experience.

Two projects formed the core work of PRASI at the beginning: to train and support practitioners, especially practitioners of color, to write about their experience and insights; and to collect literature about conflict resolution in communities of color in a volume that would be equally useable by students, researchers, and practitioners: this anthology.

Through retreats and trainings, conference presentations and networking, the work of stimulating new writing has been rich and fruitful. The anthology changed course, becoming a mixture of existing writing and new papers, inspired by the process of creating the volume itself.

PRASI continues today as a loose and vital network of practitioners, multicultural in the truest sense of that world: a place where different worldviews challenge and inform each other, giving rise to new relationships and new literature.

# Acknowledgments

Like most birthing processes, writing is something few people can do alone. Some of the finest minds on the planet have collaborated to bring this anthology from conception to fruition.

We are indebted to every participant in the telephone seminars, writing retreats, and workshops and to every reader of the manuscript. Your enthusiastic comments energized us and each other. We thank you for using the power of your words to build writing communities.

Even though this project represents the efforts of many, there are some individuals whose invaluable contributions nurtured this vision of a literature that would join conflict resolution research and practice. They include Michelle Armster, Linda Baron, Marge Baker, Sharon Perkins Bailey, Millie Carvalho, Ladan Cockshut, Aron DiBacco, Nan and Evan Freund (the most hospitable people in Chicago), William Jones, Lou Kriesberg, Kumarian Press, Debbie Lewites, Cynthia Luna, Rick Rapfogel, and Willie (Chuck) Wright.

We are deeply grateful for the financial support of the William and Flora Hewlett Foundation and for the practical guidance and support of Steve Toben and Terry Amsler. We also thank the JAMS Foundation for their generosity.

Finally, we offer thanks to countless practitioners and scholars, named and unnamed, whose efforts have enriched and broadened the field of conflict resolution. We build on your foundation.

As editors, this collaborative process has enabled us, and sometimes forced us, to grow immensely as we have shared our hearts and wisdom and work.

On a personal note, we offer the following personal thank-yous:

Mary: I thank God and my family—Amber, Lara, Gabriela, Anika, Siembra, and Jonas Chaney for staying excited throughout.

Beth: I'm grateful to my family (and most especially to my partner Mariah Breeding) for their generosity in supporting me, picking up the slack, and forgiving my preoccupation throughout the years of conferences and conversations that formed the communication backbone of the anthology.

S.Y.: I would like to acknowledge my family—James Gleason Jr. and especially my children James and Justus—for their understanding and sometimes ingenious ways of engaging me when I was present and absent from their sight. It is in this collaboration I have hope for a different, peaceful, and just future.

Linda: Special thanks to my family, in particular to my mother, Fay Brown James, for the time she sacrificed and honor she deserves. To my fellow editors for their hard work and the joy of our engagement, I say much love.

Phil: I would like to thank my fellow editors for allowing me, an outsider to the field, to participate in this project. They listened to my critiques even while I was introducing myself to the materials in the collection. They showed extraordinary generosity of spirit, and I am indebted to them.

# Contributors

**Mary Adams Trujillo** received her Ph.D. in communication studies from Northwestern University in 2004. Her professional experience has ranged from mental health practitioner to higher education administrator, from elementary education to her current work as professor of intercultural communication and conflict transformation at North Park University in Chicago.

**Damien Basey, Valarie Carey, Andrew Chang, Angel Coleman,** and **Katt Hoban** are graduates of University of California at Berkeley. While students in Beth Roy's course on conflict resolution, they conducted a collaborative research project into forms of structural racism that resulted in the paper included in this volume. Andrew and Katt were founding members of the Conflict Resolution and Transformation Center, a groundbreaking peer mediation and training group on the Berkeley campus, organized and operated by students.

**Hasshan Batts** is an experienced life coach, personal consultant, mediator, facilitator, and professor who is recognized nationally for his dedication and contribution to the fields of peacemaking, conflict resolution, trauma-sensitive mental health services, and social justice. In addition, he is the principal consultant for Bonafide Life-Enhancement Services, director of Children Services for NHS Human Services of Lehigh Valley, past associate director of Southmountain Children and Family Services, past co-director of the Conflict Resolution Center and maintains a leadership role on numerous local, regional, and national Boards. Hasshan brings a broad range of experience working in the public sector with individuals, families, schools, grass-roots organizations, private agencies, and diverse communities to address effective conflict management, cultural competence, personal and organizational communication, program development, and evaluation and strategic planning.

**Valerie Batts,** Ph.D., is executive director and cofounder of Visions, Inc. She leads the consultation and training components of the company. Author of *Modern Racism: New Melody for the Same Old Tune,* she is the originator of the Visions consultation and training model and experiential workshops. Dr. Batts earned her doctorate in clinical psychology from Duke University. As a licensed clinical psychologist, she provides consultation and training to human service providers, educators, and managers in a variety of areas. Working both nationally and internationally, Dr. Batts works with people and with organizations to develop and maintain environments that support, respect, and appreciate similarities and differences.

**S.Y. (Sandra) Bowland** was born and raised in Harlem and earned her B.A. in Social Relations from Colgate University and her J.D. from the National Law Center at George Washington University. S.Y. is a mother who is dedicated to the survival of African American males, the study of conflicts, people, and culture, as a conflict resolution practitioner and an educator. She is committed to understanding conflict resolution processes and their impact specifically on Black and multicultural communities.

**Mariah Breeding,** Ph.D., does consultation and counseling in the San Francisco Bay area. For many years she worked primarily in the substance abuse field, helping individuals and groups identify and resolve issues of personal and structural violence and oppression as part of the recovery process. Dr. Breeding served as clinical coordinator of the New Bridge Foundation and co-director of day treatment at a regional Kaiser Permanente Chemical Dependency Recovery Program. As part of a lifelong involvement in community activism, she helped found the first queer political center in Northern New England. Enlarging upon her doctoral research, she is currently finishing a book about violence and domination in childhood sibling relationships.

**Roberto M. Chené** has a B.A. in philosophy and an M.A. in pastoral theology. He has done postgraduate work in social welfare policy at Brandeis University. He is the director of the Center for Intercultural Leadership Training and Conflict Resolution in Albuquerque. He is deeply rooted in the Chicano-Latino community and has taught classes on cross-cultural education and Latinos and public policy at the University of New Mexico. He consults with many organizations in multicultural organizational development and is currently working with two major religious organizations as they initiate programs to eliminate institutionalized racism. He has conducted trainings, presentations, and lectures throughout the United States and has worked in Mexico and South Africa. Roberto is motivated by his deep commitment to transform relationships of dominance into relationships based on equality. He is currently working on a book of reflections and lessons gleaned from his more than thirty years of practice in the building of multicultural community.

**Ted Coronel** graduated from the University of Washington with B.A. degrees in history and international studies. He is actively involved with the King County Dispute Resolution Center. He serves as a member of the Diversity Committee within the organization and is establishing a new position as a mentor conciliator to assist the new volunteers with the center. He has taken basic mediation training through the City of Bellevue's Neighborhood Mediation Program. Ted was a PRASI Fellow in 2003–4. He also manages a restaurant, brewery, and bar in Seattle.

**Cherise D. Hairston** has been involved in the field of conflict resolution for the past ten years as a mediator and graduate student. She is currently a Ph.D. candidate at Nova Southeastern University, School of Humanities and Social Sciences, in the Department of Conflict Analysis and Resolution. She lives in Dayton, Ohio.

**Ray Leal** is a faculty member in the Department of Criminal Justice and Criminology at St. Mary's University of San Antonio, Texas. He holds a B.S. in drama from the University of Texas at Austin; an M.A. in international relations from the University of Arkansas; and a Ph.D. in political science from Indiana University. He has received conflict resolution training from CDR Associates, the Harris County Dispute Resolution Center of Houston, and the New Mexico Center for Dispute Resolution. Ray has trained over two hundred university students in peer mediation and with his students has trained close to one thousand teachers and students in secondary schools in central and south Texas. His most recent presentation, "Mediating Among Diverse Cultures," was given at the First World Mediation Congress held in Hermosillo, Mexico, in November 2005.

**Selina C. Low,** M.S.W., A.S.W., has been involved in conflict resolution since 1991. She received training as a mediator, facilitator, and trainer through community boards in San Francisco and continues to work with other programs in the Bay Area. Ms. Low was selected in the first class of writers for the Practitioner Scholars Writing Project. In addition to her volunteer and consulting work in mediation, Ms. Low is currently collecting her hours toward her clinical social work license. She works at a day treatment program at a nonpublic high school, providing therapy and behavior management to adolescents with severe emotional disturbances. Her future plans are to work in family therapy and family mediation and to continue to work with clients in crisis and who have experienced trauma, particularly in communities of color.

**Lucy Moore** specializes in natural resources conflicts throughout the west. Many of her cases involve Native American governments or communities. Lucy is an active mentor, believing it is the right thing to do both for the field and for those who might not otherwise have a chance in the profession. Her education includes a B.A. from Harvard, years living on the Navajo Nation, and lessons learned from many challenging cases. Lucy is the author of *Into the Canyon: Seven Years in Navajo Country,* a cross-cultural memoir about finding an identity and a role in a foreign land. She lives in Santa Fe with her artist husband and cat Fluffy.

**Onaje Mu'id**'s thirty-year history of activism explored the piercing questions of creating culturally appropriate healing human services in the context of social justice, reparations, and human rights for oppressed nations, especially for descendants of formerly enslaved Africans in the Western Hemisphere. His United Nations work culminated in declaring the transatlantic slave trade a crime against humanity at the seminal United Nations World Conference Against Racism, in Durban, South Africa, to which he was a delegate. Onaje holds an M.S.W. and is an alcohol and substance abuse counselor. Inspired by the works of Maria Yellow Horse Brave Heart-Jordan, Ph.D., and Joy Leary, Ph.D., he has focused his life's work on researching and understanding historical trauma in oppressed communities and creating the healing modalities, policies, and structures to alleviate it.

**Jelvas Musau** holds an LL.B. (Nairobi), LL.M. (London School of Economics), and Certificate in International Legal Drafting (Tulane Law School). He is an advocate of the High Court of Kenya and an associate at the Dispute Resolution Centre, Nairobi. Jelvas has an interest in the use of societal and communal understanding of and approaches to international dispute resolution. He works with the United Nations High Commission for Refugees in refugee protection work, a project replete with conflict management and resolution within, among, and between the various communities.

**Linda James Myers** is a scientist of the soul and a healer, a black intellectual and cultural critic whose research and scholarship places African Diaspora studies and psychology at the forefront of the paradigm shift occurring in Western science and converging with Eastern philosophies. Her research has lead to the development of optimal psychology, a theory of divine consciousness grounded in the wisdom tradition of African deep thought and contemporary experience. Dr. James Myers has held appointments in the departments of African American and African studies, psychology, and psychiatry at the Ohio State University. She currently serves as academic vice president and dean of the School of Graduate Psychology of New College of California in San Francisco. She is the author of numerous journal articles, book chapters, and three books.

**Anona Napoleon** is a native Hawaiian great-grandmother, scholar, and storyteller who continues to learn and accept the gifts and challenges life offers and the decisions she has made during her journey, moment to moment. She earned a doctorate in education from the University of Hawaii.

**Phillip M. Richards** received a B.A. cum laude from Yale and a Ph.D. from the University of Chicago. He is the author of *Black Heart: The Moral Life of Recent African American Letters* and co-author of *Best Literature by and about Blacks*. He has published in professional sites such as *American Quarterly, Style,* and *Early American Literature* as well as in literary journals such as *Harper's Magazine, Massachusetts Review,* and *American Scholar.* He has held fellowships at the National Humanities Center and the Institute on Race and Social Division. He has been a visiting professor at Boston University and most recently at the University of Grenoble in France. He is currently an associate professor at Colgate University in Hamilton, New York.

**Beth Roy** is a long-time mediator in the San Francisco Bay Area. She writes books on social conflict, including *Some Trouble with Cows: Making Sense of Social Conflict* (an oral history of Hindu-Muslim clashes in South Asia), *Bitters in the Honey: Tales of Hope and Disappointment Across Divides of Race and Time* (an exploration of race relations today based on stories by ordinary people involved in the desegregation of schools in Little Rock in the 1950s), and *American Skin: What Amadou Diallo's Story Says about Policing, Race, and Justice.* She holds a Ph.D. in sociology from the University of California, Berkeley. She is a founder of the Practitioners Research and Scholarship Institute (PRASI), and she teaches in the Peace and Conflict Studies program at the University of California, Berkeley. Her most recent book, *Parents' Lives, Children's Needs,* is a practical guide to addressing all the many conflicts and stresses in modern family life.

**Marlon D. Sherman**, J.D., is Oglala Lakota (born and raised on the Pine Ridge Reservation in South Dakota) and teaches in the Native American Studies Department at Humboldt State University in Eureka, California. He also consults in the areas of peacemaking, mediation, facilitation, leadership and multicultural issues. Mr. Sherman has an extensive background working directly with tribes and Native groups in the areas of negotiation, mediation, tribal self-governance, economic development, and government-to-government relations. He has served as the program director of the Bear River Band's Governance and Economic Development Project, and later as the self-governance director for the Yurok Tribe.

**Roberto Vargas** is an educator, community organizer, planning consultant, and ceremony leader. Nationally recognized for his skills in meeting facilitation and leadership development, Roberto has over twenty-five years of experience providing consultations on community problem-solving, multicultural team-building, and strategic planning throughout the United States, Canada, Mexico, and Sweden. His clients have included colleges, corporations, public institutions, Native American reservations, and more than one hundred fifty agencies and organizations dedicated to community service. Founding director of several Latino counseling centers, his theory and tools for people empowerment, leadership development, and *porvida* activism (the activism of using love to transform the world) are used by many. Roberto received his doctorate in public health and master's in social work from the University of California at Berkeley.

**Leah Wing**, Ed.D., is on the legal studies faculty at the University of Massachusetts at Amherst. She has taught dispute resolution since 1993. She developed and taught the nation's first courses in critical race mediation, examining ways in which the dominant approach to mediation can reinforce white privilege. Leah has been mediating and training interveners since 1985. As a white woman working on antiracist projects, she consults with educational institutions and nonprofits on the intersections between oppression, diversity, and conflict resolution. Leah developed an approach to mediation training and intervention that incorporates a social justice lens, and she is on the Board of Directors of the Association for Conflict Resolution and the editorial board of *Conflict Resolution Quarterly*.

**Dileepa Witharana** holds degrees in electrical engineering, but worked as a community peace worker in the midst of civil war in Sri Lanka.

Working with Quaker Peace and Service (Sri Lanka)/Thirupthiya from late 1990s to early 2000s, he was actively involved with community peace initiatives and conducted and attended numerous peace workshops. He is the author of "Community Peace Work in Sri Lanka: A Critical Appraisal," a working paper of the Centre for Conflict Resolution of Bradford University.

# Introduction

## *Conflict, Culture, and Knowledge*

Language explains ... and language obscures. Take the word "we": it can identify a meaningful group, but it can also submerge important differences in assumed likeness.

"Conflict resolution" is one of those phrases denoting a category that different people understand in different ways. Yet many people, and many textbooks about conflict resolution, assume a uniform meaning: "A process involving a neutral third party who facilitates not the content but the form of a dialogue so that the parties to a dispute can arrive at a settlement of their own making, to which they both/all agree."

WHAT IS CONFLICT RESOLUTION?

For the editors of this volume, and for many of the authors who appear here, several parts of this definition are questionable.

- Is there such a thing as neutrality, and if so, is it desirable? Can a dialogue in the midst of conflict ever be facilitated without regard to the content? Is settlement always the most desired end to the process, or are there times when changes to the relationships among the people involved are more important? Behind these questions lie a thick bunch of deeper questions, touching on matters of culture, power and knowledge.

- Who decides the meaning and definition of conflict resolution and when? How does the meaning of conflict resolution change in different settings—a school playground, for instance, versus a court of law, versus an Equal Employment Opportunity Commission hearing on a matter of discrimination?

- What happens when the work is defined by those in power (in this context, typically the authors of textbooks and training manuals or accredited researchers in prestigious universities) in ways that marginalize people with crucial ideas about social change, ideas that are evident only to them precisely because they *have* been marginalized?

It was the afternoon of September 11, 2001. In the multicultural conflict resolution class, students and teacher were still in substantial shock at the morning's attacks on the World Trade Center and the Pentagon. They were trying to talk about their feelings, but tempers ran high and the talk kept turning instead to what the American response should be.

"We need to understand the reasons behind terrorism," some students argued. "No, we need to strike back, fast and hard!" proclaimed others. Again and again, the teacher urged the students to return to their reactions rather than what should be done. "How was it for you to learn of the attacks?"

Suddenly, one young man, a vociferous advocate of "We have to retaliate!" stopped in mid-sentence. "I just realized something," he said reflectively. "Today when I walked on campus, for the first time in my life I felt like an American." The class looked at him quizzically. "Every other time," he explained, "I knew I was an *African American,* different from almost everyone I saw around me."

The African American student's "we" had shifted in the face of an assault on U.S. territory. The white students, a majority of the campus population, assumed a "we" that meant all members of the university community, whereas the young man in a minority had a sharply different understanding of the nature of that "we."

Whose "we" takes precedence is determined by relations of power in complex and often subtle ways. In each of these circumstances, people may come to conflict resolution from different cultural experiences, different social identities, different takes on what's important, what's true, and what's legitimate. To discuss culture, practice, and knowledge in relation to each other is to talk about *politics.*

Thus, the meaning of conflict resolution changes depending on who is asking the questions, who is answering them and under what circumstances, and depending on who is listening as well. Information changes depending on who has the power and who has been marginalized—and who fits into each of those categories changes, too, depending on contexts and moments in history.

As we use the term in this book, conflict resolution is a way of seeking change, social justice, social responsibility, health, freedom, liberation, and the elimination of oppression for all. Conflict resolution is a way to explore the solution from inside out and outside in. We understand that politics enter into every conflict resolution experience, but the ways in which that is true are not always addressed or expressly stated.

For those of us represented in this anthology, conflict resolution is about relationships and ways of approaching methods for problem solving. These relationships and approaches vary from one person to another, one family, business, community, country, society, culture to another, as they combine and recombine in a great variety of ways.

A conflict resolution practitioner needs to be an artist. To practice effectively involves an understanding of the human spirit and an appreciation for the many types of people in crisis, and the many ways they have of being in relationship. Conflict resolution is the art of creating or facilitating an appropriate process for the people in dispute to problem-solve together and, through that process, to reconstruct their relationships with each other. Yet many teachers and training programs do not include very important information, centering around culture, conflict, and politics, that lies at the heart of understanding how to do those things.

WHY THIS ANTHOLOGY?

This anthology is a rich collection of papers by conflict resolution practitioners who conduct their practices in a wide variety of ways. Most of the authors are people of color, or, if white, have substantial experience working in multicultural settings. What appears as a conflict in one culture may be something else entirely in another. Intervention must of necessity take different forms. People of one culture may be aware that others have different cultural experiences, but the details are likely to be hazy, the significance of different feelings and ideas unclear, as they were to the white students discussing 9/11. That absence of detail is especially true for those people whose cultural standpoint comes closest to the writers of textbooks and the teachers of how to practice, who most often are themselves culturally grounded in a hegemonic cultural and political center.

The authors in this book give us vivid pictures of how conflict, indeed of how life, appears from the center of each person's cultural universe. The volume offers to the reader a sampling of cultural voices essential to effective practice, yet not commonly heard in the discourse of conflict resolution. The authors suggest effective models for practice, ways of balancing the work between culturally harmonious approaches and socially compelling needs (see, for instance, Dileepa Witharana on peacemaking in Sri Lanka, Roberto Vargas on organizational work in Latino environments, and Ted Coronel on mediating Filipinos) and for research, engaging, for instance, in activist methodologies that frankly aim at goals of social justice (examples are Anona Napoleon's use of Ho-oponopono with Hawaiian school children, Ray Leal's work with students and staff in multicultural public schools, and Onaje Mu'id's intense examination of the horrors of rape in the Black community). The anthology is born of our collective commitment to provide the field with an opportunity to translate theoretical openness into practical inclusion in order to meet the needs of the diverse populations conflict resolvers encounter and seek to serve.

Because conflict resolution is a relatively new profession, the creation of a literature has great importance. What do we know, what do we need to learn, how do we need to go about learning and teaching it? But, as with the conflict resolution class, the "we" in those questions tends to eclipse multiple forms of knowledge. Indeed, an active contest over knowledge exists: where does knowledge reside? What makes some knowledge of central importance, other knowledge marginal? How must knowledge be articulated to communicate across cultural lines?

RE-CENTERING CULTURE, KNOWLEDGE, AND PRACTICE

Fundamental to these questions is a central understanding of power dynamics; papers by Beth Roy, Roberto Chené, Leah Wing, and Valerie Batts, among others, speak to matters of power. Respecting the perspectives of others and their ways of knowing requires critical self-reflection about our society's bias toward a myth of objectivity. Sometimes talked about in terms of center and margin, we think about a culturally dominant mainstream that tends to overwhelm (or to appropriate in distorted forms) expressions of diverse cultural stances. In other words, as we've suggested, where the center lies depends on where one stands. When an individual lives daily and intellectual life in a cultural community rarely if ever reflected with any accuracy in mainstream images, the center quite naturally occurs where the person eats, sleeps, talks, learns, thinks, breathes.

Unfortunately, people told often enough, in the form of media images, assumptions embedded in textbooks, standards of physical beauty, and so much more, that their experience is less worthy than others' may develop a tendency to discredit their own knowledge. What do I have to contribute? I don't talk the way the "experts" speak; I can't write the way the "scholars" write. In this way, a great deal of valuable and necessary knowledge is lost to the building of a field like conflict resolution. Our effectiveness in confronting urgent problems of today's world is impaired. The barriers are not only internal, though. Peer-reviewed journals, university professors, and book publishers pass judgment on work written in unfamiliar idioms, rejecting crucial ideas along with manuscripts.

What makes research credible? Where do narratives of experience pass into shareable knowledge? The editors' vision is to encourage practitioners of conflict resolution to treat their experiences as the basis for research, to move the site of knowledge making from academia to the field of practice, from dominant culture assumptions to culturally specific practices. In the process, we have intentionally blurred lines between analysis and data, between research and personal narrative. Mary Adams Trujillo explicitly speaks to the value of unifying subjective and objective perspectives, and the discussion with Hasshan Batts exemplifies that usefulness. We have found that it was only in the reordering of these categories that we could engage our primary theme: the contested nature of knowledge in a multicultural society in which inequality reigns.

Although this volume is not designed to resolve the question of inequality, we have begun a process of addressing relationships of primacy and marginality. Not only does each author work from the center of her or his experiential world, but we have created a volume that positions the authors as a group at the center of a "live" collaborative process. We think of the anthology as a text-based dialogue among the writers and readers. The papers we have selected do not seek to quarrel with dominant ideas, but rather to exchange information among equals.

Readers in different relationships to the material will no doubt read the papers differently. We invite and encourage those traditionally defined as "in the center" to listen in, to broaden their scope, and to join the conversation as they wish and are able. We believe readers will find insights here that promise to enrich not only their work with "others" but all conflict resolution practice at its core.

## HOW THIS BOOK IS ORGANIZED

Three questions define the mission of the anthology.

First, what is culture? What do we need to understand about how culture influences conflict resolution knowledge and practice? The first part of the volume explores worldviews, *putting cultural perspectives at the center of the inquiry.*

Second, what must practitioners and theorists know in order to understand and expand the learnings of the field and make these available for creating ways to address the urgent troubles that afflict the globe? This section *puts experiential knowledge at the center of research.*

Third, what values, beliefs, and expectations inform fundamental paradigms of practice? This section *puts knowledge accrued through practice at the center.*

## STYLE AND CONSEQUENCES

As we editors crafted the anthology, our theoretical orientation showed up in terms of stylistic choices. We have tried to put into literary practice the principles we espouse in the volume. Four choices we made exemplify that process:

• We encouraged our authors to use the word "I" copiously. We believe that knowledge and experience cannot be disconnected. Using the academic third person suggests impersonal objectivity; we dispute notions of unbiased scientists presenting factual information validated through processes of review by peers who share a positivist worldview.

• We use citations sparingly. There are two reasons for notes: to provide the reader with references and to provide the writer with legitimacy. If what the author has to say rings true to the reader, if it tests positive in the laboratory of lived experience, then that is, to us, a more useful measure of legitimacy. Therefore, we reserve citations for places where they direct the reader to a web of discourse on the subject at hand, including where available suggestions of selected further readings.

• We combine narratives recounting authors' stories of their work, including transcripts of interviews and conversations, with essays theorizing controversies within the field of conflict resolution. These "unlike" structures inform each other, drawing lines of interconnection between practice and knowledge building.

• Some authors have capitalized "white" or "black" referring to racial groups. Others have not. We have maintained their usage.

For people new to the work of conflict resolution, we've provided context in our editors' comments. For those who are involved in the field, our editorial comments highlight and engage some of the controversies current among practitioners and scholars.

Finally, this anthology is a beginning, a work oriented toward process rather than product alone, both ours and yours to explore. We hope to stimulate more dynamic dialogue, to contribute a richer language in which to capture broader ideas and insights, and to challenge the narrowing of dimensions that, we fear, is increasingly besetting the field of conflict resolution as it struggles for professional legitimacy. The voices represented in this volume call out for more comprehensive, inclusive, and effective practice so that the peaceful resolution of conflict can become a reality for and in all communities.

# PART ONE

# Re-Centering Culture

# Introduction

What is culture? What do we need to understand about how culture influences conflict resolution knowledge and practice? The first part of the volume explores worldviews, *putting cultural perspectives at the center of the inquiry.*

Culture is one of those words tossed about so frequently that, like conflict, it means many things to many people. Culture is used generally to connote a social grouping with shared viewpoints, experiences, histories, or identities. We talk about "popular culture" or "mass culture" or "consumer culture."

Although these designations address different aspects or levels of culture, for purposes of this text when we use the word we are referring to *the complex system of socially constructed and generationally transmitted patterns of meaning, aspiration, and behavior.*

Culture operates at many levels and over long periods of time. Culture is communicated symbolically through language, as well as nonverbally. Because culture is a system, its goal is to reproduce itself and is therefore, at its deepest levels, resistant to change. At the core of a culture are its values and its worldview. Values, the enduring, deeply held and felt underpinnings of a culture, carry a people's important beliefs and supply much of individual and collective identity. Worldview goes beneath the surface level of culture and provides, as Linda James Myers describes it, the philosophical assumptions and principles that give life to the perceptions, beliefs, patterns of interpreting reality, and designs for living.

For some people, culture is a clearly defined matter, but for others, it is a thing of mystery. "We don't know who discovered water," said a deep thinker, "but we're pretty sure it wasn't a fish." When one's cultural identity is challenged, the water becomes vividly tinted. "I know who I am, and I'm proud of it whatever you say!"

But for people who swim in the main currents of a society, culture is more amorphous. White teenagers turn to black musicians to define a generational culture. A white woman commented that she never understood culture until she heard a black woman say, "The only thing I can trace my roots in this country to is a bill of sale." The comment evokes a sense of how connected culture is with identity, and identity with history. Who we see ourselves as being, who we are seen by others to be, when one identity matters rather than another (for we all have many identities), these markers of where we live in a complex, shifting social geography tie us into the variety of cultures each of us inhabits. Culture, as we have defined it, is generationally transmitted, and our linkages to the past form one strong thread in our identity in the present.

Culture shapes how our inner life works, how we think and feel. It marks our location in social orders of inequality. Thus, culture informs how conflict is lived, conceptualized, enacted, and ultimately how it is resolved or transformed. Although much of the discourse about culture in the world of conflict resolution centers around honoring diversity, counteracting bias, and becoming culturally sensitive, we approach the subject here from a different angle. We are concerned with specifics of differing cultural practices and sensitivities—the things that culture defines—as well as with limitations of awareness brought about by our socialization within particular cultures—the things that culture blurs.

Culture influences what people think by building certain boundaries to consciousness. Cultures give rise to worldviews that in turn focus attention on only some aspects of life. In modern market-based societies, for instance, we are directed to see the individual in bold relief, but in turn we may have difficulty understanding our social connections, the profound ways we are part of a whole. We may be able to define a dispute we are engaged in but at the same time lose sight of the relational context for the fight: who we are to each other and the greater history out of which this conflict grew. In the absence of clarity about all that surrounds a given conflict, our vision is directed toward dichotomies:

"Who's to blame, you or me? If you, I'm furious; if me, I'm guilty and ashamed."

"I'm right so you must be wrong."

"What I want precludes what you want, so I'll fight you to the finish."

If conflict resolution is to make substantial contributions, it must be able to bring into awareness that which has been made invisible by our cultures. Both in order to understand conflicts contextually and therefore avoid the trap of blame, and in order to imagine new directions that push outward defined limitations, the constrictions of cultural assumptions need to be challenged. Some of the unhelpful ideas may be about race or gender or other contested identities, others about the possibilities of change in the world surrounding the disputants.

OVERVIEW OF PART ONE

Taken as a whole, the essays in this section form both a theoretical—and movingly personal—foundation on which to build skills for conflict resolution in our diverse society. The first set of papers in this section help us to see connections between identity and culture, culture and history, and point us toward new conceptual realities.

Marlon Sherman's essay opens the anthology with a specific illustration of the interrelationship of language, culture, worldview, and conflict. By exploding common meanings of the word "wild," Sherman takes apart the history of the concept of wildness, as it has come to be applied to land and to Indians. In a metaphoric sense, Sherman positions cultural conflict within the North American landscape itself. He literally grounds issues of neutrality, for example, in the history of oppressive relationships between Native and nonnative peoples.

Linda James Myers then offers a critique of the ways in which we become imprisoned in our worldviews. Juxtaposing dominant Western cultural assumptions and values against African-based ones, she calls for individual and collective analyses of social policies and practices. Through this process, James Myers challenges the reader to think beyond cultural limitations.

Roberto Chené questions the "problem" of diversity. Discovering that the real issue lies not in difference but in domination, he concludes that the often-invisible fact of power inequity creates conflicts that are always with us.

Mariah Breeding makes visible the connection between personal practice and social oppression. By linking structural violence to the threads of common life, she exposes our complicit involvement with injustice.

Onaje Mu'id further focuses the discussion of structural violence to specifically include rape. He puts into historical context the suicide of his twice-violated daughter. Through this examination, he encourages black men to take back their power to intervene in such tragedies. As an activist scholar and a bereaved father, he calls for change in the course of the internalized oppression.

Jelvas Musau closes the circle. Presenting a graphic picture of how a Kenyan people, the Akamba, externalized processes of adjudication and punishment by relegating them to the supernatural powers of an object called a *kithitu,* the author calls us to consider the ways in which supernatural phenomena or spiritual practices can assist in the restoration of social justice.

# 1 Wilderness

*Scared of the Sacred*

MARLON SHERMAN

The white man does not understand the Indian for the reason
that he does not understand America. He is too far removed from
its formative processes. The roots of the tree of his life have not
yet grasped the rock and soil. . . . The man from Europe is still a
foreigner and an alien.

> —Luther Standing Bear, *Land of the
> Spotted Eagle*

Words have power. Madison Avenue types know it; political strategists know
it; we all know it, if we just think about it. Words have power because they
are catalysts. When we see or hear a word, our minds form images of particular concrete objects, or recall certain concepts. To most people, the word
"apple" brings to mind an image of a shiny, red fruit. However, a farmer who
owns and works a 600 acre orchard of yellow delicious apples will probably
associate the word "apple" with a yellow object.

Because of the power of words, advertising can make or break a political or advertising campaign. The main idea behind this theory states that
when strong images are used often enough, whether they are well accepted
or controversial, they can indelibly tattoo a particular product or idea on the
minds of the consuming public.

The theory has certainly proved true in the case of Native Americans.
Since the first writings of Christopher Columbus, Indians have been portrayed

at different times by non-Indians as innocent, depraved, gentle, savage, intelligent, stupid, loyal, untrustworthy, superhuman, and beastlike. These sometimes similar, sometimes opposing views of Indians have appeared in travel journals, academic writings, religious tracts, popular novels, and magazines. They have also been passed on through campaign rhetoric, oratory, storytelling, and plain gossip. The various images have served specific purposes in justifying oppressive behaviors on the part of Euramerican groups in dealing with Native Americans.

Through the many differences and similarities of the stories, one fact remains the same: The overwhelming majority of images of Indians originated with non-Indians, and especially with Euramericans. Native Americans have had little say in how they have been portrayed. Even today the number of tribal voices writing and speaking in a national forum about who and what constitutes Indianness is insignificant in comparison to the multitude of so-called authorities who have already saturated the fields.

In the same way, non-Indian sources have defined human relationship with the land, at least as far as America is concerned. Where Indians were savages, the land was "wild." Non-Indians have defined humans as separate from the land and have defined land as a commodity to be tamed, owned, bought, and sold. In this manner, Euramerican intruders were able to separate Native tribes from the land they had occupied and used for uncounted thousands of years.

> If the land was vacant of any human occupancy, then a nation could claim both land title and political jurisdiction on the grounds of vacuum domicilium. . . . Such title and rights in the land and in political power offered no problem in White opinion, but the degree of vacancy was often a matter of differences in European and native land usage. What to White eyes appeared empty or underutilized according to European practices was seen as owned and fully utilized according to tribal custom and economy.
>
> Since large areas of America were occupied by tribes who moved their housing often by European criteria or who pursued hunting as well as horticulture, the Whites quickly leaped to the conclusion that such land awaited their immediate settlement because it was vacant. Europeans also believed that sparsely settled and underutilized lands could be shared by the Indians

with the "higher" uses of the Europeans without harm to native economy and lifestyles, and perhaps to their improvement.[1]

Whether intentional or not, using the word "wild" to designate landscape and environment sets the land apart from us: Americans are "civilized" and the land is "wild," untamed. As Ralph Waldo Emerson said, "The world is all outside; it has no inside." Because of American formal education and informal acculturation, Americans believe that they can visit the wild, but can never live in it. Americans are trained to think that those who do choose to live in the wilderness are either Indians (noble or savage, it does not matter) or half-crazed tree huggers.

But the concept of wilderness was obsolete the minute it was born. The original concept came from the old German words for wild land.

> Wildness meant more in the Middle Ages than the shrunken significance of the term would indicate today. The word implied everything that eluded Christian norms and the established framework of Christian society, referring to what was uncanny, unruly, raw, unpredictable, foreign, uncultured, and uncultivated. It included the unfamiliar as well as the unintelligible.[2]

Those old Germans believed witches, goblins, ghosts and other evil creatures lived in the wild lands. Children were told tales about wilderness to scare them into obedience. In America, kids were told American Indian stories—captivity narratives—to keep them in line. Indians and wild beasts were an important part of the new/old story. The stories played on European fears of the unknown.

The difference between European wilderness stories and American ones was that the people were afraid, not just of Indians or ogres, but of the land itself. The only way to conquer the fear was to tame the land and the Indians, to make the land like their European home. That pragmatic belief complemented biblical commands to subdue the earth.[3]

In the past two hundred years America has shifted away from Old Testament values and Old World fears to the romanticism of Jean-Jacques Rousseau and James Fenimore Cooper. No more do the romantics want to tame the land. Rather, they want to become like the noble savage, the frontier superman overcoming all natural obstacles in order to show mastery over the land.

The present obsession with wilderness, then, stems from a sort of stereotypical hero worship, whether it is of Odysseus, Beowulf, or the noble savage (à la Hollywood these days). It is loosely related to rock climbing, bungee jumping, parachuting and, yes, river rafting. Coming out alive with an adrenaline high is a sort of natural form of drug abuse, only it is not drug abuse, it is earth abuse, using the more violent aspects of the landscape for self-gratification, for what Wallace Steiner called the "incandescent excitement of danger and the unknown."[4] The present obsession with vertical rock faces and white water is merely the modern version of taming the wilderness. The difference is that now people don't want to change the face of the wilderness, but would rather skate across it. The ultimate meaning is the same: Humans need to know that they have the power and cunning to conquer something they see as far more powerful than humans.

Today the "wilderness" belongs to those who can afford to use it. True, wilderness areas are on so-called public lands. However, these areas are so far from population centers that few of the urban, economically disadvantaged will ever see them, much less use them on a regular basis, riding over them on $3,000 bicycles, hiking on them wearing $300 boots and carrying $1,000 worth of equipment and dried food on their backs, or parachuting off steep cliffs into deep river canyons. America's publicly owned "wild" lands are as much a myth to city dwellers today as they ever were in the nineteenth century. Dime novels about Black Bart and Calamity Jane have been replaced by glossy infomercials disguised as nature magazines. (I call the magazines glossy not because of the paper on which they are printed, but because they gloss over environmental issues and concentrate on selling exotic alloy bike frames, specialized climbing shoes, and group vacations in Nepal.)

The basic Euramerican aspiration has not changed appreciably because of any environmental movement. It has merely been informed with a self-conscious awareness that if humans persist in careless misuse of resources, we will all die a slow death. Even an environmentally sensitive thinker such as Donald Worster seems to misunderstand the basic reason we should treat Earth well. He says, "We ought to begin by getting outside our regional provincialisms, overcoming our insistence on American uniqueness, and trying to situate the cowboy and his ranch in the broad panorama of human adaptation to the earth."[5] Worster, as far-seeing and well-meaning as he might be, still looks at the earth from a distance. He cannot see the intimate relationship we have with Earth. He sees Earth only as something separate, something to which we must adapt, not as some*one* with whom we should develop a closer relationship. Life should not be a process of adaptation, but rather one of getting to know a long lost relative.

Even Mary Blue Magruder, spokeswoman for Earthwatch, commented that "[Harvard scientist E. O.] Wilson says biophilia involves waking people up to a love of biological diversity and increasing their awareness by exposing them to nature."[6] Neither Wilson nor Magruder conceive of Earth in other than lifeless terms. They do not see Earth as someone with a life, a spirit, a cognizance. They see Earth as a combination of forces known distantly as "nature," and the only relationship we can have with Earth is an appreciation of her, a "biophilia."

At bottom, the rhetoric never addresses any sort of respect of the earth, but only that we must preserve the earth so we can be positively impacted by "its" health. The positive impact may be physical, having to do with clean air and water, or it may be spiritual, causing us to feel good when we see large, green areas of healthy forest or grass, but it seems to be a one-way proposition: "I want to preserve the earth because it will make me happy and healthy," not "I want to show respect to my true mother."

We need to look deeper beneath the selfish surface of our desires. Minnie Reeves, a Chilula elder from the Redwood Creek area of Northern California, gave one reason why we should seek to protect the things of Earth:

The redwood trees are sacred. They are a special gift and reminder from the Great Creator to the human beings. The Great Creator made everything, including trees of all kinds, but he wanted to leave a special gift for his children. So he took a little medicine from each tree, he said a prayer and sang a powerful song, and then he mixed it all with the blood of our people. Then he created this special redwood tree from this medicine. He left it on Earth as a demonstration of his love for his children. The redwood trees have a lot of power: they are the tallest, live the longest, and are the most beautiful trees in the world. Destroy these trees and you destroy the Creator's love. And if you destroy that which the Creator loves so much, you will eventually destroy mankind.[7]

Oren Lyons (who was born into the Onondaga Wolf Clan) said simply, "Being a Wolf myself, I have a feeling for the mystery of that animal. . . . I think that whatever happens to the wolf happens to us. And whatever happens to us will happen to you."[8]

But simply setting aside geographical areas in which humans are not allowed to impact the land in any way (except to build trails and bridges) is not the answer. That is merely setting up a false ecosystem, one that in all probability has not existed for thousands of years. Samuel Purchas, a seventeenth-century Virginian, was and is typical of those who saw America as an uninhabited wilderness. He described the Virginia tribes as "more wild and unmanly then that unmanned wild countrey, which they range rather then inhabite."[9] Contrast this with the words of a wild and unmanly Lakota elder, Mathew King:

> I had a talk with a congressman about why we won't sell the Black Hills. He asked me, "King, why do you Indians need all that land? You don't do anything with the land you've already got. Why do you need more? We'll give you some money instead of those hills."
>
> I told him, right there in the halls of Congress, with people all around listening, I told him:
>
> "You say I don't do anything with my land? Well, what do you mean by doing? To the White Man, doing means changing things, destroying everything, chopping the forests and damming the rivers and polluting the skies. White Man wants us to be like him and build factories and motels and hamburger stands. We don't want those things!
>
> "You say I don't do anything with our land? What I do is I live there by God's Law. That's what I do there."[10]

In the days of this author's golden (or brown-haired and brown-skinned) youth, when I was studying wildlife management at Utah State, the academic party line defined ecological zones as disturbance, liminal, and climax. The professors classified most American forests (before the ax) as climax ecosystems.[11] But never once did they mention humans in the ecological equations. Never once did they mention that Native communities managed their particular home areas for maximum use of all resources, and for ease of travel. All of those top-notch environmental professors had it wrong, because they left an element—humans—out of the ecological equation. The idea has carried over until today, in the push for so-called wilderness areas that will supposedly be untouched by human hands. But leaving humans out of the equation is setting these areas up for failure.

This is how an elder Navajo woman views the relationship between humans and Earth:

> In English they call me "Kee Shelton's Mother." In Navajo my name is Asa Bazhonoodah, "woman who had squaw dance." I am 83 years old.
>
> A long time ago the earth was placed here for us, the people, the Navajo, it gives us corn and we consider her our mother.
>
> When Mother Earth needs rain we give pollen and use the prayers that was given us when we came from the earth. That brings rain.
>
> The Earth is our mother. The white man is ruining our mother. I don't know the white man's ways, but to us the Mesa, the air, the water, are Holy Elements. We pray to these Holy Elements in order for our people to flourish and perpetuate the well-being of each generation.[12]

Whether or not one believes Native American medicine people can bring rain upon request,[13] it is by now a widely accepted fact that lightning was not the only precontact source of forest and grass fires—indigenous peoples also started fires. The old Indians were not stupid, and they were certainly not unobservant. They knew that regular fires controlled certain trees, shrubs, and grasses and that some animals preferred recently burned-over areas. Those old people knew where, when, and how often to burn in order to achieve the desired results.

So, whether the tribes used spiritual or physical means, they definitely attempted to control their environment, and in many ways were successful. The Lakota Ecology Stewardship Model developed by the Oglala Tribe states:

All beings, both living and nonliving, were related in that all shared and depended on Mother Earth for survival. The Lakota believe that humans were the newest nation on Earth, and as such were instructed to learn from the older nations: the rocks, animals, and plants. Thus, natural laws and relationships were carefully observed and emulated. This Lakota Knowledge System was enhanced by each member of the Tribe, and has been passed orally from one generation to the next for greater than 10,000 years. Unusual phenomena that could not be explained were considered part of the great mystery, and retained until clarified by additional information.[14]

Unfortunately,

European values and colonization philosophies imposed on "conquered" peoples have caused near or total cultural genocide by assuming human domination over the earth, identifying non-Christian religions as pagan and uncivilized, promoting destructive exploitation of natural resources, believing that farming is the "backbone" of a civilized society, equating worthwhile livelihoods with consumerism, and measuring the quality of life with money. The disregard for Indigenous knowledge systems has resulted in severe and crisis-oriented problems, including degradation of cultural identities, poverty-level economies, and destruction of the environment.[15]

It is obvious that Euramerican husbandry practices are not as successful as indigenous stewardship models.[16] Euramerican husbandry has oppressed the land on this continent, sucking the vitality from much of it, replacing it with lifeless fences, tree farms, fertilizers, and pumped water, all in the name of taming the wilderness. Now that the wilderness has been mostly tamed and is far removed from most of us, how can we revitalize ourselves in this "technomod" society?

Because of the meanings attached to the Euramerican concept of wilderness,[17] Gary Snyder, the poet, told us to get in touch with the wild within ourselves, which is a strange concept coming from an avowed Buddhist.[18] The essence of Buddhism is that all things have the same spirit, that all things are part of a larger whole. Yet here is the poetic guru saying that we have a wild within ourselves. We must, he says, use the animal in ourselves, the wild beast, the untamed savage, to break out of our tame, urban selves. This is conceptually similar to the back-to-nature movements such as the Fraternal Order of Red Men, Boy and Girl Scouts, and other organizations that advocate returning to nature, to a primal environment, in order to improve our "civilized" selves.[19] In effect, Snyder says we can be like the earth, and the earth can be like us: we can have farmlands, cities, and wilderness. This sort of anthropomorphizing can be harmful in the long run, because—although we are made from the earth, although we can have the earth's spirit and body running through our veins, although we are completely dependent on the earth's good health and good graces—in many ways, in very many ways, the earth is not like us at all. Ascribing human emotions to natural processes can have harmful effects.[20]

There is no duality in Buddhism, yet America's beloved Buddhist teacher tells us that we have two separate parts that we need to know. That belief implies a dichotomy: we have a wild part and a tame part; the two are in opposition to each other. Only by getting to know the wild, untamed, random part within ourselves will we become more creative. Not only does this seem to be in opposition to Buddhist beliefs about the totality of nature, it also goes against the beliefs of most of the indigenous tribal peoples of this continent, whose beliefs Snyder also claims to have embraced. Oren Lyons says:

> Every inch of this land is Indian country. Every inch. The West didn't get wild until the white people got there. There's no such word as wild in the Indian languages. The closest we can get to it is the word free. We were free people.[21]

There is not now, nor has there ever been, a "wild" or a "wilderness" on this continent. All things are related. All of the animals, plants, rocks, and waters are cousins to the humans. There is no such thing as a wild animal or an untouched wilderness area. Nor is there any such thing as an inanimate object, a dead rock. All things have a spirit. All things are capable of giving themselves so another part of creation might benefit. A "wild" deer or buffalo might give itself so humans can have food and warmth. A human might give him or herself in a ceremonial way so other humans or other parts of creation may benefit materially or spiritually. Water, rocks, trees, animals, humans—all are capable of giving of their spirit, their power, their corporal bodies, so one of the relations might continue living or thriving.

Wildness, then, is a concept that should not exist on this continent. Wildness connotes fear. A thing that is wild is a thing that is out of our control, a thing that might possibly harm us, a thing therefore to be feared and either avoided or conquered before it conquers us.[22] Many people approach the wild thing as a means to prove they are able to overpower it and thereby prove they can overpower their fear. "Public wilderness areas are, first of all, a means of perpetuating, in sport form, the more virile and primitive skills in pioneering travel and subsistence."[23] Some people parachute, some raft white-water canyons, some climb sheer rock faces, drive overpowered cars on racetracks, go winter backpacking in avalanche country, challenge deep, dank caves, and some climb down into live volcanoes. Some even try to conquer their fears by besting other humans in the wild world of business competition.[24] Many adventurers and sports enthusiasts crave the adrenaline rush they feel when they face the dangers inherent in any of these types of activities. They have replaced reliance on artificial or natural hallucinogens with the surge of power they receive when in danger. Danger, and the flood of adrenaline it causes, can be as addictive as any drug.

The world is beset with a mental disease—a fear, a neurosis, a global paranoia, and inferiority complex. Millions of people, when they have enough food in their bellies, begin to look about for ways to prove their superiority in some way, begin to look for things to conquer. Or fear overtakes them, the fear that another person or group of people will take the food from their mouths. Hatred follows fear, and thus is born nationalism, racial, and ethnic strife, wars. Wars, hatred, and feelings of inferiority are all interconnected. They begin when people take more notice of themselves than of their neighbors on this planet—humans, animals, plants, earth, and water. They begin with a hunger, whether a physical hunger (or fear of physical hunger) or a hunger to prove individual greatness.

But all of these methods of proving bravery are totally unnecessary on this continent. We must realize we are related to everything and everyone on the surface of this land, and we need feel no fear.

Whenever we come upon a new thing, a new person, a new experience, we should meet it and greet it as if we are seeing a cousin we have not seen for a long time. We should in effect open our arms and embrace it. Ideally, we do not meet relatives and challenge them, doing our best to show we are better in some way, physically or intellectually. Instead, we try to remember what we have in common, try to make our relative feel at ease, comfortable. If we react to land in this welcoming way, a mountain will no longer be a hard-faced obstacle in the way of finding our bravery; instead, it will be a grandmother to be respected, revered, and loved. A river will not be an exciting opponent to make us flex our muscles and show our agility; it will be a life-giving ancestor who slakes our thirst and provides us with steady strength. A human will not be a threat to our way of life, but a cousin with whom to feel at ease. When dealing with family, there should be no need to prove ourselves greater than anyone else, because we are all essentially equal, even though our abilities and experiences may differ.

So, while the idea behind keeping certain areas relatively free from human despoliation is a good one, calling these areas "wild" may eventually cause damage. Over time, trying to achieve a climax ecosystem that discounts and excludes human interference will likely have deleterious effects on those systems and could conceivably lead to the loss of entire species of plants and animals, with the resulting loss of ground cover and soil, and eventually the loss of clean rivers and aquifers, leading to the possibility that worldwide climate patterns will change so much that humans are taken completely out of the picture, bones to be studied by future nonhuman archaeologists.

"Wilderness"—the concept that this was an uninhabited land untouched by human hands—is a European construct and is totally inappropriate on this continent. People lived here long before Europeans first contacted indigenous nations, people who never saw the land as wild or threatening. Rather than referring to the natural, precontact state of this continent as wild, one should talk instead about a well-managed environment. Or, considering the basis of Native beliefs—generosity, reciprocity, and respect—maybe we should call it a well-respected environment.

Words have power. They shape the world in which we live and help form the maps by which we move through it. My grandmother told me to "be careful what you say, because putting words out there will make it true."

Given this enormous power of words, we must be careful which words we choose to describe anything outside ourselves or our sphere of experience.

Calling the earth a resource rather than a relative invites buying, selling, use and abuse, to the short-term detriment of those lower on the economic pyramid and to the eventual detriment and possible extinction of all who live here. Portraying land as an empty wilderness may lead to fear of the unknown within it or competition for ownership of the supposedly unoccupied spaces. It may also lead to a view of those who originally occupied the land as wild savages, hardy but uncivilized less-than-human creatures.

Who can say how much better it would have been if the European explorers had greeted this land and its occupants as long-lost relatives, in the same manner that those occupants greeted the newcomers. Rather than treating the indigenous peoples as a lesser species, rather than enslaving, raping, robbing, and killing them, the Europeans might have found a shared home in which they could have lived healthy, productive lives. Instead, they chose an attitude of purposeful and relentless ignorance, misunderstanding all the laws and customs of the peoples they encountered.

Calling the land a wilderness and the people savages made it easier for the interlopers to act in ways that were contrary to their publicly stated religious beliefs and principles. The words they chose reflected an intent to conceive of themselves as superior beings and assisted them in rationalizing a genocide that the world had not seen before nor has seen since.

People fear difference. Anyone who is different is something to be either feared or looked down upon, or both. The moral strength of a culture depends upon whether it can accept difference without feeling threatened or acting upon those perceived threats. It is particularly and specifically hypocritical for a culture such as, generally speaking, the Euramerican Christian culture of the 1400s onward to treat non-Euramerican, non-Christian peoples as anything but human.

In order to treat people of other cultures, communities, and nations as humans, it is not absolutely necessary to know and understand everything about them. It is not necessary to study them exhaustively in an effort to comprehend their every nuance of thought. What is basic, though, is that if four billion humans are to coexist on this earth, other cultures must be treated with respect, must be accepted as they are, must be allowed to live their lives as their cultures dictate.

Each of us should be strong in our own cultures and beliefs, and although we should not make it our life's work, we should also spend all our lives learning about those cultures that surround us. Some of what they believe will be irrelevant to us. Some may be extremely important to understanding our present situations and the situations of our particular people. One thing that is essential is to understand how different cultures relate to each other, to insiders and outsiders. Why might they choose certain words to describe certain things or concepts? Then, whenever possible, we will use those words or their nearest equivalents when speaking about relevant issues. This shows we respect them and expect they will reciprocate.

Our beliefs are reaffirmed daily in our interactions with those within our particular culture or community. However, there can be no ultimate and absolute understanding between cultures, or between genders, or even interpersonally. We simply cannot know all of the events that cause each human's emotions and thought processes. All we can do is accept each other. All we can do is work at lessening the paralyzing fear of anything we think of as the unknown, as the Other. Understanding and acceptance of differences do not scientifically negate emotions; instead, they add reason, an awakening to human relationships.

We must each accept who we are. We must accept our cultures and our places within them. We must accept the history of our peoples on this Earth. The history is neither glorious nor pedestrian; it simply is. Recognizing the limitations of our histories, of our cultures and of our selves, we should be able to move away from selfish name-calling and toward an acceptance of those with whom we must work to stay alive. We have a duty to ourselves and to our communities and cultures to ascertain where our interests touch or intersect the interests of all others and to forge bonds along those tangents.

Now let me see. What shall we name those bonds . . . ?

# 2 Toward Fuller Knowledge in Peace Management and Conflict Resolution

*The Importance of Cultural Worldview*

LINDA JAMES MYERS

> He who knows only one side of a thing, knows little of that.
> —African Proverb

As a descendant of enslaved Africans and Native Americans, I have had the opportunity to see first hand the devastating impact of the dominant cultural worldview on oppressed people. I am also aware that my own cultural heritage has fostered a worldview that is the complete antithesis to that of the West. Most of my academic career has been spent researching, seeking to understand, and writing about the implications of these differences in cultural worldview for human experience. This essay will explore some of those findings as they relate to peace management and conflict resolution.

## BACKGROUND

More than thirty years ago, I became interested in social injustice, conflict, and the challenges to peace management and conflict resolution that seemed to be at the core of how people in the West tend to view the world. The difficulties became compounded, often even insurmountable, if the people involved were from groups that differed greatly in experience, such as the privileged in the society versus the historically disenfranchised and marginalized. Because social policies and practices are made from the perspective and interests of the privileged, and the prevailing mind-set is not one that encourages critical self-reflection and introspection, much that happens in the arena of justice and conflict resolution holds inherent biases hidden from the view of those given educational, social, and economic advantages due to the "blindness of the privileged." In other words, one cannot know, much less appreciate, the perspective of "the other" if one cannot hear their voice. Yet, if one's socialization is set up to believe that the "other" has nothing to say that is worth listening to—or if you retain the belief that you hold no bias and know the best—there will be a problem. Justice and peace will be inaccessible.

At some level the confounding situation appears to start with the way in which the proactive role of consciousness in the human experience and its subjective nature are not generally acknowledged in Western cultures. Trained as a clinical psychologist, I have found that even in my training we were encouraged to act as if there were a reality "out there" that existed outside of our own creation and the creation of others. Granted, it finally came to be in vogue in some circles to acknowledge the "social construction" of reality, but the role of culture (simply defined as a people's way of life) and cultural worldview as important determinative variables in that social construction are seldom taken into consideration. Literature in which these critical factors are considered is most often pushed to the margins of the mainstream discourse.

In social "scientific" venues, as people explore, interpret, analyze, and make meaning of the human experience of others, how is it that they also tend to fall into the trap of intellectual and cultural imperialism by imposing the hegemony of a Western cultural worldview applied universally to all, whether or not an alternate worldview is held by those examined? When scholars and practitioners fail to investigate alternate designs for living and patterns of interpreting reality that are uncommon in the West, is it because they believe their worldview is universal? If this is the case we can imagine that broader society is no more aware, critically self-reflective, or culturally inclusive than the professional field.

The situation becomes particularly troublesome for those from cultural heritages that are not only nondominant in the United States but also most often seen as inferior, negated, or ignored.

## WHAT IS IN A WORLDVIEW?

How can peace management and conflict resolution be enhanced for marginalized groups and everyone else in monoculturally hegemonic societies? Are there ways of being in a world that better accommodate the differences across cultural groups and individuals that may lead to conflict? Is there a social theory that can provide a social analysis meaningful enough to explain and predict peace and conflict? Can it give us insight into new strategies for intervening in society's operations in order to reduce conflict and improve the chances for peace? These are some of the questions for which we need to find answers to expand our understanding.

Seldom does critical self-reflection in this society allow for the consideration of the lived peace manifested by African Americans before their complete immersion into mainstream U.S. culture through desegregation and the advent of television.

I have always marveled at the resilience of enslaved, forced immigrant African Americans and their descendants. As a cultural psychologist I have been intrigued by several burning questions. How is it that these African Americans as a collective were able to survive chattel enslavement—the most brutal, dehumanizing form of slavery ever practiced in the history of humankind—when other cultural groups could not? How do human beings endure and survive almost four hundred years of psychological terrorism? What is the cultural knowledge and skill passed on generation after generation? How is it that these African Americans not only survived but sought strong human relationships and built extended family bonds, rather than focusing on the retaliatory retribution that may have been justified? What in their cultural character allowed them to thrive morally and spiritually, at the first opportunity leading the nation in a struggle for civil rights that would improve equality and opportunities for all, even the wives, mothers, daughters, and aunts of the perpetrator class, who would be the greatest beneficiaries of their sacrifice? What I began to see was the inheritance of their cultural heritage at the level of cultural worldview, which I will discuss later.

I have also been astounded by the heartless and terrorist-like behavior of the enslavers and their progeny. What would account for their long-standing inhumanity about which they seemed to give little conscious recognition? How does one feel justified in kidnapping and enslaving young adult men, women, and children, treating them as chattel and inflicting multigenerational trauma, all for the accumulation of personal and family material wealth? What could the enslavers be assuming about themselves and others that made them confident about passing laws stating that Blacks have no rights that Whites are even obligated to consider? What would be the reasoning and moral code of the conduct of people who felt justified in using violent aggression to take over other people's land and force them onto reservations, repeatedly breaking treaties enacted to bring peace.

In my attempt to understand how such behavior could be possible for human beings and how they seemingly have little or no collective sense of guilt, shame, or remorse, the importance of cultural worldview emerged once again. For the most part such behavior had historically been sanctioned as normal, and the prevailing ethos permitted this violent aggression in the name of the acquisition of material gain because of the assumptions, values, and principles underpinning the dominant cultural worldview.

My theory of optimal psychology (which I published in 1988 and 1992) was developed to help better understand and expand the most profound learnings around peace and make them available to address the urgent troubles that afflict people. With the intention of exploring the dimensions of culture giving rise to the perceptions, beliefs, patterns of interpretation, and designs for living characterizing cultural worldview, I was able to identify two conceptual systems accounting for the distinct differences in the manifestations of culture and human experience as just described.

A conceptual system is the set of assumptions and principles upon which perceptions, thoughts, feelings, behaviors, and, subsequently, experience or "reality" is based. The assumptions of culture underneath the surface structures—language, systems of organization and economic exchange, religious expression, and so on—can vary widely but generally coalesce around core principles, beliefs, and values that become the fabric of cultural worldview.

The theory of optimal psychology explores the continuum of human consciousness along the lines of two conceptual systems that either enhance psychological security, well-being, and peace or work against it. The conceptual system that maximizes the likelihood of conflict can be described as suboptimal. The conceptual system characterizing values, beliefs, and assumptions maximizing the potential for peace and harmony can be referred to as optimal. On the macrosocietal level or the microindividual level the principles yield the same outcomes.

## CONFLICT AND WESTERN CIVILIZATION

Using examples from Western culture and civilization, more specifically the United States, we can see the ways in which the worldview of dominant socialization, often unbeknown to us, may make it impossible to achieve peace. The contemporary global crisis of social conflict and stifled capacity for peacemaking could be improved if we were to step outside the conceptual incarceration of a cultural worldview that binds us to conflict. An optimal conceptual system that functions to enhance peace management and conflict resolution may be a viable alternative, but such a transformation of worldview is a developmental process.

The significance of conflict in Western civilization is made evident by the way the West benchmarks history, and much of it centers around materialistic values. Western historians typically recount what has taken place over time through the engagement of Western cultures in extremely violent conflicts or wars, the consequences of imperialist instinct and aggression or inability to resolve differences and conflict. Note that almost all cultures and civilizations have not engaged in war, but note also that the degree of imperialist aggression and colonial domination characterizing Western history is the largest recorded in the history of humankind. Insight into the mind-set of Western aggressive dominance is important. In my book *Understanding an Afrocentric World View: Introduction to an Optimal Psychology* (first published in 1988), I detail the ways in which the prevailing Western cultural worldview functions on both macro and micro levels, having tremendous implications for the issues of conflict, violence, and peace management. One telling feature of the suboptimal conceptual system behind the imperialist and aggressive behaviors characterizing Western cultural groups is the response to people of color. This feature can be observed in the monoculturally hegemonic nature of the suboptimal conceptual system under which the worldview functions and has fostered the West's belief in its centrality to world culture and civilization. Ignorance of previous or contemporary cultural traditions is commonplace, as if no others existed—or, if existent, then assumed to be of lesser value or of little consequence. For example, this self-consumed stance has lead the West to describe two of the wars it propagated as World War I and World War II, when the whole world was not really involved save being impacted by the massive turmoil that the engagement of Western cultures in imperialism and conflict caused.

Two features of a Western worldview become evident in this example. One, conflict and war may be seen as the historic centerpiece of the Western experience; and two, this minority of the global population has set itself up as the rightful definer and dictator of all human experience, most often through conflict, war, colonization, and other imperialist activities. The suboptimal worldview has become the dominant worldview of socialization wherever the West has won or has taken over. It is no wonder that many have come to believe, based on this exposure, that conflict in human relationships is simply the natural outcome of human nature. My theory of optimal psychology suggests that there are other variables that inform if not the probabilities of violence and aggression then the ways in which humans respond to conflict. That is cultural worldview.

Western cultural tradition has historically treated conflict in ways that are consistent with its prevailing assumptions regarding the nature of humankind or its ambivalence about it. Conflict is inevitable because the operating worldview functions on a faulty ontological premise that is inconsistent with the heights of knowledge that humanity has confirmed across cultural groups, even their own. The height of Western science is now confirming what has been a part of an African common sense for thousands of years. Eastern philosophies, being one of the first waves of the African Diasporan cultural manifestations of the wisdom tradition starting in classical African civilization (among the Ethiops in ancient Kmt, or Egypt), have long supported the assumptions of an optimal worldview. We have come in contemporary times to a place of cultural convergence, but in order to realize its benefits, a new understanding of the optimal mind-set must be adopted, displacing the cultural lag currently seen.

## THE COST OF RESISTANCE TO CULTURAL PLURALISM

The United States is a nation, like many others, born of conflict. For members of oppressed groups, particularly those who have had to engage in a long, historic battle to be considered fully human by law, much less given such social consideration, there is good reason for a great deal of cultural mistrust when it comes to the capacity of the United States for peace management and conflict resolution. Mainstream activities in the area of peace management and conflict resolution within U.S. borders for some members of this group are seen as exercises in hypocrisy. For some the United States lacks credibility in this regard. Although many would acknowledge that some progress has been made over the past four hundred years, with great struggle and sacrifice, most clearly see much that is alarming. Thus, any field identifying itself as devoted to "mediation and conflict resolution" is quite suspect to this group from the start. However, such thinkers realize that within this social context this field is what we have to work with, so we must seek to move it along toward greater awareness, inclusiveness, and sensitivity. If this arena becomes one in which the movement toward cultural pluralism is taken, then the current discourse must be expanded. There is much to learn and do on this path toward increased understanding and appreciation.

I have found that to learn the perspective of the Other, once one's own perspective has been fully examined and interrogated, is a step toward increased understanding and more complete knowledge. To deny or minimize the realities and the perspectives of the Other is to maximize the likelihood of misunderstanding, conflict, and incomplete knowledge. Although these assertions are simply common sense to some, they may be quite controversial to others.

For example, some cultures seem to intentionally (or unintentionally) socialize their members to systematically discount the perspectives of individuals who are members of certain groups (for example, the black race, the religiously different, etc.). Further, for those ethnic groups whose members have historically been seen as less than human, exploited and oppressed, an extended structural violence of socioeconomic and educational disadvantage and marginalization will ensue by virtue of the nature of the trajectory that has been set.

On this course members of these populations will lose their voice and can become invisible. Others will speak for them, but they will not be heard unless they agree to join the dominant chorus of the mainstream choir. For some, becoming a part of the "amen" choir will not be a problem, because of the limits of their own personal cultural experiences, exposures, socialization, and meanings made. For others, future generations, and humanity as a whole, the loss of the representation of alternate cultural worldviews could mean we will have cut ourselves off from the very forces and wisdom that are needed to save us and the planet from our current limitations and self-destructive arrogance.

## MACROLEVEL EXPLANATIONS AND MICROLEVEL PREDICTIONS

Common to the Western worldview is the presumption of material acquisition as a primary value and the primacy of individual over collective well-being. Such a mind-set holds the ontological premise that reality is the material, what the five senses inform. A spiritual aspect of being may be acknowledged, but it is assumed to be separate and secondary to the material. Thus fragmenting the nature of reality itself, the human personality is left with a sense of identity and worth couched in materiality, externalized and contingent on material acquisition for definition. The individual is left insecure, fearful, and unstable. Epistemological assumptions about the nature of knowledge and its acquisition, which are driving this conceptual system, follow the ontological premise. Knowledge is conceived as external and can only be known through the five senses by counting and measuring. Conclusions are drawn based on statistical probabilities. Axiologically, the highest value is placed on the acquisition of objects or materialism through competition and individualism.

When a culture socializes its members to define reality based upon an ontological premise that prevents a comprehensive coherence and cohesiveness, the suboptimal conceptual system that ensues becomes self-perpetuating. Holding assumptions that lead the society's members to incorrectly believe that there is material reality "out there" that they did not take an active role in creating, they feel fearful and insecure. Thus, the fragmented cultural worldview lays the foundation for other faulty assumptions that are incongruent with the height of the West's own scientific knowledge, from quantum theory to cognitive neuroscience. The fragmented orientation to knowledge is also manifest in artificial lines being drawn across the various subject matter of disciplines.

When cultural worldviews accurately fold the primary and proactive role of consciousness in human experience and its subjective nature into the structuring of reality, the spiritual aspects of being can come to the fore. The individual is conceived as connected with the source of life, peace, love, and justice, and then the sacred within themselves and within which they are sustains them. They are so immersed that they tend to see and seek this connection with others as well. The cultural worldview supports this connection by propagating the ontological premise of a spiritual or material unity of the cosmos and the belief that all are "living suns." This optimal conceptual system provides the basis for a comprehensive, cohesive, coherent synthesis of all aspects of life. A multidimensional sense of self ensues, connecting one with those who have gone before or the ancestors, nature, community, and future generations.

At the level of cultural deep structure, these core assumptions allowed African Americans to survive by living above conditions and accessing a "reality" beyond appearances. However, one can see a shift as African Americans become increasingly assimilated into the dominant cultural worldview of socialization in U.S. society with school desegregation and the advent of television. When this socialization replaces that of the cultural heritage, materialism and acquisition of objects become the source of identity and worth, yielding the same consequences for everyone who embraces those assumptions.

## THE NATURE OF HUMAN NATURE IN CULTURAL CONTEXT

One limitation we all share as human beings is that we are only capable of experiencing the world subjectively. This condition can be a shortcoming if we fail to acknowledge its importance in determining whatever it is we accept as reality in any instance. Although we experience the world subjectively, most people experience it in the terms propagated by the society into which they have been socialized; thus, our reality becomes socially constructed. If the society into which we have assimilated supports a worldview that is fragmented, we become conceptually incarcerated without a way to make meaning beyond our own limited point of view. In this case, the human tendency seems to be to assume that everyone sees the world in the same way, because what each person knows becomes all he or she knows. Failure to entertain the idea that points of view different from our own may have validity makes it impossible to acknowledge and honor the reality and experiences of others. This error is further reinforced by a corollary logic of a suboptimal conceptual system or system of reasoning that tends to be dichotomous; that is, it leads to conclusions such that only one of us can be right. If I am right, you must be wrong.

As we are exposed to points of view that are different from our own, depending on our previous conditioning and the cultural worldview we have adopted, we tend to either become interested in learning more about and from others and trying to understand, or we tend to become arrogant, defensive, and guarded when other perspectives are expressed with which we disagree or are unfamiliar. Most people simply comply with the designs for living and patterns of interpreting reality as defined by the cultural norms dominant in the society to which they belong. The assumptions of their cultural worldview may unwittingly impair their capacity to effectively resolve conflict or build and support institutional structures that would promote peace management. This state of affairs is most probable in a society in which the cultural norms of the dominant worldview do not encourage critical and independent thinking. The danger increases if the values promoted by the society foster institutional structures privileging one group over another and if the "blindness of the privileged" causes loss of interest in anything not supporting perpetuation of the status quo. Conceptually incarcerated, we are prevented from breaking out of mind-sets that bind us, because doing so would require that we entertain a worldview or conceptual system that is different from our own.

## QUESTIONING ASSUMPTIONS

Western practitioners could benefit from questioning assumptions underlying their cultural worldview and taking steps to develop an appreciation for a set of assumptions more in line with those contributing to the unity and peace management that unity consciousness provides. At the deepest structural level, culture embodies every aspect of our way of life. Cultural worldview, which informs our perceptions, thoughts, feeling, and actions with the greatest of specificity and distinctiveness, requires cultivation in order to become optimal. If one has the capacity to think critically and deeply, then examining the assumptions behind the realities, social policies, and practices that have been created is a worthwhile endeavor. Formulating strategies to more effectively address conflict and trauma becomes a natural consequence. Using this method is how practitioners can marshal the resources of distinctive linguistic, religious, kinship, or communal forms in order to better understand or resolve conflict.

The social actions that these analyses call for must occur not just on individual levels but also in society's actual operations, policies, and practices. This culture-centered approach must not be "soft" in the sense of intellectual rigor; critical and deep thinking is required. Help may be found among those whose perspectives have not resonated well with our own cultural worldview in the past. Those seeking a deeper understanding should search out the voices of those previously overlooked. With such assistance the political, social, and economic role of the practitioner within the society's legal structures is given direction and made clear. The challenge for many is to become aware that there is a valid and viable way of seeing and being in the world that differs from their own. We must move beyond the limited conception that only certain knowledge is of central importance and that other knowledge is of marginal value.

CONCLUSION

This essay was designed for readers to consider the importance of cultural worldview in all aspects of life, particularly peace management and conflict resolution. When this consideration is given, a new world of possibility emerges in which the symbolic and material meld and thus empower the confronting of social, economic, political, racial, and class issues at a depth that inspires creative and fearless solutions.

# 3  Beyond Mediation — Reconciling an Intercultural World

*A New Role for Conflict Resolution*

ROBERTO M. CHENÉ

In 1987 two significant things happened to me.* I do not recall the exact sequence of these events but I know that in my mind I put the two together and it has made a difference in my work over the past years.

Encouraged by friends, I attended my first mediation training in Santa Fe, New Mexico. At about the same time I read an article in the progressive journal *Social Policy*. The article I read listed the elements of an emerging American progressive ideology for the year 2000. An ideology that rejected relationships of dominance was central to this list of elements. The article went on to say that progressive morality should be based upon a rejection of relationships of dominance and subservience: "In our private and public lives we seek relationships not based upon coercion but trust and equality. Transforming relationships of dominance to ones of equality and cooperation is an unending personal, social, and political process. There is no single, final magic moment of liberation."[1]

*This chapter is a revised version of an article originally published in *Conciliation Quarterly*, Winter 2001 (a publication of the Mennonite Conciliation Service) and is reprinted here by permission of the publishers.

The mediation training added a new tool to the peacemaking work I had been doing for many years and introduced me to a model of conflict resolution that seemed to have great utility for peacemaking. The article in *Social Policy* validated a path I had already chosen but its language further clarified for me the essence of my choice. From the outset of my formal introduction to mediation I perceived it as simply another resource that should be put at the service of the broader and never ending task of transforming relationships of dominance into ones of equality and cooperation. I took relationships to mean both interpersonal and institutional. I believed and still believe that mediation and other conflict resolution skills are indispensable tools in the process of social transformation and the struggle for social justice and equality. The critical variable in how these tools are applied, however, is the knowledge, worldview, experience, and values that the peacemaker brings to the practice of conflict resolution.

## SOCIAL CONTEXT

It is critical to be fully aware and cognizant of the social reality in which we are practicing conflict resolution. We live in a diverse, multicultural society in which the beautiful differences between human beings have been institutionalized according to a dominant, power-over model of resolving differences. When we talk about racism, sexism, homophobia, and so on, what are we referring to if not a model of dominance and chronic conflict? For problem solving around race and ethnicity, it is helpful to include the concepts of white cultural dominance and assimilation. It is not commonly referred to, but the coercive nature of the Americanization process generates a tyranny of conformity that places people of color in the untenable position of being the "wrong" kind of American.

The point I want to make here is that according to our differences we are already institutionalized into conflicted, unhealthy, and ultimately unimprovable (within the dominance paradigm) human relationships. The conflicts between us are already set in the dysfunctional paradigm that we have constructed for relating to each other. What we are mediating are the frequent overt flare-ups of a fundamentally unworkable system. We need to think about the role of conflict resolution in addressing the chronic undercurrent of conflict that is always present even when it is not overt. We need to think about how to intentionally address a situation that most people think of as "normal."

I realize that in this brief piece on social context I am stating the obvious, saying once again what every person who does mediation or conflict resolution understands or should understand in depth. But perhaps stating the obvious is necessary. From my point of view, for example, much of organized mediation remains predominantly white monocultural in its worldview and general participation while existing in the midst of a multicultural reality. It often acts as if it has not heard of the social context I live in. The people it recruits are not trained in an intercultural paradigm. As a result many mediators are naïve about the depth of the institutionalized intercultural conflict. They are also naïve about their already conditioned and socially assigned role as participants in the conflict. As an institutionalized entity mediation tends to function on the dominant side of our intercultural conflict. It is one more institution that is relatively low on the spectrum of cultural competence and inclusion. Some mediators within it function according to an intercultural paradigm; most do not. Some people of color who participate do so at the cost of keeping parts of themselves invisible. Many others of course work to change it. Basically, it has not worked out for itself its inherent intercultural conflict.

Approaches to the use of mediation, such as community mediation and culturally specific and relevant approaches by Hispanics, African Americans, Native Americans, Asian Americans, and others, help fill in the gaps but even these gaps get harder to fill as the professionalization of mediation has escalated and become subject to dominant culture bureaucratic social norms. Efforts to make the professionalization process culturally inclusive, which I have often been a part of, are very problematic and inevitably result in a cultural clash between people of color and white Anglos. We then face the dilemma of having to mediate ourselves as we try to collaborate. This of course leads to the question of whose leadership, mediation, or facilitation we are going to accept. It also leads to the question of how much intercultural capacity we can all bring to bear on sustaining our dialogue long enough to actually create inclusive intercultural policy and conflict resolution practice.

PARADIGM SHIFTS AND OTHER IDEAS

In trying to figure out new or emerging roles for conflict resolution, one's point of view and one's understanding of the social context obviously makes a tremendous difference. There are some aspects of intercultural conflict resolution that merit some reflection and that when well understood can determine how an intervention is designed or at the very least can help provide a reality-based expectation of what can be done in a particular situation.

There is a common assumption out there that we get into conflict because of our cultural differences. There is no doubt that there are conflicts related to misunderstandings, language, values, worldview, and so on. In my experience, such conflicts are relatively minor. *Dominance, not difference, is at the root of cross-cultural conflict.* As a rule, it is the dominant side that wants to believe that it is only about the differences. Attempting to reconcile diversity without addressing the power relations results in what I call *pretend diversity,* an attempt to create inclusion without the dominant culture having to reciprocate and take responsibility for its side of the inequity. This model is common in the workplace and allows organizations to pretend to become inclusive without acknowledging the oppressive nature of the workplace structure. Nor do they have to acknowledge that bureaucracies, through their policies, exist to socialize us all to the white cultural worldview. It also perpetuates the tension placed on people of color to carry the burden of "fitting in" while the dominant culture gets to call itself diverse because there are people of color among them. Practicing mediation in the workplace does not substitute for the fact that the workplace ultimately needs to be restructured interculturally. Mediation, though helpful for immediate problem solving, allows the postponement of addressing the real source of conflict: the oppressive nature of many hierarchies, which includes the lack of caring for the workers. Control of employees becomes a substitute for vision and leadership. Actual inclusion happens when *unique* cultural, gender, and other voices are actually reflected in policy outcomes. We need to address the roots of intercultural conflict that tend to reside in top-down, poorly led structures.

CONCLUSION

The goal of recreating, and restructuring, and ultimately transforming inter-cultural relationships at all levels of society, which is what diversity is really about, needs to be moved to center stage. If we hope to move beyond treating diversity as an "add on" or "after thought," which is its current status, we must shift to a paradigm that acknowledges as primary that diversity is *the problem* we need to be always solving. If we conquer the intractability of this problem, perhaps many of our other problems will appear solvable.

In the field of mental health we see that the lives of families are transformed every day by facilitating mutual respect, power sharing, ventilation of past grievances, and forgiveness. In organizational contexts we are learning how to mediate conflicts as they arise, how to be quiet and let other voices take their power, how to nourish relationships versus mandating conformity. *We already know what to do.*

As we know, one cannot accomplish paradigm shifting without conflict. We choose to uproot a comfortable, anachronistic model in order to grow into a more workable one. I and others have learned from our work that it is possible to facilitate groups and organizations past the fears of raw conflict; mediate, nourish, and educate them through the process of creative conflict; increase their practice and knowledge of intercultural competence; and help them become inspired to want to learn more. We have also learned that it is incumbent upon those who practice conflict resolution to teach and help others embrace what I think of as *creative conflict resolution* and *creative discomfort* as being essential components of recreating intercultural community. We can help others acquire a spirit of embracing, not avoiding, conflict. Framed and creatively mediated and facilitated properly, our conflicts are simply grand opportunities to learn and be transformed.

# 4 The Shirt on My Back

*The Daily Continuum of Violence*

MARIAH BREEDING

For some weeks now, I have been preoccupied with violence; the more I con-template violence, the more blurred the boundary becomes between violence and other sorts of oppression. Perhaps the best way, maybe even the only way, for me to illustrate this dilemma is with an examination of my current lived circumstances.

I will begin with myself, as I sit here in San Francisco at a kitchen table, dressed for the day, drinking tea. Consider the very shirt on my back, made of cotton picked (for $2 per day) in pesticide-soaked fields by women in El Salvador (!) and shipped by Exxon (remember the *Valdez,* whose oil spill of 20 years' past still poisons the Alaskan coastline?) through the Panama Canal (an early harbinger of the global economy to come, built by slave labor on first stolen and then decimated land) to mills in South Carolina where it was woven (for minimum wage and with concomitant brown-lung disease) into material that could then be transported back across the Caribbean *(Valdez II)* to Haiti (!) where women assembled a shirt (for $3 per day) after which it was shipped for the last time across the seas *(Valdez III)* to wind up on my back via a Lane Bryant's 2-for-1 special (Lane Bryant—do their workers have quality medical coverage, earn enough to support a family?).[1]

And that's just my shirt. Marx, that incomparable analyst of the violence of labor, identified commodities with poetic precision as "definite masses of congealed labor time"; material goods are wrapped about—shrouded—by a densely packed history of the labor that produced them: what was done, by whom, under what conditions, and for what wages. Suffice it to say here that each of the commodities my body is adorned with/encased in/protected by have a similar history to my shirt, as do the commodities around me: the mug from which I drain the last dregs of my morning tea, the table on which I rest the mug, the teaspoon with which I stirred the tea that stood in the mug that rested upon the table.

I could go on here, in any one of many divergent ways, dense as thickets in their wildly branching complexity:

There is the electricity (from where, gotten how, and by whom, whose profits power what projects?) that heats the water (through what systems of dams, locks, and reservoirs, built and maintained by what people, under what conditions?) that floats the tea (imported from India, in a trail undoubtedly not a whit less convoluted and oppressive than my shirt's path). Or I could examine the land literally underneath all of these commodities, tracking its trail back through the chains of contractual exchanges in the Anglo-American system to the Spanish conquistadors to the nearly seventy Native American tribes that lived in the greater Bay Area of California before the arrival of the Europeans.

I am not going out of the house today, but if I were, perhaps, to go grocery shopping (what food: genetically modified in secret? irradiated? picked by which undocumented workers, for what wages?), I would have to step over and around the bodies of homeless people, about whom the *New York Times* recently noted:

> At the richest time in the nation's history, housing that the poor can afford is at an all-time low, fueling an increase in homelessness, according to the U.S. Conference of Mayors. And with complaints about beggars and bag ladies and mumbling, stumbling vagrants growing as well, cities are fighting as never before to move homeless people out of public spaces.[2]

And what about the familial and ancestral histories of violence that have vitally, albeit sometimes subliminally, informed my experience of this morning, the ubiquitous underlayment of past and personal violences that have prepared me both to endure and to participate in today's violence? Thick family legends woven of Huguenots fleeing genocide in France lead to English/Welsh southerners leaving Maryland in the wake of the Civil War with a retinue of slaves too "happy" to leave their masters. There is my mother's Depression-era job daily administering dozens of X-rays without protection, followed by her death of cancer brought on by glamorously packaged cigarettes smoked from the age of ten. There is a childhood punctuated by physical and sexual abuse, meted out by loving parents who had themselves been locked in closets and sexually appropriated by the adults who cared for them.

I want to move toward articulating a theory of violence that rests on the notion that all of us—even those of us fortunate enough not to be slicing-up/sliced-up-by our neighbors with machetes or bombed by terrorists or invading/being invaded by other countries for their/our own good, even those of us privileged enough to be living overtly peaceful and protected middle-class lives in the wealthiest of countries—exist drenched in violence; exist in a world of institutionalized violence, structural violence, symbolic violence, everyday violence;[3] a world where a hundred necessary and utterly commonplace daily acts are laced with either the performance or reception of violence; a world at its very best filled with mornings like the one I have just described.

The so-far-buried-it-is-almost-invisible bedrock upon which all of this continuum of violence rests are the accepted, "legitimate" sites of blatant physical coercion:

• The hands of the state, most notably in the conduct of war and in the treatment of criminals, the insane, and those who threaten the smooth operation of society or the amassing of wealth

• The hands of "mankind," via the controlling of nature

• The hands of the family, most notably in the rearing of children

One result of this legitimated daily and global exercise of raw physical force is that the experience of it—whether as practitioner, witness, or recipient—always has enduring transformative effects, one of which is often an increased capacity for collusion in violence in any and all of its many possibilities. Here it may be particularly important to consider the situation of children and adolescents. As a group, they are subjected to socially sanctioned violence from both state and family. They are under double jurisdiction. In the case of adolescents, at a time when they are becoming capable of acting as agents of violence, they are being bombarded by the structural and symbolic violence of the larger society. The rash of schoolyard shootings suggests what a powerful and powerless time adolescence is, and how desperately we need to understand what messages about violence have been internalized by youth, and how and by whose hands and words they have learned these lessons. Perhaps here, in the particularly potent crucible of violence received and the beginning of the capacity to inflict widespread violence, we can begin to stop the cycle.

What is at stake here is the situating of public acts of the most extreme and florid forms of violence, from schoolyard murder to state-sanctioned genocide and torture, firmly within a hegemonic continuum that also contains both acceptable, legitimated covert violence and activities and structures whereby their potential ultimate enforcement by violence is so mystified that they are not conventionally recognized as being associated with violence at all. The acceptance of violence anywhere makes possible the rationalization of violence everywhere, albeit with endless qualifiers, caveats, and the reassurance of rules and regulations. When we work from a theoretical framework that accepts the interconnectedness of the most mild of oppressions and the most heinous of violences it becomes possible to move beyond framing violence as an ever-surprising aberration committed by monstrous alien others to a logical and thus understandable—and ultimately preventable—human activity.

# 5 The Rape of Black Girls

ONAJE MU'ID

In September 1996, my daughter committed suicide. She had been raped twice in her life. This is the first, written acknowledgment of her tragic, traumatic life, and as such, is a public statement of advocacy for Taisha and her sister, aunts, cousins, nieces, friends, and other women who have experienced this wicked oppression. I tell my story with the hope of igniting a fierce, antirape Black activist movement that will successfully halt the strewing of bodies, minds, and souls in the wake of sexual violence.

I am not an objective observer of the rape of Black girls. Nor do I use analytical social science research methodology in this discussion, but, in fact, I strongly affirm and adapt an evaluative critical method that contains prescription. Like researchers Elizabeth A. Stanko[1] and Susan Hippensteele,[2] who speak to the correctness of emotionality and activism as research, I bring who I am and what I experience into my work to inform it and to present my social narrative "as evidence in ongoing struggles for social change."[3] I am emphatically against rape of all kinds. Therefore, this inquiry is intended to be a contribution toward the alleviation of human suffering and oppressions of all kinds, especially the sexual oppression of women and young girls. The backdrop for my paper is a form of research grounded in community and culture that leads me into another realm and level of understanding internalized oppression.

The raping of young girls in the Black community is a problem, both historically and currently, of enormous, complicated, political, moral, and social proportions that defies any simple explanation, and yet it demands an explanation. Sexual tyranny is not committed because of who individual

41

women are or what they do, but because of institutionalized systems of male inadequacy, insecurity, power, spiritual underdevelopment, moral bankruptcy, and lawlessness. Historical trauma theory and posttraumatic slave syndrome suggest that a connection exists between cultural and historical experiences of trauma, inflictions of sexual violence on young Black girls, and the presence of socioculturally adaptive mechanisms acquired as a result of sustained psychological multigenerational trauma. In order to find where personal and historical trauma intersect, I will examine my own tragedy in a larger context of violence and oppression.

The concept of trauma, originating in the Greek *traumat* meaning wound, has been a part of the human language for some time, although its systematic study is fairly recent. Trauma is the result of a "complex interrelationship among psychology, biology and social processes—one that varies, depending on the maturational level of the victim, as well as length of time for which the person was exposed to the trauma."[4] Historical trauma response, a concept elaborated by Mary Yellow Horse Brave Heart-Jordan in the context of Native American experience, is a constellation of features that are prompted by and is a direct reaction to a traumatic event or series of traumatic events. Symptoms may resemble formerly established trauma responses such as war neurosis, posttraumatic stress disorder, or psychic trauma. Further, Brave Heart theorizes that there exists a historical unresolved grief. This social and emotional phenomenon is produced when grief is delayed, impaired, or denied expression or societal sanction and manifests as socially maladaptive behaviors, such as prolonged signs of grief, depression, substance abuse, and somatization.[5]

Additionally, many researchers and clinicians describe a constellation of symptoms specific to rape trauma. Rape operates in a sexual context, but rape is fundamentally an outward statement of power, vulnerability, and exploitation. Power is at the essence of human relationships. By virtue of being human, we have inherent power. When our inherent human power is denied by ourselves or by oppressive systems, that denial is expressed in three basic ways. First, denial of oppression causes us to be ahistorical; we do not have a sense of how we got here. Second, oppression and its denial lead us to be apolitical; we do not have as sense of ourselves and the power we have in the world. Last, we become afuturistic, without a sense of hope for our future.

Hopeless people resort to drugs, rape, and other expressions of internalized oppression. Thus, rape occurs when societal powerlessness gets transformed into deformed, interpersonal power relationships, where subordination is transposed. In other words, rape occurs as a result of powerless people seeking to fulfill a need to exact power from or at the expense of someone else they perceive as less powerful.

## A POSTSLAVERY HISTORICAL SOCIOCULTURAL CRITIQUE OF RAPE

To fully understand contemporary sexual violence against Black girls and women, one must acknowledge the historical legacy of the raping of Black females. This long-standing social problem assumes a particular, grotesque entanglement with the historical legacy of slavery and its many facets. The raping of black females started in Africa prior to transport with the first rape in the "slave dungeons" or "castles" where special rooms were created for that special purpose. Rape continued in the "slave"[6] ships during the middle passage across the Atlantic Ocean, then continued during slavery and after slavery. Given the relatively minimal resources expended to stop it, it can be said that rape has enjoyed a general semisocial acceptance for nearly four hundred years. In addition to being used as a human baby-making machine for the production of "slave" labor, the Black female was the object of socially legitimated power violations, control, and exploitation. In a very real sense, a system of ill-gotten, stolen wealth could not have existed without her. Thus, rape was intentionally embedded in the history of a slave-o-cracy culture. First came the raping of indigenous women and then rape against Black women and girls, where sexual violence became routine, celebrated, perfected, and *legal:* sexual oppression as a legal means of enhancing the economic gain of slaveholders.

To emphasize this point of the connection between slavery and rape, and the legal protection for white male rapists, Lori Robinson provides an important historical overview of the rape of Black women. She states: "From slavery's end through the first two-thirds of the twentieth century, no southern White man was convicted of rape or attempted rape of a Black woman."[7] The National Commission on the Causes and Prevention of Violence stated in 1969 that "white males have long had nearly institutional access to Negro women with relatively little fear of being reported."[8]

Young Black girls suffered multiple forms of victimization, unimaginable for us today. They endured rape not only at the hands of the enslaver, but also from their male enslaved counterpart, maybe their father, uncle, brother, or cousin, plus a society that raped them of their dignity. The permissible raping of Black girls by Black men has a legal root in this racist-slave society where enslaved Africans had no rights save the right to abuse each other without punishment. Crimes committed against children were historically unpunishable. In 1859 when an attempt was made to hold an African enslaved male accountable for his act of raping a girl younger than ten, the Mississippi judge's response was bewildering: "There is no act (of our legislature on this subject) which embraces either the attempted or actual commission of rape by a slave on a female slave."[9]

Further, the effect of "breeding" slaves formed a rape-infested social context. An enslaved, brutalized people were forced to have sex for the sole purpose of procreation for the enslavers' power and material benefit. Oral historians report that slaveholders reached barbaric lows of human decency by forcing young black men to have sex with their mothers, hence the term "mother-f——" readily used today within some black communities. This term, as well as the word "nigger," is a sad, sorrowful, foul social commentary. What happens to the collective psyche of men who are forced into such behavior patterns? Is an injury of this magnitude ever resolved? How does it manifest in social behavior? This forced breeding conjures up the image of someone who, while eating food, is also forced to consume their own feces for survival; the poisonous elements ingested along with actual food form a diet that is functional for keeping the entity alive but prevents the entity from truly living. The entity is inherently diseased.

Clearly, the topic of Black males raping Black girls and women is a social problem that is connected to and complicated by historical and internalized oppression whose depth and meaning are not fully comprehensible. Historical trauma scholars suggest that trauma can be examined along three dimensions: (1) physical to psychological trauma, (2) individual to group trauma, and (3) trauma experienced in the moment to trauma passed down and reexperienced across time and space and then transmitted from one generation to another. The Holocaust is an example of the combination of group, psychological, and transgenerational trauma. Stories from Holocaust survivors have been used to provide a conceptual framework for analyzing historical trauma for other groups.

In 2005 Joy DeGruy Leary published a book endeavoring to explore the vestiges and internal consequences of slavery.[10] She identified the transgenerational trauma of African Americans as posttraumatic slave syndrome (PTSS). Leary asserts that psychological and emotional injury occurred as a direct result of slavery and that descendants of African slaves continue to be wounded by the larger society's inequality, racism, and oppression. The PTSS theory suggests that the consequences internalized by formerly enslaved people of African descent include self-destructive behaviors such as those psychologists identify as symptoms of posttraumatic stress disorder. These symptoms include feeling of detachment or estrangement from others; restricted range of affect, for example, unable to have loving feelings; sense of foreshortened future, for example, not expecting to have a career, marriage, or children or a long life; irritability or outbursts of anger; unpredictable explosions of aggressive behavior; difficulty concentrating; hypervigilance; and exaggerated startle response. Today, the African American community is made up of individuals and families who collectively share heightened anxiety and adaptive survival behaviors resulting from prior generations of African Americans who suffered from PTSS. In other words, as Africans were forced to function in a system that was in conflict with their own traditional customs, values, and needs, the original slavery trauma, compounded by intergenerational trauma, was internalized as socially learned maladaptive behaviors. Rape and sexual violence toward Black girls and women remain a specific outcome of this intergenerational trauma.

Both the terrorist and the terrorized find comfort in "let the past stay in the past." But as Judith Herman (a groundbreaking student of the consequences of sexual assault) insists, the unspeakable has to be spoken.[11] However, even as victims and survivors break the silence of not only their rape but also its connectedness to slavery and the rape of their mothers and forebears, rapes continue to be underreported because of societal stigma. When one looks at reporting mechanisms over time, their deficiencies become apparent. For example, the National Crime Victimization Survey recorded

197,000 incidents of forcible rape and 110,000 incidents of other sexual assault in 1996, but only for those twelve years of age or older. The Uniform Crime Reporting Program reported 96,000 forced rapes but left out rape by objects and other critical categories, including forced fondling.

Further, considering the numbers of victims and the magnitude of the problem, this entrenched social problem still has relatively few champions. Black girls and women, the persons who most obviously benefit from documenting, reporting, and indicting those involved in raping young Black girls, are least likely to be successful in bringing rape accountability forward, let alone resolve it, because of their relative powerlessness in society. Who then is in the position to make sexual violence a truly visible public issue?

I suggest that it is Black men. The degree of involvement in antirape activism by Black men who had a loved one raped appears to be woefully low. Wouldn't fathers of raped Black women be invested in stopping rape behavior? As a fairly educated Black man, I can recall little conversation, let alone instruction, from other Black men about the critical need to be an antirapist, even in so-called progressive circles. Further, as a father whose daughter and other female family members have been raped, I would think it stands to reason that there would be a visible presence of this cohort in the community voicing disgust and total opposition to rape, since their loved ones have been victimized. But why are Black men, for the most part, silent?

*The answer to this question might be found by studying how trauma and historical oppression intersect.* Black men were forbidden to defend their women during slavery. Today, silent victims, in this case Black men like myself, struggle with the pain of our loved ones being harmed, our inability to prevent it, our inability to bring appropriate retribution, and the apparent gross powerlessness that surrounds the entire phenomenon of our social oppression. Black men's fear of exposing to full view our real powerlessness, our inability to alter oppressive circumstances, causes activism to be suppressed at the cost of social change. The necessary activism that would in fact correct the problem is muffled by the risk of talking.

Ironically, both white and Black men are explicitly or implicitly implicated in the rape of Black girls and women. The former initiated rape through the institution of slavery and the latter mimicked it through the internalization of oppression. The presence of rape in the Black community gives whites the evidence to indict Blacks as savages. Black men in turn fail to confront rape and therefore support it by default. We fear that making rape public may be seen as "airing dirty laundry." Placing rape in historical context, recall, we know that white enslavers not only sanctioned rape against rebellious women and men, but even instructed it. Oral tradition has also passed down, and therefore kept alive, these acts of "seasoning" in the collective memory of the oppressed. How relevant is that history to current reality? Although each case may be different, it appears to me that learned behavior theory would suggest that the fear factor that prevented Black men from protecting their women and girls then in slavery for fear of reprisal is still in place today, on some subliminal level, and could very well be a function of PTSS.

On one hand, rape is a constant reminder of powerlessness for Black men. Acknowledging and reporting it, as well as other forms of antirape activism, carry a high price tag. On the other hand, the raping of Black girls and women has the dubious position of having the full support and weight of the male supremacist superstructure hierarchy. Neither white nor Black men have a superordinate commitment or incentive to stop it. Placing rape behavior in a social-cultural-historical context does not absolve the individual rapist, but rather it suggests that these populations were injured and therefore require healing and repair. In the same way that we do not call a family in a car accident dysfunctional as they are on their way to or coming back from the hospital, we are obliged to reframe how oppressed people of color are defined.

A sense of helplessness can turn to desperation fairly quickly. How easy it is for me to relate to young Black men who live, die, or kill by the affirmation, "Don't dis me." I clearly understand this. Because I felt unable to protect my daughter Taisha, I have felt the need to resort to the maximum retaliation possible to protect my living daughter. It is difficult, in fact impossible, for me to separate the two issues, rape and suicide, because both happened to my daughter. I cannot hold one without accepting the consequence of the other. It is impossible to think of Taisha's suicide without thinking about her rapes. How many rapes are responsible for the numerous suicides of young people? What can we do about it—NOW? The rape of my daughter and the perceived pain of her injuries were compounded by my feelings of failing to be her protector, hero, and leader. I felt that I wanted to *fight—to actually kill*—because to do anything else was to die, to disavow my person-hood—MY manhood. Eventually, with therapy, I found a way to relate to myself again as a human being, capable of all the feelings that humans have in desperate, unspeakable, and helpless situations . . . and not be drawn into the cycle of violence that consumes this society in so many ways. But fighting we must do, to create a better society.

## CONCLUSION

I assert that our mission must be to "create a rape-free society." Too many women have been waiting for us, as men, for so long, for so very long. Let us not keep them waiting any longer. Let us save the babies, the boys, the girls, the women, the men, the community, the society. The conspiracy of si-lence can only be broken by our words, our thoughts, and our actions. As an antiracist, anti-imperialist, anticolonialist, I am against all oppression, but fervently declare myself an antirapist. All acts of oppression are violations, but rape illustrates how power and terror are used as weapons of domina-tion and exertion of one's will over another. Rape comprehensively attacks the body, mind, and soul of the victim. Although rape is committed against the "person," rape leaves residual effects on family, community, and society. Sexual violence is the fullest abandonment of humanity, the ultimate act of self-centeredness and savagery.

For my daughter Taisha, I declare my allegiance to this cause, and ask your forgiveness for not protecting you when it counted most. I am sorry from the bottom of my soul. I am no longer helpless, and I will fight against this vile behavior and mentality that defiles so many men, women, boys, and girls. For a while I was numb, but now I am awake. I promise to be relentless in mobilizing this society to be absolutely against the raping of any human being at any time, for any reason. I commit myself to changing the condi-tions that perpetuate membership in this wretched cohort—fathers whose daughters have been raped or committed suicide.

# 6 Appellate Recourse to the Supernatural

Kithitu *among the Akamba*

JELVAS MUSAU

The Akamba occupy the central and southeastern parts of the Kenya, with some pockets of population in the coastal strip and along Kenya's border with Tanzania.* It is a community about which Gerhard Lindblom and several other social anthropologists have written.[1] The present study is not ethnological. It is an analysis of a cardinal dispute resolution mechanism within the community.

Prior to colonialism, the Akamba did not have a centralized form of governance in the genre of chief or kingdoms. Governmental organization was family[2] and clan[3] based. At the family level, the leader was usually the eldest male while at the clan level an elected council of elders[4] would sit as court to determine disputes, provide guidance on care and maintenance of religion, and make decisions with respect to wars and aggression. Social norms and traditional values were passed down through generations—many of them in the form of indelible imprints written on ritualistic tablets. Lindblom is fascinated by what he perceives as the Akamba love of law and dispute resolution and notes that it was the pride of every Akamba to be part of a dispute process at one time or the other.

---

*The views expressed in this paper are those of the author, not of the U.N. High Commission for Refugees.

This article looks at dispute resolution in the community and particularly, the resort to supernatural through the *kithitu* oath or fetish. It is a practice that strikes at the very nerve of dispute processing in the community. We begin by a general overview of dispute resolution.

## DISPUTE RESOLUTION

Kinship, family loyalty, and a strong sense of values and customs have always held the Akamba community together. The starting point of Akamba government was the family; being a patriarchal society, the oldest male would be umpire in all disputes that arose within a household.[5] The main arena for dispute resolution was at the *nzama* (elders' convocation). At this level, there was no obvious leader, though the most outspoken of the elders would normally preside for the purposes of order and reporting the verdict reached to disputants.[6]

Dispute resolution among the Akamba was primarily a peacemaking process, with its cardinal objective being the restoration of existing relationships. Justice was first and foremost a communal rather than an individual right. Individual rights generally existed within and in a subordinate position to the closely knit and integrated framework of familial, social, and communal networks. This probably explains why, besides bipartite negotiated compensation, all disputes were resolved through the involvement of respected third parties (elders) whose main role was mediation. They would bring pressure to bear on disputants because of the elders' esteem in the community, to find some common ground and reinstate previously existing relationships.

Most disputes had properly established and predetermined punitive sanctions.[7] This was subject to the unequivocal and unchallenged apprehension of the culprit. To resolve disputes, heads of families of the feuding parties would appear before the *nzama* for a hearing. The injured party, if not one of the family heads, would be called to testify as witness for the complainant. Each party would present their case and call witnesses to testify on their behalf. There were no rules regulating the presentation of evidence, and decisions handed down after the hearing would become binding on the parties.

There were instances where resolution could not be reached, probably because the wrongdoer was unknown or where available evidence was insufficient to unequivocally indict. In these instances, the dispute would be presented to an appellate platform at which more often than not it would, in the words of Gulliver,[8] be "transformed and redefined in symbolic and supernatural terms." The *kithitu* oath would be taken to determine the dispute conclusively. It was the ultimate source of justice.

## KITHITU

Many a commentator has observed that *kithitu* is the most distinctive and important feature of Akamba legal life. It is the most solemn and revered recourse in dispute resolution. Owing to its importance and the threat attached to it, it is only resorted to when absolute justice can not otherwise be achieved. It is scarcely in use presently, having been swept underfoot with the transposition of the various customary methods with the Western judicial system in Kenya.

The concept of *kithitu* defies accurate and precise English translation. Though it involves an oath, its embrace goes beyond the kind known to the English. The ritualistic approach, gravity of expected consequences, or even the respect given to the object[9] of *kithitu* vindicate its sanctification in the community.

Among the Kikuyu,[10] a close replication of *kithitu* could be found in the *muma*[11] oath, *Koringa thenge* (to swear by killing a male goat), and *gethathi,* the three oaths in dispute resolution. They were solemn practices, immensely respected and revered. It is worth noting that *kithitu* seems to have survived the Westernization of dispute resolution more steadfastly than the aforementioned oaths. One would speculate this to be so due to the stronger belief in ritual and supernatural power[12] among the Akamba.

We refer to it as a *kithitu* oath because in all its manifestations, it involves some swearing of an oath. In Kikamba, language of the Akamba, the concept is also referred to as *muma,* which probably derives from the word *uma,* meaning "bite" or "curse." It has been suggested that the word *kithitu* obtains from *thita,* which means "strangle," or *kuthita,* which is "to bind absolutely" or "to tighten a knot." The fundamental essence of *kithitu* has always been that whoever engages in it knows precisely the issue at dispute and that the consequence of "perjury" is death. The effects would manifest themselves through a mysterious and sudden succession of deaths within the family or among close relatives of the perjurer or wrongdoer, suspected or unknown at the time of administering it.

Several items are blended to make a powerful *kithitu* and only a handful of people, who possess the object, would be versatile in the art of administering it. Typical ingredients of the object would include human parts such as hair or nails; earth, plants, animal teeth, parts of a porcupine, hyena's excrement and others; all contained in an antelope horn or other hollow horn.

*Kithitu* has normally been categorized by those whom it is sought to affect.[13] Two distinct ranks on the basis of the kinship character of antagonists exist: the common *kithitu* or *muma* for those who are unrelated and the *ndundu* variety for people of the same family. The difference in this variation is that for the latter only the perjurer would be affected and not his whole family. It is the family and clan *kithitu*. Despite the digression, the baseline structure is the same: the ultimate recourse in dispute processing and resolution.

The swearing ceremony for the *kithitu* oath is characterized by striking the object a number of times (normally seven) with a special piece of wooden rod and uttering words to the effect, "If what I say is not true, may the *kithitu* eat (kill) me" or "whoever took my cow (the subject matter of dispute) may this *kithitu* eat (kill) him/her." The other party to the dispute frames these words where it is an adversarial controversy. In all other instances, the elders contrive the words with the acquiescence of the owner of the *kithitu*. The elders must approve and control the process of swearing *kithitu*. In *James Mainzi wa Muthiani v. Kimatu wa Mbuvi*,[14] the elders rejected the first *kithitu* brought by James on the grounds that it was too potent. This was because it was made of a piece of iron, considered completely binding and irrevocable. It could not be stopped and its power was associated with that of a blacksmith's hammer.

Upon swearing the *kithitu*, parties are not allowed to perform coition for a week or such other period as the proprietor of the object may specify. Failure to observe this leads to the death of the transgressor.

The mechanism of cleansing or purifying exists to arrest continuing oc-currence of misfortune once it becomes evident that *kithitu* has taken effect. The owner of the object would normally be able to perform the cleansing where it became necessary. Penwill[15] illustrates this with a case that came be-fore the Iveti Native Tribunal[16] in 1924. Wambua wa Ngwilo sued Kithuku wa Nzinga on the ground that his brother had been struck by Kithuku's brother and had subsequently become sickened and died from the blow. Wambua swore to the *kithitu* that had been brought by Kithuku and was duly given the first cow of the blood price.[17] Being a strong *kithitu*, the pe-riod of effect was given as nine days and at the end of the time, no death had occurred. This was an unusually short period for blood price cases where common practice was that the stipulated period would last until the person swearing "had drunk the milk of the *ng'ombe ya mbanga*" (cow of acciden-tal killing). Wambua asked for, and received, the remaining stock due to him. Within three months there followed a spate of deaths in Wambua's family. Those that died were Wambua himself, his wife, his two young sons, and a daughter; his brother Nzau, Nzau's wife, son and two daughters, and a brother who had emigrated to Ngoleni and who took the cattle saying that he had no fear for *kithitu*. The latter died slightly over a month later and the clan hastily seized the cattle and returned them to Kithuku, who organized a cleansing of the *kithitu*. No more deaths occurred.

A RITUAL?

In *The Elementary Forms of the Religious Life,* a pioneering work of early sociology, Emile Durkheim points out that rituals are determined modes of action distinguishable from other human practices by the special nature of their object. He further points out that the object's special nature is ex-pressed through beliefs.[18] Anthropologist Hans-Georg Soeffner looks at them in terms of a repertoire of preconditioned conduct obtained through symbolism: some kind of ignition for a stimuli-like chain reaction whose stretch is preinterpreted.[19] These are certainly not the goalposts for ritual; they are the most fitting definitions of the concept for our purposes. The categorization they give eclipses *kithitu* and are based on which concept is characterized as a ritual. It is a "plastic stay in Kamba society's corset."[20]

Like many societies, the Akamba were highly ritualistic. This was especially accentuated by the fact that it was an acephalous community (without a ruling head). The rituals were the convergence zone for the various clans and subcommunities within the larger Akamba nation. *Kithitu* may be placed within the context of rituals designed for societal control. Besides the fact that it always involved some repetition of liturgy, the reverence for the object firmly implants it in the classification.

## DISTINGUISHED FROM WITCHCRAFT AND ORDEALS

Though sharing many characteristics, to assume that *kithitu* is some form of witchcraft or ordeal is to clothe three different phenomena with simplicity and cloud them with obscurity. Each has always existed among the Akamba to serve its distinct social function. If precise difference is not to be found elsewhere, then social conceptualization, perceived and actual, functions of each may provide the elusive answer.

Although *kithitu* has always been accepted among the Akamba as a necessary means of dispute resolution, witchcraft is an evil that was associated with "old, wrinkled, ugly people, cripples, squint eyes, ugly facial features or any crudeness in a person."[21] Nobody would admit to being a witch, and the traditional Kamba method of dealing with witches was banishment. This would be after having the concerned's house burnt down. If the banishment order was not heeded, the *king'ole*[22] would lynch the condemned to death.

Under Kenyan law witchcraft is criminalized.[23] *Kithitu,* however, was accepted into the postcolonial legal system as part of customary law.[24] This may be attributed to the perception of witchcraft's association with evil supernatural power, ugly oracles, jealousy, and injustice. Although *kithitu* is applied to restore order in the community by conclusively determining a dispute, witchcraft has always been a source of tension and suspicion partly because of the secrecy around it. For whatever else it is, witchcraft often is believed to involve the application of supernatural power for an evil rather than a good end.

In a sense, *kithitu* operates like some kind of an ordeal, especially when applied to investigate the guilt or innocence of a person in a group or class of suspects and nonsuspects. Refusal to swear is taken as admission of guilt, a starting point in its difference with ordeals among the Akamba. The ordeals determine guilt by instantaneous physical effects on parties to whom they are inflicted; *kithitu* takes some time to show results. Ordeals do not go beyond the determination of guilt and could be challenged; *kithitu* is an arbiter of final and conclusive resort. Ordeals could not be used to determine guilt of an absent party nor were they ever applied with death as a consequence for the guilty. Although ordeals involved a severe physical exertion, trial, or examination, *kithitu* did not.

## SUPERNATURAL IN DISPUTE RESOLUTION: THE CASE OF *KITHITU*

Conventional dispute resolution mechanisms thrive on evidence and issues that involve some degree of empirically verifiable content. Courts and other alternative dispute methods have this as a thread of commonality and even where a dispute is resolved by the unilateral decision to avoid, an important feature of such decision remains that it derives from an authority (self) that the disputant can see. Where naming, blaming, and claiming forms the basic processual shape of a dispute, the all-important question of the authority to which the claim is made is at the core of a discourse on the involvement of the supernatural in denouement.

What we refer to as the supernatural is basically that which transcends our perception, a power beyond the natural sphere. The supernatural has been associated with spiritual powers, belief, and influence of magic. In the religious arena, it may be taken to encompass the all-powerful, invincible, and invisible Supreme Being responsible for the state of nature. The existence of a supernatural power thrives on the parallel subsistence of a belief in the same; after all, it is the supernatural that is beyond rational definition. Like religion, faith, belief, and acceptance are the pillars upon which supernatural power is erected. A characteristic of these pillars is that believers and non-believers alike have no empirical proof. This notwithstanding, a common feature among all societies throughout the world has always been the existence within their structural realm, a belief in some form of supernatural.

In widely appreciating disputes, one observes that the practice has often been to seek solutions in available options based on the factual bases of the altercations. Justice is thus a function of the formulation of the options into perceived categories of logic whose force derives from an acceptable societal response to the given infraction. Articulation of the formulated logical response is entrusted on some accepted "hand of authority." In supernatural dispute denouement, "logic of faith and acceptance" may arguably be the fuel for the process. Response is observed through the occurrence of expected (or at times unexpected) events that are conveniently associated with the supernatural.

The study of the supernatural involvement in dispute resolution under the Akamba *kithitu* practice invariably calls to imagination the sophisticated and "remote control" attributes of primordial juju and fetish. The nature of the object and reverence that attaches thereto make a case for the classification of *kithitu* with juju and fetishes. Suffice it that it is a practice that has utility to parts of the population in the community to date. Educing from its practice are some fundamental attributes of supernatural involvement in dispute resolution process, the most fundamental being the shift of power in the resolution process from the disputants and any third parties who may have been involved to the supernatural.

The reliance on the natural occurrence of a succession of misfortunes culminating in deaths within the family of one that lies under the *kithitu* oath is illustrative of this shift in power. The elders were completely removed from the penalty and outcome of a dispute once the oath was resulted to. The handing over of the dispute to some unseen force is akin to religious reliance on an all-powerful and unseen God to perform a miracle. The parties to the dispute would have to believe in the external force and accept it.

The shift from a bilateral or trilateral temporal resolution process to a unilateral supernatural umpiring process is also significant because it opens up room for questions as to where the power derives from; whether it is the object itself or whether it is from the psychological effect on the wrongdoer, or if indeed some powerful external power exists whose justice is as final as it is accurate. For the Akamba, it has been argued that the silent arbiter is the fetish (object of *kithitu*) itself; that its power derives from its secret ingredients and is measured by its reputation for inflicting sickness and death on false swearers and their families.[25] The fact that the object that was so elaborately constructed and the intrigue in the fact that it seems to have effect on some people who clearly disclaimed it add to the argument. It became the community's ultimate ritual in its search for justice.

It would be difficult to sustain an argument of the existence of some external entity with the power to resolve the disputes short of falling back to faith and belief—the essence of many a ritual. This may be getting into quicksand because the presupposition that one would draw from such assertion is that some minimum element of faith and belief runs through the entire community. Besides this, one would rightly wonder why an object that is evidently revered has to be in the picture if all it takes is faith in some supernatural power. This is only half the argument, however. As a rite, enough homage cannot be paid to the handing down of the same across generations and the inevitable "legendization" through the period.

The modernist argument is that some form of psychology of fear has a role in the operational effects of *kithitu*. It is indeed no falsity to argue that *kithitu* works almost in the same manner and evokes almost as much fear within the community as witchcraft does. Whether this fear is sufficient to lead to a succession of misfortunes is the point at which the "psychology of fear" argument may meet its demise. That the whole concept of *kithitu* is feared is a fact, but whether this fear is capable of causing the effects associated to the oath is another thing altogether. As a source of power in dispute resolution, the fear blends with awe to ensure the complete trust and reliance in the outcome.

Having noted that the strength of *kithitu* depends on what it was made of, it would be accurate to appreciate it in the wide concept of communal rituals whose stimuli effect was conditioned on its composition. The owner of the object is seen as a vessel in the journey to justice, and the whole dispute and antagonism are shifted from the parties or the elders to the inanimate object. It can be argued that this has the advantage of having parties relate without suspicion because the bearer or owner of *kithitu* does not really play a role in the final outcome of the matter. Faith in the removed power within the object promised "absolute justice."[26]

A CRITIQUE OF *KITHITU*

It is curious that legislative authorities in Kenya proscribed witchcraft but at the same time took up *kithitu*. In all fairness, they operate in a similar manner save for the fact that one is overt, sanctioned by the community, and believed to have social utility. The skeptic could argue that *kithitu* comprises a power that cannot be defined, like witchcraft, and that the effects attributed to it cannot be proven to derive from it. In dealing with this thesis, it should not be forgotten that supernatural power or magic could be good or evil and that good magic was especially esteemed among many African communities.

It has also been argued that the use of *kithitu* in dispute resolution is an abdication by the courts of their role of adjudication to a medium that they have no control over. This follows on an assertion, based on the embrace of Western court structures, that a court of law can ill afford to operate on supernatural and empirically unverifiable factors because it adjudicates disputes on the basis of evidence adduced. The weakness in this argument is that it deals not with efficacy of the dispute resolution method. It appears to delve much more on process, swallowing hook, line, and sinker the supposed superiority of the court system.

On the argument questioning the validity of a dispute resolution method because it is based on faith in, and the acceptance of, some supernatural elements, it is submitted that such reasoning goes to the very heart of the jurisprudential debate on law as a social control mechanism. The acceptance by societies to be bound by rules posited on their behalf by their representatives should not be construed differently from the choice of a people to place that faith in an external force in resolving their disputes. It has, in fact, been observed (by Kenyatta, for instance) that the advantage of this is that it guards against the fabrication of evidence or bribery of the adjudicating personnel.

*Kithitu* cannot stand as firm against the assault of utilitarianism, related penal theories, and human rights arguments. Its finality is as disturbing as its effect on innocents (family members of suspected wrongdoer). It appears that the traditional Akamba community was concerned with "justice for the complainant" seemingly to the complete indifference toward the rights of the suspect. This is cognizant of and notwithstanding the fact that the situation changed considerably once a suspect took the *kithitu* oath and nothing happened to him or his family within the prescribed period for its effect. The ceding of all control over the penal sanction that a wrongdoer is to face is manifestly dangerous for a variety of reasons, ranging from the fact that dissimilar crime may be treated the same, to the extreme that it may be impossible to undo a wrongful punishment.

The fact that its main effect is the death of the victim as well as family members clearly places it at odds with modern human rights thinking, which looks upon life as the sacred basis for all other endeavors. The death of a common thief who had the temerity to lie under the *kithitu* oath would today be considered a most cruel and inhuman punishment; the extension of the increasingly out-of-vogue death penalty.

The chance that the psychic effects of the oath may be exploited should not be ignored. In *Mulwa Kyambino v. Ndunda Nduto,*[27] the appellant died of pneumonia, according to a medical diagnosis. This was after the court had granted permission and *kithitu* oath had been taken. The respondent went ahead to poison the deceased's cattle, thereby frightening the family into seeking to be cleansed. Though he (the respondent) was sentenced for the crime, his actions and their effect clearly show that a party could rely on the fear that accompanies *kithitu* to exploit a weakened adversary.

CONCLUSION

This paper has attempted to present a method of dispute resolution from a traditional African perspective. It is a system with considerably less application today but one from which several broad propositions may be made:

1. *Kithitu* and other supernatural dispute resolution methods have the advantage of being systems through which no party would suffer from power imbalances. The transformations of the dispute into a supernatural appeal for justice and subsequent removal from human authority, the task of handing out the decision, and sanction neutralizes any power imbalances.

2. The wrath of the supernatural depicted by the successive occurrence of misfortune and the inability to control it, short of admission of guilt and responsibility, is the coercive and policing authority analogous to the more conventional imprisonment or incarceration by a state authority.

3. On a criterion of simplicity, *kithitu* has an edge. The fact that it hardly requires testimonial evidence saves time. It involves a one-off flexible process and has the added advantage of religious reverence by disputants who choose it. This acceptance is in itself therapeutic for the aggrieved party. The

faith in the system proliferates over likely areas of miscarriage of justice in the present-day popular adjudication process, for example, unlikelihood of bribery and corruption.

4. Coming from a background of elaborate and binding oaths at the pain of death, it was not easy to transform the believers of such phenomenon as *kithitu* to similar reverence to an oath under a Bible or other fairly alien object. In spite of the fact that Christianity and other religious groups have infiltrated the traditional African way of life rather deeply, the threat of criminal and religious sanction on commission of perjury is normally insufficient to discourage lying. The threat is not immediate, real, or fatal.

In the search for alternative means of dispute resolution, it may help to look at and pick out strong points of traditional practices. Supernatural appeal in present day, largely manifested in various religious practices, may not count among the most immediate and effective resolution methods. This is with a caveat. The larger part of humanity is schooled (during childhood) in some supernatural law. The same cannot be said of temporal law. Though many people (irrespective of religious affiliation) can tell a sin or transgression against the Supreme Being, few will be able to tell the municipal laws that regulate their day-to-day activities. Religious regimes have developed "inculturation" programs.[28] It may be time that legal regimes attempted the same to develop and strengthen the civil justice system.[29]

# PART TWO

# Re-Centering Knowledge

# Introduction

What must practitioners and theorists know in order to understand and expand the learnings of the field and make these available for creating ways to address the urgent troubles that afflict the globe? This section *puts experiential knowledge at the center of research.*

The anthology began with the premise that some of the conflict in conflict resolution involves a contest over knowledge: where does knowledge reside and what makes some voices more valuable and important to be heard than others? "Cultural worldview" plays a major role in that determination, a reality that the profession of conflict resolution has not escaped.

Knowing how profoundly conventional scholarly rules of knowledge making daunt and suppress voices of people whose cultural and political experience lies outside the boundaries of academia, this anthology seeks to redefine the concept of knowledge to reverse that dynamic. Instead of insisting that everyone must write in one style, in one conceptual framework, in one structure, we insist on honoring and including the widest possible range of peoples and perspectives. That goal leads us directly to issues of credibility. Who decides which story is legitimate? More specifically, how does it come to be accepted that certain practices of conflict resolution are acceptable and others not? Based on whose experience, ideas, and worldview is legitimacy achieved? What turns perception into knowledge, narrative into literature?

In a splendid book called *Talking Power,* Robin Lakoff, a professor of linguistics at the University of California, Berkeley, wrote an essay on the hidden rules of writing in academia and their connection with hierarchy. The business of the university, she opined, is to produce knowledge, a goal we share. Undergrads, at the very bottom of the pile, are expected to regurgitate that knowledge without critical reflection. Graduate students are allowed to venture tentative analyses of what they are learning, thereby putting a toe in the water of knowledge making, but mostly they must demonstrate their command of the body of knowledge defined as crucial to their field. In staying strictly within the parameters of "objectivity," they also demonstrate their command of the unspoken rules of their discipline. Junior faculty not yet admitted to the ranks of the tenured must produce knowledge legitimated by the achievement of publication. But they must not challenge too profoundly the canon. Once tenured, however, professors may relax the rules. Only at the apex of the pyramid may professors write personally and entertainingly, for they hold the keys to the door of the house of legitimacy.

In contrast to this assigned hierarchy, you the reader are invited to decide what is useful to you in the papers we have assembled. What provokes inquiry and what engages thoughtful reflection? The more you know—about who the authors are, where they fit in their own stories, from what experiences they have formulated their wisdom—the better you can weigh and sort the knowledge contained within these covers. We wish to share that power with you. We use our resources (our power) to inspire writing and collect materials here, and we trust you to use yours to take the process of knowledge making wherever you want and need it to go. In other words, you and we together form a partnership in the production of knowledge. By insisting that people without degrees, sometimes without academic credentials of any kind, know things that others need to know, we seek to create a new power order based in functionality.

This section opens with a grounding paper, followed by three critiques of the field, and three examples of alternative approaches. Finally, we end with a critical essay from the perspective of an outside observer. We urge our readers to welcome, with openness and pleasure, the variety of approaches to knowledge making presented here.

OVERVIEW OF PART TWO

Mary Adams Trujillo's paper echoes themes of worldview and culture struck in the first section. Reflecting her own multiple cultural standpoints, she brings academic knowledge making and the street into relationship with each other. Her account gives substance to the theoretical concerns articulated by

Linda James Myers and Mariah Breeding. As a long-time resident of a community beset by violence, and a newer member of a task force charged with finding roads to peace, Mary combines tools of academic analysis and lived wisdom, two forms of knowledge making often in contention with each other.

Leah Wing analyzes assumptions about neutrality in the field of mediation. Using critical race theory, she explicitly interrogates the politics of standpoint and worldview through an account of a failed mediation involving disparate power relations. Through this story, she critiques the use of neutrality as a canon of the field, demonstrating the ways apparent impartiality can in fact act as bias and evoking the fundamental chords struck by Marlon Sherman in the earlier section.

A group of undergraduate students contribute a collaborative paper expanding Leah's critique to dynamics of racially based exclusion in the field of conflict resolution. Starting with an account of various forms of structural racism in America, they go on to an examination of conflict resolution literature evaluated for its relevance to the dynamics they have described. As enthusiastic entrants to the field, lead author Andrew Chang and his fellow students, Damien Basey, Valarie Carey, Angel Coleman, and Katt Hoban, hold the field's feet to the fire in an even-handed and thoughtful critique of the current canon's relevance to today's most pervasive racial problems.

There are two chapters of culturally specific work. A seasoned practitioner, Lucy Moore, offers advice about working with Native American tribes to address environmental problems in the southwestern United States. She describes in detail the framework within which her constituents negotiate water rights. Lucy offers non-Native practitioners a concrete guide to ways for meeting at least halfway across cultural divides.

Anona Napoleon then gives us a vivid account of work decidedly grounded in the specific cultural approaches of her community. A grandmother living in Hawaii, she was awarded a doctoral degree late in life based on research in a style true to her culture, values, and voice, in both content and presentation. Excerpted here, she writes a narrative describing the introduction of *ho'oponopono*, a traditional form of conflict intervention, into nontraditional public schools. Through metaphor and poetry, she tells her own story as she presents her research.

Cherise D. Hairston revisits research she completed in 1999. By counting the number of papers appearing in the primary journals in the field that addressed issues of relevance to African Americans, she demonstrated the extreme absence of such a literature. In her chapter, Cherise comments on her experience as a practitioner of what has and has not changed since that time, and she challenges the field of conflict resolution to develop a research agenda relevant to people of African descent for the future.

Writing almost a decade later than Cherise's first paper, Phillip M. Richards, a professor of literature, concludes this section by contrasting what he terms "the new class of minority professionals" in conflict resolution with those in his field. With an academic outsider's eye, he independently confirms Cherise's assertion. Phil highlights claims to legitimacy as they draw on cultural warrants.

Taken together, these nine essays hold the prism of knowledge to the light, reflecting differences and at the same time illuminating ways to broader approaches to the art of knowing.

# 7 Why Research Matters

*The Reciprocal Nature of Knowledge*

MARY ADAMS TRUJILLO

Before enrolling in a graduate program in communication, I assumed that the worlds of practitioners who "did" conflict resolution and academics who (only) studied conflict were separate, distinct, and mutually exclusive. Prior to graduate school, I was a practitioner in various areas of conflict resolution work ranging from client advocacy for people diagnosed with mental illness to teaching mediation to children to affirmative action dispute resolution. My original goal in going back to school was to develop conflict resolution models applicable for multicultural contexts. As one who defined herself primarily in terms of the outcomes of her work, I had little knowledge of (and therefore little use for) formal theory or research and certainly no models for activist scholarship. I assumed a kind of chauvinism based on the presumed superiority of "real world" experience versus intellectual constructions. However, I found that exposure to formal academic research required me to question whether all knowledge is valid and whether all forms of knowing are equal. Now, as a faculty member in an "institution of higher learning," I can see that research and practice are natural allies. I am proposing that we rethink possibilities for future researcher-practitioner collaborations. Thus, I offer the story of my own experiences with research as both an example and justification.

Conflict resolution practitioners are fundamentally problem solvers. We tend to approach situations from a problem-solution orientation. Our assumptions tend to be experientially based. That is, we give credibility to what we have seen or heard as valid sources of knowledge. Our tendency is to focus on the tools we need to address the immediate problem. We tend to be result oriented and dismissive of, if not suspicious of, knowledge without "results." For our profession, the practitioner's bottom line is *what do we need to do in order to bring about change?* From that perspective, it is difficult to imagine that a formal academic structure might benefit the practitioner. However, two among many benefits stand out. First, we are required to question which knowledge claims are legitimate. How do we know what we know? In applying a formally established methodology, one has the benefit of a review of the literature, some level of "testing" of the knowledge claims, as well as a systematic process of scrutiny by a community of interested others. Second, the most striking and practical benefit of academia is access to tools, resources, and information that allow practitioners to convert experience to social change.

Academics, however, want to know, "What is the nature of knowledge and what is the relation of knowledge to truth?" Academics have their own brand of chauvinism. We privilege what is written (not transmitted orally) by scholars like ourselves. We are dismissive, if not suspicious of, experience without critique. Indeed, we love even the sound of the word, "critique." We love the pursuit of knowledge for its own sake and may look askance at the work of people who are not really "scholars." Our intellectual training teaches us as well as provides the tools to be skeptical, cynical, and critical. We often exercise our privilege to be apolitical, not acknowledging that "legitimacy" of knowledge is politically determined, socially constructed, and culturally informed.

However, the Academy and the Real World are not mutually exclusive places. Just as academic settings offer systematic investigations in which to develop theory, practitioners bring the ability to test out theory in the real-life settings and contexts where they occur. Practitioners theorize (a.k.a. "problem solve" or "brainstorm") in meetings, through case conferences, with colleagues in parking lots—often sharing information and knowledge informally. We distill the learnings and make the ever-evolving final product (applied knowledge) available for others' use, often through the use of anecdote. Clearly, neither a purely academic nor a purely practical approach could be sufficient. Rather, both approaches cry out for a more inclusive definition of scholarship, one which demonstrates the complementary and reciprocal nature of theory and practice. Further, this new-style scholar can be an activist who is empowered to use research and research methods to bring about social justice.

INITIAL INVOLVEMENT

As the old adage suggests, much practical knowledge is born out of necessity. Through several serendipitous occurrences, my notions about the interrelationship of academic research and practical knowledge changed drastically. First, I lived in a neighborhood that had been the site of several murders of young men. Second, motivated by concerns about the safety of my own and other children, I joined a community task force that had been formed in response to the murders of several young people. The task force's stated goal was to prevent violence. Third, I was privileged to study an innovative approach to critical ethnography with the late Dr. Dwight Conquergood, a true scholar activist. Critical ethnography is distinguished by its attention to the political economy of the studied community. Critical ethnographers are interested in analysis of power relationships as well as observations about cultural forms. Finally, as a result of needing both a dissertation topic and a safe neighborhood, I set out to formally investigate what happens when institutions and community-based organizations attempt to collaborate for the "common good."

The task force had been formed about three years prior to my involvement. Leaders and representatives of various community organizations were invited by the local school board to share violence prevention strategies and resources after several young men were killed. The original group developed a community civility campaign and generally tried to mobilize various community stakeholders, without much success. The group did not have outside funding, and much of the administrative support was provided by the high school's staff. A friend from the university was a member of the task force and asked if I would join. Because I had significant community organizing experience and had worked with a number of the individuals on the task force in varying capacities, there was no overt resistance to my involvement. Although membership in the group seemed to be based on status as a community "leader," I think that I was accepted simply because I showed up and continued to show up. By the time of my involvement, most of the original thirty-nine members were gone, replaced by heads of civic organizations, municipal departments, and social service agencies. The group met once a month, on Tuesdays from noon until 2 PM.

Since the task force was composed of leaders of organizations, group decision making and relationships between members held added significance. Some members participated in the meetings because they felt politically obligated to do so. I know this because several members confided to me that they felt their agencies would be negatively viewed if the leaders were not part of the task force. ("How can you not support violence prevention?") Some others were genuinely troubled by the conditions in the community. Some members had sincerely and deeply examined their own racial and class biases. Other members were very comfortable referring the "those people." In general, due to the relatively high stakes of public opinion, and the relatively low level of intragroup trust, meetings tended to stay fairly superficial.

Before continuing, let me warn the reader that this story, like most research, does not have a tidy ending. My research did not transform a violent environment. To this day, people continue to kill each other. Many of the same issues that existed before the task force was formed still exist today. Why then, should we care about communication research that does not change the status quo? At a practical level, should we assume that talk is just a poor substitute for action? On the contrary, in the case of my work, conflict resolution practitioners need to know how to observe and analyze group talk because conflict resolution practice virtually always involves group work at some level. Knowing how to examine group communicative practices across a variety of contexts and relationships can be used to (1) facilitate group conceptualization of roles and tasks, (2) strengthen intra- and intergroup relationships, and (3) foster awareness of the ways in which cultural identity, community, and conflict intersect. Further, by detailing what prevents social change agents from, in this case, preventing violence, the practitioner is in a position to facilitate specific corrective outcomes.

METHODOLOGY

Clifford Geertz observed that groups construct "structures of signification" and roles as allegories for their identities.[1] As I looked at the task force there seemed to be so many symbols, structures, roles, allegories, and identities operating within it that numerous frames of analysis seemed possible. The first step was to design a data-gathering strategy that would capture the subtlety and texture of interaction, yet be flexible enough to accommodate that which could not be predicted by theory. In other words, how would I figure out what exactly was going on? As a methodology, critical ethnography offers a "remaking of social analysis" by integrating theory and practice.[2] The ethnographic method lends itself to naturalistic contexts, such as community relationships where human interaction is messy and not always easily categorized. My overall goal was to see and experience the subjective realities of a community member as well as a task force member. Both perspectives were necessary to see, interpret, and contextualize the culture as a whole. This dual perspective simultaneously allowed and required me to fully immerse myself into both worlds. Thus, this method served as a starting point for interrogating and unraveling power relationships, social structures, and assumptions operating in both the community and the task force. In this case, the resulting data exposed the enmeshed relationships between political structures and communicative microstructures, between organizational structures and the discourse of community members. I ended up with four strategies for gathering relevant information, that is, data about the local community:

- Participant observation
- Content analysis
- Survey of citizen preconceptions
- Survey of member resources

Although each strategy provided a different perspective, offered advantages and disadvantages, and allowed for a different level of involvement with task force and community members, most germane to this paper are participant-observation and content analysis methodologies. In practical terms, a participant observation model meant that I attempted to balance my modes of being and doing in the group. These modes were documented in two ways: through the use of field notes and ethnopoetic transcription processes. As a participant, I attended task force meetings, subcommittee meetings, and community events for more than three years as a working member. I was involved in developing and evaluating activities, facilitating group sessions, building relationships with task force and community members, and interviewing applicants for the coordinator position. From my vantage point as an observer, I wrote detailed field notes after every gathering. In these field notes, I instantiated types of verbal interactions, frequency of speakers and speech patterns, tones of voice, indications of nonverbal channels, and especially individual and collective use of language. In some field notes, I transcribed conversations and interactions through a method of ethnopoetics, which I will describe momentarily. When all my research was completed, I used the field notes to determine categories and themes for analysis. I made field notes to document observable realities as well as my perceptions. The usefulness of field notes is their consistency over time. Individual documents can be compared to photographs, moments frozen in time.

THE CASE EXAMPLE

During the time of the research, I lived in the house where I had grown up. My childhood and adolescence had been shaped by the neighborhood's Fourth of July barbecues, the trees and vacant lots that were our playgrounds, the sounds of the tambourine and organ spilling out into Sunday evening. Virtually all of the houses and many of the same people who stayed in the neighborhood in the 1950s were there in the late 1990s.

However, some of the old familiarity was challenged. I no longer knew the young men who leaned on my car in the evenings, drinking beer and playing their music. Nor was I comfortable telling them to pick up the beer bottles that they left on the sidewalk. No matter how tired I was, I could never forget to lock my car or the doors and windows to my house. In addition, there was a kind of casual violence that hung in the air. Today's fights, fueled by alcohol, drugs, and guns, seemed to easily become fatal encounters, unlike the fist fights of the old days. In sum, I was ambivalent about my neighborhood, wanting to change it, but also wanting to defend it from its critics. I found myself in the position of having potential access to community improvement resources by virtue of my involvement with the task force. In exchange for access, however, I felt obligated to translate, interpret, or otherwise represent a population that was viewed as deficient. In this way, my experience was like that of many practitioners who earnestly desire to make social change but find themselves mired within the limitations of personal experience or, as I discovered in this case, by the confines of organizational structure and discourse.

Participant-observation of the formal meetings provided a clear picture of the group's discursive relationship to violence prevention. By paying systematic attention to the discourse of both the task force and its larger community constituency, I began to observe and track embedded patterns of relating, decision-making structures, conflict engendering and resolution processes, and overarching values.

At the same time, I found it necessary to keep a human face on the experience of violence, in order to balance the abstract nature of observing group talk. In the course of three years' work, I made intentional efforts to build relationships with and be around individuals in the community as well as task force members. These relationships provided insight into the relational nature of both collaborative and ethnographic work.

In the process, I had to learn about which personal boundaries to establish and keep. Sometimes the boundaries between participation and observation were painfully difficult to maintain. There were times when someone would disclose information to me as a friend that I could not ethically include in the study or disclose to other group members, even when the information "should" have been out in the open. In research, as in life, privilege requires a level of ethical responsibility. Rosaldo situates the scholar as a member of a privileged community that has historically used academic forms and practices that manipulate, usurp, or distort the experience of studied populations for the academy's benefit. He calls out for the researcher to instead use his or her tools for the "full enfranchisement" of diverse groups. Additionally, when the researcher is also a member of the studied population, as I was, the researcher must be willing to acknowledge that absolute neutrality is neither possible nor desirable. Nor can the researcher become overly self absorbed. To illustrate the complexity of balancing ethical research and personal boundaries, I offer the following example from field notes.

### MORELIA

She called and asked if she could come over. I told her to come on, that dinner was almost ready, and she was welcome. By the time she arrived, I was going over homework with my two daughters. Morelia said she was amazed that I cared. My family always jokes about being dysfunctional, or at least nonnormative, but I'm sure that to Morelia we are the Cleavers.

I offered her something to eat, which she hungrily accepted, and then I left to make phone calls. As she chatted with my daughters, I half listened to their conversations. I know that Morelia always tries to "tone it down" for my girls because she knows that their experience levels are very different, but her conversation is usually still way above my comfort level.

After the girls went to bed, we talked. There were good things like winning an essay contest on one hand, but not getting the job she expected, on the other. She shared her notebook with me. Her poems are very dramatic, honest, graphic, direct, painful, explicit. Sometimes I have to stop reading. She writes about the sexual abuse she has experienced from father, brother, uncles, pimp, strangers. She always ends up, no matter how our conversations begin, trying to make sense of the sexual violence that has characterized her life since she was a child. Sometimes, I can't hear any more.

I offered to let her spend the night at my house when she told me some of the things that were going on, but she preferred to stay at her brother's house. So, I dropped her off at her brother's house which is in a high violence, high drug area of the city. We had to go to the back, through the alley, since she didn't have a key. There were no lights and I felt very vulnerable amidst the men in the alley. I waited with my headlights focused on the house while she broke in. It seemed to take forever and I was relieved when she finally turned on a light to let me know she had made it inside. The question that this raises for me is how do I do ethnography without getting involved? She needs so much help—a friend, a therapist, a lawyer, a different home situation. But I also know that I need to talk with the figures in the shadows, the people on the corners, the kids hanging out in order to get the whole story. This is the dichotomy of participant observation. I have to continually weigh and balance the advantages and disadvantages.

These notes illustrated what became a growing dilemma. On one hand, I was a student, a researcher looking for information to complete a dissertation. On the other, I was a real person dealing with other human beings whose lives were not such that they could be summed up in a chapter on results. In order to fully comprehend the nature and impact of violence in the community, I had to be willing to suspend my fears about dark alleys, judgments about the types of people who committed crimes, and preconceived notions that what I saw was the only reality.

Documenting my dual participant-observation strategy, one face toward the task force, the other toward my fellow community members, involved a technique taught to me by Conquergood called ethnopoetic transcription. The technique involves learning to listen uncritically and recording exactly what one hears and sees. Ethnopoetic transcription is the human equivalent of videotaping, tape recording, and photographing. The physical and emotional self of the researcher is the medium for documentation. Like any skill, ethnopoetic transcription is perfected through consistent practice. Through this process, the researcher listens carefully for content as well as nuance for the purpose of accurately representing and reproducing the Other's voice. The purpose of this technique is to enable or force the researcher to meet the studied Other as they are, not as who the researcher wants them to be. The voice of the researcher is deliberately silenced in order to "hear" the experience of the "subject" from her or his own perspective. Ethnopoetic transcriptions are usually shorter interactions with relatively fewer voices. They may be used as a part of field notes, or may be separate constructions.

I offer the following interactions with neighborhood residents as examples of ethnopoetic transcriptions. The examples are followed by analysis of the methodological tool.

EX. 1: ETHNOPOETIC TRANSCRIPTION (SEPTEMBER 2000)

See, Brown is Crips territory.
Dewey and Simpson is GD territory.
They parties be—WHOA!!!
The dead end of Darrow?
They parties always get broken up by the cops.
(Deep sigh) (pause)
But Brown and Church, it's a drug war. Tha's why people always be gettin'
shot.
They
ALWAYS
in the WRONG PLACE
at the WRONG
TIME!

The reader should read the words just as they are written. They should reflect rhythm, spacing, inflection, pronunciation, and tone of the speaker. Ethnopoetic transcription forces the listener to take down the words, just as the individual says them. As a narrator-interpreter, I would likely offer some background information to introduce the speaker to the reading audience. I could say that the speaker was a young man of limited education, whose purpose was to inform me about the community I was researching. As a narrator, I might be tempted to explain the sociological implications or ideological differences. I might even acknowledge my perceptions or feelings about the interactions. However, ethnopoetic transcription is not designed to interpret; the researcher's opinions or feelings do not matter. Rather the focus is on the lived experience of the speaker. For the purposes of this explanation, however, I will dissect this verbal communication.

EXPLANATION

*See, Brown is Crips' territory.*

"See" is used to indicate that the speaker is explaining or clarifying information. Brown is a street in the predominantly black Fifth Ward. The Crips are a gang.

*Dewey and Simpson is GD territory.*

Dewey and Simpson are also streets in the Fifth Ward, almost a mile apart, but this is considered the area governed by the Gangster Disciples, another gang. Territory has several connotations. First, territory is a geographical area in which revenue-generating activities, such as selling drugs, are overseen by that organization/gang. Territory also means that recreational facilities, "hanging out," or places of refuge are provided for members of that organization/ gang. Both Brown and Simpson and Dewey are perceived as violent places and both have highly visible police presence, especially during the summer.

*They parties be—WHOA!!!*

Parties are gatherings of people, mostly young, but not always. These gatherings are often spontaneous. Admission may be charged if the party is in a house. Usually, the activity of the party spills over into the streets or yard. Drugs or alcohol are often present, but the emphasis is on having unrestrained fun ("WHOA!!!") Parties near Brown and Church are likely to be livelier and go on for longer.

*The dead end of Darrow?*

Darrow is a street near Simpson and Dewey where the street ends in a cul de sac (a dead end).

*They parties always get broken up by the cops.*

Police tend to intervene fairly early at the Simpson/Dewey neighborhood. One reason might be because the mayor of the city lives near the intersection. The statement could also mean that these parties tend to ("always") end up with fighting, resulting in police intervention. The statement may also imply the speaker's perceptions of the sociability of GDs (a gang) versus Crips.

*But Brown and Church, it's a drug war. Tha's why people always*

On the other hand, when people fight at Brown and Church, it's often about money for drugs. The speaker emphasizes the words, speaking more slowly, showing inflection, and increasing volume on the words of which the listener needs to be aware.

*be gettin'*

*shot.*

*They*

ALWAYS

*in the* WRONG PLACE

*at the* WRONG

TIME*!*

Subtext: Be careful at Brown and Church. Innocent bystanders, or people who just want to have fun but are not paying attention to the social cues, may end up hurt (or dead). And to some extent, it will be their fault. He makes an oblique reference to a shooting where one woman was killed and another injured as they stood talking to the intended recipient of bullets in a drive-by shooting. To some extent, the speaker blames the victims.

In this next field note, I include myself in the interaction. Because we ascribe meanings and motives to speakers that may not actually be what the speakers intend, this technique is a method of moving the listener beyond her own perceptions. In this situation, had I not forced myself to focus on the production of sound, my attention would have wanted to linger on the scar at the base of the speaker's throat and speculate on how he got it.

EX. 2: ETHNOPOETIC TRANSCRIPTION

(Daniel is an African American male in his late thirties or maybe early forties. He and I used to live on the same block.

I see Daniel crossing the street just as I arrive at the intersection. I offer him a ride.

He's going to the welfare office. He carries a fat manila envelope. My eyes are drawn to a healed-over scar at the base of his throat.)

His voice is both deep and hoarse:

You know, I went to that church over there on
Dodge. Is it on Dodge? Yeah. I went there. Got to the
door, but I couldn' go past the door. I *couldn' make myself* go in. Yeah. But I'm gonna go. I was gonna go wit'
you but there isn' never anybody home at your house.
I never see the car there. (pause) Yeah. You know I jus
got outta jail?

(No, I didn 't know that. Did he get the scar in jail?)

Yeah, I was in there for a few days. This girl who
has a lot of drugs in her life told some lies about me.
Said I was in the bushes selling drugs and what not. But
see, it's not like that. See, she ain' about nothin' BUT
drugs. I like a woman who has a mind.

The ethnopoetic transcription allows me to record the interaction, concentrating on Daniel. Of course, Daniel is also reading me at the same time.
His conversational rhythm was slightly asymmetrical and his speech was
pressured, suggesting to me that his thinking was perhaps impaired. He
spoke "yeah" to punctuate his sentences. "Yeah" was the period at the end
of a thought. Sometimes the period came at the end of a statement, sometimes at the beginning, as if the conversation was as much with himself as it
was with me. I acknowledged him when I saw him and asked if he needed a
ride. Other than that, the only words I spoke were "No, I didn't know that."
Although I rarely saw Daniel, he let me know in the beginning of the conversation that we have something in common—going to church, although he
is a little fuzzy on the details. Again, the use of the word "see" signals that
his intention is to share information or to explain something to me. In the
end, he obliquely compliments me by comparing me favorably to another
woman. This attention to the verbal communication allowed me to glimpse
into Daniel's daily life, his worldview, his attitudes toward women, his values, and a sense of how he structures his thinking with his language.

The above ethnopoetic transcriptions and field notes are examples of
participant observation strategies to generate fuller, richer, and deeper perspectives of the task force and its community.

CONTENT ANALYSIS

As a second data-gathering strategy, I performed two types of content analysis to explain, confirm, and contextualize the operating assumptions of the task force. The idea for the analysis first occurred to me because of the conspicuous absence of discussion about the role of race in violence prevention. In attempting to determine the nature and source of the group's perceptions about race and violence, I turned first to the media to see how the community's thinking was informed. In the absence of a local television outlet, I examined forty-six issues of the local weekly newspaper over a period of eighteen months to see how race, violence, and crime were depicted. I looked for and found links between race and violence, race and crime, and crime and violence. These connections were established through placement of stories (in the "Police Blotter"), descriptions of the neighborhood or exact address of the offense, descriptions of offenders, addresses of offenders, and description of clothing or African American identified artifacts ("a young male wearing a 'doo-rag'"). I established categories for explicitness versus implicitness to capture a sense of degree as well as frequency. From this I began to develop a sensitivity to the language.

I next sorted through public documents, such as previous minutes of the task force and grant applications. I began to see similarities in the content and form of language and how violence was conceptualized in racial terms. By systematically tracking language, I saw a pattern of thinking emerge. The thinking of the task force mirrored the thinking represented by the language of the newspapers. I observed that although the task force did not specifically articulate that African Americans were the intended focus of violence prevention efforts, it was apparent to me from their language that there was a definite perception of race as a variable in violence. The consensus of the discourse was that crime and violence were synonymous, and that the bulk of crimes were committed by a racialized Other. This Other was variously and synonymously depicted as a gang member, young, black, and male, and his offenses tended to be reported as occurring in one of three minority neighborhoods. The presence of these commonalities of thought between media and task force established the foundation and supported the contention that groups are influenced by their environmental context.

Within the task force meetings, as in life, language functioned as both an instrument and a system of culture, simultaneously reflecting and shaping ideas. Language and thought formed discursive building blocks that served to subtly reinforce and reproduce members' perceptions linking crime, violence, and race. In this way, group members collectively negotiated meanings through specific use of connotation, professional jargon, and oft repeated phrases from the media. In other words, as members talked about "learned helplessness," "inadequate lighting," or descriptions of "perpetrators," "lowest achieving students," "neighborhood action," to name a few, they simultaneously created a rhetorical identity for the community and distanced themselves, through their use of language, from that community.

Social distance between task force and community was manifested in two significant ways. First, none of the task force members, except for me, lived in the neighborhood. Second, as heads of social service and civic organizations, they were primarily trained in a model that focused on social deficits. Essentially, the group was composed of practitioners who tended to see the predominantly black Fifth Ward in terms of what was wrong with it.

In addition, the group seemed unable or unwilling to address the subject of race. Instead, the group developed all kinds of code language that subtly equated crime, race, and violence. For example, words like "young men hanging out on corners" or "truancy problems" were encoded to mean "young black males." "Civility" was a code for an accepted standard of suburban middle class public behavior. Thus, "young men/truants hanging out on the corners posed a challenge to civility." The implicit imperative in this statement is that the young men must be removed from the corners. I was intrigued by the coded language and began to document how what I saw seemed to relate to what was going on in the meetings.

FIELD NOTES FROM THE INTERSECTION OF CHURCH AND BROWN

Both the task force and neighborhood residents noted the presence of people, mostly young men, who "hang out." There are two types of people who hang out on the corner. There is the lone young man in the dark. Sometimes there are two or three young men who stand near each other. Sometimes they approach cars directly, sometimes passengers in cars approach them. On occasion, there is the lone young or not-so-young woman peering into the cars that cruise Church Street.

The other group of people are what might be called a social grouping. Young men and women, mostly men, drink beer, smoke cigarettes and blunts, listen to music, and literally hang out on the corner. The fence around the house on the corner has been bent beneath the weight of the partygoers. The visible presence of the hanging out participants evokes a strong response. I suspect that they are a human graffiti, "a very ambivalent form of human communication."[3] Like most subordinate groups, the street crowd suffers from both too little and too much visibility. Homi Bhabha spoke about "the marginalized, displaced . . . whose very presence is both 'overlooked' . . . and, at the same time, overdetermined."[4]

However, the group's insistence on the racialized Other as the source of the "problem" tended to overlook the pervasive nature of violent conditioning among children in general. The following field note illustrates this observation.

EX. 3: FIELD NOTE FROM MIDDLE CLASS HOUSEHOLD
OUTSIDE OF THE NEIGHBORHOOD

The driveway is an abrupt turn off a busy road. The house faces the street but the family enters and exits on the side. Inside the porch are hiking boots, a 25-pound bag of dog food, an umbrella, a pair of hockey skates and various other accoutrements of middle class life. Inside the family sits in the living room. The mother, a middle aged woman with red hair, is having dinner and "family night" on this Sunday evening. There are four children, two preteen girls and two fifteen year olds, one boy and one girl. The girls are reading. The boy sits in front of the television set, playing with his most recent gift from his father who is recently divorced from the boy's mother. Nintendo blaring, he is James Bond seeking out and destroying his prey. There are weapons, there is blood as the boy methodically shoots his victims, one by one. Split screens and geometric images efficiently record each hit. The techno soundtrack underscores the sterility of the kill. The boy has just returned from a visit with his father, who shares custody with the boy's mother. The Nintendo blares. He is 007. He stalks his targets, surprising each with gun blast from behind.

WHAT DO I DO WITH ALL THESE DATA?

A second form of content analysis occurred as I typed and read through my three years of field notes, looking for themes, patterns, and other interesting features. I listed everything on pieces of butcher paper and taped the papers to the walls of my dining room. I categorized first by topic, looking for specific discussions of violence or prevention. Next I looked for functional characteristics of verbal communication such as prioritizing the task, maintaining relationships, and streams of narratives.[5]

Unsatisfied, this sorting led me to discursive elements and processes essential for collaboration. I matched elements, such goals and tasks, identity and role, and norms and rules with specific examples and ended up with numerous categories but no unifying theme. I also found myself with too much seemingly unrelated data. My response was to narrow the scope of the inquiry. Grouping field notes according to themes they illustrated, I chose to examine one year's worth of representative data, instead of three years' worth.

The issue of a unifying theme was resolved as I forced myself to look at the obvious: conflict was a consistent but overlooked presence. Violence occurs because of unresolved conflict. The meetings themselves were full of conflict over goals and tasks. Conflict was a consistent feeling that I experienced as I attended meetings, thought about the work, and observed interactions between task force members. Conflict occurred simultaneously on several levels. I discovered that by positioning conflict in opposition to collaboration, I could see the various conflict avoidance discursive elements worked together to protect important economic and political realities for the group.

First, as human and social service funding decreases in many communities, economic competition forces organizations to either collaborate or compete for the dwindling pot of resources. If collaboration is seen as a survival strategy, "getting along with each other" is a necessary survival mechanism. Although the economic imperative is seldom the sole reason for avoiding conflict, in this case group members may have recognized that overt conflict lessened their chances for future collaborations. Second, there was an inherent contradiction in eliminating conditions that would eliminate their jobs. Although task force members were publicly committed to a course of action for the common good, this course required competition with other nonprofit agencies for funds and social recognition. Third, the public nature of the leadership positions of the task force members required an appearance of unity. Literally, they could not talk about this conflict. Thus, code language permitted the group to talk about potentially divisive issues without overt conflict about substantive issues. Consequently, conflict was more likely to be manifested or expressed indirectly, often nonverbally, and outside of group meetings. Conflict was evident in the following behaviors: task force members used questions to make statements; had side conversations; tended to interrupt frequently; and established a pecking order of who was able to speak about what. Further, an executive committee developed an agenda prior to the regular task force meeting, in effect deciding what topics could be discussed and for how long. Though many meetings had a prearranged agenda, one must ask to what extent regulation of member speech effectively silenced dissent in this group.

EX. 4: FIELD NOTES FROM TASK FORCE MEETING
WHERE THE QUESTION WAS ASKED, "WHY CAN'T WE
GET THE GUNS OUT OF OUR COMMUNITY?"

Although I attempted to be "objective," clearly my opinions and feelings were engaged.

Cast:

Tom, white male religious leader

Pete, middle aged white male police dept representative with many years of experience

Dana and Pam, two middle aged African American women, both CEOs of their organizations

Ed, African American public school official. Planning to retire, which no one knows

Victoria, a middle aged, well intentioned, but naïve white woman.

Chairman, white male head of the largest nonprofit in the city. Very charismatic.

Kathy, a middle aged white woman, a former social worker

Jean, African American school board member

Art, high ranking public school official, white, very popular

Connie, middle aged white woman, school board member

*Tuesday, 12:30 pm*

*Before task force meeting begins:*

We are in a conference room at the University. There is a massive table dominating the room. Chairs are arranged around the rectangular structure. In one corner of the room, next to the window is a coffee pot, several bottles of water, and assorted sodas. The police department's two representatives choose seats together, close to the door.

TOM: (speaking to police department representative) What
    happened on Emerson street the other night? (Emerson
    is a street in an African American neighborhood.)

PETE: Drunk got hit. Man wandered into the street. He's
    okay.

TOM: I was driving by there and was afraid that there was
    some neighborhood action.

Dana and Pam come in and choose seats at the opposite end of the table from the police.

There is conversation in pockets. There are guests present, but they are not introduced. Several other African American women come in and cluster around the end of the table.

TOM: Who's running this meeting? (The chairman comes in, but another member who has moved into directing the meeting suggests that the chairman and an official from the school district [Ed] answer some questions about truancy that came up in the previous meeting.)

CHAIRMAN: Refresh my memory.

(Ed indicates that he reports truancy to the county superintendent.)

ART: (interrupts) We stopped reporting since there was no enforcement.

GUEST #1: Aren't there state requirements?

ART: Of course.

POLICE REPRESENTATIVE #1: It's not a criminal offense. (The other representative drums his fingers on the table.)

DANA: Let's rewind. (Reviews the discussion of the previous meeting. The concern was that there were children of school age in the streets during the day when they are supposed to be in school. She thinks that the schools should be able to do something about truant children.)

VICTORIA: Can't the police do something?

POLICE REPRESENTATIVE #2: It's not a criminal offense.

(Art suggests that a member of the high school staff could ride along with the police and identify the young men in the streets who are not in school during school hours. Several people talk at once.)

KATHY: Get the community involved.

PAM: (voice quavering) It's got to be multi-tiered. We have to work with the businesses. (She turns away from the group and talks to her neighbor.)

DANA: Whose responsibility is it to make sure that kids make the transition? (from high school to successful postsecondary plans; her tone suggests that this is not a question, but an accusation.)

ART: Some of the lowest achieving students have parents who are the latest in registering their kids for school.

(Since the local media has published much talk about lower achieving minority students, "lowest achieving students" is an agreed upon code referring to black/Latino students. Like most codes, this one is not stated explicitly.)

DANA: As a community, we have to deal with it before it becomes a problem.

(Ed reports on a strategy that another local community has used to address the problem of "hanging out." He describes a program in which youth interventionists go out to where the youth are and try to "reach" them.)

JEAN: The idea is to find out how we might engage the young people in the community.

POLICE DEPARTMENT REP #2: We hired two men last summer and had two youth outreach workers in two of the high crime areas and tried to do one on one interventions with the young adults. I thought the program was good, but the money ran out . . . We've started the program again with funding to September . . . Trying to do the same stuff. We have a contract with—

JEAN: We're talking on two levels.

TOM: The ecumenical action committee has a similar sense of need. Maybe we could partner with them.

KATHY: I think we should do an asset inventory of the group.

GUEST #2: Is there a crisis line?

(The discussion grows in a disjointed fashion. The group eventually decides to delegate a subcommittee to map the community's assets. There are side conversations. Two people leave. . . . A high school student has come in during the discussion. She stands up and speaks in a clear voice:)

STUDENT: I sense that there are people here who don't care. The first time I came to a meeting, I felt that there was potential, but then we let the *hierarchy of ourselves* get in the way. (When she said "hierarchy of ourselves," there was an electric stillness in the room. I suspect this was because her words exposed the falseness and insincerity of the adults, as children's honesty has to capacity to do. The atmosphere was changed.) Professionalism, professional identity versus heart involvement. We have to really believe that it is possible.

(There is silence.)

CONNIE: I think we need to move on to the program report.

(The energy of the group is immediately dissipated.)

Like many community groups of which I had been a part, I began to observe that this group had a definite preference for *talking about the issues,* as opposed to *doing something about the issues.* Because much of my professional work had centered around listening processes, through careful and structured observation of the group's talk about the issues, I began to see over time that their talk *was* the *action.* I began to understand, as I analyzed the group's talk in a systematic way, that the members of the task force saw themselves as powerless to stop the violence. Talk was their way of addressing the unsolveable.

In contrast, I include the example of members of a local neighborhood church and their use of talk to address the community's issues.

EX. 5: "THEY WILL NO LONGER BE ABLE TO STAND HERE . . . "

Early hours of a bright Saturday morning in August.

Members of church in the neighborhood.

Five women and two men walk from the church, covering a semicircle of the neighborhoods east of their building. They walk, leaving flyers about upcoming church events, praying, picking up trash, and making conversation with people they passed. In front of the high school, they gather on the lawn, put down their flyers and trash bags, form a circle and begin to pray.

Father, we thank you for this school, for the resources to educate our children. We thank you for the
administrators, the teachers, the support staff, and the
students. We pray, Lord, that even as the students enter
the building this year, that they will come to know that
this is a safe place. We invite a spirit of hopefulness,
of excitement, of friendliness. We bind and cure spirits
of drug addition, alcohol use, cynicism, spirits of suicide, gang activity, violence, sexual impurity, lawlessness, and disrespect. We ask that you raise up children
who will be examples to their peers, who will not be
ashamed or afraid. We call forth teachers and counselors who will pray over their charges . . .

They walk across the street to the corner of Church and Dodge.
They stop and talk to Janice, a woman who lives in the neighborhood.

"It's so depressing living here. I hate the trash, the people who
stand—hanging out—taking up space on this corner with their loud
music and their drugs." She shakes her head. "It's just depressing. I
have a seventeen year old son and he wants to get out in the streets.
It's hard enough, tryin' to raise him—without *this*." She gestures
toward the street.

Once again, the group forms a circle, holds hands, and bow
their heads.

A man prays quietly, firmly, earnestly that the activity on this
corner will cease:

Prostitution, drug dealing, hanging out
can no longer happen. People will not know why,
but they will no longer be
comfortable
on this corner
They will no longer be able to stand here.

The sky darkens with rain clouds and the group decides to walk
back to their church, talking to the people that they pass, handing
out flyers, picking up trash, and praying for the neighborhood.

(For about three weeks the corner stayed completely empty.)

As task force members expressed their particular values and experiences, the group verbalized wanting to find points of agreement and collaboration, but in reality usually found more opportunities for disagreement. The one event that the group agreed on was a gun and toy gun buy back. With much zeal, several members of the committee arranged with local merchants to offer vouchers for adults who brought in guns to various law enforcement spots. Children who brought in violent toys were offered certificates for ice cream or movies. Most of the guns that were turned in were old, or nonfunctioning, not the hoped for sophisticated weapons in use on the street. Prior to the event, several community members voiced opinions that this was a meaningless gesture and that responses in other cities could predict what the return would be. The resulting discussion exposed the deep fissures in the group. There were those who wanted to *do* something, those who wanted to support the efforts of the organizers, but there were also those who recognized the futility of the exercise. As a result, the in-meeting talk supported the toy/gun buy back, but outside talk was very critical of both the initiative and of the organizers. Months later, when a group of students from a local university performed a communication audit of the task force, a number of group members expressed resentment because they felt that they had been left out of the decision making for this event.

Eventually, the group reached a stage where they could see the ways in which their goals, strategies, values, or attitudes differed. When that happened, there seemed to be more bickering during meetings, and more outside-of-meeting criticism of other members and speculation about their motives. Often these differences seemed to be perceived as irreconcilable, and there was little effort to address differences in a substantive manner within the meetings.

Actual structural power imbalances and inequities between group members exacerbated interpersonal difficulties. Because the group was composed of both community organizations and major community institutions, there were real differences in power and status. The opinions and suggestions of the director of the largest school district, for example, carried more weight and credibility than those of the small grassroots organization. These power and status differences were reflected in the amount of time that leaders of these organizations spoke, who interrupted or disagreed with whom, who sat next to whom, as well as how well ideas were received by the group. Not surprisingly, the organization with the largest budget and whose leader was also very charismatic was also the leader of the group. Power challenges were discursively enacted as pointed questions, talking over, sitting next to or directly opposite the leader, looking away from or performing other activities, and coming in late or leaving early. Sometimes a member decided to chair the meeting before the chairman arrived.

Conversely, deference to the leader was enacted by choosing a seat in close proximity, directing comments to the leader as opposed to the group as a whole, maintaining longer eye contact with the leader for visual approval, asking his opinion, and agreeing with his opinions.

CONCLUSION: WHAT DIFFERENCE DOES IT ALL MAKE?

As I mentioned before, this research did not stop the killing in the community, nor did it directly transform the activity of the task force. However, the research, based as it was in practice and experience, provided an opportunity to meld the boundary between practice and theory. Additionally, the ethnographic methodology I used was a research tool that allowed new insights and clearer understandings to be generated. One cannot gain new research tools without practice, nor new insights without analytic tools. Because this research was for a dissertation, the work itself allows me to present it both to fellow practitioners in their language and cultural terms, as well as to an audience of academics.

What has been most useful, however, is that as I train future generations of scholars and practitioners, I have a solid body of evidence and examples, supported by a methodology that will enable both scholars and practitioners to do their work more comprehensively. Although description is greatly abbreviated in this essay, the research clearly documents how discourse both reflects and structures thought; how discourse and thought both enable and constrain action; that language and culture are inextricable; and that social change in communities may begin with something as simple as identifying the meanings and functions of language. Ethnographically oriented strategies can provide a means of seeing the realities of persons other than ourselves. They are especially useful in making evident the political and social realities of marginalized groups.

Certainly, ethnography is not the only research strategy that can be adapted and used toward a goal of producing social change. For those of us committed to making a better world, all knowledge can be applied to this task. Previously rigid categories of scholar and practitioner, within a paradigm of activism, are outmoded and need to be discarded. Theory and practice nurture, reinforce, and transform each other.

# 8 Whither Neutrality?

*Mediation in the Twenty-first Century*

LEAH WING

In discussions of dispute resolution, we begin these days with the assumption that neutrality in mediation is essential. That we should even concern ourselves with where neutrality is going, therefore, may appear superfluous. Since the eighteenth century, neutrality has been a core element of dispute resolution theory and practice, both inside and outside U.S. courts. As we embark upon the twenty-first century and find ourselves in the midst of one of the periodic resurgences of dispute resolution in the history of the United States,[1] I believe we do well to examine mediation's core values, its effectiveness, and its ability to respond to the material conditions of U.S. society as well as to an increasingly global economy and political reality.

In the early years of the twenty-first century, what role does neutrality play in the structure of mediation and does it attend to the needs and expectations of the users of these services and of society? In what ways have central values of mediation such as neutrality been upheld or eroded by its increasing institutionalization and the formalization of its practices? And perhaps most importantly, whose interests are being served by mediation and other alternative dispute resolution (ADR) processes based on the concept of neutrality?

This chapter looks at the role of neutrality in the mediation field, followed by an exploration of its problems. I conclude with some recommendations and predictions about the role of neutrality in mediation's future in the United States. My primary interest in this interrogation of neutrality is to challenge the discourse and mythology of neutrality that it serves all equally. As a consequence, the analysis of problems associated with neutrality and my attending recommendations will not be aimed toward demonstrating how our attempts to be neutral fail nor will I propose pathways to rectify shortcomings. Rather I wish to engage the reader in considering how a focus on neutrality is misplaced and actually perpetuates a hegemony that serves some better than others. Such results fall far short of offering everyone a fair and accessible process for self-empowered relationship and agreement building. We can undoubtedly do better, and both participants and the visions offered by our own field demand no less.

From the beginning of this new wave of attention to mediation, the goals of those promoting it have been diverse: increasing the efficient administration of overcrowded courts;[2] offering opportunities for self-determination and mutual problem solving,[3] transforming individuals into more morally developed human beings,[4] and using its "magic"[5] to aid in the healing of relationships and communities.[6] Nonetheless, there is a unifying set of beliefs that ties together these seemingly disparate visions of mediation as a tool of volunteers, as a profession, and as a field of study.

These shared beliefs are manifested in the typical descriptions of mediation. For example, mediation is commonly defined as a neutral process for resolving conflicts in which a neutral third party—someone not involved in the dispute—facilitates communication and resolution of a conflict.[7] These "neutral third parties" are framed as unbiased, impartial, and "disinterested" in the content of the discussion and any agreement to be reached by the parties. In fact, mediators are seen as only interested in the *process*, in ensuring that it is fair and that parties to the dispute are the decision makers on any mutually acceptable agreement formulated. The combination of these characteristics mark mediation as fundamentally different from other methods of dispute resolution. And central to the success and popularity of mediation, it is argued, are these qualities of self-determination, of win/win agreements grounded in a voluntary and fair process.[8]

It is instructive to unpack these core attributes and note their relationship to neutrality. Neutrality is seen as the condition making it possible for parties to raise any topic that concerns them, negotiate with other(s), and come to a resolution of their own accord. This aspect of neutrality supports empowerment and self-determination and is referred to as impartiality because the mediator does not take sides over the content of the conflict or its resolution. The other element neutrality consists of is defined as equidistance—how mediators should position themselves in relation to the parties and to the content of their discussions. Equidistance requires mediators to balance their interventions equally (symmetrically) between all disputing parties, not favoring one person over the other. In other words, equidistance requires a symmetrical relationship between the mediators and the parties.[9]

Therefore, symmetry (as demonstrated by procedural fairness) and impartiality are the key components of neutrality and are the raison d'être for many intervention strategies. Procedural fairness (read symmetry) is believed to create a legitimate process, thereby *serving all participants*. This approach to conflict resolution reflects a particular cultural worldview that, for the most part, has gone unnamed and unexamined in the field.[10] Ironically then, while articulating a commitment to neutrality and presenting it as universally applicable and value-free, in actuality, the mediation field has routinely espoused a particular set of cultural beliefs that have been its driving force in this country.

These values are imbedded in a Western ideology of positivism that assumes it is possible for the observer to be separate from the observed; that one can conduct an intervention (whether it be as a scientist leading an experiment or as a judge, jury, or mediator engaged in a proceeding) without having one's own experiences or values permeate the process.[11] This outlook does not take into account that valuing distance between a conflict intervener and disputing parties is a cultural belief; it does not consider the impact the intervener has on the course of a mediation as he or she guides the process by asking certain questions and not others.

A commitment to the Western values of positivism and its attending concept of neutrality are at the core of the hegemonic paradigm permeating mediation literature and practice in the United States.[12] A desire for neutrality and symmetry is a part of Western liberal philosophy[13] that offers both as the antidote to inequality. Although this is undoubtedly driven by a care and concern for fairness, it raises the question, What are the consequences when a mediator treats equally those who are on an uneven playing field?

In a stratified society, we must ask what is the meaning of being neutral, of seeing oneself as capable of being neutral, and what is the result of treating all participants in the same manner? When differing experiences of violence and of access to power, decision making, and respect impact the lives of the participants, who is better served when power inequities are attended to by symmetry and neutrality? Such questions lead us into an examination of the scholarship of the field.

Interestingly, what has been central to the literature of both the champions and the critics of mediation is a discussion of fairness and its relationship to the sacred value of neutrality. In fact, critics have argued from early on that attempts to offer a fair and neutral process in private settings without the protection of public scrutiny and the ability to appeal or enforce agreements can reinforce power imbalances and steer disenfranchised populations further away from rights protection and enforcement.[14] In other words, a process may offer neutrality on its surface through procedural fairness, but despite this, it can reinforce those inequities that exist outside the mediation session and on a grander scale within society. Critics have been particularly concerned about how mediation can prevent or undermine structural changes based on precedent-setting legal decisions.[15]

Such critiques have focused primarily on mediation's role within a larger social system rife with inequality. And their conclusions have been that dispute resolution must be grounded in and responsive to the larger societal context, and that individuating and privatizing disputes within a so-called neutral setting violates this requirement. This literature—generated primarily by critical legal and critical race scholars—has challenged the heart of the mediation field and its belief that neutrality on a micro level is possible and is valuable.

Despite these attacks—and at times because of them—the vast majority of those defending and promoting mediation have focused on the positive aspects of neutrality for empowering people and resolving disputes on the individual, organizational, and community levels. Scholarship (both qualitative and quantitative) has rigorously sought to demonstrate—and many believe has done so successfully—the ability of mediation to achieve a neutral and fair process.[16] From theoretical analyses of why mediation works to training manuals and how-to books, the literature of the field is saturated with the language of neutrality. It is presented as a central tenet of ethical standards for practitioners[17] and as *the reason* the field can offer procedural fairness. In this way, the neutrality of an intervener is offered as *the guarantee* of a fair process. According to this discourse, neutrality makes possible the resolution of disputes through a truly democratic process of empowered, participatory discussion and self-determined decision making by parties. It thus maintains its hold as the sacred fabric of mediation in the United States.

NEUTRALITY'S LIMITATIONS

Over the past two decades, as a mediation researcher, teacher, trainer, and practitioner, I have witnessed what many refer to as the "magic of mediation"[18] as it seemingly lives up to its promises of empowerment and mutual engagement in democratic dispute resolution. I have also seen its ability to replicate disenfranchisement. Given its capacity for both, can an interrogation of the underlying principles and practices of mediation unearth identifiable patterns as to who is being better served by mediation's commitment to neutrality? Will it illuminate ways in which this is being carried out by mediators? How might increased understanding in these areas lead to meaningful changes in theory and practice? These are some of the questions that are driving my research.

This task has required examining the environment in which mediation is practiced. In 2007 as I write, U.S. society—similar to all time periods throughout its history—continues to be stratified, with resources differentially distributed based on socially constructed social group memberships such as age, ability, class, gender, race, sexual orientation, and religious heritage and affiliation.[19] Access to housing, employment, bank loans, educational opportunities, and health care are unevenly divided among social groupings.[20]

In such a society, mediation is challenged to consider its relationship to stratification. This is both problematic and necessary for a field that is concerned with procedural fairness and neutrality. Yet, for the most part, the field has failed to respond at all, let alone successfully, to this challenge.[21] Instead, it has lacked a sufficient critical analysis of social justice[22] concerns as well as the necessary intervention techniques to assist in navigating the realities of inequality. And those whose works have scrutinized mediation with an eye to social inequities and power imbalance (who have been fortunate enough to have them published) have come almost entirely from outside the field. This gap in the scholarship speaks to the strength of the master narrative[23] of neutrality within the field.

Seeking to address this gap, I conducted a literature review of the field and identified themes relating to neutrality that are outlined below. Then, they are unpacked more fully in an exploration of an actual case. Critical theory provides a useful lens for analysis, and it illuminates both the centrality of neutrality to mediation as well as its ability to reinforce larger social inequities. The four themes relating to the problems of neutrality are as follows.

1. An approach to mediation organized around the principle of neutrality assumes that all parties have equal access to narration in mediation. In other words, this assumes that all parties feel equally comfortable and capable of raising any topic, the mediators will treat all narratives in the same fashion, and, therefore, all narratives have an equal chance of being addressed. Recent research has demonstrated that this is not the case specifically with respect to age, gender, and race issues.[24]

2. The second theme emerges directly from the first. Both qualitative and quantitative research demonstrate that parties have disparate procedural and substantive experiences in mediation.[25] Therefore, symmetry and neutrality fail to offer symmetrical experiences, and those who belong to groups in society with more power are often further privileged in mediation.[26]

3. The belief in neutrality results in diverting attention from the likelihood of mediator bias by assuming that it does not occur unless it is proven otherwise. This faith in neutrality belies research findings regarding the commonplace experience of bias in this society.[27]

4. The realities of those who experience systematic inequality in society do not drive the research agenda, intervention strategies, or models for mediating (which I believe explains why there is an assumption that a neutral approach to mediating is universally useful and applicable).[28]

A critical interrogation of neutrality reveals that not only despite its use but directly *as a result of its imposition*, those with greater power can become more enfranchised in mediation than those with less power.[29] This observation serves as the focal point for examining the four thematic problems of neutrality.

First, let us examine how narrative processes work within mediation. Despite the mythology and common rhetoric of mediation as merely an alternative forum for solving problems, in actuality it is a complex process of story facilitation. *The ability to tell one's story* in a mediation—to describe the events and circumstances involved—*and to have this responded to and built upon by others is a key unit of power.* Therefore, it is participation in a legitimized narrative that provides one empowerment in this setting. And the mediator's facilitation of narratives influences whose stories are told, responded to, and built upon.[30]

If a story is not fully told in mediation, it cannot be adequately engaged with, and therefore it will be left out as the parties develop a plan for the future. Such a plan is commonly referred to as the mediation agreement and is actually a future story. The results, then, of the underdevelopment of one's story about the conflict leads to disenfranchisement in co-constructing a future story.[31] This issue relates to the second theme of problems associated with neutrality: that the results actually are frequently asymmetrical in terms of both procedure and outcome. Mediators' microlevel decisions about questioning, summarizing, and other typical strategies significantly influence story development.[32] There is a direct correlation between mediator decisions and whose stories dominate not only the discourse of a session but the outcome as well. In fact, one study reveals that in more than 80 percent of the cases researched at numerous mediation centers, the mediators favored the story of the first party to speak and that the final agreements were designed in accordance with this speaker's narrative framing of the conflict.[33] What was found was that it is the mediator's reliance on turn-taking that discursively reinforces the first speaker's story, and this reinforces the second speaker into a defensive position. The mediator responds to accusations and then the turn-taking, based on symmetry, establishes a pattern that interferes with an ability to narrate a different story of what has occurred, one that comes from the second speaker's own perspective.

Thus, a mediator's assumption that all parties have an equal opportunity to narrate actually serves to undermine their full narration and participation.

The pattern of the domination of the first speaker is only one of several reasons why some stories are more fully engaged with by mediators. Another is that those stories that resonate with larger cultural stories—the master narrative—in society have reinforcement and are more easily understood and identifiable since they are mirrored by the culture at large.[34]

Story facilitation strategies privilege stories that resonate with the master narrative in a number of ways.[35] For example, mediators strive to achieve neutrality by alloting the same amount of time to speak to each party. However, this often results in privileging the speaker whose story is most easily understood by the mediators. This description of events does not require detailed explanation and justification because it reflects the master narrative and therefore resonates with their experience.[36] The facilitation and elaboration of a counternarrative[37] often require additional time and patience for those unfamiliar or uncomfortable with the essence of it. Despite this and in the service of symmetry, mediators often use the party who needs less storytelling time and support to have their story fully told and understood as a baseline for the amount of time each party gets to speak. This focus on symmetry undermines full access to storytelling and story development, and in this way it limits access to complete participation, empowerment, and decision making in mediation. Ironically, then, with an inherent asymmetry in their storytelling needs, many participants are faced with a process and outcome that structurally determine the perpetuation of inequality *because* of the focus on neutrality and, specifically, symmetry.

A look at an example may bring to life these concerns with neutrality as we move from abstract discussions to the way they play out in a real session. In this case, all the problems described above occurred as the parties attempted to narrate their stories. In a mediation between a tenant and an apartment manager, despite *repeated attempts* by two people who are Latinas[38] to engage in a narrative about the negative racialization[39] of the Puerto Rican tenant, this story (basically one of racism) never fully emerged during the mediation. As a result, the agreement made by the two participants (one of whom is a White Anglo[40] and one of whom is a Latina) was not based on this underdisclosed story.

In fact, six months later the Latina participant reported that the mediation had not taken care of what she had considered the *"real problem"*: being negatively racialized at her apartment complex, which had lead to false accusations, misleading police reports, and threats of eviction. Concerns about and experiences with racism were at the center of the narrative that was not fully told or dealt with during the mediation. The story that had been fully articulated and built upon was about accusations of rule violations; this was the story presented first and by the White Anglo party. The Latina party, who spoke second, spent much of the session defending herself against what she stated were false accusations. The narrative about the future—the agreement that was reached—was primarily about rules violations as well.

In the end, the Latina tenant was pleased to have her "name cleared" with the manager for not having violated the rules, but she was also disenfranchised both procedurally and substantively. At the same time the White Anglos associated with the mediation—the apartment manager, one of the mediators, and all the residents of the apartment complex who were affected by the mediation agreement—did not have to deal with the Puerto Rican party's experience of being negatively racialized. In effect, then, the mediation resulted in White Anglo racial privilege in the procedures and in the substance of the agreement reached.

In this case, the pattern of the speaking order influenced narrative domination. What of the pattern of domination by those stories that resonate with the master narrative? In this case, the narrative about negative racialization, and racism was repeatedly interrupted by a narrative about rules; this included discussions about the rules of a traditional mediation process as well as discourse on rules in society at large. I argue that this is not circumstantial or random; rather, it was a manifestation of a thematic in the master narrative that is replicated in mediation as it is elsewhere in society.[41] The master narrative is saturated with the valorization of rules as we are a "nation of laws not of men." I argue that this thematic of the master narrative gave strength to the discussion of rules violations in the mediation as problems worth discussing and solving.

Accusations of racism, however, do not resonate with the master narrative. This is not surprising since the master narrative reflects the experiences of White Anglos and not of people of color and therefore essentially reflects and legitimates the viewpoints and interests of those in power and then frames them as universal. A direct result is the belief perpetuated in the master narrative that racism is a deviation from the norm; that it does not exist unless it violates a law, can be proven, and was *intentional*.[42] Therefore, the functioning status quo is to assume that racism is not at play unless a narrative can properly justify that it actually exists. Despite the assumption of fairness imbedded in a "colorblind" approach, in reality what results is that stories that do not acknowledge racism are favored, placing additional burdens of proof on narrators describing racism. Forsaking any appreciation for the reality of an uneven playing field, a colorblind assumption hides the fact that racial stratification can be reinforced by aracial rules.[43] Instead, this dominant narrative promotes a belief that "the exercise of racial power . . . [is] rare and aberrational rather than as systemic and ingrained . . . [a] deviation by a conscious wrongdoer from otherwise neutral, rational, and just ways of distributing . . . power."[44]

Therefore, telling a story about the reality of racism is a counternarrative, and in order to be seen as legitimate and resonant with the master narrative, such a story must provide proof of intentional race-based harm and a violation of a law. Strikingly, even in this dispute resolution forum, which does not require proof and does not engage in the official imposition of the law, the master narrative on racism and law invaded and impacted the storytelling process.

In this case study, the narratives about rules immediately and systematically followed attempts to engage in the narrative of racism. The mediators and the parties then proceeded to build upon the stories of rules and leave behind discussions of racism. Once again, neutrality was both procedurally and substantively a culprit in this domination of rules narratives over the narrative of racism. Time after time when the issue of race or racism was raised, the topic was changed to note that apartment complex rules and Federal Fair Housing laws were applied symmetrically and in accordance with a colorblind approach and that therefore racism could not have occurred. This repetition disrupted and finally ended all narration on race that had been undertaken by the Latina party and the mediators. In addition, during a mediators' caucus when discussions ensued about the need to address the story of racism with the parties, the mediators were reminded of the norm of giving equal amounts of time to speak by the mediation coordinator as a way to ensure neutrality. He pointed out that since the White Anglo party had already spoken less, it could be problematic from the standpoint of procedural fairness and neutrality to pursue further conversation with the Latina party.

This demonstrated a common pattern, that the narration structure of a session uses the person speaking from the master narrative to set the standard for the entire session. For example, here the coordinator assumed that if one participant had concluded telling her story in a certain amount of time, then the other participant should only receive approximately the same amount of time to speak. Otherwise, ironically, in mainstream mediation practice it is argued that the mediators are creating an imbalance and favoring one party over another. In this case, the participant who spoke English as her first language and was telling a story of rules that resonated with the master narrative completed her story more quickly than did the participant who was speaking English as her second language and was telling a counternarrative. Holding the entire mediation in English and then using the Anglophone's time frame as the standard is a way in which an attempt at symmetry—without accounting for the realities of each party and each mediator—privileged the Anglophone party at the expense of the Spanish-as-a-first-language speaker.

The mediators' lack of attention to (albeit due to a lack of knowledge of) the impact of neutrality on reconstituting racial and linguistic privilege is also reflective of the master narrative. The faith that symmetry and equidistance are salves for inequality does not provide mediation practitioners with the theory or tools they need to tackle the realities of mediating in a stratified and multicultural society. Since "racism is embedded in our thought processes and social structures . . . [and] the 'ordinary business' of society—the routines, practices, and institutions that we rely on to effect the world's work . . . [then] only aggressive, color-conscious efforts to change the way things are will do much to ameliorate [this] misery."[45] Recognizing this, then, challenges the mediation field to rethink the place of neutrality in light of the reality of racism.

The findings of other studies should add to this call. Strikingly disparate results from mediation for White Anglos and people of color emerged from the findings of quantitative research conducted by the schools of law and sociology at the University of New Mexico in Albuquerque. In their study, parties of color consistently fared worse than White Anglo parties whether they were the plaintiff or respondent in small claims mediation, and these results were more extreme than in the adjudicated cases to which they were compared.[46] These data are consistent with other findings on disparate outcomes from mediation that have uncovered the pattern of reconstituting privilege along group membership lines.[47]

The final theme of the problematics of neutrality is clearly elucidated by what has been previously outlined: the realities of the lives of those experiencing systematic racial inequality in society do not drive the ways in which mediation has been designed or functions. Therefore, it is not surprising to find that the majority of mediators are from racially privileged backgrounds; further, we find that most who are published and practicing in the United States are White adults who are middle class, able-bodied, and Anglophone, for example.[48] Therefore, many of the counternarratives attempted by parties in mediation will not reflect the life experiences of a mediator nor resonate with the master narrative. Rather than responding to the needs of each participant to fully tell their story of the conflict, an emphasis on neutrality actively perpetuates unequal access to storytelling, causing the colonization of counternarratives and the disenfranchisement of their narrators.

CALL FOR CHANGE

When we look beyond the mediation room it is noteworthy that the scholarship and research agenda of the field has not made even peripheral, let alone central, the concerns of those who are systematically discriminated against in society.[49] Universalizing the experiences of those in higher power groups has been a pattern of the vast majority of research—ironically, a discrepancy inconsistent with the rhetoric of neutrality and symmetry.

I do not argue that this flaw is intentional. However, in the long run, perhaps that is a moot point as it once again steers us to engage in the master narrative's definition of discrimination. Instead, my research has focused on identifying some of the ways in which not attending to the realities of inequality have perpetuated it. By implicating neutrality in this and by demonstrating how strategies carried out in its name structurally determine inequality, a centerpiece of mediation theory and practice is challenged.

Once we consider the impact of people's material realities on their participation in mediation and its outcomes, we begin to make a paradigmatic shift away from neutrality. As we move from assuming that neutrality and its components symmetry and equidistance are universally valued and applicable, the dispute resolution field faces new research questions and new possibilities for intervention.

Uncovering the political nature of facilitating narratives in mediation has demonstrated that relationships between all the players in the room are often asymmetrical, and so mediators need to be prepared to intervene asymmetrically to offer full access to storytelling and story construction to each participant. With this knowledge, research questions then emerge regarding how to create intervention models and train mediators to understand the politics of story facilitation and how to develop strategies that can effectively interrupt oppression dynamics within a session.

Given these indictments of neutrality, we must consider, "whither neutrality?" Additional research is needed to further investigate the problems fostered by efforts promoting neutrality. And we must explore what teaching and training methodologies, models of intervention, and programmatic structures might best respond to the needs of parties who come from differing positions and identities within society.

The research findings point to the importance of providing mediators and mediation program coordinators with both theoretical and practical tools for facilitating the narratives in a mediation from a critical (race) perspective. In addition, they need an in-depth understanding of narrative theory and processes; learning how stories are constructed and how facilitation techniques can foster or hinder story development. On a programmatic level, mediation centers may want to consider structural changes based on the assumption that the participants attend mediation with different needs and resources, specifically with regard to narrative participation. Therefore, having a diverse pool of mediators who can mediate in a number of languages is particularly important.

Just as important is in-depth training on issues of oppression. If mediation training is grounded in a social justice approach to critical race mediation, interveners could learn how to mediate with the assumption that racism and other forms of oppression are commonplace and that privilege is more likely than not to be at play in a session. This will require teaching a counternarrative—that the status quo is not neutral or colorblind and that symmetry does not invariably create equality in a mediation process.

What we must still research further are the techniques and strategies that mediators can apply for disrupting oppressive narrative processes. It is this, much more than merely understanding and appreciating the theory and values behind social justice mediation or critical race mediation, which can prepare mediators to encourage and protect full storytelling for all participants. Finally, as part of training and ongoing support for mediators, opportunities for reflective practice could provide rich learning experiences. The use of videotaping, jointly analyzing interactions with one's co-mediator and coordinator, and receiving feedback from role-players and, most importantly, from actual disputants can foster constructive critique and encourage experimentation.

New questions for investigation have emerged out of my research related to identity, power, and conflict narration. We are in need of furthering our study of the relationship between these elements in mediation if this method of dispute resolution is to serve all parties based on the realities of their lives. Historically, the field has underserved large segments of the population, making it urgent that mediation participants themselves help to define the research agenda for the field and not remain invisible or merely become objects of study. In fact, there is a role in research for listening to those who are *not* choosing to come to mediation. And if we do not take these new paths as researchers, then whose interests will our research serve?[50]

Dispute resolution educators are challenged to introduce students to mediation by *presupposing* that racism and other forms of oppression are tied to the participation of both the mediators and the parties to a conflict. We must search for new and creative ways to generate understanding that these experiences are intertwined. How might this objective influence our teaching modalities? What texts can we include in our introductory and advanced courses on mediation, dispute resolution, and conflict theory that can encourage critical thinking about these issues? An introduction to critical race theory could provide a new generation of students a useful prism through which to view mediation and, I hope, invigorate ourselves as well to creatively take on the challenge of eradicating racism and other forms of oppression from mediation practice.

All these recommendations require that we turn away from a focus on neutrality and symmetry, building a counternarrative to that thematic imbedded in the master narrative. As scholars, educators, and practitioners we are conduits for narrative advancement; the question becomes, In the service of which narratives will we work? There is no room for neutrality in the answer to that question.

There is a rising awareness—a more visible critique of neutrality underway from *within* the mediation movement than ever before. There are several factors influencing this development. Previously, critiques of neutrality from within the movement were ignored or ostracized[51] as irrelevant or undermining to the growth of a movement. Although some mediation scholars and practitioners, overwhelmingly people of color, have long articulated the problematic nature of a lack of attention to cultural and power inequities in mediation, their voices have not set the research agenda for the field. This must change if the field is to reflect and serve all members of our communities.

Interestingly, as the field has begun to reach maturity through its institutionalization in society[52] the attending security has fostered opportunities to reflect and critique *from within the mediation movement.* This is increasingly being valued within the field. Note, for example, the Symposium on Intentional Conversations about Race, Mediation and Dispute Resolution at Hamline University School of Law, annual conferences on Eliminating Barriers to Minorities in Dispute Resolution at Capital University Law School, and the Seventh Annual Facilitated Discussions on Racism and Conflict Resolution at the Association for Conflict Resolution conference in Fall 2006. The field has become secure enough that inside critiques are not considered threats to its relative stability. This bodes well for furthering a research and practice agenda that scrutinizes and deconstructs neutrality. However, it also denotes that such efforts are likely to stay as relatively contained counternarratives, with the thematic of neutrality being buttressed by the master narrative throughout all of society's cultural and institutional apparatuses— even dispute resolution.

# 9 Race, (In)Justice, and Conflict Resolution

*Injustice in the African American Community, Effects on Community, and the Relevance of Conflict Resolution*

ANDREW CHANG, DAMIEN BASEY, VALARIE CAREY, ANGEL COLEMAN, *and* KATT HOBAN

In the fall of 2005, we attended Professor Beth Roy's conflict resolution course through the Peace and Conflict Studies program at the University of California, Berkeley.* This paper began as a group project for that class and emerged from our respective academic studies and lived experiences—either as African Americans who are personally and intimately aware of continued oppression and racism in our society or as student-allies beginning our journey into peacemaking and social justice activism.

As students of other disciplines of study and only newly becoming oriented to conflict resolution, we have had a unique and naturally interdisciplinary perspective approaching this field and practice of conflict resolution. Admittedly, our experiences in and loyalties to the field do not run deep—at least in comparison to some of the seasoned professionals writing in this anthology, who individually and collectively embody decades of wisdom and actual lived experience as peacemakers and educators. However, in a

---

*With thanks for the contributions of Terrell Williams.

108

sense, our position also offers us a degree of separation, which perhaps helps facilitate critical analysis and fresh insight.

Although we do not wish to overgeneralize and obscure the heterogeneity within and between various ethnic and racial groups, we do believe that this analysis of the structural racism affecting African Americans is relevant to the experiences of many other marginalized or underserved communities as well.

## INTRODUCTION

Today in the twenty-first century, the African American community continues to experience significant forms of systemic injustice. In mainstream discourse, race is often seen as existing only superficially, as conservative politicians and aggrieved applicants for university admissions increasingly advocate for "race-blind" social policies and lament the supposed "reverse discrimination" of affirmative action-type policies. In this nation founded on slavery, however, with its history of atrocious—and for centuries mostly government-sanctioned—racism, racial injustice continues to thrive. Furthermore, in its evolved, postslavery and post–Jim Crow form, this racism manifests itself not only as individual-level prejudice and ignorance, but also most threateningly in the economic, political, and social realities of the United States. In this context, African Americans are in conflict with the institutional structure, a system of inequality and privilege, of oppression and power that belies the existence of racial equality or a "level playing field."

These forms of injustice and oppression have tangible and serious consequences, negatively impacting individuals, interpersonal relationships, and efforts at attaining mobility or justice. Such a problematized understanding of conflict and its structural context and implications is a necessary foundation for any discussion of resolution; after all, this is the context in which all American conflict resolution practice takes place. It is in light of this sociological and racial analysis that paths toward justice may potentially be forged and that an examination of conflict resolution and the field's literature may become meaningful. Specifically, the ways in which conflict resolution can either aid injustice or contribute to oppression will become more apparent, as we proceed with an exploration and critique of conflict resolution, focusing on issues of culture, race, and power.

Although studies and books have tried to illuminate these particular issues and propose possible responses to these conditions of oppression, it is also clear that this significant and unjust reality still remains hidden to the majority of society as well as unaddressed and absent from most discussions of conflict resolution. Within this context then we must now ask the question: how might those in conflict resolution begin walking against the flow of oppression and racism to create positive change? More specifically, how can conflict resolution, as an established field but also more generally in all its various forms of theory and practice, be relevant and ideally serve as a tool for promoting change and discovering actual justice?

## STRUCTURAL INJUSTICE IN THE AFRICAN AMERICAN COMMUNITY

Structural levels of racism tend to be invisible to those not personally experiencing them. Dynamics such as "redlining" of neighborhoods that result in higher home buying costs for people of color or the multiple forces that result in higher rates of incarceration of African American men are sometimes in the public eye, more often not. We begin by describing a few examples of realms of injustice that affect the African American community: education and employment and the resulting impact on the family.

### Education

Although education is often lauded as an enabling and "equalizing" tool that can aid positive change, it is clear today that educational stratification in fact plays a significant role in maintaining and reproducing the injustices that African Americans face. Statistics and studies illustrate that there continue to be significant educational disparities between blacks and whites. For instance, according to a report by the Department of Education in 2000, on average only a third of blacks ages eighteen to twenty-four attend college, and overall blacks make up only 11 percent of U.S. college students. Similarly, throughout the 1990s, the national college graduation rate of African

Americans, roughly 39 percent, has been 20 to 25 percent lower than that of whites. Even among those who do finish college, the grade point average of black students is two-thirds of a grade below that of whites.[1]

Socioeconomic, historical and other factors do undoubtedly help explain these academic discrepancies—as financial pressures and inadequate financial aid are indeed the most important explanatory dynamics contributing to college dropout rates.

The association between poverty and youth problem behaviors may be explained by possible links among the educational quality of home environments, academic difficulties, and increased problem behaviors. Poor families have fewer resources to commit to educationally related tools such as computers, books, and calculators. This type of impoverishment is associated with academic failure, which, in turn, may prompt or sustain misbehavior or emotional distress in school.[2]

However, class factors alone fail to explain why virtually all aspects of underperformance—lower standardized test scores, lower college grades, lower graduation rates—persist among students from the African American middle class. What does help to explain such underperformance is the existence of such structural factors as tracking, bias (conscious or not) of teachers, insufficient funding of schools in low-income and black neighborhoods, inherent biases in standardized tests and college admission tests, government programs such as No Child Left Behind that rely on results of such standardized tests, isolation amid a hostile climate once in college, and more. It is informative that African American students graduate at their highest rates at the most prestigious colleges and universities, schools that most commonly have forms of racially preferential policies as well as increased retention efforts.

*Employment*

In turn, educational inequities set the stage for discrimination and inequality in employment. Further, as both spatial redlining and overall racial discrimination contribute to greater unemployment, today these substantial inequities for African Americans exist in every aspect of economics and employment: hiring (and firing) practices, unemployment levels, representation in managerial positions, and overall wealth, to name a few. As our economy becomes overwhelmingly service-sector oriented, African Americans remain underrepresented in "white collar" professions; not surprisingly, African Americans are also the "hardest hit by downsizing and unemployment and are most often the workers to lose jobs across all industries."[3]

Statistically, according to the Urban League's 2005 report, "More than 1 in 10 African Americans are now unemployed," making the national unemployment rate for blacks (10.8 percent) more than twice the rate for whites. Most disturbingly, the "median net worth of an African American family is $6,100 compared to $67,000 for a white family—an outrageous $60,900 difference."[4]

*Family*

All of these dynamics—in housing, education, and employment—are among the stressors on families. Of all ethnic groups, African American households have the highest number of single family households. As resilient and inventive as many single parents are, nonetheless a higher proportion of single-parented youths end up involved in some kind of youth violence. A 2001 report by the Surgeon General notes:

> No single risk factor or set of risk factors is powerful enough to predict with certainty that youth will become violent. Poor performance in school is a risk factor, for example, but by no means will all young people who perform poorly in school become violent.[5]

This being said, youth in families who possess all of these risk factors are at high risk for youth violence. At the front lines of where all of these risk factors overlap is the single-parent family.

The single-parented child often lives in poverty, performs poorly in school, is unsupervised after school, lacks a relationship with his or her father, and is exposed to violence in his or her community. The single-parented child experiences this reality because of the shared reality of the single parent, most often a mother. The single mother is commonly low income, works one or more jobs concurrently, cannot be with her children during the workday or night, has little if any support from the other parent, and has experienced domestic violence. However, though raising a family with one parent instead of two for whatever reason is tough, single parenting as an isolated factor is not an indicator of violent children. It is the conditions under which many single-parent families live that create a healthy breeding ground for youth violence.

Poverty is an issue with many repercussions for the single-parent family. It disallows them from living in better neighborhoods and sending their children to better schools. It sends children to school hungry and keeps them from engaging in any capital-intensive extracurricular activities, such as school trips. It creates homelessness, chronic illness, and depression. According to Parents Without Partners, $28,000 is the family income average for a home with custodial parents. Many single-parent families have more than one child, and "over half who do not have joint custody or agreements do not receive any payments" from fathers to assist with child rearing.[6]

Poverty has a big hand in determining school performance of single-parented children. Many single parents live in underfunded school districts like those described above, institutions where students are often tracked into negative categories for the wrong reasons. With few resources, the single parent may be incapable of fighting for a child's educational rights, and the child, soured by the experience, may turn away from education. When they go home, these youths then avoid discussing their academic problems with their parent. They understand that the parent cannot afford the resources available to help them excel academically, and they want to protect the parent from experiencing more stress.

Single parents often have less time for supervising homework; there are simply not enough hours or dollars in a single mother's day. In *Youth Violence: Do Parents and Families Make a Difference?* researcher Laurence Steinberg estimates that "30 percent of parents [do] not know how their child [is] doing in school."[7]

Frustration may lead the teen to emotional outbursts. The instructor immediately labels the teen instead of attempting to identify the problem. The teacher's fear is transparent to the teen, and classrooms become unruly and disorganized when teens realize that teachers are just other disempowered adults incapable of righting wrongs. This reality leaves the child stifled and overwhelmed with anger. "Not surprisingly," concludes Jennifer Roback Morse, "kids in these families have inferior grades and drop out of school more frequently."[8]

The single mother finds herself trapped in a system of ineffective parenting, but she continues on alone. Just as her mate is absent from her children's lives, the single mom is surrounded by other single mothers who have absent male partners. Many of their partners are incarcerated. "55% of incarcerated males have a child under the age of 18. 32% had two or more children. . . . Of male inmates with children, 89.6% indicate the child is now in mother's care."[9] With problematic role models and few mentors to guide them through their maturation, many young males find comfort in joining a gang where older men become father-like figures for them.

The single mother is associated with the problem of youth violence because she comes from the very conditions that produce it. She is not a cause; she must not be the only defense. By putting ourselves on the front lines of this issue in our communities, we can lift up the single mother and her family and build communities with more hope, more parenting, and less violence.

*Relationships*

All these systems—housing, employment, education, and family structure—have an impact not only as external social forces; they also greatly affect interpersonal relationships. African American people experience the effects of these systems in their relationships with co-workers, friends, family members, and other members of their community. With internal relationships strained, the community's capacity to organize in an effort to change these social forces is inhibited. Racist social systems are at times internalized and represented in poor self-esteem and negative perceptions of other community members. Moreover, frequent discrimination builds pain and anger, making constructive communication in an effort to overcome injustice all the more exhausting and difficult. Systemic racism disrupts the community by co-opting efficacy in one's life and draining the psychological resources people have available to invest in relationships.

Yet healthy relationships within the community are crucial to empower the community to make positive changes toward social justice. Only with positive relationships and a sense of empowerment can the African American community engage in the social activism and organizing necessary to fight against racial inequality.

CONFLICT RESOLUTION FOR JUSTICE?

Conflict resolution skills and practices, and particularly the more progressive and transformative kinds, can potentially help. At the same time, the limiting and problematic aspects of conflict resolution practice also inhibit the field's social/racial justice potential. We first briefly explore the former, the positives, in general terms before proceeding onto a more critical analysis.

John Paul Lederach's conception of conflict transformation emphasizes that conflict, as a naturally long-term and dialectical process, need not be a negative experience and can instead be engaged constructively and expressed nonviolently, through dialogue or nonviolent direct action, for instance. Similarly, Baruch Bush and Joseph Folger's conception of transformative mediation emphasizes that mediation has positive effects on individual empowerment and recognition. Empowerment refers to individuals' personal clarity about their goals and thus greater efficacy to make decisions for themselves.[10] In turn, "recognition" refers to giving consideration to and feeling empathy for others and an Other. With both types of transformative conflict resolution practices, emphasis is placed on relationships and on empowering individuals in the community, not simply on reaching an agreement.

Can the processes advocated by Bush and Folger, Lederach, and others actually produce such results effectively in spite of the obstacles of culture, race, and racism? The overarching intent of these ideals and philosophies—to enable individuals to handle conflicts and conduct their relationships in more constructive and amicable ways—are clearly positive and especially useful for a community striving for justice. If a community embraces the potentially productive and constructive nature of conflict and expresses intracommunity conflicts in more nonviolent and collaborative rather than self-destructive ways, then a positive spiral of change could begin on an individual level. Such a community, with empowered individuals and curbed violence, might then have greater energy to address external and institutional issues and to organize for both individual-level mobility and social justice activism.

Theoretically, even in its relatively more conservative form of alternative dispute resolution (ADR), conflict resolution has several positive effects that could help poorer people of color in the legal system or in business areas. For example, Sara Kristine Trenary discusses typical items that are believed to be benefits of ADR's integration into the judicial system. These include "savings in time and cost," "improved accessibility and empowerment," "flexibility," and "durable resolutions." Court-related ADR and alternative judicial options such as restorative justice hold much potential. Conflict resolution practitioners in these areas believe that they are furthering the collective good with this type of "procedural" justice. "ADR specialists tend to believe that formally uncoerced agreements negotiated by parties themselves . . . are more likely to prove mutually satisfactory than agreements imposed by officials or precedential rules."[11]

Despite these apparent positives, some critics suggest that ADR in the courts proves in reality to be just as oppressive to minorities as traditional adjudication forms. These critiques should be considered seriously, even as there is evidence to indicate that these sorts of alternatives are improvements, simply in their existence as alternatives, over the more traditional punitive and adversarial models of (in)justice.

In the area of "intercultural communication," there is a way that conflict resolution can also potentially help individual and community struggles for peace and justice. Particularly over the past decade, an extensive body of literature has been compiled about the ephemeral and abstract idea of culture, making conflict resolution, in all its various mainstream, conservative, and progressive forms, a leader of sorts in increasing society's awareness about issues of diversity and cultural difference. Though we will later explore the ways in which the conflict resolution discourse of culture is problematic, the existence and expansion of the discourse itself does represent laudable progress (at least relative to mainstream "colorblind" society). In its ideals, the conflict resolution discourse on diversity calls for a more egalitarian and multicultural society, where people of different worldviews, values, and cultural identities may coexist rather than conflict.

Finally, there is potential for individual resolution of intercultural conflicts to become meaningful at a larger structural level as well. If conflict resolution can transform individual people and increase their recognition of and empathy for (those usually seen only as) Others and increase the degree to which individuals feel empowered, then these individuals will be fundamentally changed and improved. Such transformation at the individual level might lead people to make different decisions, hold different values, and lead different lives. As Lederach states, conflict transformation interventions can also lead individuals to a greater understanding of the "root causes and social conditions that give rise to . . . harmful expressions of conflict" and in turn, encourage individuals to develop alternative structures that are more participatory and just.[12]

In areas such as antioppression education or conflict transformation, the transformative potential of these practices is exciting because it speaks of the potential for bottom-up forms of change. Although the structures of injustice and oppression must be directly addressed as well, because these are the conditions that produce further destruction and suffering on the individual level, change is also possible from the other direction: change happening in individuals and those individuals in turn affecting and dialectically transforming the structures and power dynamics around them. If such profound transformations can occur in individuals—for instance, with those previously unaware becoming allies and those previously discouraged becoming empowered—transformative practices may help enable and promote peace and justice on a larger scale. This is the promise of conflict transformation. Viewed through a transformation lens, this is also the promise of all conflict: for individuals to become empowered and able to minimize the destructiveness of conflict, while transforming conflict into a choice as well as an opportunity for structural change and personal growth.

*Conflict Resolution's Shortcomings and Oppression*

Although there are many good things being done by conflict resolution practitioners, there are also ways in which conflict resolution generally fails to live up to this potential and may even contribute to greater injustice, particularly when it fails to engage the influence of structural injustices. Many conflict resolution forms lack a means or a built-in conscientiousness to acknowledge important factors that lie outside the interpersonal dynamics immediately visible at a mediation table. Even while individuals (both disputants and mediators) are shaped by the socioeconomic, political, historical, and cultural conditions around them, conflict resolution practices may fail to explicitly take these factors into consideration in the process of diagnosing and attempting to resolve, manage, or transform conflict. Additionally— and most startlingly—as Roberto Chené points out, from the perspective of people of color within the dominance paradigm:

> According to our differences, we are already institutionalized into conflicted, unhealthy, and ultimately unimprovable ... human relationships. The conflicts between us are already set in the dysfunctional paradigm that we have constructed for relating to each other. What we are mediating are the frequent overt flare-ups of a fundamentally unworkable system. (See chapter 3 by Chené in this volume.)

In other words, to reappropriate a common metaphor used in conflict resolution, individual conflicts themselves may represent only the tip of the iceberg. Meanwhile, during many conflict processes, the remainder of the iceberg, representing our fundamentally violent and unjust society, remains mostly invisible but unquestionably real. In Chené's analysis and in this analogy, conflict resolution practices that focus only on the individuals and their immediate conflict and fail to see the rest of the iceberg that is the social context may in fact be futile or misguided. In light of this reality, those involved in conflict resolution need to undergo a vast transformation in the way they perceive of themselves and of the purpose of mediation.

This problem of mediation has been articulated internally by several scholars within the conflict resolution field. For example, in her article "Rethinking Neutrality: Race and ADR," Sara Kristine Trenary criticizes ADR as also potentially a drain to community-organizing efforts against racism and injustice. This "privatization of justice ... diverts public, group issues into private settings. The result is that collective actions are fractionalized and reduced to individual disputes, robbing society of class remedies and publicly articulated norms."[13] Similarly, David Turner and Elias Cheboud discuss this issue in their exploration of antioppressive approaches to advocacy and conflict resolution in social work. Referencing writings by Baruch Bush and Folger, Turner and Cheboud give an example of how mediation "privatizes and depoliticizes sexual discrimination (the power context), downplays the structural context, and reduces a matter that should be a public issue to merely a private concern." Further, Turner and Cheboud cite Whittington's assertion that:

> In sum, the overall effect of the [mediation] movement has been to neutralize social justice gains achieved by the civil rights, women's, and consumer movements, among others, and to establish the privileged position of the stronger classes and perpetuate their oppression of the weaker.[14]

From this most dramatic criticism of conflict resolution, it becomes clear that in practice conflict resolution's ideals and claims of doing good do not always hold up. Conflict resolution can also be a tool of oppression and not just a positive and constructive force producing peace and justice. On what side conflict resolution falls and whose interests it serves are determined by both the process and the content of how it is practiced—namely, its methodology—and by the values and assumptions—the epistemologies—that inform its praxis.

Any proposed prescriptions must attempt to address (or at least understand and acknowledge) all the various levels—individual, interpersonal, cultural, and systemic—of injustice and conflict. As conflicts are built into the structure of our society, conflict resolution praxis cannot focus only on the level of individuals and fail to recognize the root socioeconomic and political causes of violence and inequality. Such a positioning would place the conflict resolution field in the same paradigm as that of prisons and other typically oppressive institutions of mainstream society: a paradigm that perpetuates oppression by salvaging and veiling the unjust system while scapegoating individuals. In this sense, conflict resolution mechanisms without a sociological imagination and some pragmatic peace studies idealism would be of no use to anyone but those currently enjoying power and privilege. At the least, what is needed is, in the words of Chené, for conflict resolution practitioners to "think about the role of conflict resolution in addressing the chronic undercurrent of conflict that is always present even when it is not overt. We need to think about how to intentionally address a situation that most people think of as 'normal.'"

In light of these critiques of the field's ignorance and complicity in oppression, it should be clear that conflict resolution has much work to do.

## CONFLICT RESOLUTION, MULTICULTURALISM, AND RACE

Having analyzed how conflict resolution can serve either social justice or oppressive ends, and pointing out a few general areas in need of reform, we may turn our attention to the final focus of this paper: conflict resolution's relationship with and treatment of race and multiculturalism. Although mainstream conflict resolution has been working to improve its "cultural competency" for the past decade or two, there remains much room for progress. Having undertaken a broad survey of conflict resolution literature written specifically on race or culture, we explore some of these articulations from the literature, offer some of the field's critiques of itself, and propose an alternative measure for diversity and multiculturalism that goes beyond the current discourse.

### A Critique of Conflict Resolution's Culture

To begin, we question the content and assumptions of traditional forms of ADR and conflict resolution. In recent years, assumptions about mediator neutrality and the overall universality of mainstream mediation models have been called into question by several writers. These issues rest on the cusp of discussions of power and structure on one hand, and culture and identity on the other. Trenary concludes that "remaining neutral in a mediation where there are significant power imbalances is acting to permit them and even to facilitate the manifestation of these imbalances in the outcome of the mediation."[15] Turner and Cheboud give further voice to this significant position:

We believe neutrality is a myth which ostensibly whitewashes the natural standpoint of the mediator. This false objectivity creates an illusion of "fairness" which is hard for the marginalized party to challenge. Mediators are essentially middle-class mainstream professionals with a privileged experience . . . which impairs their sensitivity to marginalized experience.[16]

Unable to truly ameliorate feelings of hurt and injustice, a mediator may unintentionally validate dominant cultural narratives over those from the cultural margins. A simple change of rhetoric to describe mediators as "impartial" rather than "neutral" is insufficient. Instead, all of these writers propose a more antioppressive or justice-oriented approach where intervention on behalf of the oppressed party is justified and where mediators are required to take greater efforts to determine whether particular conflicts may be mediated or whether these should be referred over to other more advocating and organizing-oriented responses. When race and power are brought into the conversation, what may also be read in these critiques is the reality that mediations do not operate in a vacuum and that whether or not one chooses to recognize them, unequal power relations, reflecting societal injustices, *always* exist and always matter.

This challenge to a significant tenet of mediation—many mediators have always proudly described themselves as neutral or impartial third parties—speaks to the overall transformation that conflict resolution is currently undergoing at its progressive fringes. There is increased awareness of the culturally specific nature of the traditional mediation model. For instance, in her article "Mediation and Multicultural Reality," Michelle LeBaron describes the cultural roots and limitations of mainstream mediation:

Mediation in dominant cultures of North America tends to be characterized by overt communication, structured confrontation and intervention by a "neutral third party with no decision-making power." . . . The cultural indebtedness of [this] model is clear: that values and approaches to communication reflect individualistic, low context, "modern" societies.[17]

This culturally specific model based in white middle-class values and assumptions should not be asserted as one that is universal. However, without other alternative models that are as widespread or accessible, this limited model is still often forced upon people in conflict whose cultures are different from the model, the mediator, or their fellow disputants. The effects of this cultural misalignment can be seen clearly in the difficulty many U.S. and Canadian community mediation programs have, according to LeBaron, in "attracting and engaging members of ethnocultural minority groups as interveners, staff people and parties."[18]

Cynthia R. Mabry applies a similar critique to family mediation, in "African Americans Are Not Carbon Copies of White Americans." She lists various ways that the reactions by African American cultures and people to the traditional ADR model are different than those of whites, and she discusses the need for these differences to be recognized by mediators as well as in the design of the mediation. Some of the differences to be taken into account include the experience of African Americans with racism and prejudice and the effects they have on trust and rapport between disputant and mediator, as well as the subtle forms of stereotyping, prejudice, and communication ignorance that might exist in the mediator. She emphasizes that a "mediator must examine cultural influences and methods by which African American families adapt to segregation and discrimination . . . [and] be sensitive to how racism and prejudice have affected African American family life."[19]

Laura Ward Branca gives a most complete critique of mainstream mediation in "Culture Is to People Like Water Is to Fish." Besides the culture of mediation being more "consistent with the norms of middle class white people," Branca also points out that mediation often is "viewed cynically as whitewashing . . . [or] as window-dressing to put a good face on dishonesty, stupidity, and misuse of power, with no intention of touching what is really going on."

> People of color in mediation are often resigned to the likelihood that the institution or the mediators themselves will reflexively see them as the source of the problem. The referring agency will probably not be able to see how systemic exclusion and insensitive practices have contributed to or even created the problems that bring them to mediation. . . . Mediation can seem contrived and unlikely to really resolve matters.[20]

*Attempted Multicultural Practice*

Significant cultural and racial critiques of conflict resolution, such as the ones we have cited here, have led many practitioners and academics to elaborate various methods of valuing and recognizing culture, signs of progress in conflict resolution's complex and evolving relationship with culture. Nonetheless, although the need for intercultural capabilities and multiculturalism in conflict resolution is becoming more widely understood, writings in the field suggest that attempts at implementing multiculturalism into actual practice have not yet been fully successful.

For those practitioners and scholars who have taken up the challenge of making their practice and models more multicultural, culture has proven to be an unwieldy and uncontainable entity. Michelle LeBaron, a scholar who has focused on the question of multiculturalism in mediation, points out that "when conflict is understood as interrelated with culture, every dimension of analysis and intervention is affected." Illustrating this complicating reality, LeBaron poses a laundry list of questions challenging fundamental assumptions or components of a mediation, from "what constitutes a conflict" or a resolution, to "the identity of the parties," to "whether, how, and with what processes or interventions a conflict should be approached." Her point is to emphasize the dynamic and "complex nature of culture as a foundation of standards of reality, knowledge and power." Additionally, the "aspiration to design culturally appropriate processes" becomes even more complicated when one recognizes "that cultures are constructed from deeply shared meanings, that each individual is a part of multiple cultures, and that there is wide variation within cultures."

For all these challenges and complexities, LeBaron emphasizes the need for both "deep awareness of culture, both of self and other" and for "the development of capacities for flexibility, creativity and innovation." She introduces two of the primary ways that culture has been incorporated into and dealt with in mediation: awareness building and (in the tradition of Lederach) elicitive process design, in which mediators remain flexible and encourage disputants to participate in the actual shaping of the mediation process.[21]

In a more recent and helpfully field-encapsulating article, Mark David-heiser includes these two, as well three other approaches, as the most common answers to culture in mediation. The other three are "adjusting the communication framework to make it amenable to other communicating styles; following checklists of cross-cultural mediation techniques" by measuring "various dimensions of culture;" and "matching ethnicities" or having multicultural mediation teams. Davidheiser explores various strengths and weaknesses of each approach. To summarize for our purposes here, he finds essentially that the latter three approaches are useful to some degree but can all be guilty of essentializing culture and ignoring the heterogeneity and dynamism of culture within and between individuals and groups.

Meanwhile, the opposite dilemma exists with awareness building and elicitive design. Building "internal awareness of one's own cultural orientations" is a positive step for mediation and for people in general. However, as of yet it is unclear how to translate this awareness into practice, or "how mediators can optimize their practice when dealing with diverse disputants." As for elicitive design, including models such as transformative mediation and conflict transformation, it is most promising for minimizing ground rules (which are inevitably culturally particular), aiming for empowerment of disputants rather than simply for settlement, and overall for allowing disputants to participate in the process of the mediation and not only supply the narrative content. There are, of course, also potentially problematic elements. For instance, Davidheiser points out how "the conceptualization of empowerment is specifically Western ... reflect[ing] a liberal trend of thought traceable to the Enlightenment ... [and] central to Western cosmology" and individualism/self-determination. Additionally, besides the significant question of practicality—how exactly do you create and maintain such a flexible and dynamic practice?—there is also the chance that with less formal checks and facilitative power, coercion and power imbalances may be more likely to subtly influence the mediation. However, despite these pitfalls this "process model" does represent "an ambitious effort to counteract problems of power disparities and cross-cultural applicability."[22]

In sum, from this analysis, a combination of awareness building and elicitive design practices seems to represent the conflict resolution field's latest and most progressive endeavor to become honestly and critically multicultural. "Our accumulated knowledge of culture suggests that an open and integrative praxis is essential to mediation becoming a truly multicultural field." Further, given that "on some level, all mediations are 'intercultural,'" Davidheiser sees crafting an "adaptive practice that still minimizes the risks that accompany a lack of structure" as the positive direction. While no one can yet claim to be fully multicultural in their mediation approach, there are clearly efforts being made. The continued progress—or lack thereof—over the next decade or so should be a good measure of whether the fact of cultural diversity can ever be completely reconciled within a mediation practice, or whether practitioners and scholars need to begin recognizing the impossibility of being universally adaptable and no longer claim to be able to serve every person equally and justly.

*Conflict Resolution by People of Color*

We return once more to the question of race and racism to address one final issue: the amount of diversity and culture within the field of conflict resolution.

In his seminal work *Pedagogy of the Oppressed*, Paulo Freire states an obvious point that too often goes unsaid: "The pedagogy of the oppressed [is] a pedagogy which must be forged *with*, not *for*, the oppressed."[23] We believe that the same holds true for conflict resolution for African Americans, or more generally for people of color, the underserved, and all others who face forms of oppression in our present society. In fact, conflict resolution has become so institutionalized as a field and practice that from our culturally biased lenses, it likely has become difficult to recognize other existing forms of ethnic or indigenous conflict resolution because they do not fit the norms of the current white middle class traditions. In this sense, the field of conflict resolution has become culturally hegemonic.

While researching this paper we had a surprisingly difficult time discovering articles by or about conflict resolution practitioners or scholars of color. We also were unable to find much conflict resolution literature explicitly discussing race. Moreover, of the articles talking about culture or multiculturalism that we did find, nearly all seemed to be written by white Americans or Canadians from one of the relatively few established conflict resolution departments in North American universities. In essence, perhaps because of how conflict resolution has been monopolized by this normative institution, we were unable to find any alternative, community-based, bottom-up forms of problem solving and conflict resolution. This absence is both curious and problematic and raises the question: why are these people of color and these alternative methods and models not prominent and visible to students just becoming oriented to conflict resolution, and also, more importantly, to those in need of these more authentic forms?

When we finally stumbled upon one organization, the Alliance of African/African American Peacemakers, our fear that there were in fact no people of color in mainstream conflict resolution was somewhat assuaged. Through linking together African and African American peacemakers, this organization envisions fulfilling its "mission to develop, disseminate and provide African centered peacemaking models, strategies, and interventions to, for and with African people and communities around the world."[24] It is exciting and heartening to see that there are in fact African Americans working to represent themselves and assert their voices and perspective in conflict resolution.

It will not be enough for mediation to serve as a tool of social justice for people oppressed by systemic racism or class injustice if practitioners fail to understand the structural inequities and power dynamics that exist and how these affect the individuals and cultures in dispute as well as every aspect of a conflict or an attempted resolution.

To review and conclude, the conflicts in the African American community are rooted in the overall racism and injustice of our society. These injustices are often negatively internalized, strain interpersonal relationships, and affect the greater community, creating more individual level conflict to further magnify structural and institutional injustices—in housing, education, and employment, for instance—that still thrive today.

Conflict resolution can undoubtedly play a role in the struggle against systemic racism, acting as a supporting mechanism in a variety of ways. However, it is a paradox that conflict resolution practitioners may sometimes contribute most dramatically to social justice by simply stepping away and refusing to play a role in oppression. Increasing their understanding of race and of the systemic roots of conflict, as well as their awareness of their own culture and contexts of privilege, people in conflict resolution may also aid the struggle by promoting and allying with African Americans and other practitioners of color. Increasing the representation and voice of people of color and other marginalized peoples in the field may ultimately be the only way to make conflict resolution theory and practice authentically diverse and multicultural.

# 10 Experience from the Environmental Dispute Resolution Field

*Adjusting the Process for Maximum Inclusion of Interests and Knowledge*

LUCY MOORE

I am increasingly concerned with two dilemmas that I frequently face as a mediator and facilitator of natural resource disputes.* The first relates to inclusion and participation of Native American parties in my processes. The second relates to what I call "ways of knowing" and the conflict that arises when different kinds of expertise face each other across the negotiating table. In the following two case studies I hope to describe these dilemmas and offer some potential solutions. It also seems useful to me to understand as well as we can the nature of each problem and the ways in which they relate to each other.

## WATER PLANNING IN NEW MEXICO: WITH OR WITHOUT TRIBES?

Water planning in New Mexico began in earnest after an attempt by El Paso, Texas, to appropriate New Mexico groundwater. This was a shocking

---

*This chapter was originally presented as a paper at the Yosemite Conference, October 2000, State Bar of California, Environmental Law Section.

prospect and seemed within the grasp of the greedy neighbor after the federal district court ruled that New Mexico's statute against exporting groundwater was unconstitutional. If the state was to deny Texas, it would have to prove that water supplies within the state were needed by New Mexican citizens. Terrified of losing out to a longtime rival, the New Mexico legislature passed legislation in 1987 to develop a water plan for the state, which would be based on regional water plans and would prove the state's long-term need for all its water resources.

Since then, sixteen separate water planning regions identified themselves on the basis of common political, economic, and hydrological interests, in hopes that the plans would both make sense and be implementable. Grants between $25,000 and $75,000 were awarded to these regions, with little guidance about what a water plan should look like. Planning processes should be "appropriate," costs and timetables "reasonable," water conservation "adequate," and *all tribal governments within a region must be included.* A *Regional Water Planning Handbook,* developed by the regional planners and the state in concert in 1996, offered a water plan outline and further emphasized the need for all regions to engage a balanced and representative group of interests in the planning process and to provide for meaningful public involvement of all interested citizens.

## The Cloud of Adjudication

New Mexico is a state rich in cultural diversity and poor in water resources. The scarcity of water adds tension and competition to the relationships among the interests and the cultures and makes planning for a balanced and realistic water future difficult. To add to the anxiety, water rights in the state are in the agonizing process of being adjudicated, and New Mexico boasts the oldest case in federal court in the country—the *Aamodt* case, which is in its thirty-eighth year. Adjudications like this one are feared by everyone involved, except perhaps the attorneys. They are endless, hostile, hopeless and become bound up in hydrological, political, and legal minutiae, leaving neighborhoods divided and turning neighbors into enemies.

The *Aamodt* suit has been particularly damaging to relationships in the communities bordering the Rio Grande north of Santa Fe. With priority dates superior to any others, the four Native American Pueblos[1] in the region have a measure of security, but the price they pay in hostility is enormous. Many in the traditional Hispanic communities checkerboarding the area are related in one way or another to Pueblo members, and the two cultures have shared lifestyles, food, music, and farming practices for generations. Both cultures have viewed with some suspicion the arrival of the "newcomers," relatively wealthy Anglos who have bought traditional compounds and remodeled them into luxurious haciendas. But the adjudication has exacerbated tensions among the three cultures and thrown any alliances into question. Many Hispanos have sided with Anglos in opposition to the Pueblo claims; old friendships have been lost, and new ones prohibited.

*The Jemez y Sangre Water Planning Council*

Against this backdrop, the local governments of the region are attempting to undertake together regional water planning to ensure a water supply for all interests in the region. Three counties, two cities, numerous irrigation interests, business interests, and environmentalists began to "plan to plan," forming the Jemez y Sangre Water Planning Region and receiving a grant from the state. Their first task was to form a steering committee that would follow the guidelines in the *Regional Water Planning Handbook* and be representative of all interests in the region. They carefully identified stakeholders in the process, and among those were, of course, the four Pueblos mentioned above, and two others. As the organizers visited each stakeholder group, they described the process and invited participation on the Water Planning Council, which would take the lead in creating the plan. They created an agreement for each member to sign, pledging good faith, energy, and optimism for the effort. They were careful not to include any implications in the agreement that would bind any signatory to a certain action or implementation of the plan. The process was to be voluntary, and planned actions would be optional for those involved in the planning.

Part of the impetus behind this deliberate vagueness was to entice, or at least not frighten off, the six tribal governments. But, the reassurance was not evident to the tribal leadership, and none of the six Pueblos signed the agreement to become members of the Jemez y Sangre Water Planning Council. They each explained the hazards of tribal participation in processes over which the tribe has no control. A state process, like this one, was particularly suspect, since tribes must be extremely careful to protect their sovereignty and not put themselves in a position where that sovereignty might be compromised. Although implementation was not part of the planning process, the Pueblos feared that commitments or agreements might emerge that would result in a tribal community being subject in some way to another authority. They also explained that their involvement in the adjudication of water rights in the region meant they should be extremely careful about revealing data about water supplies or use, now or projected. Even population figures could be sensitive. Finally, some of the Pueblos expressed a reluctance to enter into a non-Indian-dominated process, where tribal values, beliefs, and cultural information might not be respected or included in the discussions.

### The Process Adjusts to Accommodate Tribal Interests

Council organizers understood and let the invitation to join stand. But they knew that without the Pueblo interests represented in the process, there would be no way of realistically assessing current and future supplies, and current and future uses. If tribal representatives or members ever wanted to attend a council meeting, they urged, or participate in any of the subcommittees, or other activities of the planning process, they were more than welcome. Pueblos could join and become council members, or they could come and observe. In any case, their presence would be welcome. In addition, the council organizers offered to help the Pueblos secure water planning funds from the state to hire experts of any kind to help them develop their own water plan and, it was hoped, link in some way with the Jemez y Sangre Regional Water Plan. The Pueblos accepted the offer of resources for planning expertise, and $72,000 was awarded the six Pueblos as a group.

Four of the Pueblos also accepted the invitation to attend council meetings and observe the discussion. The monthly council meetings were held at a local community college, where those attending sat at tables arranged in a large hollow square. There was no distinction made between council members who had signed the agreement, and nonmembers or observers, some of whom were Pueblo and some not. All sat together as equals. Pueblo observers offered their perspective freely, always prefacing their remarks with a statement about the impossibility of their Pueblo participating in the planning process, and the sanctity of tribal sovereignty. As the non-Indian members would nod in acceptance, the observer would proceed to offer a substantive comment that was relevant, and often key, to the discussion.

The council formed subcommittees to focus on different aspects of the plan, such as population projections, water supply, conservation alternatives, and public involvement. Two Pueblo representatives even agreed to form a Pueblo Subcommittee of the Jemez y Sangre Water Planning Council, with an eye to at least informing, if not coordinating, tribal and non-Indian water planning.

### When Is Observing Not Observing?

The progress to date has not been without crisis. Perhaps both sides have learned most about each other during these moments when it is tempting to give up and walk away. One such moment came as a result of an article in a planning council newsletter. The editor wrote what he believed was a simple, uncontroversial description of the Jemez y Sangre Water Planning Council and the process they were undertaking. He listed the council members and in another column he listed the observers who also attended meetings regularly. The list of observers included the Pueblos who sent representatives. In response, the editor received an angry call from a tribal official at one of the Pueblos. How dare the council print the name of the Pueblo in the list of observers? Yes, maybe people from the Pueblo staff did attend council meetings, and did observe and even speak, but this did *not* mean that the Pueblo was an "observer." It was a great affront to the Pueblo that they had appeared in the newsletter and that the insinuation was made that the Pueblo was participating in the process in any way.

The editor struggled with the issue, confounded by the apparent fact that one could "observe" but not be an "observer." As mediator and facilitator for the council, I supported his efforts to make it right with the angry

Pueblo official, who was demanding an immediate retraction be mailed to everyone who received the newsletter, or he would go to the media and severely criticize the planning process. We learned the reasons behind the outrage—some relating to the council and some not—and we explored various resolutions. There were several phone conversations back and forth—the official wanting the retraction, the editor offering that the next issue focus on the tribal perspective and include a full apology for the inaccuracy about "observer." Eventually, the tribal official agreed to an apology and explanation of the tribal perspective in the next issue, if the issue schedule was speeded up, and if the editor would allow all the Pueblos to review the articles before publication.

The process of writing, reviewing, correcting, and educating each other has been a good way of developing some degree of trust. The articles are actually co-written by the council and the Pueblos, a painful but effective way of really understanding each other. Not only is the issue extremely instructive for all readers—Indian and non-Indian—but the way it was produced, through delicate negotiations of words, will carry the planning process a long way toward being inclusive in a genuine sense.

*Guidelines for Including Tribal Governments and Communities*

The Jemez y Sangre Water Planning Council solution to the tribal dilemma seems to be a good one. The process is flexible. If the point is to include all key stakeholders, then the people take precedence over the process, and the process should accommodate the players to every extent possible. In this case, the council has let the issue of membership slide, and Pueblo representatives are included as equals and with seats at the table. Pueblos have felt comfortable enough in this setting to participate in some important ways, offering perspectives, sharing plans, even submitting some data. And, as we saw, the council and one Pueblo survived, and learned from, a misunderstanding that could have sunk the whole effort. Some council members are concerned that relations will not be as smooth once the development and consideration of alternatives begin—when amounts and destinations of water will be negotiated and values will win or lose. But, in the meantime, there is a feeling of good will, of two parallel tracks undertaking plans with knowledge of each other. When the tough times do come, it is hoped there will be a degree of trust that will see them through.

The lesson for non-Indians who attempt to include tribal interests in their processes is clear.

• It is necessary to approach the tribe with true respect and without prejudging the result of the visit. Each tribe is different, each encounter will be different.

• Understand that tribal governments may have very different operating principles and structures from those we are used to. You will need to understand the nature of the government and its accountability to its members in order to work together successfully.

• Be ready to listen carefully to what is said. The message may be clear and cordial. Or, it may be confusing and offensive. Or, it may be something in between.

• Clarify. If you are confused or do not understand, say so. Do not be shy. Make sure you leave understanding what the tribe needs, and that they understand what you need.

• Be prepared to make a mistake. We inevitably make mistakes with each other. If you are willing to learn from them, chances are you will be easily forgiven.

• Be patient. Keep pursuing a better understanding, a better relationship.

• Understand the stress on modern tribes. They are pulled in many directions at once, and the leadership has enormous demands placed on them. Where we may wear one or two hats in our work life, a tribal leader may wear five or six.

• Adjust your process—whether it is a mediation, a negotiation, a public meeting, or a pot luck—in ways to accommodate those tribal needs.

## SUMMITVILLE: A BATTLE OVER WAYS OF KNOWING

Background: High in the San Juan Mountains in south central Colorado sits the Summitville site. Since 1870 Summitville has been a magnet for gold seekers, but at an altitude of almost 12,000 feet mining has always been a risky business, both in physical and economic terms. An equally hard life, and one also with great rewards, lies downstream of Summitville in the

Alamosa River Watershed. Here, for generations, farmers and ranchers have struggled to make a living and protect their rural lifestyle in the beautiful San Luis Valley, surrounded by spectacular peaks that are the source of the Rio Grande and tributaries, including the Alamosa. It is a hard life, they say, but the beauty of the valley, the fish in the river, the cranes migrating in the spring and fall, the picnics, the sense of community all make it worthwhile.

In 1984 the Summitville Consolidated Mining Company opened a large open pit gold mine, operating until 1992 when they abandoned the site and declared bankruptcy. Uncontrolled acid mine drainage from the site carried contamination down the river to the valley below. In scientific terms, the exposed earthen materials from the mining operations generated acid, which in turn mobilized a variety of metals including copper, zinc, and aluminum that contaminated the river system. In community terms, the fish died in the river, irrigating sprinkler systems turned into metal lacework, property values trembled, and surviving as an independent farmer or rancher became even harder.

Although the responsible party, the mining company, fled to Canada, cleanup at the site began immediately. Declared a Superfund Site in 1994, the U.S. Environmental Protection Agency (EPA) and the State of Colorado jointly oversee the ongoing cleanup activities. With the mining company bankrupt and extradition denied by the Canadian courts, the bill is being paid 90 percent from the Superfund trust fund and 10 percent from the Colorado Hazardous Substances Response Fund. As part of the Superfund requirements, a technical advisory group (TAG) was formed to serve as liaison between the community and the state and EPA, interpreting data to the community and concerns to the agencies. The TAG has been an important voice for community anxiety about Summitville, and the community representatives that serve on the TAG have become active in pursuing community agendas with respect to the cleanup.

*How Clean Is Clean?*

No one disputes that damage has been caused by the drainage from the Summitville mine. But, it is also indisputable that acid *rock* drainage is naturally occurring in these mineral-rich mountains. The same effect can be caused by water flowing from a mine over large amounts of disturbed earth and rock, *and* by water flowing over earth and rock that is not disturbed. It is the greatly increased surface of rock exposed during mining that has raised the level of acid drainage to Superfund levels. But the question remains: How much of the total contamination is the result of Summitville, and how much is naturally occurring? To what level must the state and EPA clean up the Alamosa River? How clean is clean?

With no baseline data, the answer became a moving target. For the community, the quality could only be described in terms of what life was like then, and how it should be now. For the state and EPA, the appropriate level of cleanup could only be determined through modeling, through analysis of comparable sites, and through certain factoring of conditions, such as temperature, turbidity, flow rate, and presence of other minerals. In the eyes of the community, this was hocus-pocus at best and deceit at worst, all in an effort to keep costs to a minimum.

## Enter the Mediator

In 1998, EPA decided to attempt to reduce the hostility and perhaps come to some agreement on the water quality standards for the Alamosa. As mediator, I was to convene a small group representing those most involved from the state, EPA, and the community and begin discussions. The participants included the two key state staff from the Department of Public Health and Environment, who were responsible respectively for the site remediation and for community relations, and the two key EPA staff, with roughly the same roles. The third party was to be the community but was in effect represented by five TAG members.

I spoke privately with each of the three parties before the process began and heard the community's deep resentment of both the state and the EPA. The state they held responsible for permitting, with virtually no bonding, a mine at 12,000 feet that was inevitably going to cause serious environmental damage. They blamed EPA for some early cleanup decisions at the site that they felt only prolonged and increased the problems. And with both agencies, the community had had bad personal experiences with individuals assigned to defend and implement state and federal plans. The level of frustration and suspicion was extremely high, and their willingness to try mediation was almost buried in an avalanche of anger.

State and EPA representatives were frustrated, too. They had tried over and over to make the community understand the technicalities of water quality standard setting processes and to convince them that the cleanup decisions at Summitville would be made on the basis of the best science available. They were harangued over and over, they said, by emotional local people, who only wanted to talk about the old days and were unwilling to face the facts of the Summitville site. As agency people, they were responsible for carrying out certain functions, and they were doing the best they could. In fact, they said, the local people should realize that "we are on their side—we are the ones working to clean up the river." They were hurt and confused to find themselves cast as the enemy, every bit as evil, it seemed, as the mining company itself. The state was willing to try mediation, although not optimistic, and like EPA, they were exhausted from the regular beatings from the community. Both agencies hoped for some way to deflect the heat from themselves.

*A Shift in the Process*

The first session was a disaster. Although the state and EPA staff felt quite satisfied with the caliber of their presentations, the community members confessed later to me that they were confused, intimidated and bored—all at once—by this foreign techno-babble. And, if I could not recognize that this performance was all part of the ongoing manipulations by the state and EPA, then I was truly of no use to them. They made it clear that there would be no more meetings like that, and in fact that they would not meet ever again with the state or EPA to talk about water quality standards. Realizing that if I was to be of use, it would have to be in another context, I asked if there was anything that they *would* like to talk with the State and EPA about. "If we thought they cared about the future of the watershed, we would like to meet with them," was the reply. There were economic development needs, riparian restoration needs, irrigation structure needs, and information needs—about how to get things done.

During the next year and a half, we met almost monthly. There were three milestones that helped move us forward, and they all related to a reconciliation in "ways of knowing," as the technical and the anecdotal found some kind of common ground or language.

*Maya's Map*

After the group had drafted a tentative mission statement that included a vision of a healthier and more functional watershed, an EPA representative asked just what the watershed looked like. Everyone glanced around the room (at the local Water Conservation District Office) for a map. There was none. "Well," she said, "someone just draw one for us. Just show us what the watershed looks like." A TAG member drew on two pieces of flip chart paper taped together the watershed, complete with tributaries, grazing sheep, abandoned mines, campgrounds, the best spot to catch a fish (in the past), dams, reservoirs, and key roads. Each community member put his or her house on the map. This map, known as "Maya's map," became a centerpiece for discussions at that meeting and subsequent meetings. It was always on the wall at mediation sessions, and when other maps were brought in to illustrate some technical aspect of the watershed, someone would invariably say, "Well, where would that be on Maya's map?" and everyone would turn attention to that alternative view of the watershed.

*A Field Trip*

After six months of meetings, in the fall of 1997, the mediation group took a field trip together to the Summitville site, and down the Alamosa River, through the valley where the TAG members lived. The trip was another step in reconciling different worldviews. The two views were becoming clearer—the technical and the on-the-ground grassroots—but they were no closer to reconciliation. The community members had suggested a field trip, hoping that would bring Maya's map to life for the rest of the group. They believed that without *seeing* and *experiencing* the land and water in question, no one could really understand the community perspective. The state and EPA were glad to oblige, and suggested that a larger group be invited on the trip, including other stakeholders not in the mediation session, such as environmental organizations, private landowners, and other agencies. Twenty-eight people took the trip.

Community members planned and hosted the trip. They produced a guide sheet that identified problem areas and points of interest mile by mile and arranged for one of their own technical experts to speak at each stop along the way. Agency experts, also included in the field trip, spoke as well, and in some cases a healthy debate resulted, with a backdrop of a mountain peak or a lifeless green reservoir. Vans were provided by the agencies, and different mixes of passengers rode together from one stop to the next. The change in setting, the informality, the beauty of the day, the picnic lunch, and the addition of other stakeholders all contributed to a different dynamic among the parties. State, EPA, and TAG members were relaxed and at times friendly; differences were handled with more respect and a little humor. There was a feeling of equality, with the bureaucrats on community turf, which allowed the community to relax. The trip ended with margaritas at a community member's house on the banks of the river and group pictures of people in combinations never before dreamed of.

## A Different Quality of Caring

The field trip helped the mediation group understand more clearly their differences with respect to the land and water resources in question. For community people, the trip was in their backyard. Their livelihoods, their recreation, and in some cases their spirituality were all rooted in that landscape. For them the Summitville site, with half a mountain peak cut away, was a mutilation of something personal. The deathly green reservoir evoked a personal fear for the health of families and wildlife downstream. What was a personal investment for them seemed to be a only technical game for the agencies. Their choice of words, their voices, and their faces communicated this attachment. State and EPA mediation group members could not miss the point.

For the bureaucrats, the mountain, river, and reservoirs were also tragic. As scientists, they had a professional commitment to reclaim, remediate, and restore to the highest level of health possible, and they saw a monumental task before them. Their heads were spinning with water quality models, state-of-the-art water treatment systems, pilot projects for re-seeding, and budgets to make it all happen. This was a job they took seriously, and for many of them it was a job that manifested a deep personal commitment to the environment. But these federal and state employees went home to Denver, or other parts of the state; their personal history and culture were not rooted in the Alamosa Valley.

What was needed was an acknowledgment of this different quality of attachment, a different level of investment, from the bureaucrats. They had already tried to compete with the community in commitment to the problem and its resolution. "This is our job, and we are committed to righting the wrongs that have been done," they had said over and over. Finally, in a meeting following the field trip, when emotions were at a peak, a state representative at the table said what needed to be said. She was the latest target of community anger, a scientist from Denver who appeared to local people to be arrogant and uncaring. She volunteered that she had really come to understand what the community meant, and that she knew that she could not care at that same level.

"I hope you know," she said, "that I care very much about the health of this watershed. As a scientist, it is very important to me to find the right information and develop the right technology to make things better, and I am working very hard to do that. But I also know that my attachment to the Alamosa is different from yours, and I want you to know that I appreciate that difference. For you, this is your life, your history, your future. For us, it is our job. We care, too, but it is a different kind of caring, and I know that."

This was a key acknowledgment from a suspect bureaucrat. She spoke a truth that was not easy to say and that reflected a level of understanding that surprised the community. She had also granted the community a kind of power, by admitting that theirs was the substantial interest.

*Battle of the Sciences—Technical Versus Anecdotal*

Once this issue of a different relationship to the land and resources was recognized and validated, there seemed to be an opportunity to review the definition of science and expertise. The EPA and the state had made it clear from the beginning that answers to questions such as "how clean is clean?" come from good science, and for them science was technical, numerical, formulaic, provable on paper or in the lab. Decisions about water quality, about cleanup strategies, about schedules are all based on good science, and good science happens in a university or an agency laboratory. Data are gathered "in the field" but the science is done elsewhere. For the community, science is a hands-on experience. Science is looking at water, crops, wildlife, and making observations and comparisons. Science is remembering past conditions, noticing trends, making predictions based on those trends and other cues taken from the land and water. Taking information to Denver is not the way to understand the Alamosa or make predictions about it.

As the meetings progressed, water quality standards in the river returned to center stage. The group was discussing the feasibility of a fishery just below the mine site. Community members insisted that, in spite of naturally occurring contamination, fish did exist in a certain segment of the river below Summitville before large-scale mining began. EPA and state representatives maintained that their scientific models and formulas said fish "could not have existed in that segment." A many-generation Hispanic farmer from the valley exploded. "How dare you say that??!! There have always been fish above that reservoir. We used to go on picnics up there when I was little and catch fish for the picnic. We were too poor to have hamburgers, so we caught fish, or didn't eat, and believe me, *we ate fish*!" At a later meeting he brought pictures of one of the picnics, old black and white snapshots from the 1940s. That was *his* scientific evidence—those pictures, his memories, the stories of his community. No amount of river modeling could convince him his science was wrong.

Eventually, the state incorporated in its proposed changes for water quality standards in the Alamosa what became known as the "fish stories." They called this "anecdotal data," and attached over twenty survey forms filled out by those in the community who had seen or caught fish in certain segments of the river. They also withdrew their request to downgrade from cold water fishery classification that segment of the river where most of the fish stories were set.

*Year 2000 Update*

In 1998, as a result of political pressure brought by the community, the governor of Colorado formed the Alamosa Watershed Restoration Task Force with a mission almost identical to the mission of the mediation group: to restore the watershed to a healthy and functional condition. The task force, peopled with state, federal, local, and community representatives, met for a year and raised over $300,000 in grants to begin restoration projects. Several of those projects are being implemented, and the health of the river is improving.

*The Role of the Mediator*

Looking back, it is difficult to evaluate my role as mediator. I believe that I was brought in for the wrong reason—to develop a common set of recommendations on water quality standards for the Alamosa River. At the first meeting, the state made it clear that they were legally bound to base their recommendations solely on science and that their science was technical, not anecdotal. They were willing to listen to community views and needs, but this would not change what science told them was true. The community was enraged at this apparent devaluing of their lives and refused to engage in further discussions about the very topic I was hired to resolve.

Believing that my *real* role was to bring these parties together, improve their understanding of each other, and help them develop some kind of working relationship, I hung onto the people and gave up the topic. I performed radical surgery on the process in order to keep the people at the table. I was lucky that the client EPA was flexible about this rather irregular move and allowed me to proceed with new goals in place. Our common goal, then, became something large enough to keep everyone at the table—the vision of a healthier and more functional watershed. And although we had on every agenda implementation of this vision, that item always took a backseat to the communication issues and trust-building needs of the group. Again, that was consistent with my priority, that the relationships were the real topic, and where we needed to apply ourselves.

I believe that this goal was accomplished. The fifteen people who flowed through the process, as membership and jobs changed, developed honest relationships with each other. Some were, of course, more successful than others, but all participants have a deep understanding of each other, which serves them at Summitville, and in other contexts as well. Insights that were gained during the process are not lost and will undoubtedly carry over to other issues, other projects, and other opponents. Those at the state and EPA have told me that current conversations and exchanges of information would have been unthinkable before mediation. Their jobs are easier because of the experience . . . not easy, but easier. Community members say that they never would have believed they could feel such a degree of comfort, trust, and equality with state and federal bureaucrats. This has given them confidence to push forward in other arenas, such as the task force.

If the mediation process helped the parties develop valuable relationships, it was the energy, determination, and anger of the community that made the real difference, that made those in power take note and respond. They insisted that they be taken seriously, as stakeholders in the future of the valley and as experts with great stores of experience and knowledge about the watershed. As mediator, I enforced an equality among the participants in terms of power and reconciled the two "ways of the knowing." I helped parties understand the different quality of caring for the land and water, the different relationship each had to the resources in question.

Within the mediation, they were equal, but the truth is that outside the mediation they are not. Government, politics, and money are all powerful in the outside world, away from the mediation table. The mediation process gave the community members a chance to experience equality at some level and to exercise their power. But it was their seizing power that has moved the healthy watershed agenda forward. They have broken into the system, that seemingly impenetrable bureaucracy, and attracted the attention of those with political power. And that is where the solutions to their problems lie.

# 11 *'Ike Ho'oponopono*

*The Journey*

ANONA NAPOLEON

I thank you, reader, for taking the time to read this narrative of my life experiences of *'Ike Ho'oponopono:* The Journey. During this reading, you might see, or come to know, or even be transformed along the way; you are welcome to the seeing, the knowing, and thus the transformation(s). If any one of these three things should happen to you and you are able to make a connection, then I have honored my ancestors, my teachers, my mentors, every living creature in nature, as my grandfather would say: the East, the West, the North, the South, everyone and everything Above, Below, and Within the universe.

## *'IKE HO'OPONOPONO:* THE JOURNEY

Beginning with the title: *'Ike* is the Hawaiian word to see, to know (knowledge), and to transform (to be transformed). *Ho'oponopono,* on the other hand, means to make right, to set to right, to bring about harmony. But *Ho'oponopono* goes deeper than just the above. To be *"pono"* with the present helps you become *"pono"* with your past, only so you are free to move into the future. To *'Ike Ho'oponopono* is to see something that is not right and to try to make it right.

*Ho'oponopono* is a Native Hawaiian problem-solving process that literally means setting to right: to make right; to correct; to restore; and to maintain good relationships among family members and between family and supernatural powers. *Ho'oponopono* is the specific family conference in which relationships are "set right" through prayer, discussion, confession, repentance, mutual restitution, and forgiveness.

Always embedded in complete *Ho'oponopono* are the following:

Opening *Pule* (prayer) and prayers any time they seem necessary. *Kukulu kumuhana* is a statement of the obvious problem to be solved or prevented from growing worse, a discussion of the purpose of the process. *Mahiki* is opening the issues, followed by *Hihia* or separating the issues. Next comes *Hala*, identifying the problem. The final steps are *Mihi*, asking and giving forgiveness; *Kala*, release; *'Oki*, which is to sever or cut; and *Pule Ho'opau*, the closing prayer. These steps are applied to each successive problem that becomes apparent during the course of *Ho'oponopono*, even though this might make a series of *Ho'oponopono* sessions necessary. A quality of absolute truthfulness and sincerity is needed, called *'oia'i'o*, the "very spirit of truth."[1]

Control of disruptive emotions is achieved by channeling discussion through the leader, facilitator, or *Haku*, and the questioning of involved participants is also traditionally conducted by the leader. Honest confession to the gods (or God) and to each other of wrong-doing, grievances, grudges, and resentments were met with mutual forgiveness and releasing from the guilt, grudges, and tensions occasioned by the wrong-doing *(Hala)*. This repenting-forgiving-releasing is embodied in the twin terms, *Mihi* and *Kala*. This process was followed by a closing prayer—*Pule Ho'opau*. *Ho'omalu* (time out) was often invoked to calm tempers, encourage self-inquiry into actions, motives, and feelings, or simply for rest during an all-day *Ho'oponopono*. Once a dispute was settled, the leader decreed *ho'omalu* for the whole subject, both immediately and long after *Ho'oponopono* ended.

As a graduate research assistant, I was part of a collaborative university team that developed two *Ho'oponopono* curricula. The intent of my research was to examine the self-described changes in knowledge and efficacy in the behavior and attitude of teachers and counselors involved in the *Ho'oponopono*/educator training process, after their initial introduction to this curriculum. At first, I wanted just to examine the effects of presenting an educator's in-service training curriculum, based upon a *Ho'oponopono* curriculum, on the participants (teachers, counselors, teacher trainees.) Later, as one Hawaiian grandmother who constantly references her learning to family and grandchildren, I came to realize that the "heart and soul" of *Ho'oponopono* is not a script and cannot be rewritten into a "Western" curriculum. However, after spending many hours interviewing people such as Aunty Abbie Nape'ahi, a native Hawaiian grandmother, *kupuna,* and elder and master of *Ho'oponopono,* I came to realize that the values of *Ho'oponopono* can be effectively taught through personal talkstory or *kukakuka.*

Through Aunty Abbie, I saw that *Ho'oponopono* resides within each of us. It is a process of discovering and telling our own stories, and in so doing becoming responsible for our own very personal choices and actions. Thus, I have included voices other than my own to enhance my research. These stories are presented as a way of viewing and experiencing, of authoring the life that I have lived as a Hawaiian child, student, educator, mother, and grandmother here in Hawai'i. I have interwoven the story of my research with a streams metaphor to illustrate life's journey from the credible to the incredible, from fact to truth. My personal story is not meant to be viewed as representative of all Hawaiian life but only as a sample of my experience.

As a child I had valuable learning experiences in special places (such as the streams) and made connections that have led me to inquiry, action, and knowledge about places that are grounded in firsthand shared experience of my homeland. I have learned through my upbringing and through the lives of my ancestors, children, and grandchildren, to bond with the natural world and identify with the place where I live and to learn to love it before asking this place to heal wounds. Place is very important to most Hawaiian "locals" living in Hawai'i. It's a kind of identification—for myself it is "identity." For example, my surname is Naone. In the Hawaiian language this means sands. I have paddled in the black sand bay called Taone (sands) in Tahiti and have swum in another black sand bay in Tutuila, American Samoa, in a village called Leone (sand). There is also a place here called Naoneala'a that means sacred sands, on the windward side of O'ahu. (The word *la'a* by itself also means holy, consecrated, dedicated). Naoneala'a is a black sand "place" located in Kaneohe Bay, an important bay in the Polynesian connection.

For me this story begins with a stream.

Streams

They are gifts that flow, some fast some slow

Over and around rocks big and small.

Be still, listen, and you can hear them speaking, sometimes soft, other

times thunderously loud.

Yet they are forever moving.

Their waters are mostly cool depending on where you are when you enter.

If one enters close to the source you can find it quite cold, but at the same

time very refreshing.

When you find a stream, sit, be still, listen. You may like what you hear.

Since the 1970s there has been a resurgence of writing and public information sharing about *Ho'oponopono*,[2] including growing anecdotal evidence that the traditional practice can be "accommodated" to the public school environment.[3] Writing from the perspective of a Native Hawaiian teacher and counselor, with a lifetime of experience teaching and counseling Native Hawaiian youth, I have observed firsthand what is now well documented in Western literature: namely, that there are many incongruities between the educational and counseling practices of Western schools and the cultural experiences of Hawaiian and part-Hawaiian youth in their homes and communities, including all of the now expected related factors, such as school failure, abuse of drugs and alcohol, violence and suicide, and general malaise.[4] Reports suggest that Hawaiian, part-Hawaiian, and non-Hawaiian youth respond favorably to cultural processes, even with facilitation by non-Hawaiian leaders, under certain circumstances.[5]

Typical high school teachers and counselors in the state of Hawai'i have received little if any cultural sensitivity training specific to the needs of Hawaiian and part-Hawaiian youth. Most school-based professionals are Japanese-American or Euro-American with cultural backgrounds and experiences that are radically different from Hawaiian and other Polynesian youth. Many of the teachers and counselors in Hawai'i come from the continental United States and received their university training there. Their first and often only encounters with Hawaiian youth may occur when they are fresh off the airplane and already responsible for managing classrooms, teaching, and counseling. The Hawai'i Department of Education recognized the need to train and support school-based professionals to be responsive to Hawaiian and part-Hawaiian youth.

In the year 2000, the Hawai'i Department of Education and Alu Like, Inc., contracted with the Center on Disability Studies at the University of Hawai'i to develop the Ho'oponopono Curriculum and the Educator's Training Curriculum, an in-service training based on the former curriculum. Alu Like is a private, nonprofit service organization that has assisted Native Hawaiians in their efforts to achieve social and economic self-sufficiency since 1975. I was part of the university collaborative team that developed Ho'oponopono Curriculum and the Educator Training Curriculum. Both were field tested during the 2002 academic year, with a cross section of counselors, teachers, and teacher trainees at the University of Hawai'i.

There is overwhelming evidence that alienation among Hawaiian and part-Hawaiian students outnumbers in occurrence among all other ethnicities, according to the High School Youth Risk Behavior Survey.[6] Comparing general education and special Education students for the 2001–2002 school year, students of Hawaiian ethnicity are overrepresented in special education classrooms by approximately 50 percent. It has also been found that these students (Hawaiian and part-Hawaiian), in both general education and special education populations, are more likely to be suspended from school.[7] In a presentation to the White House Commission on Excellence in Special Education, D. J. Reschly suggested that among Hawaiian and part-Hawaiian populations, it is important that the practice of *Ho'oponopono* be carefully researched and, if found to be successful, disseminated throughout the Hawai'i public schools.[8]

THE STREAM CONTINUES

Pukele stream—Fast moving—North

My family has lived in Palolo valley for the past 32 years, within a house that Nappy (my husband) and I bought, and where we raised our children. There are "grandmother" mango, plum, papaya, tangerine, and lychee trees that have given us nourishment all these years. Their fruit has been shared with all of our family and neighbors. The land is good. There is a stream called Pukele that flows on the North side of our property, and when the boys were young they played in its cool refreshing water, as their mother played in her stream.

It is possible that *Ho'oponopono* would be better practiced within family or "natural groups" within Hawaiian and part-Hawaiian communities, rather than within public schools. However, given the fragmentation and disintegration of many families and communities, and the now recognized importance of guidance and counseling within the school curriculum, it certainly seems worthwhile to explore other possibilities. It is noteworthy that many Hawaiian, part-Hawaiian, and non-Hawaiian youth report that when they are in trouble, public school teachers and counselors are the single most important resource for these students. This evidence alone supports the value of training in-school professionals in culturally congruent conflict resolution practices.

It started when my thirty-six-year-old son Aaron (one of my twins) shared with me his recent trip to the Big Island, with his teammate Kai, the day after they both won the Moloka'i to O'ahu channel one-man canoe relay race. They had been asked to speak with a group of at-risk youth. While Kai was speaking, Aaron said he was looking at the pictures hanging on the walls of the room. When it was Aaron's turn to speak, he asked the youth what was the story behind the pictures. One youth shared that most of the pictures were of their *kupuna* (grandparents), while others were of special people they knew. All photographs were of *'ohana* (family) in some way.

Aaron then asked, "Do you pray to them?" Many of the youth, according to Aaron, "sighed" and then one pointed to another and said, "She does." Then Aaron said that he was taught to pray to his ancestors in times of need. At this point Kai shouted, "Tell them about the 'wave'!" Then the youth group stepped down off of the bleachers and came and sat on the floor in front of Aaron. Several shouted, "Yeah, Uncle, tell us about the 'wave'!" Aaron was stunned by their sudden movement and shouts. When they had all quieted, he continued. "It's not the wave or experience, its about the lesson you learn from the experience." He continued to share about some of his ancestors who lived on the Big Island. He was sharing the who, what, when, and where of our families, thus making connections with these youth. And again a resounding: "Tell us about the 'wave', Uncle!"

"All right the 'wave' story," Aaron said. "Here it is and you are the first to hear this. I haven't even told my wife, or Kai, what really happened. Anyway, after Kai and I made a change and I came back into the escort boat, we were about three hundred feet behind the leaders (Maui and Karel). I was sitting on a cooler in the back of the escort boat and wondering what happened because we were in front when I got into the canoe and now we were behind. Just then, the captain of the escort boat's girlfriend (and I don't even know her), turns to me and says, 'suck it up'! Wow! Who are you to tell me what to do, I think to myself. After a little while Kalani, our coach, yells, Aaron, you ready to relieve Kai? Yep, I say. So I dive into the ocean. By now we're in the middle of the Ka'iwi channel (between Moloka'i and O'ahu). I dive deeper than usual and open my eyes. I see a ray of sunlight filtering through the deepest blue ocean that I've ever seen. I spread my arms and call on all my ancestors, 'aumakua (family gods), and God for strength. Then I enclosed my arms around me and broke through the surface where I tread water and wait for Kai to exchange places in the canoe. After the change and after about ten or more paddling strokes a wave comes and I surf it, on and on, until Kai is in the water waiting to change. Then I'm back in the escort boat, and we are three hundred feet in front, and we kept the lead till the finish."

An incredible story for some, and a lived experience—just doing what comes naturally, for Aaron. This story produced a strong connection with all the persons present that day, especially those at-risk students.

When Hawaiian and part-Hawaiian students are living in their own homeland, why should they have to have such a drastically hard time in the classroom? It is my contention that exposing these students to culturally relevant curricula and cultural and pedagogical processes, such as Ho'oponopono, will bring their school experiences into cultural congruence with their experiences at home and make school more "real" for them, thus engaging them. In this way, more students may be encouraged to work harder and to stay in school.

## THE STUDY

Fifty-five participants were involved in my study of ho'oponopono in the schools. Teachers and counselors and their respective trainees volunteered to participate. Nineteen, or 35 percent, were male, and thirty-five, or 65 percent, were female. Of the fifty-five participants, thirty-five were educator trainees and twenty were professional educators. The professional educators' years of service spread throughout the categories of one to five years to thirty-six to forty years. All the ethnic backgrounds listed were represented, so there was a good cross-section of ethnicities.

Each participant was given a folder and asked to select a goody bag that contained sweets and munchies. Included in the folder were the agenda; a cover letter including a consent form asking for participant's voluntary and confidential participation; the demographic survey of the respondents; and the twenty-question survey (six point Likert-type scale). Before the presentation began, participants had been given directions to complete these two forms and the surveys, and then the completed forms and surveys were collected. (This survey was the pretest.) Also included in this folder were handouts on both the Ho'oponopono Curriculum and the Educator's Training Curriculum, as well as four research articles supporting the work of teachers and counselors.

The intervention began with the first *oli* (chant)—an invitation to the ancestors to come and be present, and a second *oli* welcoming everyone. This was done in the Hawaiian language. This was followed by a two-hour presentation that involved two videos, talkstory (making connections via storytelling), an activity (connections via hands-on activities). After the activity, we ended with a song during a period of reflection. Directly after the presentation, a second survey (posttest) was handed out to the group. These were completed by the participants and collected as people exited the room. Six weeks later a first follow-up survey was mailed to each participant who had agreed in writing to participate further. A second follow-up survey was also mailed to those who had not returned the first follow-up. However, because of the small number who had responded to both follow-up surveys, we were unable to conduct an analysis. Results of the demographic survey, the pretest, posttest, and the questionnaire from the cohort director were statistically analyzed.

### Stagnant Stream in Moanalua Gardens

There are times in life when it seems that all or everything is at a stand-still, as if waiting for something or anything to give.

Unexpected changes continually surfaced while doing my quantitative analysis. For example, I combined the ethnic groups into only two large groups: HAAPI (Hawaiian, Asian American Pacific Islander) and white, instead of the original ten groups—for the sake of simplifying the data analysis. At first, I had classified the first group AAPI (which included all the groups except white); however, upon further consideration, I wanted to distinguish Hawaiians as a separate group, but for the purposes of traditional data analysis, the results of the demographic "ethnic group" fell into these two larger groups, thus the change to HAAPI. In *Eliminating Health Disparities: Conversations with Pacific Islanders,* Dr. Aiu states: "One of the main things is that Hawaiians are an indigenous people, not immigrants. So when you put Asians and Pacific Islanders and Hawaiians in one group, then Hawaiians get treated as if they're immigrants."[9]

The results of the quantitative analysis were anything but stagnant. These two interaction effects between subjects "Ethnicity and Test," on two questions that were culturally sensitive, and then conducting cross tabulations on all the demographics and finding a significant difference in the "years in Hawai'i" as well was quite exciting. My statistics and analysis revealed that many of the participants who were fairly new to Hawai'i and its culture were possibly at risk because they knew what worked for them, yet they weren't able to know what worked best for the "local" or Hawaiian culture. Cross-tabulations were significant in the "years in Hawai'i." This pointed out again the fact that many teachers would benefit from culturally sensitive educator training and curricula. The individual teacher's self-efficacy would be enhanced, and thus they would empower their students to approach learning from a positive and culturally relevant vantage point. In this way, the students could be more involved in their own education, and by extension perhaps their families would become more involved in the school as well, as this is the Hawaiian model of education within the 'ohana.

During the analysis of my data I had to try to explain the what, where, when, how, and why of my study and the results. I attempted to find possible explanations for the results. Stories were the "proof" to support the results of my quantitative analysis. As my research progressed, I discovered elements of surprise waiting to be unveiled and (in Hawaiian "ho'ike") exhibited.

The HAAPI (Hawaiian, Asian American Pacific Islander) group, which had been living for many years in Hawai'i, had become part of the "local" culture. Knowing and experiencing these kinds of family roles on a daily basis make them real and give this group an advantage. Their learning is primarily related to family background and may differ among individuals in small ways depending on the predominant ethnic experience(s) of their family. However, as the results of this study suggest, they all have had a "local" experience, which sets this group apart. The white group, having not lived as many years in Hawai'i, and perhaps not noticing Hawaiian/part-Hawaiian families interacting or not living in proximity to Hawaiian families, have a kind of learning about them that exists from a distance. They might know a lot about Hawaiian "sights," such as where to go or what to see culturally, and this could explain the high score in the pretest. But after the intervention, the posttest score was low, which suggests that they learned more about the family background of Hawaiian and part-Hawaiian students from the presentation and realized that they really do not know enough. Role patterns in the four types of institutions mentioned do interact. Patterns of parent/child interaction in a society are carried over into teacher/student and boss/subordinate relationships, and thus the teachers do need to acquire understanding of local culture, wherever they teach, in order to really connect with their students.

The first step in the original 'ohana-based traditional Ho'oponopono (which for some practitioners is the only true Ho'oponopono) is pule (prayers) directed to one's 'aumakua or family gods, "ancestors" and/or a "greater power." Some practitioners think that when doing the pule one must include the words Akua, Ke Akua, and Iesu (Jesus). In her book Nana Ike Kumu, Mary Kawena Puku'i and her co-authors combine both of these schools of thought and adds biblical context, a third school.[10] The linking factor between these opinions is that if the spiritual element is left out, then it isn't *Ho'oponopono*. This thinking was shared by almost all traditional practitioners. A fourth school of thought can be found in Victoria Shook's book *Ho'oponopono,* where some modern facilitators purposely left out prayer and were successful in maintaining peaceful relationships using the *Ho'oponopono* process.[11] However, some counselors mentioned more meaningful maintenance in relationships occurred when the spiritual element was included.

### Our Family's Ho'oponopono Story

Within my family, I have been taught, and have also taught my children and grandchildren, that we are "endlessly bound to love and forgive."[12] We try to be one and right with self and family members. It is not easy and takes hard work to maintain a loving relationship. As a family, we have had many highs and lows, good and not so good, and sometimes really painful encounters where *Ho'oponopono* was needed. Within this love and forgiveness resides hopefulness (hope for the future) for each individual and for the family.

Our sons were teenagers and we had packed our car with surfboards on the roof. The cooler was in the trunk, filled with food to fuel the boys for their surf contest at Makaha beach on the west side of O'ahu. My husband, Nappy, was driving over the speed limit and I had asked him to slow down. Because we were late, he continued at this high speed and then "PAK"—the straps holding the surfboards broke, and the boards went flying and landed on the five-lane highway. When the car stopped, the boys opened the doors and ran out, thinking only of retrieving their surfboards while both Nappy and I were screaming at them to stop. Luckily, no one got hurt, and the screeching cars finally came to a stop, and all the boards were picked up and roped more tightly to the surf rack this time. Every board had 'dings' or damage that needed repair, and that day our sons had to borrow surfboards in order to compete. It wasn't a good day and they didn't do well!

When we finally arrived home that evening. Nappy told David to get the Bible, open it (at random), and read a paragraph. The paragraph had to do with forgiveness (1—Pule wehe). After the reading, Nappy told each one of us he was sorry, and asked us, individually, to forgive him—which we did (emotions were quite high). Nappy was the *kupuna* and also the troubled family member, so he was able to, in shortened form, go through all the major steps in Ho'oponopono: (2) *Kukulu kumuhana*, (3) *Mahiki*, (4) *Hihia*, (5) *Hala*, (6) *Mihi*, (7) *Kala*. We each said a prayer of thanks prior to our meal (7—*Pule Ho'opau,* closing prayer). After dinner, Nappy and the boys went downstairs to the garage to repair the damaged surfboards (restitution). This was our family's *Ho'oponopono.*

Our sons have always remembered this experience because it was the first time they heard their father say he was sorry and ask for forgiveness from them. They have shared the story with their children. I learned a lot that day.

Education matters; however, what matters more is making the connection(s) between nature, child, home, and the place (community). In the traditional *Ho'oponopono* session, children were always included, thus Hawaiian children's early participation and learning in most families matters. Today, too many families are fragmented and too many of our children are preoccupied with material gain and have little understanding of the other treasures one stores and enjoys. Teachers who seek to acquire understanding of the "local" culture are more effective with their students, and wherever they teach, they will really connect with their students. Schools that emphasize community and service can help balance acquisitiveness, and these schools will support the teachers' efforts in validating the students' culture.

Auntie Abbie Nape'ahi says that before you begin a *Ho'oponopono* (as the facilitator), you are to pray and you must *"pono"* yourself. This is not unlike Shakespeare, who has Hamlet saying, "To thine own self be true." Another anonymous person answers with: "If it is to be, it's up to me." After my own extensive research, and after reflecting and writing, I found myself developing my own formulaic expression: Action and Reflection and Contemplation (thoughtful inspection) equals Learning. This expression evolved as I wrote my stories about nature, child, home, and place. I was looking for a connection between the curricula research results and my stories, and, more importantly, between myself, the author, and you, the reader.

*Ho'oponopono* is not a "curriculum" in the Western sense. It is a way of living. It is a view toward life (past, present, and future). It is a reverence for place. It is sacredness in relationships, especially within the family. For me this way of life can only be expressed through stories. As I discovered, after action and reflection, *Ho'oponopono* cannot be quantified and examined scientifically. The process of reduction limits the essence of *Ho'oponopono*. For me, *Ho'oponopono* is the greater story of my Hawaiian family and community and their struggles in their land to reclaim their place, to find peace with their gods, and to live together in harmony under extreme hardships. We will not let the "revisionist historians" redefine the history of our people as lucky, happy Polynesians who fish and surf and gather coconuts—the Native Hawaiians who are "always smiling and friendly."[13] This is not the way it was. It is not the way it is. It is not the way it will be. Again, it involves making a choice!

Auntie Abbie Nape'ahi, who was my primary spiritual and "data" source, shared many stories of her own life experiences with me, and I realized after these conversations that the values of *Ho'oponopono* can be better taught through personal stories. My stories give voice to my own relationships within the Hawaiian and "local" culture. Stories are a direct passage from the world of thinking to that of day-to-day living. The more recognizable the connection between the story and the reader's or the listener's own story, the better the chance that some learning will take place.

The only disappointing factor during my work on this study was the follow-up survey. There were not enough responses or numbers to the follow-up survey that I had mailed out, so we had to omit the ones for which we did have responses. It is possible that further tracking of participants (those who gave their written consent) could still be done to see if they are using any of the materials introduced at the workshop.

The final revelation for me has been the importance of telling my stories. To act, to talk, to reflect, to contemplate, to make connections, to research, to write, to learn: these are also other ways healing can take place. As Martha Noyes notes, "Previous generations masked that pain with an outward aloha spirit and an inner silence."[14] I saw the pain in my father's eyes as he shared his stories. His parents were living and giving love and allegiance to a Queen (Liliu'okalani, the monarch and ruler of Hawai'i), and overnight that was changed. The ideological and political conditions that produced these changes caused much suffering for the masses of Hawaiian people.

My father inherited his father's stories and those of his 'ohana. These stories live within me and my 'ohana today. In the beginning of this paper I told a story of the place of a stream in my life that is no more but a memory that no one can take away. I began with the "place" as it connects to people, including self and family. I have discussed some of the lifestyle changes in Hawai'i that have happened in my lifetime in the place that I love and belong to and that I want to take a part in healing. Though I experienced my father's pain, I have been able to share his stories with my 'ohana, so that they will remember the path we have taken on this journey of life, and also share my hope for the future of living here in Hawai'i.

As I reviewed the results of this study, I realized that I am building on the work of my ancestors, and others will build on my work, and still others will likely be motivated to start other research projects that may study similar questions over a longer time period. My learning has continued through the use of kukakuka—I have discovered several schools of thought by practitioners of Ho'oponopono whose common focus was in the area of spirituality.

I am very thankful for having been blessed by my family. I am referring to all family members from the beginning of time to the present. I am also so grateful for the results of my research project, in which the main research findings effects obtained through the general linear model were consistent with findings from the paired sample T-test (with only question nineteen not showing significant changes across pre- and posttest). Two significant interactions between "test" and "ethnicity" that were unexpected at first were completed after cross tabulation and confirmed my own beliefs about the importance of culture in learning.

### Waikahalulu Stream

Isn't it amazing no matter how many pohaku, stones and boulders, are there, the stream always finds a path. So are we being taught in life to seek, to ask, only to find our path. For some it begins early in life, others take a lifetime, and for someone like myself, the path and I have now found each other. I've come to realize and understand that, like the pieces of a puzzle, everything fits or happens in due time. It doesn't fit or happen when I want it. Sometimes when I least expect to receive this gift of understanding, it arrives. Most times, when I've been *li'u,* or "seasoned" in Hawaiian language, then *maopopo ia 'u,* I understand. This has been my experience.

# 12 Reflections on "African Americans in Mediation Literature: A Neglected Population"

CHERISE D. HAIRSTON

It has been eight years since the publication of my article "African Americans in Mediation Literature: A Neglected Population"[1] in *Mediation Quarterly* (now *Conflict Resolution Quarterly*). It seems timely to step back and re-examine the issues raised and to assess how far we as a field have progressed in addressing the major knowledge gaps discovered in the mediation literature with regard to our collective understanding and knowledge about the conflict resolution needs, concerns, and interests of African Americans.

When I wrote the article, I called attention to several serious problems. First, I reviewed 420 articles in *Mediation Quarterly* from 1983 through 1997. As a result of this content analysis, I was unable to locate articles by, for, or about people of African descent.

Second, and more importantly, I made an argument that the lack of conflict resolution literature and research on African Americans posed a serious ethical dilemma for practitioners in the field. I asked in 1999, "Can African-Americans be served effectively and appropriately by mediators who have limited academic access and actual multicultural (cross-racial and cross-cultural) interaction with this specific population in mediation?" My argument was based on a simple premise: without knowledge and understanding of African Americans, or any marginalized group for that matter, how can we as practitioners provide socially responsible and culturally appropriate mediation services that are guided by the ethical principles of do no harm (malfeasance) while promoting the growth and development of the parties (beneficence)? I believe that it is not possible, and we do harm to African Americans with our collective ignorance.

Finally, I made a call to action for concerned practitioners and offered several recommendations. For the purposes of this chapter, I would like to briefly explore a few of the recommendations that I believe have not been adequately addressed and that are still critical concerns.

## PROFESSIONAL REFLECTIONS

One of the central problems back then that continues to pose a problem now is that the field of conflict resolution is "a primarily white, middle-class, English-speaking field" that is "solidly located in a larger society that is struggling with issues of diversity, racism, and exclusion."[2] For me, this contradiction continues to be problematic because issues affecting African Americans as participants in conflict resolution processes and as practitioners continue to be marginalized, as evidenced by the fact that "many dispute resolvers of color have been meeting informally to discuss their displeasure with conflict resolution organizations that they view as unresponsive to their needs."[3]

Centuries of social exclusion and exclusionary social practices have shaped virtually every society.[4] In the United States, intergroup conflict, beginning with the arrival of Europeans in 1619 and the encounter of Native peoples, set the stage for an enduring legacy of social exclusion as exemplified in the narratives of the experiences of people of African descent. The institutions of slavery along with the founding documents of the society (that is, Declaration of Independence, Bill of Rights, the Constitution) set the stage for modern manifestations of social exclusion and exclusionary social practices as manifested in Jim Crow laws. It is the legacy of this social exclusion and its enduring and continuing effect in exclusionary social practices on people of African descent. This area of inquiry, as it relates specifically to the field of conflict resolution, has largely remained unexamined in terms of practitioners of African descent and their contributions to the development of the field, their development as practitioners (that is, purpose for entering the field, the values that guide their work, along with their training, skills building, and reflective practice), their unique experiences and interests in the role it plays in theory and practice-model development, and the effects of policy on their continued development, opportunities, and practice.

It has been a struggle to continue in the conflict resolution field at times because I have been "tracking human hypocrisy" in the field. In *Prophetic Thought in Postmodern Times,* Cornel West describes this phenomenon as the "gap between principles and practice, between promise and performance, between rhetoric and reality."[5] The rhetoric we hear so often about the value of diversity—the importance of having people from diverse social backgrounds—rings hollow for many of us. Marvin Johnson argues that the field is beset by the problem of "diversity resistance." Diversity resistance is maintained by those people in the field who oppose the concept of diversity and resist change. Diversity resistance consists of an unwillingness to acknowledge and recognize the contributions of people with diverse backgrounds and to include people with diverse backgrounds at all levels of the field.[6] The concept of diversity is typically used to mean acknowledgment of differences and respect for people's cultural background; however, "In the real world, the fact of diversity is typically correlated with forms of inequity and stratification."[7]

For me, diversity resistance is seen most vividly in the fact that there continues to be a lack of mainstream scholarly attention to the needs, interests, and concerns of African American conflict resolution practitioners. It is my contention that the social exclusion of African American conflict resolution practitioners (and African Americans in general), as evidenced by our underrepresentation as practitioners and the field's collective failure to explore research issues despite an espoused rhetoric of diversity, is firmly rooted in racism. Racism at its base is the "denial of the humanity of a group of human beings, either on the basis of race or color"[8] and oppressive relations that involve people engaging in "strategic decisions that exclude certain groups or individuals from formally and legitimately accessing power and resources."[9] Until we can eradicate diversity resistance and cease to downplay and ignore the interests of oppressed groups, I do not believe the field will live up to its ideals.

KNOWLEDGE GAPS

In my 1999 article, I made a "call to action" to increase published literature written by, for, and about African Americans that "describes, understands, and reflects the realities of African-Americans by placing their worldviews, values, beliefs, and life experiences at the center of empirical investigation and analysis."[10] Why a focus on literature and research? Because it is apparent that in a field that is dominated by European American conflict resolution practitioners, those practitioners will write about and research issues that are most relevant to them or that they have curiosity about.

It is telling, then, to examine the conflict resolution literature now and see minimal progress. A body of literature and research is a prerequisite for an academic and professional field,[11] and "discipline-specific literature" reveals the areas of research that are deemed important and worthy of scholarly attention.[12] López and Parker argue that "as scholars of color . . . we have a duty to create our own theories and transform the 'theorizing space' from which we and our theories have historically been excluded."[13] It has become apparent that most likely the only way the knowledge gaps in the knowledge base of the field will be addressed is if African American conflict resolution practitioners continue to step forward to fill the gap, and we are.

What remains to be seen is whether this growing body of knowledge produced by African American conflict resolution practitioners is taken seriously and used by others in research projects. The new knowledge that comes from the work of these writers is very important because it can fill the gap in knowledge about the contemporary conflict resolution needs of African Americans. Although there is some acknowledgment that knowledge gaps exist, my contention is that these gaps have never seriously been addressed. In fact, there continues to be a conspicuous absence of literature on important issues that affect African Americans. For example, certain issues have been identified, such as the effect of race and gender of the third party on the conflict resolution process[14] and other issues around race, ethnicity, and cultural competency,[15] but these issues continue to remain underexamined. It is as if the mere mentioning of issues means that the issues are dealt with sufficiently. But, as we know, this is not the case, and huge knowledge gaps persist.

Why do these important issues remain marginalized in conflict resolution research? Our collective understanding could be greatly enhanced if these research issues were taken seriously and engaged in empirical investigations. The practice of conflict resolution will become unethical without knowledge of the real world conflict resolution needs of African Americans and African American conflict resolution practitioners.

## COLORING THE FIELD

As in most academic disciplines and professions that have excluded African Americans from participation, the values, beliefs, and processes that prevail in conflict resolution reflect European American practitioners and participants. Irvin, Benjamin, San-Pedro, writing in the context of working with Latino families in mediation, argue that "most of the models of our field implicitly impose white, middle-class norms and standards which oppose mediation's value on self-determination."[16]

Christy Cumberland Walker argues that African American conflict resolution practitioners currently involved in the field struggle against experiences of exclusion in the field, suggesting that some African American conflict resolution practitioners believe "their voices and opinions are not given the same weight and respect as those of others."[17] This contributes to feelings of isolation and disempowerment born out of asymmetries of power, privilege, and forms of dominance and subordination. The result is that African American conflict resolution practitioners must seek to create their own organizations and practices to address their needs and the needs of participants of African descent.

When African American conflict resolution practitioners typically raise concerns about their marginalization in all aspects of the field, these issues are rarely addressed "courageously, openly, and frankly";[18] they receive little critical assessment. It is crucial then that more African Americans (as well as other marginalized groups) are welcomed and encouraged to join the field. More importantly, African Americans must be provided the support and resources that allow African Americans to develop their skills, contribute to theory and practice, and engage in research. If the field continues with business as usual, the participation of African American conflict resolution practitioners will continue to be marginal, and experiences for practitioners currently in the field will continue to revolve around daily experiences of social exclusion.

## CONCLUSION AND RECOMMENDATIONS

Although there is a growing body of conflict resolution literature written by, for, and about African Americans, this body of literature must be taken seriously by others, particularly when it comes to theorizing and conducting research. Unfortunately, there are still few profiles of practice on African American conflict resolution practitioners. What literature does exists does not adequately portray or reflect the needs of African American practitioners and participants; it renders African Americans as voiceless objects instead of active subjects that actively reflect on and shape their world. Conflict resolution theory and practice cannot continue to develop in an ahistorical context free of race, ethnicity, or culture. African American conflict resolution practitioners, as well as others who are concerned about this population and sensitive to the issues that affect this group, are creating the base from which a deeper understanding will provide the basis for developing knowledge that addresses conflict resolution needs, interests, and concerns for African Americans in general. If we, as a field, care about the well-being of all practitioners, then we must find ways to walk the talk of inclusion and truly create a field that lives its declaration of valuing diversity and inclusion.

# 13 The Language of Culture and the New Practice of Conflict Resolution

PHILLIP M. RICHARDS

A new class of minority practitioners in the field of conflict resolution is serving minority or otherwise marginal populations, often as court-assigned mediators outside of the justice system. These practitioners find themselves located amid the interfaces of conflicting American populations. Largely engaged in the de facto promotion of social order, these new professionals frequently go between legal-judicial institutions and minority populations apart from the mainstream in segregated schools, neighborhoods, and social services. The chapters in this book represent the new class's confrontation with its complicated professional, social, and political situation.

I approach these issues not as a practitioner in mediation but as a student of literature, interested in the predicament of a similar class of newcomers to my own field. In a recent book, *Black Heart: The Moral Life of Recent African American Letters,* I examined the professional languages, institutions, and cultural sensibility of minority entrants to the field of literary studies. This new academic literary class has engaged many of the foundational tasks that now occupy the minority practitioners of the PRASI group. The experience of both groups confronts conditions faced by new minority practitioners in professional life. Considerations of these issues have forced minority scholars into an ad hoc sociological consideration of their professional procedures, canons of knowledge, and claims to legitimacy. The great majority of writers in this book face these issues in the essays collected here, and they do so with the same urgency displayed by scholars in my own field.

Like many other minority middlemen and go-betweens, this new class of mediators frequently finds itself caught between various interests and institutions. In their practice, they often fall within the interstices of a practice now including marginalized client populations and an older guard of white, male—often legally trained—mediators, mediators who have hitherto dominated the profession, servicing mainstream American economic, social, and political institutions and setting the profession's norms and standards.

No one can therefore be surprised that the new class of minority mediators frequently describes its professional experience in terms of impasse—breakdowns of communication, understanding, and institutional function. The theme of interrupted social functioning pervades these practitioners' language. Minority professionals describe these impasses in their encounters not only with their lower-class minority clients but also with the profession's established old guard and its academic representatives in a growing number of graduate degree programs. Indeed, the new mediators describe these impasses in the experience of mediation itself—gaps of silence, the recalcitrance of offended clients, and disruptive antagonism. These impasses also occur in the newcomers' professional lives—the refusal of the profession's establishment to grant legitimacy to the acquired wisdom of its most recent class of practitioners. On the level of their academic experience, these impasses take their most compelling form: the difficulty experienced by minority newcomers in completing dissertations and finishing graduate degree programs.

Members of the new class have often invoked cultural difference as an explanation for these breakdowns. This invocation is, I argue here, largely pragmatic. It has, despite obvious advantages, clear disabilities. Most importantly, the invocation of "cultural" explanation in the breakdown of mediation thwarts a political and social self-consciousness that should be fundamental to minority activity in the profession. Race and culture have come, often through the intellectual efforts of minority intellectuals themselves, to mystify the heart of political, class, and economic structures conflicts in which the new mediators engage.

It is not surprising that this professionally marginal class of practitioners should rely on a pragmatic cultural style that has growing cachet throughout the academy, the professions, and American society itself. All fully extended societies deploy forms of conflict resolution. Mediation inevitably involves cultural entities, conceived as programmed social life, legitimizing beliefs, or rituals. As a society regulates and socializes itself it mediates class, communal, interest conflicts by an appeal to cultural norms. These cultural norms are embedded in language, religion, kinship network, legal systems, and economic exchange, the components of culture itself. Indeed, mediators must synthesize these components when they resolve conflicts. And such mediation has a cultural style, which makes conflict resolution in Islamic Malaysian society different from that practiced by Baptists in the American South.

Such a conception of culture inevitably leads to a consideration of social, political, and economic structures. The pragmatic notion of culture invoked by the new mediators evades social and political considerations in a freewheeling, vague, and ultimately deceptive style. With few exceptions—usually investigations of non-American and non-Western cultures—these practitioners ignore the specific linguistic, religious, communal, and kinship elements that make up a particular mediatory style. Consequently, they often bypass the social, economic, and political dimensions of conflict.

The new class of mediators often defines culture in such all-embracing terms that it seems to embody every aspect, no matter how central or peripheral, of a society's worldview. Given this spacious definition of culture, these practitioners easily interpret mediation as wholly "cultural" or discover socially dysfunctional worlds in which culture has disappeared. As an all-inclusive category, culture may exist everywhere or, given its lack of distinctive definition, nowhere.

It is easy to see the pragmatic usefulness of this culture-centered language, given the social and political world in which the new mediators find themselves in a professional predicament. African American, Latino, and Native American communities find themselves beset by extremely high levels of conflict in domestic households, the schools, the prisons, and the hospitals, all of which are central sites of day-to-day life for the poor of whatever color in American life. Conflict resolution represents a means of social control carried out by indigenous community mediators who squelch political tensions (indeed the crises) of social stratification, gross economic inequality, and hopelessness in the lives of underclass blacks and Latinos. As social explanation this "cultural" approach tends to delimit the scope of a crisis by refusing to summon up its political, economic, and social dimensions. This intellectual style, however, clearly reproduces the inegalitarian, racially divisive structures often underlying the conflict that the mediator faces. Work by minority mediators may control or abate the violence that imprisons so many blacks and Latinos by refusing to make their ideological context more volatile.

Furthermore, the cultural approach of conflict resolution speaks to the increasing academicization of conflict resolution practice. To define indigenous cultures as a source for resolving cultural disputes draws upon many current trends in the scholarship of African and Latino studies that have a similar orientation. Through this borrowing, the new minority mediators may make cultural allies already entrenched in the academy and foundations.

Drawing upon these culture-centered approaches within the university, students of color will find as they have found in ethnic studies, romantic, sentimental, and therapeutic languages that seem to offer real explanatory force. The therapeutic and sentimental discourse of the new mediators may represent a minority professional style that facilitates relations with white colleagues. Certainly, the academic community has been willing to create ethnic, culturally centered enclaves in which minority students isolate themselves away from the tensions of integrated life.

Even the most progressive, newly minted professions, committed to multicultural breath and acceptance, must seek legitimacy. Legitimacy after all reassures potential customers of the practitioner's competence, whoever he or she is. Just as "minorities" (a necessarily inaccurate name for a newly emerging professional class of women and nonwhite Americans) have had to force their way into the academy, so have the new mediators entered their professions against the resistance of its entrenched and legitimacy-granting elite. This resistance has not been a disinterested action on the part of the elite, which at least partially legitimizes its professionalized knowledge and expertise by excluding "minority" outsiders.

Professions create legitimacy by organizing canons of knowledge that constitute expertise. This expertise largely defines the boundaries of a professional group: those qualified to do the particular professional activity, whether it is litigation or medicine or alternative dispute resolution. Bodies of "experts" who certify practitioners not only create public legitimacy for the profession but also extend or withdraw its approval of persons and practices. Professionals must maintain a body of knowledge so clearly defined that applicants for admission to the field can be trained, tested, and qualified.

Professional legitimacy demands that a given person or group must define its relation to these canons of knowledge in an institutionally sanctioned way.

Inevitably, this new class of practitioners confronts the structural political and economic means in which the established profession frames its institutional wisdom. The new class will have to define—in highly explicit ways—its relationship to the professional activities of litigation, medicine, or alternative dispute resolution. Such a claim on the profession's "knowledge" will usefully define the newcomers' confrontations with that hierarchy mirroring the majority's power in American society. A serious reflection upon the new mediators' practical experience is an inevitable start in the exercise of this claim.

The new class's stress on vaguely defined "cultural" modes of explanation complicates this problem. Put bluntly, the established profession does not recognize the culturally based languages (or experiences) on which the new class seeks to draw. Ironically, the profession of mediation has historically drawn on non-Western cultural sources. In its beginnings, the discipline of conflict resolution drew freely on traditions from China and the Pacific Islands. The established profession defines itself in the highly refined canons of law and medicine for legitimacy. With the passage of time, professional awareness of the non-Western or otherwise "marginal" origins of the field has withered away. The field as a result now presents itself as a taken-for-granted cultural and political product of a white male Western social and political elite.

To a large extent the impasse of canonical knowledge that divides the professional establishment and its newcomers is defined by white privilege. The newcomers find themselves excluded from the profession by bearers of a white privilege implicit in both the Westernization of the professional field and the discipline's appropriation by established legal and therapeutic professions. This racial exclusion trumps even the legal or therapeutic credentials that people of color may bring to a field grounded in traditions in which a "Westernized" facade amounts to code for its identity and consequent legitimacy as a "white" American institution.

The present experience of the new class of conflict resolution specialists, however, shows the way in which people in color have created forms of mediation in order to conduct their day-to-day lives. The methods of the new practitioners continue the discipline's now unacknowledged persistence in "traditional," "indigenous," and "ethnic" sources. This practice has, for the new practitioners as well as for the old, been pragmatic and more or less inevitable. It has only become marginal in the light of the racial and national identity of the people, both professionals and clients, involved.

I suspect, however, that the failure of the new class to engage in an inherently confrontational analysis of the social, political, and economic dynamics of conflict is part of the impasse. The claims by the established professions to legitimacy represent claims to power sustained not only by knowledge but also by particular interests. An approach to conflict grounded in the realities of social life might discern the heart of conflict between the old and new guards. A clearer, more specific articulation of the cultural components of indigenous means of mediation might show the points of connect and disconnect between the worldviews of the establishment and the newcomers.

The present state of the profession has cast the new mediators into a marginal role, turning their cultural understandings and practice into "hidden transcripts." To a certain extent the marginalizing of the new mediators follows from the nature of professionalism itself. From the beginning of this process, the practitioners found themselves addressing and returning to questions about culture—that body of assumptions that encodes patterns for knowing, acting, and being in the world—as well as questions about the way in which the field of conflict resolution has organized its "knowledge," its "institutional wisdom" about the processes of mediation so central to any culture. The result of these conversations has not only been a new questioning of the nature of the conflict resolution, transpiring in these unofficial sites, but also an implicit questioning of established "professional" knowledge and procedure.

This situation has had a number of consequences. Practitioners of color struggle with how they might define themselves as professionalized intellectuals. This question flows not only from their political differences with the old guard but also from an increasing sense of themselves as bearers of "legitimate" knowledge. Processes of description and dissent by both the new mediators and the "old guard" have become the first stages of the creation of a professional identity.

# PART THREE

# Re-Centering Practice

# Introduction

What values, beliefs, and expectations inform fundamental paradigms of practice? This section *puts knowledge accrued through practice at the center*.

How does the experience of practitioners of color and others working from "the margins" challenge the growing body of theory that has become the canon of the professional field over the past thirty years? The writers in this section provide ideas for working effectively with people from their various communities.

Each of the papers in this section exemplifies power dynamics in some fashion. Many of the authors do not use the word "power" and do not explicitly address questions of power. Nonetheless, power is often the unspoken heart of the matter. Culture, legitimacy, and power form a thick bundle of interlocking issues that lie at the heart of conflict resolution. Cultures are imposed and suppressed; voices are deemed legitimate or illegitimate: in both these ways power is used to privilege some and oppress others. Yet these issues are rarely addressed in ways that enable practitioners to integrate their importance into day-to-day practice.

One consequence of power dynamics is to subvert the flow of information. For example, in our discussions leading to the anthology, a conversation something like this often happened:

FIRST PRACTITIONER: You know, I don't usually admit this, but what I do when I'm alone in the room with disputants who look like me is not at all what I was trained to do.

SECOND PRACTITIONER: Really!? Me neither. What do you do that's different?

FP: Well, for one thing, I don't do that turn-taking thing. Just won't fly in my community.

SP: Yeah, and sometimes I'll leave the room when feelings get hot—let them shout a bit and cool off, and then talk it through when I come back.

Practitioners admit to not talking publicly about their true practices for two reasons. First, many of them work in organizational settings where they are supervised. If truth were out about what they actually do, they fear they might be fired. Second, they subject themselves to self-supervision; the internalized boss casts doubt on the validity of their practice. If there are "legitimate" methods, as evidenced by what is taught and written, then practitioners may feel that they are wrong to deviate. Maybe they question their effectiveness. Often, these doubts fester in secret.

One result of these dynamics is that people whose cultural inclinations may be toward collectivity end up working in isolation. Solo practice is the norm throughout the field (despite the early insistence by some community mediation groups such as the San Francisco Community Boards to always provide two or three mediators). What working alone means is that conflict resolvers have few sources of evaluation and continuous learning. For practitioners of color, this deprivation may be yet another way of being trapped inside structures that grate against most other behaviors in their lives.

In consequence, writers of color are often more comfortable critiquing the "mainstream" than revealing their own practices. The papers in this section break out of that constriction. Many were written when the authors were inspired by support from other practitioners of color. Collectively, the papers constitute frank dialogue as the authors share perspectives on creating models of practice culturally relevant to their communities.

OVERVIEW OF PART THREE

Beth Roy provides a theoretical framework for understanding how power operates in multiple realms and then applies theory to practice in two extended case histories. The first involves a biracial couple, the second a multicultural organization.

Dileepa Witharana next addresses strengths and problems in conflict resolution workshops introduced into Sri Lanka by British Quakers. As a participant and, eventually, a leader of the work, Dileepa explores a number of contradictions between imported forms and local needs in a war-torn society. In essence, he writes about relationships between colonizers and colonized, dynamics that echo Roberto Chené's essay in this volume, as well as Lucy Moore's discussion of working with Native American peoples.

Four examples of work in culturally specific sectors of American life follow. The first is vividly provided by a conversation with Hasshan Batts, a young African American staff member of a community mediation program. Through an account combining his personal history with his professional experiences, he deepens insight into frontiers awaiting the work of conflict intervention in diverse communities.

Roberto Vargas describes his approach to working with organizations utilizing Latino traditions. Through ritual and long-term consultation, he midwifes collaborative growth, often by attending to conflict as a constructive process. His approach draws on ceremony and traditional knowledge in a vein similar to the Hawaiian processes described by Anona Napoleon in part two of this volume.

Ted Coronel next tells the story of his development from formal training in mediation to a vision of how to work with Filipinos in ways consistent with community values and traditions. Next, Ray Leal provides a case example that demonstrates how history and worldview can be successfully taken into account in a school setting. Both papers illuminate Leah Wing's critique of neutrality in conflict resolution work in the context of specific cultures.

Finally, two papers raise questions of racism on institutional levels. Selina C. Low offers a picture of obstacles as she transitioned from community mediation volunteer to professional mediator. By addressing that most crucial of practices—the recruitment of a diverse body of people working in the field—Selina brings together the volume's discussions of culture and knowledge as they enrich—and constrain—relevant work in conflict resolution.

Valerie Batts writes about an approach to overcoming "modern racism" that elaborates in practical detail understandings of how systemic oppression works to distort interpersonal relations. Finally, S.Y. Bowland gives us a personal critique of training that belies its multicultural intentions.

Through theory and narrative, these authors teach ways to advance equity and justice, and they raise exciting questions for conflict resolution as it comes of age as a force for progress.

# 14 Power, Culture, Conflict

BETH ROY

In 1996 I was asked to participate in a project to produce a collaborative book about power and conflict resolution. My assignment was to write a chapter called "Power: The Pitfalls." I puzzled over the concept: is power something subject to pitfalls? A pitfall is something you fall into, unawares. The metaphor suggested that power might be a journey, with a beginning and a course and an end—and with some dangers here and there along the way. Presumably, one might avoid those dangers by recognizing them from a distance, for pits have clear edges and are separate from the road itself.

On reflection, I suggested to my fellow writers that power *is* a pitfall and that perhaps we needed to step back and talk through how we each conceptualized our subject. We were all involved in conflict resolution as practitioners or administrators or teachers; it seemed inevitable, and interesting, to me that we would have different ideas based on our different experiences and theoretical inclinations.

For a variety of reasons, that level of collaboration never happened. And the book never happened either. A structure of roles was created (editors and subeditors and writers and commentators) that generated conflict. Some people moved on to other jobs; others simply got busy with other projects. In that indefinable way things sometimes fall apart, the book died.

My own view is that we failed to address our own power dynamics, an absence that was fatal to the project.

Four years later, the editors of the *Mediation and Facilitation Training Manual* published by the Mennonite Conciliation Service approached me to contribute something about how power dynamics work in conflict resolution.[1] I gratefully submitted a shortened and revised version of my chapter for the defunct book. That piece of writing has now been reproduced in a number of places. I begin this essay, focused in more detail on how culture and power intertwine, with a revised version of the article from the manual.

I then question the ways in which conflict resolution theory imagines the role and functions of culture, viewing it as a category distinct from dynamics of power except insofar as facilitators fail in their obligations to be "culturally sensitive." Through an exploration of two case histories, I seek to bring culture, power, and conflict into vivid relationship with each other.

When Juliana Birkhoff explored the ways mediators think about power in her pioneering doctoral research,[2] she found two prevailing concepts: power as "a thing," something people "have"; and power as a negotiating position, deriving primarily from "batna" or "best alternative to a negotiated agreement."

In contrast, I think of power as something we *do*. It is the means by which we accomplish, or are denied, well-being. Power is a process going on between and among people, a multilayered and ever-shifting set of relationships. *Shaped* profoundly by the social structures within which we live, power is *internalized,* manifesting as feelings of entitlement and insecurity. It is *enacted* in transactions between and among people, *embodied* in cultural practices, and *played out* in organizational roles.

## WHY POWER MATTERS IN CONFLICT INTERVENTION

In ordinary life, process and possession are vaguely interwoven in the ways we talk about power. It is something bad, a process of exercising control over people and resources. Power is seen as ruthless, uncooperative, competitive, and wounding. But sometimes power is a good thing, an ability to get things done, a set of admirable attributes. In either rendition, power is laden with value judgments; the concept itself reeks of power.

These common concepts of power show up in conflict resolution theory as acknowledgment that inequality is a problem. Mediators are cautioned to intervene in a way that "balances the table." An underlying assumption is that many inequities can be left at the door and a conversation constructed that establishes equality in the room. Sometimes that may be true, but often it is not. Research on outcomes of divorce mediation, for instance, demonstrates the subtle and profound ways that gender styles of negotiating combine with material inequalities in men's and women's earning power and with the still-gendered imbalances in child-rearing to disadvantage women in mediated settlements.[3] Similarly, in the aggregate, people of color mediated by white mediators in cross-racial disputes end up with lesser value outcomes than they achieve in court adjudication.[4]

Developing a holistic understanding of power dynamics allows mediators to understand ways in which imbalances remain inherent in any process, however carefully arranged. Even if mediators are able to intervene in a way that "balances the table" in the room, they are working on a transactional level that does not necessarily address many other realms in which power may be decisively skewed. Lacking that awareness, people may leave a mediation more mystified and unprepared for the realities they face out in the world. Like physicians, conflict interveners need to "do no harm." That commitment requires asking the hard questions and having far reaching answers: Is mediation a possible and advisable course, for one thing, and, if so, how can inequities be described and confronted directly and effectively?

The mediator's power is a fluid and complex matter. Who the mediator is, of what cultural heritage, matters of gender and race and age, language spoken, transparency, and so much more—all affect the flow of power in the course of the work. One example lays in the ways mediators encourage or control the expression of emotion during a session. If the process is focused on settlement, emotional communication may be subjugated, by subtle or overt means, in favor of the negotiation of interests. If a participant speaks an emotional language, holds the healing of relationship to be more important than the resolution of disputes, or needs to work through emotional hurts as an integral part of the journey toward solution, then the mediator's actions seriously disadvantage that disputant and bias the outcome. The mediation table is itself a social structure, and as such it can reinforce or encourage renegotiation of power and well-being.

Power in and of itself is not an evil. Indeed, people come to mediation because they hope and believe the mediator has some power to help them. But such a negotiated use of constructive power is only possible when power is understood complexly and negotiated openly.

DOMAINS OF POWER

When I analyze power as I practice conflict resolution, I think of it as operating dynamically in five domains.

• *Internal:* One's sense of confidence, ability to articulate thoughts, skills for recognizing emotion and for managing it, and command of language all become factors in how powerfully one operates in transactions with others.

• *Transactional:* Everyday behaviors that occur between and among us—choice of words, body posture, eye contact, and so on—communicate and negotiate power.

• *Organizational:* Sets of agreements, tacit or explicit, create environments in which power is distributed in particular ways. Roles in families, organizations, communities—those institutions we experience personally on a daily basis—may be assigned by agreement or assumed de facto, and power accrues to them.

• *Cultural:* Particular histories and identities influence individuals to behave in particular ways and also influence the meanings attributed to behaviors by others. Ethnic origins, religious communities, racial identities, gender, and physical abilities all have associated with them sets of cultural habits and assumptions that are brought to bear on power dynamics.

• *Structural:* Both face-to-face transactions and group situations exist in the context of greater social structures, which define an underlying set of power relations. Often, these structures appear to be abstract (the economy), distant (the government), impervious to the wishes of individuals. Relations in this realm attach to cultural identities and attributes and become internalized in a sense of self (as a global sense of powerlessness, for instance).

Like all theoretical constructs, this one is less than exhaustive, a step in the ongoing process of evolving more comprehensive tools. In each of these arenas, power is exercised differently, with particular consequences for collaborative work and particular challenges to the practitioner. None of the domains I have described is independent of the others; all intertwine in mutually generating dynamics. Take shame, for example. It is an intensely internal sensation that at heart is the product of cultural and social-structural forces. Often, it causes people to keep silent about what they truly feel and think. Silence is a significant transaction between people; silence can be very loud. That which is not said shapes roles and relationships, becoming an organizational principle.

## CULTURE AND POWER

Of the realms I have identified, culture is in some ways the most talked about and the least understood. I hear mediators identify certain differences in behavior or style or sensibilities as "cultural" with an implication that the word ends the story. To say that Tisha comes from an African American culture in which yelling is normal and okay, and Annie comes from an Asian American culture in which silence and subtlety are honored may or may not be helpful on a descriptive level. But do these generalizations contribute to parsing the complex and interactive ways those two mannerisms also serve as conflict strategies?

Just as substances can be used constructively (for ritual, celebration, aesthetic pleasure, and so on) or destructively (abused, overused, used at inappropriate times, used in addictive ways, and so on), so too can power be used or abused. I find helpful a concept of *power play,* defined as any act intended to get another person to do something he or she would not otherwise do. A power play is an act of coercion, whereas power is a relationship of people to possibilities. A raised voice, for instance, may be a genuine expression of emotion for the purpose of communicating something that adds to the listener's power to accomplish something mutually desired. Or that same expression may be a threat; power plays have both the intention and the consequence of intimidating and overwhelming others. They represent "power over" rather than "power with."

Annie may keep silent to marshal her power strategically. Withdrawal from engagement can be the ultimate power play, effectively wielded universally by people who lack more overt forms of power. (Think of the teenager whose favorite word, said with a shrug and a turn away, is, "Whatever!") In this sense, nonviolence is a political power play that has demonstrated great effectiveness to change the world.

If Tisha and Annie come to a point of genuinely understanding each other's acculturated styles, if they therefore become capable of hearing each other with no loss of self-determination, then we are truly talking about culture. But to the extent that their forms of expression, however true to their cultures of origin, impact their abilities to negotiate their differences cooperatively—which is to say, with each of them acknowledging the other's equal right to satisfaction and each of them powerful enough to hold her own—the possibilities of mediation become problematic. What is a mediator's role in this case? I believe we need to be willing and able to talk fully and without judgment about both intentions and consequences of cultural styles, as we see them occurring in the room, in the context of people's historical and cultural experiences in the world.

I have said that nonviolence can be seen as a form of collective action that uses powers available to dispossessed peoples who may not have other forms in which to assert their interests.[5] Identity politics can have similar functions. My study of a Hindu-Muslim riot, *Some Trouble with Cows*, revealed the ways in which this conflict, seemingly based in religious identities, more truly reflected the absence of a political venue in which people could pursue needed changes in their lives.[6]

So too in interpersonal and organizational settings, cultural identities intersect with clashes of interest in often-complex dances that interveners need to understand in a thoroughgoing way. I offer two examples (both fictionalized composites of several actual stories).

DYNAMICS IN INTERCULTURAL MEDIATIONS: A COUPLE

Mapping dynamics like these onto intimate relationships may seem a contradiction in terms, but in reality it is an opportunity to unravel some very common problems and build toward greater love.

By the time Taritha and Alyssa came to me, they had almost given up on that possibility. After twelve years of being together as a couple, they had split up three months before. They came to me for help figuring out how to be apart, a project that was going just about as badly as being together had gone. But they also both confessed to a hope that they might find a way to put their relationship back together, "Although not the way it was before!" Taritha declared.

Taritha was the mother of two children, a fifteen-year-old girl and a thirteen-year-old boy. When she and Alyssa met and fell in love, Alyssa proclaimed her willingness to co-parent actively. Never having had a strong desire for children, she was clear that her devotion to Taritha was sufficient to motivate her to the project. Besides, she thought it was right that she do so; love, she believed, required certain sacrifices. She liked the kids well enough; they were fun and brought out a playfulness in her that had never been encouraged in her white, work-oriented Midwestern family. Nor did her career as an in-house lawyer for a large corporation leave a lot of space for fun.

Moreover, she could see that Taritha really needed help. The father of her kids had been in her life only briefly and was long gone. He had walked out when he learned of the second pregnancy. Taritha had a large and loving family, but they lived 2,000 miles away in the extended African American community in which Taritha had grown up, and no one had a lot of extra money for travel. Working as a first-grade teacher in a public school was satisfying, but it paid badly.

When they started their relationship, the women had talked extensively about the many differences between them. Race and sexual orientation headed the list. Neither woman had been in a cross-racial relationship before. Alyssa proclaimed herself to be color-blind and therefore considered race to be a nonissue. Taritha was alarmed by that formulation. "How can you be color-blind," she asked, "when your life as a white woman is so incredibly different from mine as a black single mom!?"

Taritha thought for a moment and went on, "I've never been with a white lover before, but one thing I know for sure: If we're going to make this work, you better develop a whole lot more color-vision, fast!"

Neither had Taritha ever been in a romantic relationship with a woman before. She was "coming out" by being with Alyssa, a process Alyssa had experienced at fourteen. "I always knew I was gay," Alyssa told Taritha. "It's a lot different now, but when I was growing up it was a big deal to be openly lesbian in high school. No way was I going to date anyone who hadn't already figured out she was a lesbian, too.

"You're my first relationship with a straight woman—something most of my gay friends are warning me not to do."

They moved in with each other three months after they'd met. (Old joke among lesbians: How does a lesbian show up on the second date? With a U-Haul.) At first, keeping house together was divine. Alyssa had never set up a home before. Sure, she'd paid the rent on apartments, but she'd always furnished them with spare utilitarianism. Taritha brought to their cozy house a sense of aesthetics, and the children contributed noise and mess and warmth. Alyssa felt like she was playing at a storybook life she'd never imagined for herself, and she was happy.

On Taritha's side, for the first time in her life she could truly experience aesthetic choice. When she mooned over a gorgeous, colorful rug that cost far too much, Alyssa insisted they buy it on the spot. "It's not *that* much," she said. "I can afford it, no problem."

Gradually, though, the glow faded and problems set it. Now the pain of separation had brought them to mediation. I asked them to speak about whatever emotions might interfere with their negotiating their breakup in a cooperative fashion, and the hurt and anger rolled out.

First came issues of class. Alyssa was generous to a fault, willing to buy whatever luxuries Taritha wanted. But in the absence of thoughtful dialogue, Taritha quickly began to experience troubles in two realms of power. First, she found herself guessing whether Alyssa really wanted to buy what she wanted, bowing to styles and colors she intuited Alyssa preferred, and then resented those compromises. Second, Alyssa found herself subtly, and guiltily, expecting that Taritha would do more housework in return, a dynamic that plunged them into the subject of race.

For Taritha, any expectation that housework was her greater responsibility evoked symbolic shadows of her mother's and grandmothers' lives as domestic workers. She'd put herself through college, the first generation to experience substantial upward economic mobility. She might offer to wash dishes or do laundry out of love and cooperation, but not out of expectation.

Although both partners were women, this equation of money and domestic labor evoked deeply imbedded power dynamics of gender. Both had internalized the value judgment that work at home had less value than work for wages. Alyssa had rebelled against that assumption very early in life, challenging a profession that was moving toward gender equality. Taritha still did "women's work" for pay, and she doubly bridled at the idea of doing it in a home shared with a woman partner as well.

Class, race, and gender—the *structural* realm of power relations—had thus actively undermined the women's relationship. On a *cultural* level, Alyssa was strongly attracted to Taritha's warm and freewheeling family, idealizing them in a way that Taritha resented. She loved her kinfolk, but she'd also moved far away from them as a way of escaping some of their cultural attributes. Primary among these were matters of child rearing: she wanted to raise her kids through persuasion rather than punishment. She especially quarreled with her mother and grandmother about hitting kids: they maintained it was necessary in a racist world to make sure young Black people, especially boys, knew how to show respect, and they considered Taritha's ideals to be elitist, impractical, and dangerous.

*Interpersonally,* all these domains came together in patterns of silence and explosion. Over time, a tilt developed: Alyssa became more silent, Taritha more explosive. Each berated herself for her own behavior, even as she lashed out at the other for hers. To Taritha, Alyssa's habit of disappearing emotionally for days at times of tension was a power play. It left Taritha helpless to either resolve her feelings or fix the problem. On the other hand, Alyssa felt intimidated by Taritha's greater emotional expressiveness, and all the more fell silent out of fear, gravely underlined with resentment. These *internalizations* of power further undercut attempts to talk out their problems and left them both feeling all the more depressed and hopeless.

These dynamics showed up in their *organization* of parenting roles. Alyssa tended to be the playful parent, and Taritha felt herself to be a martyr, the one who had to do all the hard work of getting kids to school on time, supervising homework, setting curfews, and so on.

For the first three hours of the mediation, I guided Alyssa and Taritha in a dialogue about the those things that weighed on their hearts, all the old resentments and hurt feelings that lingered. The goal of this part of the work was threefold: to clear the air through the ritual of expression, to practice a kind of emotional dialogue that they could use in future when the going got heavy, and to make explicit from a subjective perspective those core dynamics that had strained their relationship to the breaking point. Some version of this work was necessary no matter what they decided in the end, to separate or to reconcile, because in the absence of dealing with their feelings, it was unlikely they could manage to problem solve or negotiate with the cooperative mind set needed for collaboration.

To understand their problems in terms of power dynamics in all these realms helped Taritha and Alyssa reduce the amount of blame they had been directing at each other, and it also suggested ways to think about the changes they would need to make either to stay together or to separate and co-parent cooperatively.

That was a decision they were not yet prepared to make. They agreed to go slowly and see what they could rebuild, either together or apart.

### DYNAMICS IN INTERCULTURAL MEDIATIONS: AN ORGANIZATION

A colleague and I were asked to work with a research department in a large health organization. About six years earlier, the all-white, all-male, very prestigious team had hired the first woman of color, an African American of considerable standing in the field. She in turn recruited another woman of color, a Latina who was younger but also had impressive experience. Together, they argued for further increasing cultural diversity on the team, especially as the patient population they studied grew ever more diverse, but to no avail. Three new hires in a row were men of European descent.

Under pressure from members of the administration who were concerned about their ability to represent the institution as multicultural to the patients and insurers on whom the finances of the institution depended, the researchers at last hired an African American man, a man who had recently immigrated from Asia, and an older woman who was a lesbian.

Relations among staff members were civil and formal. But the newer people pushed for an opportunity to talk more honestly about dynamics of race, gender, and other identities. My colleague, an African American man, and I, a Jewish lesbian, were hired to conduct a three-day retreat over a long weekend.

The first morning, eighteen people seated themselves in a comfortable room, cups of coffee and pastries at hand. We asked them to introduce themselves, describe their histories, positions, and roles in the department, and tell us why they were here: What issues did they personally hope to address in the course of the retreat? The conversation proceeded well; people were, I thought, a little hesitant, a bit formal, understandably testing the waters of safety in the room.

There were only two people left to speak. The next to last one was a middle-aged man of pleasant demeanor, diffident, and humorous. "I don't exactly know why I'm here," he began. "I'm not really on this team. I used to be, but now I'm strictly an administrator."

"Oh, but we're glad you're here," someone exclaimed from across the table. "It's always fun to have you present."

"How did you come to be here, if you're not on the team?" we asked.

"Well," he said, with a moue of humility, "our CEO asked me to sit in for him. He had to be out of town, otherwise he'd planned to be here. He wants me to report back to him."

A deep silence greeted that announcement. My co-facilitator and I exchanged a surprised glance.

Structural power had loudly introduced itself into the story of the group. At this point, my colleague and I knew we needed to assert *our* power to shape the conversation in a way that would make for openness.

We asked if people felt able and willing to talk about anything and everything they needed to discuss with a representative of the CEO present. Several of the older members, long-time co-workers of the man in question and all of the same broad identity (white and male), quickly assented. The newer hires, however, said nothing, a silence we noted as a signifier of both transactional and organizational power. Body language was eloquent. We noted who looked frankly at the administrator and smiled, who looked down or away.

Questions of safety almost always reflect inequalities. To construct a forum in which honesty is truly possible is to explore the terrain of power. When people are afraid to speak, it is because they fear some consequence that they believe they cannot control. To be sure, speaking truth, on a certain level, opens the door to unknowable results; it is always a risk. Whether or not people are willing to take that risk is a calculation about potential harm done by others with some form or forms of power, factored by the risk of *not* dealing with the problem or conflict at hand. If life is too intolerable as things currently stand, then one may be willing to take certain risks because the alternative is to quit. But that is a decision that participants in conflict resolution processes need to make individually, knowingly, wisely.

We asked the man in question to please step outside the room for a few minutes so that others could talk more freely about his presence. He agreed. Several people then said that, however much they liked Sam (the pseudonym we will give him), they were not comfortable with the notion that he would repeat everything to the CEO, a person well respected and liked by everyone in the group but still their boss. "It's not that we don't want him to be informed about what we do here. We recognize that we'll need to report some things back to him. But *we* want to make that report, based on what we together decide to say."

A different kind of silence greeted this statement. Clearly, the older researchers were taken aback. Their assumption of collegiality was in the process of being challenged. To their credit, they were thoughtful instead of argumentative. Nonetheless, not quite able to draw the lines so starkly, someone suggested that perhaps Sam could stay on a friendly basis, if he agreed to report only what the group determined and to do so in partnership with a chosen representative of the group. That suggestion stimulated a wider conversation about confidentiality, the parameters of which seemed simple but were not. Groups frequently make easy declarations of confidentiality: "Nothing said in this room will pass out of the room." But then half the people go home and talk excitedly about what they have just experienced with their significant other. That is an understandable thing to do; honest forums for dealing with conflict are intense moments of learning. They challenge assumptions, stir feelings and memories and questions for participants, who quite naturally need personal forums for sorting.

"Also," said one woman who did overlapping research part-time in another department as well as this one, "some of what we decide here might affect what I do and how I do it over there. What do I say to them?"

"Also," said a man, "my wife works in the CEO's office. What if something that comes out here involves her? Do I have to keep it a secret from my own wife?"

Not to surface and talk through details about how information flows is to gainsay a confidentiality agreement. Information is power, as wise people have long said. Better to make concrete allowance for the ways in which people *will* talk than to pretend that they will not.

Sam was invited back into the room and asked if he would promise to follow the group's wishes about information to the CEO and confidentiality in general. He said he was happy to do that, felt relieved in fact not to have to make decisions about what was private and what reportable all by himself.

We had barely begun the retreat, but already several significant things had been accomplished. We had signaled to the participants that we were attentive to power issues. We had demonstrated our ability and our intention to be attuned to subtle levels of power (especially as they impacted openness in the retreat) by questioning silence as well as verbalization. We had listened carefully to some people's need to establish conditions of safety before embarking on honest conversation, and we had reframed that need as something institutional rather than a personal weakness or disloyalty to the "team." We had demonstrated a willingness to disagree with the desires of leadership in order to protect those with less organizational power. By exploring the details of a confidentiality agreement, we had told people we were committed to respecting their real needs rather than our theoretical ones—and we were barely an hour and a half into the retreat.

Overall, we challenged the culture of the institution. I would describe that culture as polite, collegial, nonconfrontational. The rules of the place were to err on the side of accommodation rather than protest. Only after the interveners raised questions about the CEO's representative being present did others voice their concerns.

Often, collegiality in this form serves to perpetuate the status quo. The style of niceness that began the meeting may well be preferable to people's attacking and hurting each other. Indeed, if those are the only alternatives, the protection afforded by collegiality may be preferable, although I believe that it also reflects a value system so deeply assumed by people accustomed to certain kinds of privilege—typically white men with affluence and status—that it remains unnoticed by them. Things go unsaid because there is no need to say them; the CEO's belief that his oversight would be accepted by his staff without demur was consistent with his organizational position and also with many other experiences throughout his life in our stratified society.

At the same time, the discomfort of those people who, for a variety of reasons, stood outside the circle of collegiality was palpable. Had the group's initial polite silence gone unchallenged by the mediators, it would have had the important consequence of creating a structure for the retreat that silenced the less powerful members of the staff through fear. Therefore, our intervention had a visible impact on the possibilities for a more equitable conversation. In short, we made apparent some important lines of power within the institution, and at the same time we negotiated between us, the interveners, and the participants a relationship of respectful power sharing.

Talk quickly flowed among them with honesty and depth. At one point, the second woman hired (I will call her "Melisa") revealed to an older colleague ("Stanley") that she had long ago made a decision to stop expressing her opinions in department meetings. Stanley, a warm and thoughtful man, was aghast. "Why did you do that!" he asked in horror.

"Do you remember that time we were deciding how to set up the new research project on [she named the subject]? Well, twice I told you all that I had extensive experience working in that area, and twice the conversation went on around the table as if I hadn't spoken. When it came time to appoint someone to head the project, my name wasn't even mentioned by anyone.

"I got the message. You were not hearing me. I was hurt and very angry, and I made a decision to speak up only when I really needed to."

Stanley visibly reddened. He turned to Melisa with genuine sorrow in his eyes. "But why didn't you tell me? I thought we had a good, friendly relationship!"

"I didn't tell you because you weren't listening," Melisa responded. "I felt humiliated. Too often I've been discounted because I'm young and Latina."

"But," Stanley said with even more emphasis, "I never intended to offend you. I wish I had known. You never gave me a chance! Why didn't you tell me?"

We pointed out that Stanley was doing the same thing now that Melisa was grieving from years ago: he was not hearing her. He used the power of his position at the center of departmental dynamics to discount Melisa's statement. Rather than asking, "What did I miss?" he turned the question on her, "Why didn't you speak?" He assumed he was at the center of the transaction, she on the outside with a responsibility to get his attention. Moreover, she spoke of cultural assumptions about her age, gender, and ethnicity. By asking his question again and again, repetition implying criticism of her, he exercised his cultural power to deny the importance of those factors. Finally, on a subtle level, he suggested *he* was the aggrieved party because his intentions had been good whatever the consequences of his actions; why had she not forgiven and forgotten, or at least given him a chance he could recognize to redeem himself?

When we called his attention to those dynamics, he was deeply moved. He apologized and asked Melisa to give him another chance. "I really want to know when you feel overlooked or unheard," he said. She agreed to tell him, but only if the group as a whole agreed to hear her statement as worthy of attention, and if Stanley and his older colleagues committed to learning what they needed to learn from all the newer researchers, not just her. Otherwise, we pointed out, another injury would be inflicted by the imbalance of awareness intrinsic to these dynamics: precisely because she is in a disadvantaged position, she knows instantly and intensely when a discount is afoot. She cannot help but feel the injury. But Stanley and his peers can only gain awareness of what, to them, is simply the normal way of doing business—normalcy being defined as the way they do things—through exhaustive actions by a person who already feels wounded. To change their assumptions, they need Melisa and her peers to do the substantial work of articulating their perceptions. Not only must Melisa speak of her grievance (already a violation of the culture of collegiality), but she must then convince Stanley that her experience is credible. Moreover, even while she is working to overcome his defenses against recognizing his discriminatory behavior, she may also feel pulled to soothe his guilt that he has done some racial or ethnic wrong.

No wonder that Melisa opted instead to stop speaking. But the paradox is that people who, like Stanley, have lived lifetimes immersed in the culture of supremacy cannot simply will themselves to share power; they need to be taught. What they can do to at least ameliorate the consequent hardship on their colleagues to is embrace new learning with humility and enthusiasm and seek it in as many places as they possibly can. I cannot know what I do not know, but I can know I do not know it and welcome new learning. "Whites-only" gatherings to pool awareness of these dynamics are one possible step in the right direction.

Composite case histories cannot quite communicate how much pain and warmth and learning is contained in the business of understanding power dynamics in these ways. In the process of its application to conflict resolution, a subject theoretical and dry becomes a living thing, a way of casting human existence with an optimistic eye fastened on the best of possibilities. Thinking about power as process allows insight into how personal life is lived in a framework of social forces. In turn it allows each of us, in our most meaningful relationships with others, at home and at work, in the community and in the polity, to be powerful agents for change, challenging inequality and taking on the creative process of rebuilding daily relationships as exercises in justice.

# 15 Outside Interests, Inside Needs

*Tensions in Conflict Resolution
Workshop Practices Based on
Sri Lankan Experience*

DILEEPA WITHARANA

Sri Lanka has been a country in a civil war for at least twenty years.* The crux of this conflict has been the struggle by the Tamil minority for their rights and political autonomy. Since independence from the colonial British in 1948, consecutive Sri Lankan governments have failed to take Tamil demands seriously. Attempts to address the demands of the minorities, through proposals to devolve or share political power at the center, have either been rejected at the last minute, due to pressure from the majority Sinhala-Buddhist community, or not implemented properly. Until the late 1970s this struggle was mainly a political one in which senior Tamil politicians from the upper social strata played a major role. From the late 1970s through the early 1980s it became more violent as the momentum shifted to Tamil youth, who came mostly from the lower layers of Tamil society. As the civil war has raged over the last few decades, the Liberation Tigers of Tamil Eelam (LTTE) has gradually gained ascendance over the other groups representing the Tamil struggle. It is now the most powerful of the Tamil groups, with territory under its control in the North and the East provinces of Sri Lanka.

---

*This paper was originally written in 2003.

This devastating civil war has created a strong need for a peaceful settlement. There have been various peace initiatives at many levels, from the grassroots to the national. From 1998 to 2002, I participated in workshops that were facilitated discussions or activities that concern the resolution or the transformation of conflicts. I took part as a participant and as a workshop "guide" (I use this general term to encompass roles of both facilitator and trainer because, as I will demonstrate below, those functions overlap and are in tension in Sri Lankan practice). These workshops I participated were sponsored by international nongovernmental organizations (INGOs) such as Quaker Peace and Service–Sri Lanka (QPS Sri Lanka), Oxfam-UK, and Save the Children Fund, as well as by regional NGO networks, local NGOs, and community-based organizations (CBOs) in various parts of Sri Lanka. In the course of my experience, I have worked with several different Sri Lankan and foreign workshop guides.

Although the practice has spread countrywide, with many locals involved in the field on a professional basis, the idea of conflict resolution workshops did not emerge organically from the Sri Lankan struggle to find a nonviolent solution to the Sri Lankan conflict; it evolved elsewhere under different conditions and was imported to Sri Lanka by international NGOs and the Colombo-based civil society organizations. This is important because it means that the assumptions underlying conflict resolution theory, approaches, and standard theoretical knowledge are not native to Sri Lankan culture, and that, unmodified, the conflict resolution tools introduced to the situation will not ultimately be useful in resolving the conflicts they were brought here to address.

An example of this problem is the understanding of conflict itself: In Theravadic Buddhism, the religion of the Sri Lankan Sinhalese majority, conflict and peace are both seen as expressions of the internal states of individuals. This perspective differs from the Western conception of conflict and peace as external states to be managed and changed. Clearly this difference in understanding of the *source* of conflict will lead to a different approach to the *resolution* of conflict, for example, the Buddhistic approach to peace is more in line with *transcendence* of conflict than its *management, resolution* or *transformation*. Additionally, the very structure of conflict resolution workshops—agendas and discussion groups and flip charts and activities, etc.—is culturally unfamiliar to most Sri Lankans living away from the capital, making it more difficult for them to absorb already foreign concepts. Like any practice introduced from outside a culture, the practice of nonviolent conflict resolution must change if it is to be accepted and applied with positive consequences in the Sri Lankan context. Conflict resolution practice must face these challenges and undergo transformation if it is to become a genuinely Sri Lankan tool.

In this paper, I identify and discuss seven contradictions that arise, at least in part, between the foreign assumptions built into the current conflict resolution workshop model and the needs on the ground in Sri Lanka, and I explore ways that Sri Lankan facilitators have attempted to reconcile those tensions. The reasons for each of these tensions are complex, but they include cultural biases about fairness, conflicting ideas about who qualifies as the expert in a given situation, diverse perceptions of elements of peacefulness, the best relationship to time, and the question of whether it is more important to train as many people as possible or to cultivate activists.

Over my years of participation, I have observed different workshop guide approaches to conflict resolution training, diverse interests and needs on the parts of workshop guides and participants, and diverse objectives held by the general professional conflict resolution practice and by communities affected by conflict. These observations have led me to identify contradictions in the practice of conflict resolution in such areas as conflict resolution approaches, workshop formats, contents addressed, and so on: These are tensions between practices that seem mutually exclusive though they are on the same continuum; giving space or attention to one element of the pair automatically reduces the space for the other. I have observed seven areas of tensions in the workshops I have taken part in, and I think that it is fair to assume they are common in other prolonged violent conflicts. My discussion of these points of tension is based on observation, personal reflection, and discussions with my Sri Lankan colleagues since becoming involved in this field.

In an attempt to move the practice forward toward constructive uses, I will be describing each of the elements in each pair of approaches and the argument in favor of each, and discussing the contexts within which the two elements conflict with each other. Then I will discuss the factors influencing which elements workshop guides favor in which situations. Finally, I will be discussing methods practitioners have developed to incorporate the constructive aspects of each element into new ways of approaching the problems they each seek to address, taking the best from each for optimum results.

*Positive Attitude and Critical Analysis*

How should the effectiveness and content of the workshop be evaluated, given an intention of improving impact?

A *positive attitude* is necessary at every stage of any peace initiative, but especially so when the conflict being addressed is protracted, complex, and violent. In these situations, people can develop mental barriers that make it difficult to even imagine that peace is possible, let alone how to create it. Without a positive attitude, negativity tends to paint any steps toward peace as utopian and not worth trying. This negativity can defeat the goals of conflict resolution workshops before they are even held. Cultivating a positive approach can bring beneficial changes to several aspects of conflict resolution training. First, "seeing good" in each individual makes it more likely that everyone will be included in the effort, rather than excluded. Second, if people feel they are well thought of, they are more likely to exhibit positive qualities. Third, a positive approach creates space for hope that solutions can be found to the painful and difficult problems and conflicts being discussed. Fourth and finally, the deliberate practice of interpreting situations in positive terms, an exercise demanding creativity, can uncover new avenues for the peace process to move forward, avenues that usually stay hidden in a negative environment. So cultivating a positive attitude is an important aspect of a dialogue on peace to overcome the embedded pessimism of a conflict-affected society.

*Critical analysis* is also crucial. This is particularly true when conflict resolution workshops have been only recently introduced from outside, are still being developed, and are being practiced in diverse cultural, political and conflict contexts. It is important in these situations to think critically about workshop objectives, structures, themes, activities, discussions, venues, formats, agendas, facilitation, and target groups. This analysis is essential to ensure these elements of conflict resolution workshops are appropriate to local conditions. In each case, the nature and degree of the changes will be dependent on the nature and degree of the cultural and conflictual differences between where the workshop was developed and where it is being applied.

In my experience of conflict resolution practice in Sri Lanka, I have not seen examples of serious, systematic, and comprehensive attempts at critical analysis by workshop guides of their own work. What evaluations I have seen done have generally been limited to superficial feedback about workshop performance hastily done at the end of each workshop or workshop session, without integrating the evaluation feedback into an ongoing process of future workshop design. In general, workshop guides conducted the final assessments of their overall performances with the ground rule that all feedback should be positive. This approach by the workshop guides discouraged feedback that was critical of the process and suggested other ways of doing things. Also, the definitions of "positive" and "negative" may themselves be a problem. At a training of trainers workshop in 2000, local participants critically analyzed certain practices (the standard workshop format: conducted in a hotel, sitting in a circle, using flip charts, participating in "strange" games, etc.) as culturally alien to the Sri Lankan villagers they would be working with. The foreign trainers agreed the concerns were legitimate, but they warned participants of the consequences of being negative and informally made light of them during the following tea break.

The tension then is between the need to remain positive about the goals and possibilities of the work, while leaving room for critical analysis of how the work is done. Though it has not been done on a systematic basis and has not focused particularly on analyzing the workshop performance, QPS Sri Lanka and Thirupthiya[1] have tried to develop an organizational culture that reconciles this tension. In this culture team members developed the habit of critically analyzing *one's own work* along with suggestions to improve the practice. In this way they work to make a distinction between negative criticism and critical analysis.

*Equity and Impact*

Who is encouraged to participate actively?

*Equity* is a fundamental guideline in dominant-mainstream conflict resolution workshop facilitation. In an equitably run workshop, workshop guides give fairly equal time to each participant and fairly equal weight to each participant's contributions. This is important to do because each person there brings some unique perspective on the conflict—through ethnicity, religion, age, geographical region, culture, social class, life experience, life expectation, and gender—that can contribute to a better understanding of the problem and prepare the way for a resolution that addresses all the issues and is accepted by all the parties. Equitability is a powerful antidote to the currently popular political practice of using a single dominant narrative, promulgated by political elites, to explain and resolve conflicts. The value being expressed through this approach is that each participant is as important to the process as every other participant. The goal is to make heard any unheard voices.

*Impact,* on the other hand, gives priority not to "equal opportunity for all" but to the practical aspect of identifying and encouraging those who are working on peace outside of the workshop as well. In a context of a complex and prolonged violent conflict such as in Sri Lanka, conflict resolution workshops are but a single element of a larger, and longer term, peace process. This peace process is carried forward by individuals who emerge from the conflict-ridden society. Conflict resolution workshops can be ideal places for workshop guides to find and nurture these leaders from within the pool of participants. The value being expressed through this approach is that those who can serve outside the workshop have priority within it. The goal is to clarify and strengthen the voices of those willing and able to lead, so optimizing the long-term impact of the workshop.

The conflict in the *equity/impact* tension is about focus. In the equity model, the aim is to treat everyone "the same," giving all participants the same opportunities to be speak and to be validated. In the impact model, the aim is to give more opportunities to participants who are working, or may work, on long-term peace initiatives, giving them more spaces to express themselves and more freedom to define themes and to guide the discussion in directions they think important.

A training session held in Kotmale, Sri Lanka, in April 2000 demonstrates how potential peace workers can lose confidence in conflict resolution workshops organized in the equity mode. In the eastern province of Sri Lanka there is a long stretch of villages, popularly known as "border villages." One side of this stretch is Sinhalese territory controlled by the Sri Lankan army and the other side is a Tamil area controlled by the LTTE. In the middle separating the two territories is the stretch of paddy fields spreading over thousands of acres. Sinhala and Tamil farmers, who were living together peacefully before the war started, got together in 1999, ten years after armed conflict, and in a unique community peace building initiative declared the paddy fields a weapon-free zone. Instructing all parties carrying arms to respect their wishes, they resumed cultivation. It was a comprehensive community initiative, a process faced with serious difficulties and threats, but the farmers were able to cultivate paddy for two seasons before the process was disrupted. A group involved with this initiative was invited to a long-term, applied-peace-building course to share their knowledge with others. However, feeling that the workshop guides did not give them enough opportunities to guide the discussion toward what they saw as the important concerns, they left the program after the initial sessions.

In contrast to this experience, another conflict resolution workshop, also held in 2000, provides an example of drawing positive aspects from each element of the equity/impact conflict. The participants were youths and young adults primarily from Sinhalese and Upcountry Tamil communities in the central region of Sri Lanka. Some members of the group, whom I categorize as "potential peace workers," wanted to discuss and argue more on the theme of "the politics of Sri Lankan conflict." This focus was counter to the wishes of a majority of participants, who were more comfortable addressing conflict in general. The workshop guides changed their structure to provide a facilitated discussion of the political issues within the workshop for those who wanted it and also arranged an additional workshop to continue the discussion in greater depth. The workshop guides retained equity as a basic value in the workshop, but had the resources and flexibility to provide higher impact opportunities as well.

*Facilitator and Trainer*

What are the crucial roles and tasks for workshop guides?

How workshop leadership is defined influences the structure and outcomes of the work. As mentioned above, conflict resolution workshops are facilitated discussions or activities that concern the resolution or the transformation of conflicts through nonviolent means that take a variety of forms. One key variation concerns the role of the people leading the group. Generally, these workshop guides see themselves as either *facilitators* or *trainers.*

The *facilitator* role is to manage the *process,* not the *content* of the workshop, while staying neutral, to help participants conduct the discussion in a systematic, democratic, and constructive manner within a given time frame in an attempt to achieve objectives agreed to by all. The facilitator's tools are questions, clarifying comments, and selection of the appropriate participants at the appropriate times. Though facilitators may present general conflict resolution tools and skills, they are not the main providers of the content of the workshop, and they should not use the power of their position to influence the conclusions reached by the group. Facilitation is the preferred approach when the workshop participants are expected to know the nature of the conflict well and are considered able to work out nonviolent resolutions of their own design.

The *trainer* role, in contrast, is to provide content. In addition to understanding general conflict resolution skills and tools, trainers have expertise: information and opinions based on a broader contextual knowledge of the conflict. A main purpose of the workshop is for the trainer to share this expertise with the participants at appropriate times as they move from understanding the conflict to thinking about its resolution. Training is the preferred approach when the participants, even as a collective, lack information about the complicated nature of a prolonged conflict or how to resolve it.

The role of facilitator is appropriate when a workshop guide is unfamiliar with the conflict under discussion, as is normally the case in conflict resolution as currently practiced in Sri Lanka: conducting conflict resolution workshops has become a professional career, and national and foreign experts are frequently asked to work on conflicts that are not entirely familiar to them. However, when the workshop guide is as familiar with the specific conflict as the participants are, and also has some deeper, broader, or more detailed relevant information than they, then the role of trainer is more appropriate. The conflict in the *facilitator/trainer* pair is over whether we should allow workshop guides space to share their knowledge and experience or not.

What I have seen in my work in Sri Lanka is that local civil society organizations working toward peace tend to base their workshops mainly on a trainer model, while the international NGOs or Sri Lankan organizations with strong foreign influences focus more on facilitation. The question of training versus facilitation was a topic of lengthy internal discussions in organizations such as QPS and Thirupthiya, where the staff consisted of both locals and foreigners. Foreigners argued in favor of facilitation as the best model for adult learning and drew a distinction between workshop guides and participants, hence preventing workshop guides from contributing to the discussion. Some locals responded by identifying local workshop guides of conflict resolution workshops as also being "participants" in the Sri Lankan conflict (with the assumption that the entire population of Sri Lanka has experienced war in some way and shares responsibility for the conflict on some level) and arguing that these workshop guides could also appropriately and usefully contribute to workshops as participants.

In a less volatile conflict, trainers may have conflict resolution tools as the stand-alone object of their training, but this is of less use in active, violent conflicts such as currently exists in Sri Lanka. When Sri Lankans talk about "conflict," they are almost always talking about the national conflict and not about conflict in family, organizational, or other settings; there is no meaningful existence for conflict resolution tools if one isolates them from the issue of Sri Lankan conflict. Most of the tools I have come across are too simplistic to be useful in understanding and working out the full spectrum of a complex, real-size conflict. Tools such as stages of conflict, conflict mapping, models of nonviolent communication, and so on, are so simplistic that rather than using them to explain the conflict, one can use the conflict to explain them. What happens in such a situation is that rather than the conflict being the focus, the tool becomes the focus, distracting work away from the main objective.

I have seen a case where aspects of both facilitation and training were used with positive results, in a workshop held for field workers and volunteer activists of peace and development fields in the Central Province of Sri Lanka in fall 2000. The workshop was designed to permit the members of the team of facilitators to step out of their roles at specific times during the workshop to actively participate as equal members of the group in activities being run by other workshop guides. This helped to develop trust among facilitators and participants and added to the feeling that the workshop was an exercise among equals working as a unit towards a common goal.

*Agenda and Content*

How is it decided what to talk about in the workshop?

The *agenda* is the tool with which workshop guides design the structure and flow of their workshops to make sure they cover the points they want to cover. Since guides are by definition the experts on the topics of peace and nonviolent conflict resolution, it is seen as reasonable that they should present to the workshop participants the guidelines for the workshop. There is some room for modification by the participants in this model, but the agenda as presented defines the limits of those modifications.[2] The process of developing the agenda begins with deciding what objectives the workshop is intended to meet. These objectives suggest the themes that will flow through the workshop, which in turn suggest particular workshop activities. The agenda sets up the basic structure of the workshop before the workshop begins. This is important to the participants because it informs them what they are supposed to discuss in the workshop and what information they can expect to take from the workshop, and to the workshop guides because it gives them the guidelines to conduct the workshop constructively. This clarification of expectations is important; in one conflict resolution workshop I participated in,[3] the lack of a preset agenda caused frustration and loss of faith among participants. Though they were not particularly unhappy with the end results, for the first half of the training they continually asked questions about the purpose of particular activities and the facilitator's objectives for the workshop. The value supported by setting an agenda is that of having clear expectations, and the goal is to articulate and meet them.

However, if we primarily consider a conflict resolution workshop as a place to discuss issues, then it is the *content* rather than the structure that should lead the discussion. In such a model, the participants work with the workshop guides as the discussion unfolds to decide what topics to follow up on and how long to spend on each topic. This process reflects a respect for the seriousness of the issues under discussion and is particularly important when participant diversity means that previously unconsidered points may be brought to light. The value supported by allowing content to define the direction of the workshop is that of honoring the knowledge and experience in the room, and the goal is to leave space for important concerns to surface for meaningful discussion.

When conducting conflict resolution workshops for mature adults, there is good chance that the agenda-driven and the content-driven models will at times be in conflict with each other. At one end of the continuum, "sticking to the agenda" no matter what can discourage participant engagement by giving the impression that the discussion can *never* influence the preset agenda or (perhaps more importantly) the outcome of the workshop. This is particularly critical in situations where significant differences exist between the knowledge systems, worldviews, and visions of peace held by the workshop guides who created the agenda and those held by the participants. At the other end of the continuum is the case in which the workshop becomes focused on one particular point, unable to move forward toward any commonly agreed-upon goals. In either situation, the tension between the two elements of these conflicting approaches can reach a high level.

In workshops I have been part of, I have seen two ways to minimize the contradictions and resolve such tension. The first method is to include participants (or a group representative of the participants) in the development of the agenda for any workshop lasting more than a few days. The curriculum development portion of the April 2000 workshop discussed in the equity and impact section above was conducted in such a manner.

Individuals who had expressed their willingness to participate in a long-term applied peace-building course were invited to participate in a curriculum design workshop prior to the course to decide what they wanted to study. Though curriculum development is different and more resource intensive than a workshop agenda, this example suggests that a similar process could be applied to agenda development for intensive conflict resolution workshops lasting more than a few days.

The second method is to share the thinking underlying the agenda along with the agenda when it is first presented to the participants. Such disclosure can keep the agenda comparatively more flexible as the workshop proceeds and more open to changes in response to discussions within the workshop. This method was used successfully in a February 2002 workshop held for peace activists of a regional NGO network. Most of the participants of this group had political affiliations and were not limited to nonviolent means of achieving peace, nor were they familiar with the workshop concept. The facilitators spent more than half an hour discussing the thinking behind the agenda.

More generally, in the absence of an agenda, workshop guides could still influence and guide the direction of a content-based discussion by sharing their experiences in a more personal way than is customarily done and by staying aware of the overall need to build community peace throughout their entire intervention.

## Workshop Time and Informal Discussions

How is time conceived of and controlled in the workshop setting?

Conflict resolution workshops are basically forums within which participants can be brought to understand the conflict systematically and to find nonviolent methods of resolution. These objectives are realized through various workshop activities. These include activities intended to change the attitudes that promote violent conflicts and activities to make participants familiar with conflict resolution skills and tools. The more activities that are covered, the greater the chance of convincing participants that conflict resolution is a realistic alternative to violence. Given that participants, workshop guides, and the sponsoring organizations have limited resources to spend on presenting workshops, it is common practice in Sri Lanka to make maximum use of the *workshop time* by covering as many activities as possible within each workshop. Starting the workshop early, extending the workshop time into late evening, and shortening breaks are all common characteristics of Sri Lankan conflict resolution workshop practice.

Although this is an understandable prioritization of workshop resources, packing the schedule so tightly means that an important opportunity is lost: The lack of unscheduled time means that there are few opportunities for *informal discussions* between participants. These informal discussions are one of the key benefits of conflict resolution workshops in Sri Lanka, providing unusual opportunities for participants from disparate communities to get to know and interact with each other in a natural way. In contrast to the controlled introductory sessions within the formal workshop agenda, this space is used by participants to have their own discussions in small groups on themes they find important and relevant but which are not being adequately addressed within the workshop. In addition to the simple lack of time on the workshop agenda, there are other reasons for participants to find informal spaces for discussions outside the workshop, including limitations set by ground rules, fear of discussing genuine opinions in public, small discussion group formation based on artificial guidelines rather than natural interests and affinities, lack of attention for raised concerns on the part of the workshop guide or the majority of participants, and the culturally alien forum of the workshop itself.

Workshop time and informal discussions come to be most in conflict when the aim of the workshop design is optimization of positive impact, and this is most often an issue for groups that have limited time and money. In general, the international NGOs and the Colombo-based NGOs with fairly large budgets present workshops with a balance of workshop exercises and free time for participants to make informal connections. However, the small local NGOs and CBOs, which struggle to manage activism with limited allocation of funds, generally conduct workshops in small uncomfortable spaces and limited time frames, and without the luxury of ample opportunity for informal discussions.

Some important issues may come up informally but rarely are raised in formal conflict resolution workshop forums in Sri Lanka:

- Sympathies and justifications toward military actions of the regular Sri Lankan armed forces, LTTE, and so on. Sharing these is perceived to be improper in a conflict resolution workshop, which is generally understood as a forum for peace-loving people to discuss peace.
- Atrocities of one's own armies and militant groups on one's own community, as open expression of this is perceived to bring danger if the information reaches the groups carrying arms, or it is considered disadvantageous to discuss such issues in a multiethnic forum where the "other" ethnicities are present (for example, antidemocratic practices of the LTTE).
- Atrocities of one's own communities toward other communities (for example, the issue of Sinhala border villagers stealing the property of Tamil neighbors on a mass scale during ethnic riots is hardly disclosed in formal forums.)
- Contradictions, criticisms, and critical analysis of the aspects of conflict resolution practice including suggestions for improvements. Participants are either not confident enough to express themselves or just keep quiet because of the perception that such comments could hurt their career opportunities within the field of conflict resolution training.

On the rare occasions when these issues are introduced for discussion with proper facilitation, they frequently take the discussion beyond the superficial level (the level typically reached) to a more meaningful discussion, one that has more likelihood of addressing and changing attitudes that promote conflict.

Though most models still do not treat informal discussions during breaks as an integral component of the workshop, I have seen some facilitation styles that aim to expand and encourage informal discussions in the context of structured workshops. These include (1) ending an activity before a break with a relevant and a thought-provoking topic, intended to generate enough excitement that participants will continue discussing it during the break; (2) facilitation with conscious awareness of the importance of informal discussions, including getting involved with some of these discussions during breaks as a part of the role of the workshop guide; and (3) encouraging participants to critique aspects of conflict resolution workshop practice by initiating discussions of issues that are perceived to be improper under normal conditions.

*Stereotypes and Myths and Culture and Realities*

How are issues of cultural and social difference addressed within workshops?

*Stereotypes* and *myths* play a significant role in situations where there are serious divisions among communities. These stereotypes and myths are positive and exaggerated when they are about one's own community and negative and insulting when about others. They maintain and promote the existing divisions among communities as well as the conflict. Activities that challenge such stereotypes and myths are an important and necessary element of an effective conflict resolution workshop.

At the same time, when the conflict is between ethnicities and nations from different cultures, members of each group expect space to exercise their own *culture* and would like their own culture to be seen and respected by others. It is also important and necessary to address culture in conflict resolution workshops, taking into consideration the practices, beliefs, values, and lifestyles generally shared by members of each community involved in the conflict. In addition to culture, social *realities* also have to be taken into careful consideration while designing and implementing peace initiatives. Social realities are facts one has to deal with, and hiding them beneath the surface by branding them as myths does not serve the objective of long-term peace.

Stereotypes and myths, interpreted from a different conceptual framework, generally contain some form of useful information about how people live, or culture, and how things are, or social realities. For example, "women are stronger than men" is a myth, but to think that it is always a myth misses the wider truth that women can be stronger in many aspects of life and these aspects are not given prominence in a male-dominant world, where men keep the sole authority of definition. Here is the tension in how this conflicting pair is handled in conflict resolution workshops: if workshop guides seeks to address stereotypes and myths by providing counter examples, they risk diminishing or disrespecting something that is important to someone about their culture or neglecting a reality that should be dealt with. Particularly problematic is the case where counter examples are the exception or the special case and not the general population.

In workshops I have been part of, I have seen statements such as "Sinhalese cannot live in the East of Sri Lanka,"[4] "Westerners are rich,"[5] and "Sri Lankans are lazy"[6] discussed as stereotypes and dismissed as myths. However, this overly simple technique of rejecting stereotypes without exploring their roots and wider context can lead to an opposite but still incorrect set of stereotypes. More importantly, opportunities are missed to explore alternative ways of thinking about the "stereotype" information, carrying the discussion forward to address such concerns as "Sinhalese (as well as Tamils and Muslims) cannot live feely in the East of Sri Lanka," "people in the Western world have a fairly high standard of living while the majority in the third world are involved with a bitter struggle for survival," and " 'lazy' is an incorrect interpretation of the cultural trait of having a relaxed approach toward time."

A conflict resolution workshop held in Eastern Province of Sri Lanka with a group of voluntary social workers in February 2002 shows a way out. There, the stereotypes and myths were not discussed in isolation as a separate topic but as an integral part of a discussion covering all four themes: stereotypes, myths, culture, and social realities. This integrated approach brought more clarity to each of the subjects and to the activities of the workshop.

*Career Needs and Community Peace Needs*

What are the motivations and desired ends of the workshop guides, and what are the consequences for the work?

One response to the violence of the ongoing war is a search for nonviolent methods of resolving the conflict, including conflict resolution workshops. Yet, for all the good intentions, all the contradictions I have discussed so far come together in one final paradox.

The increase in available funds during the 1990s has led to an increase in demands for the services of organizations offering conflict resolution workshops in Sri Lanka. In addition to whatever peace benefits this has brought, there is also a side effect that training and facilitating conflict resolution workshops is becoming a profession with opportunities in Sri Lanka.

Conflict resolution workshops in Sri Lanka provide attractive career opportunities for workshop guides in both national and international NGOs, with opportunities to gain training and experiences at an international level. They also provide a rich environment for academic research. The problem with this development is this: Investment in a particular approach to conflict resolution workshops has created and attracted a pool of professionals committed to that approach, *whether or not it is in the best interest of the people being served.* The emergence of *career opportunities* linked to conflict resolution workshop training has contributed significantly to the establishment of the field as the assumed practice for promoting an alternative to violence.

Experience suggests, however, that the current standards of conflict resolution workshop professionalism do not always serve the ultimate goal of peace in Sri Lanka. At times community peace needs demand, within the context of a prolonged violent conflict, that workshop guides expand the boundaries of their work beyond the workshop premises. For example, instead of the professional distance dictated by conflict resolution workshop roles, the workshop guide needs to enter into close interactions with the participants when working on a long-term basis in actual community settings. Such shifts contribute two essential things: greater trust and respect between participants and the workshop guide, and the opportunity for the workshop guide to gain detailed contextual knowledge of the conflict in question and the community culture behind it. Before the workshop guide's leadership in a long-term project can be accepted, the participants need assurance that he or she is genuinely interested in community peace. This will be apparent to them if he or she has the deep knowledge of the conflict mentioned above, and if he or she has demonstrated a willingness to share the same dangers and to take the same risks as participants by living with them during some or all of the project.

An example of how this process was done well was a 2001/2002 CARE project developing a women's network in the Eastern province in Sri Lanka. The workshop guide ran a series of workshops with a group of women from that region. She developed a close relationship with the members of the group during this long period by visiting them frequently, staying with them in their villages, spending time with them in their day-to-day activities, and helping in their personal needs whenever possible. This degree and kind of participation in the lives of the participants is in sharp contrast to the standard style of strict workshop-based professionalism.

The tension within this pair of approaches exists between the workshop guide's professional success (his or her career needs) and maximum positive impacts from his or her intervention for peace. At one of these extremes, the concern that dominates is how to keep working. This is not deliberate, but is the natural by-product of the "frame" constructed by the practice: to be successful, and so get more work, a workshop guide must follow the guidelines, norms, and work styles of existing conflict resolution workshop practice—and those frames have been set mainly by international NGOs, international trainers, and international consultants. In contrast, to be successful in the larger context, that of fostering peace, presenters need to be accountable and responsible to the community as represented by the participants, requiring a willingness to adapt standard practice to local conditions, based on a collective—guide and participant—critical evaluation of the practices as they apply to the situation at hand.

The problem arises because accountability and adaptability seem to have an insignificant, or at times negative, impact on the careers of presenters. In order to avoid the negative career consequences of straying from standard practice, many presenters working in Sri Lanka avoid the flexibility and engagement that might make the peace effort more successful. Experimentation and taking the side of the community are easily interpreted as characteristics of rebellion against the comfortable lifestyles of current professional practice.

At the other extreme, the concern that dominates is how to maximize the impact of the workshop in the community. Individuals and groups whose main concerns are community peace needs tend to consider conflict resolution workshops as exercises primarily serving the community of conflict resolution professionals, and not the most useful activity for creating peace. This approach portrays the image of "peace building" as a "holy" exercise, which should not be mixed with "unholy" motives of personal gain. As a result, these community peace workers reject altogether the systematic conflict transformation tools available through the vehicle of conflict resolution workshops, not leaving themselves the option of using them, even after adaptation.

The two are not, however, irreconcilable. If funding leads the way by expanding the type of training workshop guides receive, a shift could be made to develop and reward "specialized peace workers" instead of "specialized workshop presenters." The roles and skills of these professionals would include training and facilitation, but would also include knowledge of how to notice and adapt to the needs of the community at hand. They would be expected to engage in many community peace activities besides conducting workshops.

ANALYSIS AND CONCLUSION

My identification and discussion of these conflicting approaches demonstrate some of the tensions inherent in the introduction of the foreign conflict resolution model into the context of the Sri Lankan conflict and some of the ways that Sri Lankan workshop guides have attempted to reconcile those tensions. Further research into these adaptive behaviors may indicate ways of creating nonviolent conflict resolution models that are uniquely Sri Lankan. Specific areas of research that may yield positive effects are:

• Reasons for the dominance of the *being positive, equity, facilitator, agenda, workshop time, stereotypes/myths,* and *career needs* elements over the *critical analysis, impact, trainer, content, informal discussion, culture and social realities,* and *community needs* elements of the seven conflict pairs.

• The impact of the availability of time and money on the decision of which of element of each pair to emphasize in a given workshop.

• The role of funding in how conflict resolution workshops are designed and run: which practices are rewarded and sustained, and what would it take to change them?

• What should be the guidelines of this process of transformation?

Sri Lanka is a country torn apart by conflict, and creative nonviolent solutions are essential. The conflict resolution workshop is one of these possible solutions. However, for its full potential to be realized, the priority of conflict resolution practice must shift away from unconsciously serving the interests of the conflict resolution "industry" in general and the professional workshop guides in particular toward the interests of the community being served, and the assumptions the practice is based on must be native to Sri Lankan culture. By drawing on the advantages of all the elements I have detailed here, conflict resolution workshops in Sri Lanka can better serve the one goal that all agree on: a real and meaningful peace.

# 16 A Conversation with Hasshan Batts

Hasshan Batts is a young African American conflict resolution practitioner who served on the staff of a community mediation agency in North Carolina. Quickly elevated to positions of leadership in his organization and nationally in the field, Hasshan is a member of the board of directors of the National Association for Community Mediation (NAFCM) and a participant in PRASI's seminar-by-conference-call, the weekly conversations that gave rise to this anthology. We asked him to present his experiences because we recognized that his was a fresh and perceptive voice, addressing familiar problems in insightful ways.

The names of some of the other participants as well as case details have been changed for reasons of confidentiality. Pseudonyms are indicated with an asterisk the first time they appear. Hasshan, S.Y., Jerome, and Greta are African American; all other participants in the conversation are white.

**S.Y.:** Hasshan, how did you get so involved in mediation?

**Hasshan:** I was in North Carolina, I saw a sign advertising mediation training. Mediation training was the kind of activity I wanted to pursue. Not necessarily the conflict resolution part of it, but just getting the exposure, getting the volunteer hours behind me. Putting something on my résumé. So I took the training. It was interesting. It was interesting stuff. I didn't buy into it. I mean, at this point—years later—I still don't buy into it necessarily.

I took the training. I did some volunteer mediation. Later on they asked me to be on the board—this is the conflict resolution center in Hickory,

North Carolina. They asked me to be a board member; I was still somewhat young, and I was impressed, you know, with being a board member. Happy to be involved. I got involved and tried to bring a different perspective. There was no one black on the board. Not one black involved in the organization. And in a county that's probably . . . I would say 13, 14 percent black.

So I'm on the board. And then they got a contract to go into the school system. And they needed some help. They needed a youthful perspective, as they said. That's what they considered me. So they brought me in because these were all middle-aged white women.

**S.Y.:** They probably needed a black perspective, too.

**Hasshan:** Yeah. Even though they were more focused on youth. They brought me in. These are thirty-five-, forty-five-year-old white women, I would say. And we did some work. We trained the whole ninth grade at the school—the High Brighten High School, which is in an interesting county in the area. And the kids were real receptive to me. The way that I approached them—I came dressed as myself. I brought who I was to the table. And the kids were receptive, and it impressed the director. So she later said, "Well, you need to be doing this full-time." I was working at a psychiatric hospital. She said, "You need to be doing this full-time with us."

So that's how I got introduced into the conflict resolution as an employee. I started off as the coordinator of youth services, or something like that. And the center was relatively young. It was about three years old when I got involved. It had just splintered off from a parent organization. So I helped build the center, in terms of programming, networking with the community, funding stream. And the center was really built around youth services. I mean, we had some court money coming in from the administrative offices of the courts here in North Carolina, that all of the centers get. But our funding stream came to youth services. When I came on, the budget increased significantly. I was involved with so many different things. It got to the point at the center where the ED was working maybe twenty hours, sixteen hours a week—I think. I was the only full-time employee. I was working forty hours a week.

The executive director at that time wanted me to become the executive director. This was after about three years. She presented it to the board. And for some reason that I can't explain the board disagreed with it. They didn't want me to be the executive director. They felt that we still needed her. She's an attorney. But her time had dropped so much that I was the one representing the center everywhere. I was writing grants. I was doing most of the workshops, in terms of youth and community and diversity. She was more involved with business mediations and facilitations—corporations and county employee stuff.

In the end they decided to go with a circular management model, where we had three directors—three co-directors, two of which were part-time. One was sixteen hours, one was maybe thirty hours, and I was forty hours. That was also an interesting experience for me. So we did that for a while. I attended some conferences. Got involved with PRASI and that really helped me. I met a lot of people at the NCPCR [National Conference on Peacemaking and Conflict Resolution] conference that kind of changed my perspective and let me know I wasn't alone in the field. Because here in North Carolina, I always felt alone. I mean, I was involved—heavily involved—with the mediation community in North Carolina. I did some things with youth in the state, set up some youth conferences, did some facilitation projects in the western end of the state. And I was always out there alone. And the models that we would use were, from my point of view, always Eurocentric. They weren't reality based. They didn't take other cultural perspectives into consideration. They didn't take the spiritual needs of black people into consideration, the emotional needs of black people into consideration. It was all more centered on Europeans. And I saw that I was studying a lot and looking for an answer. All of this to make sense, to resolve problems I confronted in the job.

I had seen so much violence, and I had seen so much conflict that I was trying to find a way for people to peacefully work out their issues. But I was just discouraged, I guess you could say. A lot of our clients came in because of a court diversion contract, a juvenile court diversion contract. And one thing that I found real interesting occurred when the kids would get arrested. Very few of my clients were black. Very few of the people we mediated with were black, even when we did workshops, we got very few black referrals. Then when I looked at the boot camps, there were more blacks, but still the majority were not black youth.

Then when you go into the prisons and the jails, it was 80 or 90 percent of the kids are black. And when you're talking to these kids about what they are incarcerated for, a lot of it was the same stuff that these kids were coming to mediation with me for. I mean, one kid came to mediation one time because he shot another kid. That was the most difficult mediation I ever had, because of *my* stuff. He shot a twelve year old. He's in mediation. This kid is getting no time. And I had to catch myself. I really wanted to write an article about that case. (S.Y. has been trying to encourage me to write articles for the longest time.) I had a white co-mediator, and I told her we needed to write our different perspectives about this mediation because so many things were different, in terms of the racial issues involved in the mediation. Just him [the boy] sitting there upset me. Because he shot another kid. He was crippled, I mean, for life. And it was a hybrid of a victim-offender mediation, because the victim's family was present, and it was a terrible experience for me.

And it just represented the whole system to me. He seemed unaffected. Yet here was a kid who can't walk, who can't talk because of his actions. And society told him it was okay. How does the saying go? Young, white, and twenty-one, or something like that. And my co-mediator—though she was frustrated—she didn't feel what I felt. She didn't see what I saw in that mediation.

So that was kind of the climax of my experience as a mediator. I came to understand that mediation is just another tool of oppression. And it's used by the system to meet its needs. In the case of owner-tenant relations, you have first the relations between "have-nots" and people with power, an issue that nobody really wants to address. This is the case whether you have victim-offender situation—depending on the circumstances, whether you have community mediation or barking dogs. Especially once the court system is involved. Once the court system becomes involved, there's a power imbalance. And we go into the mediation with the goal being harmony. Perfection. A balance of honesty. As Doctor Jones [Bill Jones is a retired professor who teaches oppression theory] taught me: cuss and discuss. We don't allow people to truly put their concerns on the table.

One thing I find interesting about practicing is that black parties are relieved when they see black mediators. This fact is more important than any consideration of models: getting people to come to the table when they give black parties the authority. In my three years of experience, I have found that black people often will say that only a black mediator will understand their problem. As S.Y. said to me the other day, "Everything is a model." Even the old things that her grandma used to say.

There are models that we use that aren't models that we have tested in the field with communities of color. So we ask what do you do with models that work with black problems or black disputants versus the Eurocentric models that we have encountered. I have just found that black and white people are different in the way that they see things. Our Eurocentric models have ground rules: we bring parties to the table; one person speaks at a time; let's not get too boisterous; keep your voices down; and all those things that even precede any talk. Not to say that we are a pack of wolves, but I find that we as people of color are more animated; we speak more with our hands. We may even stand up and raise our voices in a session. And that in itself is a part of the conflict. I have been black for twenty-seven years and that may not be a long time but it is an eternity, I guess you can say, as far as my attitude is involved. Black people do not approach conflict resolution from a logical perspective; we are more emotional.

However, this is a dialogue and I would like to hear what others have to say.

**Peter\*:** This is Peter and I would like to say that I agree that our white mediators are more leery of emotion, tend to be more restrictive, and try to have more well-defined guidelines and ground rules. And that I clearly see.

I guess the question I have is in terms of what defines a successful mediation. In terms of many of the white clients, that is problem solving. Let's get those issues and find out what positions are. I guess I am hearing in a little bit of what you are saying that there may not be as much of that for African Americans. That's not as important to move right through to what is the problem, what is the solution, but instead to really take the time to deal with the emotion around the relationship. I am really curious about your perspective and experience concerning that.

**Hasshan:** I have found that the voice of "how come?"—how come that created a conflict? for instance—is more holistic. Even in terms of a mediator's role, we talk about the word neutral. Peter and I have ridden together, Peter and I have discussed these terms, and I still don't know if I quite understand it.

**S.Y.:** I want to offer Peter one way of looking at this. And that is, most traditional mediations and trainings include the practice of separating the parties and the problems. And I think that separating the parties and the problems may have different meanings because of different worldviews in different communities. That practice does not particularly fit some communities' different philosophical worldviews. When you try to talk to a party in those terms, they look at you as if to say, *What* are you talking about?

**Jerome:** This is Jerome and I just wanted to say that I agree with a lot of the things that you said, Hasshan. I've run across those myself, here in Pittsburgh in the Center. I also am trying to get the Center to deal with the problem of ground rules. Mediators have an agreement-driven process: the mediation depends on whether you reach an agreement or not.

The other thing that gets me is whether so-called neutrality is in fact possible. I've always had that question myself. Can someone be neutral? You walk into a room and, myself, I've never found myself to be neutral. I've always looked at some one and thought, *They may have this issue.* And I've trained mediators and I've trained them *not* to be neutral because I don't believe that to be possible. You understand that you may have an opinion but you keep that to yourself. I'll give you an example: I was mediating with a white mediator and it was a case between a black couple and a white couple having these problems. The black woman said, "I think they are racist. I think they were born racist." And the white mediator said, "Are you sure?" And she said, "What do you mean am I sure? Yeah, I am positive."

What I started to talk about with other mediators I know is whether or not the questions we may ask in a case involving race can possibly be neutral. No mediator wants to be unsure of his questions and then say something racist. What I try to do in a case like that is to say, "If you say it was racist, then it was racist. Maybe as you work through it down the road, you may find out that what the person said wasn't racist, that there was some other intent to what was said." But training mediators I find that making these distinctions is a difficult task. Nonetheless, our mediators are starting to look at this issue. Most of them tend to assume that they are not racist or don't intend to be, but often they encounter these problems.

**S.Y.:** Jerome, can you self-identify so people will know who you are?

**Jerome:** Oh, I am Jerome.

**S.Y.:** I mean self-identification and ethnicity.

**Jerome:** African American.

**S.Y.:** This is S.Y. and I want to share two quick things and then I will be quiet for a while. Number 1, Jerome, is that the theory that we have formulated concerning this problem is the believing game. We tell mediators that they have to believe what they hear. The minute they question whether a remark is racist, they can silence the party and shut it down. That is what we call the believing game. You've got to believe what you hear no matter how difficult it is to believe.

**Stewart\*:** May I ask a question about that? I'm not sure about the procedures for working with a party when the party says, I feel that the other party is racist. Obviously, paraphrasing back that you feel discriminated against, you feel that you have been oppressed in some way [isn't adequate]. What do you do when one party accuses the other of racism and you, the mediator, believe the charge? I wasn't sure exactly what Hasshan meant in his response.

**S.Y.:** I raised the believing game as a skill building tool for mediators. The mediator engages in the believing game to determine whether the accusing party's perception accords with that of the mediator himself. At no point in time does the believing game require the mediator to draw out the allegedly racist incident. Of course, another situation exists, if A says he needs to discuss the race issue because he believes his neighbor is racist and does not want to leave until he has settled the matter for himself, as a mediator I tell the accusing party that I would like to raise the issue of race so that the two parties might discuss it.

I want to address a second issue, concerning neutrality. I have discovered that sometimes clients differ in their perception of the mediator's neutrality. A person of color who perceives disinterestedness on the part of the mediator often, in my experience, thinks that the mediator does not care. When that happens, communication is shut down.

**Hasshan:** And if you buy into a more Afro-centric perspective, then clients of color must perceive the mediator's concern because of who they are. If I take part in a court-referred mediation concerning a custody issue, divorce, or truancy then I as an African American mediator can't be neutral. I as an African American have some stake in how this community resolves this issue. I am a part of this community, and it affects all of us. In the Western model, the mediator presents the issues and offers to help the clients resolve them. I am not saying that African American mediators should impose their values upon African American clients, but I think that such mediators must see their mediation in a broad community context, particularly when dealing with young Hispanic and black people. They are particularly tuned into a sense of their place in the present-day world. I don't often see the transformative model in use.

**Victor***: Hi, this is Victor, and I just joined the call a couple of minutes ago. I just wanted to touch on a couple of points, if that's all right. First, as a community mediator in four states over fifteen years, I don't think that there is a model for mediation that is oblivious to its effects on a community. I don't think it is fair to say that there is a model out there that doesn't care about the effects on community. I know that many people started doing community mediation because they cared about their community. I self identify as an Anglo, but I don't think that that changes the fact that I have a stake in the community.

I am with you, Hasshan, when you raise questions about the issue of neutrality. A mediator is not neutral when he says that anything that goes on in this room is cool by me. I for one don't hold that to be the case. Another thing that I wanted to chime in on, and that I think you are right on is the existence of different styles of conflict. One book concerning this issue is Thomas Kochman's *Black and White Styles in Conflict*. He was studying desegregation in many cities in the North and South, and he found that the accepted social expectation in most places was that if you wanted to come to the meetings, you could not raise your voice. That was an issue for some communities, especially communities of color in which you don't divorce the emotion from the content. I think there is an extent to which many folks of different colors, shapes, or ethnicities have adapted their styles of mediation to their environment and clients. And I certainly agree that in the more formalized processes, in courts and in EEOC [Equal Employment Opportunity Commission] mediations, the mediation takes place where some folks demand that you have to play by their rules to play in the forum. I think that is problematic. I am definitely with you on that front as well.

And I think it is our responsibility to keep educating ourselves and each other around the various ways that people participate in mediation. I am not sure whether that lends itself to a model. The more that I do this [work], the more I wonder whether there is a model anywhere? The more I do this [work], the more confused I get when I try to label models and pin them down because I don't know what the hell I am doing sometimes. Thanks for letting me talk.

**Judy***: Victor, you are always refreshing. This is Judy Warner; I work with Hasshan. I just wanted to go back to Jerome's comment about someone's raising a question of racism; what do you do?

**S.Y.:** My experience around someone perceiving a statement as racist is that sometimes when the mediator hasn't set the tone for the discussion of race or ethnicity as naturally as any other part of the conversation, then it doesn't come out until caucus, and then in caucus when it comes out it depends again on who's present. The way that gets played out is that you go down a list and invite the party to ask a couple of questions around the topic: whether it is important to you to have this discussion, do you want to have this discussion here, or what is it that you would like. And in cases where it is a long-lasting relationship, it is more important to address it than when that is not the case: whether this be in the workplace or neighborhood, for instance.

And so I think that first the mediator has to convey his possession of adequate knowledge and confidence to be able to address the racial issues that come up. If he possesses these elements, the disputants may be able to see that racial difference plays a part in the analysis and resolution of a dispute. It is often quite telling when I talk to someone and they say that race never came up in an EEOC matter. Well, it may have come up but you didn't catch it. The racial issue plays itself out in different ways.

**Carol***: This is Carol. I am a white woman from the Midwest and there are a couple of things that I want to say. I think that it would be great if the mediation community had a deep discussion about the word neutral because I have stopped using it actually. There is also a woman in Massachusetts who has done a lot of work—name is Leah Wing—around the intersection between mediation and oppression. She says that you do whatever it is that you need to do so that each side can tell its story, whatever that story is.

In the work that I do with white mediators I try to teach them to see that they are white mediators, because as white people we don't have to think about our culture or identity as people of color do. So we have to figure out that we have an identity. Then the question I have concerns the types of cases that come up: how some people perceive mediation as a tool of oppression when they become connected to the justice system.

I have had at least one case like that where I was concerned about that issue. Recently I have begun to get a different angle on cases where I get people from a subsidized housing complex where there are people of color. The regulations have changed so that property managers can evict people who are not necessarily convicted of a crime but connected to criminal activity in some way. The residents have been calling me for help because they feel that there are generalizations being made about them as a group of people and about their situations. They need to be heard in order to be understood as individuals. They will admit that there are people in their families who are connected to criminal activity, but these tenants feel that these particular cases are not fully understood. So I am wondering if you have any suggestions for dealing with both the property managers who are concerned about safety and the residents who are concerned about safety as well as fairness and justice.

**Hasshan:** Let me refer to what I said about mediation being another tool of oppression. What I find is that oftentimes parties of color, blacks in particular, view mediation as a part of the system. And we have developed a lack of trust for the system because of historical circumstances. For whatever reason we have perpetuated this distrust from generation to generation, and I think a lot of time has to be spent in the field building that trust. We focus a lot on not being perceived as a part of the school system, not part of the court system. That way I think we can address a part of the organizational level. We don't support the school, we don't endorse the schools. We don't support the courts and we don't endorse the courts. And therefore the outcome is affected. I am more known for asking questions than giving the answers to the questions. And with the housing policies, I know the issue you raised is part of an ongoing debate and no one has solved it yet. I am curious to hear what others have to say on that one.

**Peter:** Going back to what was said about neutrality one of the things I have struggled with is that for the last two years I have been a part of an antiracist team, doing diversity work but realizing that you need to move deeper, to develop an antiracist identity. I have to realize that as a white mediator I am supporting a racist society if I am neutral. You cannot be neutral about racism. It is a struggle in your own life to begin to understand what impact white privilege played in your life and how difficult it is to have antiracist identity.

And then, I think about how I can encourage mediators as mediators to begin to understand the whole analysis of racism and understanding how white privilege plays into that. And then the next layer when you get down, then, to your clients you find that mediating with a black and a white client is so incredibly difficult. And I don't know the answer. This discussion has stirred up a lot though in that as a white mediator where does the antiracist identity that I am trying to cultivate come into my practice? In the short period of time that I have with clients, how can I actively promote antiracism, actively try to reconstruct race relations?

**S.Y.:** would like to reply to what you've said, Peter, but I would like to take some responsibility for a dynamic I think I have set up on the call, and I want to address it. I asked Jerome if he would self-identify because I know him and I know who he is and I wanted to take the mystery out of him as an African American male.

But I want people to feel comfortable. I haven't asked anyone else to self-identify, so I sort of imposed upon Jerome because of the relationship that I have with him, and I think that it was coming out that he was an African American male but it hadn't been stated. It also gave me a chance to build a connection between him and Hasshan, because I don't know whether they know one another. So I want everyone to feel comfortable and I was concerned about that and thought that I should speak it because any identity is worth a lot and being a soccer mom is a great thing. So I want everyone to have a sense of comfort or tell me where you lost your comfort, so that as we build our network we can help explore this.

The other reality is that sometimes it is very tough to have cross talk amongst multicultural groups. This concerns what you can say and what you can't say and what you say here you might hear some place else. And so there is sensitivity around what I say. People wonder whether I am just expressing my feelings or am I educating them in the process.

And that takes me to the point of what came up with you, Carol, about what Leah does. When people of color come in for a mediation and they realize that not only are they there to try to solve a problem but they are there to be educated, it becomes very difficult. And that is where the inquiry comes in. Are you sure, is this real, are you sure you see that? Then people have to get into defending themselves and I think that it is about education.

People want to know about the mediator's sincerity, but they always face the problem of separating the party from the person. Just because they see me, a black woman, as the mediator, I feel I shouldn't have to sit and educate them about race. So the problem becomes convoluted.

I'd love to go on longer, but I want to acknowledge the time frame. It's about 12:40 and Hasshan has to leave us about 12:45.

**Hasshan:** S.Y., I can stay until one and still make it to temple.

**S.Y.:** Oh, wonderful.

**Hasshan:** This is so good, let's keep it going, I will just rush down the highway.

**S.Y.:** Oh no, you cannot be rushing down the highway! No, uh uh, I am not going for that!

**Hasshan:** I can stay until one; it's so good to be talking like this.

For years, I felt like this little man on an island in the field of conflict resolution. I was doing research and taking certain courses and, even in terms of mentorship, there were many wonderful mentors in North Carolina because there is a strong mentorship in North Carolina, but there were no black mentors, which I felt personally is kind of what I needed, to make me aware of some of the pitfalls, the highs and the lows in the field, that I felt like I encountered. I don't want to sound as though it was a bad experience; it has been a wonderful experience.

**Greta*:** Can I add something here? I'm Greta. I am currently finishing up the conflict resolution program at a college in the South. I am in that semester where you are writing your thesis on doing an action project. And my focus, being an African American, is looking for models of African American or an Afrocentric style to conflict resolution. I have had some, well, not a lot of success in terms of finding other African Americans who are writing about the Afrocentric style of conflict resolution. I know that the African American church has a way of counseling people and taking on domestic and familial conflict. But I am looking for a broader way of doing that and there is some literature out there that says that still African American conflict resolution has to do with emotional conflict resolution. And one writer thinks that where the Western world uses logic the African American world uses emotion, and I couldn't wrap myself totally around that. I couldn't understand what he was meaning by that: if we go to a negotiation we are going to do this whole in your face kind of resolution to force the other party to deal with us on a realistic level. Now, in examining that I found it quite disturbing, just throwing it all out there that African Americans are emotional, that the only way they deal with their conflicts is through violence and emotion. So I just wanted to hear if anybody has something to say or to look at it in terms of doing research on it.

S.Y.: I find sometimes these characterizations don't hold true for lots of groups. The other day I had an Asian woman and a black woman in a mediation, and the Asian woman appeared to say: Look at me, look at me, look at me, look me in my eyes. And the black woman appeared to say: Talk to the hand. And so it is a situation where many of us were trained that Asian people may not want eye-to-eye contact, and that might be true in some situations and a lot of cases, but then the mediator encounters a difficult face-to-face problem. In this case, the Asian woman was married to a black man; I wondered if they hadn't learned some other ways of being from each other. And the mediation concerned her child, so she was particularly heated. This discussion raises questions about where a mediator can find the information and resources to think about such cases.

# 17 The Porvida Approach

*For Multicultural Respect and
Organizational Success*

ROBERTO VARGAS

I am a second generation Chicano, an American of Mexican and Indian heritage, and a product of my family's evolution. My father was born in California of Mexican immigrants and my mother emigrated from Mexico as a young adult. In English, my father's name translates into "Man who sees with vision." From him I learned to believe in myself. From my mother's family I learned about the power of love and to care for others. The result was a commitment I made as a youngster to dedicate my life to creating a better world. Within my Chicano indigenous cultural tradition, one becomes an elder at 52 years of age, the age I am now. Various responsibilities come with this milestone, including the responsibility of sharing of the experience one has accumulated over the years. From my cultural roots and my work as a community organizer, therapist, organizational psychologist, and ceremony leader, I offer several tools for community empowerment and social healing that I call the Porvida Approach. This strategy integrates healing wisdom and spirituality into organizational development work. It is relevant to all people who seek to inspire positive change on behalf of our culturally diverse communities or organizations and to professionals involved in conflict resolution or in advancing multicultural respect.

In Spanish, *por vida* means, "for life." More than twenty-five years ago I coined the term "porvida" to describe a philosophy deeply held by Chicano activists and healers, the life practice committed to advancing a better world.

We sometimes call it the good life or *la vida buena*, which to us means living with gratitude and joy and the purpose of manifesting love in all that we do. Living and working with a *porvida* consciousness one recognizes that our human essence is "life affirming and love seeking" and our human responsibility is to advance a society that supports justice, love, and respect. Given this orientation I developed the idea of *porvida activism* which is to pursue the evolution of a more caring culture and a better world. I also developed the Porvida Approach as a professional consultant strategy for people development and organizational change. Here I share the Porvida Approach as a consultant or facilitator strategy for people empowerment and organizational change.

This paper focuses on how the Porvida Approach was developed to provide insights into the dynamics of community empowerment within communities of color and the application of this approach to advancing multicultural understanding and respect. I provide an example of the use of the Porvida Approach to organizational development and end with a discussion of the relevancy of this approach to conflict resolution work.

I begin by reviewing the cultural and historical influences which shaped the development of this strategy.

## BRIEF HISTORY OF CHICANO DISCOVERIES

Chicanos are mostly thought of as Mexican Americans or Latinos. While we are members of both of these communities, many of us consider ourselves as indigenous Americans whose origins can be from any part of the Americas. We reside in the United States and seek to maintain a culture that honors the positive values of our ancestral influences, particularly of the values of family, balance, respect, and social justice. Beginning in the 1960s and through the 1980s many of us were involved in the movement for social justice and community service. I was an activist of this period and by the 1980s I recognized the need for a new type of leadership that applied attention to our cultural and spiritual potentials as well as our vision for social justice.

Many of us saw the necessity for a leadership orientation that was concerned not only about civil rights and social justice, but also with our human need to connect with spirit and to encourage respectful relationships among all people. Thus, more than twenty-five years ago, I began using the term *porvida* to mean "for life, love, spirit, and justice." I envisioned the use of the term "porvida" to capture the vision and a conscious way of living that would be "for life, love, and justice." In time porvida came to represent the worldview and practice of making all our actions and relations porvida—for life, love, and all this is positive. The inspiration for this orientation came from my life experience as a Chicano and my early activism in the field of mental health during which time we were developing theory and tools for people empowerment.

In 1973, as a young university student I co-founded a mental health center called El Centro de Salud Mental (hereafter El Centro) in Oakland, California, as part of La Clinica de la Raza. This center integrated cultural wisdom and counseling services to advance the healing and empowerment of Latino individuals and families. As one of the first such centers in the nation, El Centro provided us the opportunity to develop culturally based knowledge and tools for community organizing and healing. By healing I mean interventions that served to either resolve problems or advance personal and family well-being. From its inception, El Centro served us as a think tank and practice center to invent new approaches relevant for our community. Given our experience with institutional racism most of our staff shared a deep reservation about conventional mental health practice, which was largely based on a deficit paradigm. In other words, conventional mental health services focused on individual pathology, and as a result counseling services overly focused on seeking illness and largely ignoring strengthens and potential. We saw the necessity for a holistic model that appreciated our familial and cultural strengths and that recognized the social context in which we were surviving oppression and racism.

Familiar with our own realities, we sought to develop a mental health practice to heal those who had been damaged by racism and oppression. Given our experience we recognized that many of our community struggled with a sense of diminished self-esteem due to the negative messages received from the dominant culture, a dynamic we called EL NO. Because of the prevalence of this internalized oppression within our community, we sought to affirm the strengths of every individual to become self-confident and able to achieve success. As therapists and community educators we sought to empower—to build self-esteem, assist persons to resolve their immediate concerns, and equip them with skills to advance healing within their own families and communities.

In our work we were applying the principle "cultura cura" that culture heals. We saw the necessity of using cultural values and practices such as *familia,* respect, and courage to advance necessary healing. To apply these practices we offered within the context of our counseling services the options of home visitations, use of Spanish or English, family involvement, and the use of cultural or spiritual ceremonies. On occasions, given the spiritual needs indicated by a person or family, we used ritual or ceremony to compliment the counseling intervention. In these instances we sometimes recruited traditional community healers to assist us in our interventions.

In responding to the mental health needs of our community from a commitment to "do what works," we learned the power of integrating counseling, community learning, and cultural practices to advancing empowerment, community building, and group problem-solving. These accomplishments also reaffirmed our power as activists, that we could transform challenges into solutions and deeper wisdom for healing.

Several years later I left El Centro de Salud Mental. I had two principle reasons; new funding regulations for mental health services were beginning to restrict our creative approach and I had a desire to apply our tools to organizational development and leadership training. Actually, my time had come to take our learning regarding people empowerment and apply in within other arenas—more directly within the family as an involved parent and within my extended community as a spiritual guide. This began with the birth of my children.

With the birth of my first daughter I was immediately drawn to apply all my knowledge to raising her and then our next child to become self-confident and caring human beings. I coordinated with my wife so that I would care for our children during most of the week and use my weekends to facilitate planning retreats for organizations. This experience combined with others provided by the Creator resulted in a more profound connection to my indigenous origins and a deeper connection with the power of Spirit. This led me on to the path of becoming a ceremony leader in my community using ceremony to help families deepen their expression of love and commitment to advancing community well-being. I would assist families to transform their anniversaries, birthdays, or funerals into community experiences to nurture family unity, connection with spirit, and the expression of love. All these experiences fueled my passion to further develop the practice of porvida activism and the Porvida Approach for organizational development.

Over the years I directed my activism to empower families and communities to *be* more courageously for love and respect. This included helping communities to develop vision, plans, culture, and leadership directed toward advancing the greater vision of an "ideal world"—a sustainable world in which societies support the ability of all people to live healthy lives. Applied to organizational development this activist orientation became the Porvida Approach. My intention with this approach was to assist proactive organizations to become their best. This required working with an organization's board of directors, management team, and staff over a period of months or years to develop a culture of increased vision, courage, and respect. The strategy employed a combination of consultation sessions, workshops, and planning retreats in which each session provided an opportunity to address organizational development issues, facilitate learning regarding multicultural respect, and nurture inspiration. The intent and outcomes often included a clearer mission, deeper individual commitment to multicultural respect, increased mutual support, and the development of plans to better serve their diverse communities.

I will now discuss the essential elements that guide the Porvida Approach, beginning with the porvida worldview.

## THE PORVIDA WORLDVIEW

I believe we are born perfect beings with the purpose of discovering, manifesting, and evolving our perfection. We are not born inherently sinful but intrinsically porvida—for life, love, and respect. Our human path is to connect with and evolve our capacity to be more loving. We can do this by connecting more deeply with God, Spirit, or faith in our inherent goodness. While learning to be more loving and caring is our path, we must contend with the real challenges posed by the immature side of our human nature, our tendency toward ignorance, fear, and selfishness. Our challenge is to transform these personal tendencies within ourselves as we also confront their existence within fabric of our society in the forms of exploitation, oppression, and violence.

Our human challenge is to mature and manifest our perfection. This is where healing or transformation is often necessary. Healing is more than the curing of illness; it is also restoring our wholeness. Transformation is similarly facilitating the multiple levels of change required to get us on the path of becoming better persons. Both healing and transformation involve interacting with others so as to help them connect with their deeply held commitment to love self, others, or life. When we connect with this capacity to love we are more motivated to respect and actively care for others. We can do this by creating experiences for others that affirm their inherent goodness, expose them to the goodness in others, or encourage their personal development.

We are all born with this inherent goodness and to make the world better. We can do it by encouraging the development of others and seeking to develop a culture of more caring values and practices. Although this involves effort, it ideally becomes a labor of joy because it serves to manifest our purpose and help us grow. Within this context, cultural diversity provides us a tremendous treasure and resource. The growing diversity of our nation provides us a powerful menu of values and practices that can truly aid us in our human and social development. The prerequisites include understanding that our common purpose is a better society and world and an openness to learn from each other.

In our twenty-first century life, it is the responsibility of all professionals to engage in professionalism consistent with our porvida purpose. For me this involves continually asking myself, How can I advance people empowerment, social healing, and porvida consciousness as I facilitate meetings or assist organizations in their development? Consequently, I approach all consultation projects as an opportunity to offer organizations and their staff a means to become their best. This involves assisting them to develop the structure, relationships, and culture that can enable them to advance their most lofty goals. Similarly, assisting in conflict resolution provides the opportunity to assist persons to develop relationships and a culture that enables respectful dialogue. Respectful dialogue involves honoring the experience that each person brings and viewing conflicts as part of the natural process required to develop understandings and to grow our maturity.

## FROM RAZALOGIA TO PROACTIVE FACILITATION

Successful organizational development or conflict resolution work requires clear goals and an effective facilitator. Similarly, the Porvida Approach requires commitment to the evolutionary potential of all groups and skills in the practice of proactive facilitation. Typically, a facilitator serves as an impartial servant of the group ensuring that all voices are heard while guiding the group to address its objectives. The proactive facilitator desires more outcomes for the group's effort—that all aspects of the group experience serve to advance individual and group empowerment and overall social betterment. For this type of facilitation, I draw upon the goals and tools inherent to the community learning strategy popular within the Latino community called the Razalogia Approach and the practice of proactive facilitation that has evolved out of this application among multicultural communities.

Razalogia is a term coined by Francisco M. Hernandez, one of the early theorists of El Centro de Salud Mental, to describe a self-help community learning approach that we originated as Latinos and working-class people. Razalogia means "knowledge of and for the people." As a method of community learning, Razalogia is akin to the process of liberation education as advanced by such educators as Paulo Freire.[1] However, at the time we were not familiar with this tradition. We were simply young Chicano activists seeking to develop knowledge about ourselves, our community, and the practice of mental health that could assist us in empowering our communities.

In our effort to develop counseling methods meaningful to our community, we met regularly and in time began to systematically share of our experience. Our intent was to find insights about the influences that either undermined or contributed to our well-being, when, Francisco mirrored back to us that we were in fact engaged in a process of knowledge development. With this reflection, he unleashed within our group a tremendous reservoir of restrained power and creativity. We had all been socialized to believe that knowledge came from the dominant culture or intellectual elite who wrote the books and taught the university courses. Francisco informed us that the word education comes from the Latin word *educare,* which means "to draw from within" and that in our group conversations we were drawing from our individual and collective experience to create knowledge and understanding. Through this experience, we discovered how "oppressed" people could engage in a process that was both empowering and effective in developing relevant knowledge. For greater understanding of the Razalogia, note *Razalogia: Community Learning for a New Society.*[2]

I was moved by this experience to focus on evolving the Razalogia Approach as the art of facilitating for relationship building, group learning, and people empowerment. Through the practice of Razalogia, first among principally Latino communities throughout the United States, and then among multicultural communities both in the United States and in Canada and Sweden, did I and others discern many of the principles and techniques that made it a powerful tool for community building, people empowerment, and self-help problem-solving. Through this practice I also discovered the need to rename our Razalogia process to make the tools more accessible to non-Latinos. I used Proactive Facilitation to indicate the provision of meeting leadership for optimizing the power of groups to advance community betterment. Hereafter, as I write of Proactive Facilitation, please remember that its origins reside in the Razalogia Approach.

Proaction is the opposite of being reactive; it is ideally action in pursuit of one's vision; in other words, it is action seeking to make the ideal real. Proactive facilitation is providing group leadership to advance a group's power to address both immediate needs and its ideal potential. Four principles continually inform the practice of the proactive facilitator. (1) Ensure all voices are heard in the process of articulating needs and resolutions. Beginning with the invitation to the group meeting, the facilitator seeks to ensure that all voices of the community will be represented and an environment established that encourages the participation of all. (2) Seek to optimize the development of the individual and collective power that resides within the group. The facilitator applies special attention to develop the agenda, facilitate dialogue, document ideas, and engage participants in a way that fosters the development of individual and group power. (3) Encourage the process of relationship and community building. The facilitator mindfully provides multiple opportunities for participants to engage in personal sharing that develops relationships of trust and community. (4) Use strategic questions to encourage group members to draw from their experience and surface understandings "of and for" their community.

Here is brief example of how these principles are applied. I responded to a request to facilitate a session of culture workers who were planning to organize an event to lift the political consciousness of youth. I began by asking questions about their purpose to ensure that all relevant persons were invited to the planning meeting. With their input I developed an agenda and then later guided their meeting process toward addressing outcomes, which included a plan for the upcoming event, deeper relationships within the group, and increase clarity of their larger vision. Although it was not explicit, until I asked the questions, their desired outcome was more than just a single event, but to develop a means of involving youth in political advocacy work over time. For this reason, it was important to use their initial meeting to deepen the mutual trust and understanding that could support their ability to be more effective in their ongoing youth work.

Essential to the proactive approach is the conocimiento principle, which teaches facilitators how to develop an atmosphere of trust, communication, and group. There is no equivalent English word for the Spanish word "*conocimiento*," which means "getting to know one another by each sharing of self." The conocimiento principle reminds us of the necessity to address "relationship before task." Within this context group meetings are started with specific questions posed to the group that will facilitate the relationship and trust building required to be effective in their tasks. Questions to use might include, Where are you from? What is your cultural background? What are your expectations for this meeting? Or, for groups with longer histories, one might begin with questions such as, What is going great or could be going better? What is your vision for our project? What experience do you bring to our project?

When two individuals share conocimiento, they initiate the beginning of mutual interest that fosters rapport, deepens communication, and develops trust. Magic literally occurs when a group meeting begins with questions that foster rapport. You see relationships develop, sharing deepen, and participants become more committed to each other and the group's success. The conocimiento principle outlines a formula that asserts power as its desired outcome. Power comes from the Latin word "*posse*," which means "to be able." Essentially our objective is to lift the group's power or ability to accomplish its goals. The individual becomes more powerful because he or she has developed or strengthened relationships that can offer experience, learning, and mutual support. Similarly, the group is more empowered because it has developed internal relationships of community in which it is more aware of its collective experience and has also evolved increase commitment to each other and to common goals.

This conocimiento and question-asking process is also essential to diversity work. To develop multicultural respect among groups, people must be provided the opportunity to share and hear each other's stories. This can be accomplished by inviting participants to ask each other questions that reveal their cultural experience, for example, Where were you born? How was it growing up? What was your first experience with a person of color or a white person? How has it been being a person of color in this organization? Informed by the Proactive Approach, the facilitator creates strategic opportunities to invite responses to such questions that foster multicultural understanding, connect group members, and clarify the diverse resources available to their team.

DEEP PURPOSE AND CEREMONY

Given a porvida orientation, one's vision is for a better world for all people. I believe this world, society, or community is created in the here and now, when we choose to relate to each other and make decisions that manifest love. The political, institutional, and system change required to advance our vision requires long-term attention. Yet, at the same time we must encourage the cultural change that makes the vision of our desired world immediately present within our families, organizational environments, and communities. We must learn how to courageously express our love in all we do in our present. To address this need, I found it essential to integrate into my facilitation and organizational develop work the use of ceremony.

Within all cultures there are rituals used to aid individuals in connecting to their purpose and to mark special family or community occasions. Within my indigenous tradition, we use a particular form of ceremony to facilitate our connection to spirit or to encourage the sharing of love among family, friends, or community. Guided by a porvida perspective, I use the practice of ceremony to create the opportunity for personal and group transformation. Here proactive facilitators optimize the power of their role to guide group dialogue or planning and to encourage group members to share heart words that connect participants with their capacity to love. I first describe how ceremony is facilitated within family and community, to illustrate how it is applied when doing organizational development work.

Within every circle of family and friends there are typically several persons who by virtue of their commitment or talents possess the ability to bring people together to share heart words. When they do this they can turn ordinary family gatherings into ceremonies that encourage wellness, love, and inspiration for all participants. In our Chicano tradition we call this doing *ceremonia,* and the occasion is characterized by the use of the unity circle, sage burning, and the sharing heart words to create an experience where participants feel their connection to their spirit and each other. The gathering can be to celebrate a birthday or anniversary or to honor the graduation of a student.

At an appropriate time, the facilitator brings participants together for a unity circle. In our tradition there is then the burning of sage, which signifies the creation of sacred time and space to which we are inviting our ancestors, our spirit, and the Creator. Typically, there is the sharing of prayers, which sets forth the context for the circle, which is to recognize our loved ones who are celebrating their birthday, anniversary, or accomplishment. Establishing this context, the facilitator invites participants to share their words of appreciation or their well wishes to the person(s) being honored. This is when the magic really happens. Participants are inspired to deeply connect with and articulate their feelings to the honoree. To many witnessing this degree of sharing further connects them to their spirit, and they too find themselves expressing inspiring words of respect and love. The outcome for many is a feeling of spirit connection, love, hope, and renewed commitment to family, community, and social betterment. Growth and healing occur in these circles as persons find the courage to share feelings of love, respect, and forgiveness.

What is the relevance of ceremony to social change work, organizational development, or conflict resolution? To create the change desired in the world we need be the change. To be a force of caring and love in the world, we need an environment around us that nurtures our ability to be and express love. To assist groups or organizations to be more transformative in their dialogue or conflicts we must foster cultures where people can access their love and communicate from a place of respect. Porvida ceremony uses ritual to advance this form of inspiration and cultural development.

When the aspects of porvida are combined with ceremony, the work of organizational development, or the teaching of conflict resolution, the outcomes are powerful. Using appropriate ritual for the group can transform an organizational planning retreat into a powerful experience of personal and team growth. Participants can be invited to bring to a retreat several items that symbolize their source of inspiration for the inspiration table, then the retreat is begun with a ceremony that involves participants sharing items the items they brought. Participants will get to know each other deeper and faster and will feel inspired to be more courageous in their subsequent sharing. Or, a conference of community activists can begin with a ceremony or prayer that involves persons from various spiritual beliefs or nonbeliefs to begin fostering an environment that encourages respect for diversity and courageous optimism. Repeatedly, I have witnessed an opening ceremony create a safe space for participants to remind each other of their higher purpose. I remember the occasion when tensions arose within such a conference. A participant known for his quietness called for a break, saying "like we said in our opening prayer, let's remember to respect each other as we do good work today, so let's take a break." After the break, cooler heads and more connected hearts were able to transform the evolving conflict into a learning opportunity.

The Porvida Approach integrates proactive facilitation and ceremony as tools to enable groups to become learning organizations in which all members commit to doing their part to improve themselves, the organization, and community. Several years ago, I had the opportunity to co-facilitate a series of conversations involving community activist leaders from throughout the country. The objectives of these four-day retreats included evolving a clearer vision of the society we desire to create and increasing connection between activists from such diverse field areas as civil rights, environmental protection, philanthropy, labor, and so on. Key to the success of these gatherings was use of the Porvida Approach, particularly the use of ceremony. We documented the specifics of our method and the results in *Movement Building for Transformative Change*.[3]

Next, I provide a case example of how these tools were applied to assist an organization with issues to become a highly effective and impactful multicultural team.

## DOING ORGANIZATIONAL DEVELOPMENT: THE APPLICATION OF THE PORVIDA APPROACH

The executive director of a highly recognized advocacy center contacted me for team-building and a race dialogue session for her staff. Despite its many accomplishments, the organization struggled with internal issues of unfocused direction, insufficient trust, and an underdeveloped infrastructure. Additionally, the African American executive director felt that the organization's racial advocacy mission was being compromised. The majority of the powerful positions in the organization were held by white persons, and there seemed to be increased questioning of the organization's direction. Explaining my holistic approach, we agreed that I would interview key staff to assess the organizational needs and to design a one-day retreat.

The interviews made it apparent that the organization had multiple needs that were equally, if not paramount to, the need for dialogue regarding race. There was lack of trust within senior staff, unclarity of roles and expectations, and an unclear decision-making structure that created additional problems. I proceeded to use each interview to advance conocimiento and to build staff's trust in me as the planning consultant and in a process that could lead to a more extensive commitment to developing an organizational structure and work environment desired by all.

The theme of the first retreat was "Focusing Our Mission and Improving Our Team." The main objectives for the one-day program were to increase our ability to communicate effectively as a multicultural team, clarify the organization's direction, and identify next steps to build an effective team. I began our retreat by reviewing our purpose and then engaged staff in a dyad conocimiento in which pairs shared on questions regarding their background, cultural experience, and experience working for the organization.

After the sharing by the pairs, I asked the group, "What did it *feel* like to share?" Feelings that surfaced were "appreciative, excited, connected, and hopeful." When asked why, they said because they *were really connecting with and learning about their coworkers*. I used their words to explain the conocimiento principle and how we were going to engage in further dialogue with each other toward developing deeper trust and understanding.

The context was established—we are sharing and trust building to advance our collective power. The next exercise divided the group of twenty into three groups to share about "personal culture, oppression and their *ideal organization.*" They were instructed to use the *talking stick.* Whoever held the stick had the responsibility to speak and others to listen closely. After the speaker spoke they were to pass the talking stick. The questions for their first speaking round were, What do you like best about your cultural background? What makes it difficult being of your culture? During the second round participants were to respond to the questions, What do you like best about the Advocacy Center? What changes do you recommend to improve our organization culture? Given time for a final round, they were to take turns expressing any validations they desire to offer their coworkers. This exercise was followed by several others to evaluate the organization's mission and direction, identify developmental needs, and make recommendations.

By the end of the day, staff felt strongly connected, genuine pride in the organization, each other, and in their ability to raise the organization to higher level of effectiveness and increase their ability to impact. To advance the organization's development the group had developed a list of priority needs that included a revised mission statement, explicit organizational priorities, clear organizational structure, improved office systems, and improved staff relations. While the entire staff expressed their readiness to move forward the executive director was particularly inspired. I had strategically paired her up with the person she felt was her chief antagonist. Through their conocimiento she had discovered that her strongest critic was also her strongest ally. Although quite different, they both shared a common vision and commitment for the organization and a deep respect for each other.

Inspired by the retreat and guided by the retreat recommendations, the executive director enlisted the board chairperson's support for a major strategic planning and organizational development initiative. Together we developed a follow-up plan that included engagement of the board in strategic planning, organization of a management team, and continued support for improved staff relations. All these interventions proceeded mindful to the goal of deepening the integrity of their services to people of color. This goal required using our various sessions to both learn and plan for greater multicultural inclusion and respect.

Over the next four years we collaborated on an organizational improvement process that involved strategic planning by the board and staff, organization development planning by the management team and staff, periodic planning retreats for staff, and strategic coaching sessions for the executive director. Throughout all these interventions, I applied the Porvida Approach and proactive facilitation and was continually optimizing teaching moments to foster inspiration and practices for multicultural respect.

For example, for the subsequent staff retreat all participants were invited to bring several items that reflected their source of inspiration for an inspiration table. We began the retreat with an opening sage ceremony that I offered from my indigenous background to remind participants that our retreat was to create good for today and the next seven generations. During the course of the retreat participants were invited to share the items they brought for the inspiration table. In the sharing of artifacts, photographs, writings, and items from nature, the team deepened their learning about each other as persons and as individuals from different cultural and life experiences.

The results from the multiple interventions are telling. The staff of twenty-some became a more effective multicultural team, better able to learn from each other. Within the first couple of years, the mission statement was revised from a half-page document to a synthesized statement underscoring the organization's commitment to civil rights and people of color, the board of directors approved strategic objectives for the coming five years, and the management group became a high performance team. During the subsequent years, the organization achieved many of its objectives, including becoming nationally recognized for excellence, developing a culture of multicultural respect, institutionalizing systems and policies to ensure quality service, and becoming an organization that staff felt was a "great place to work." Additionally, the executive director, with board and staff support, was able to initiate and establish two additional state and national organizations committed to the advancement of progressive law and multicultural healing.

Did all the work move smoothly? Usually, but not always. The executive director had to personally heal from the real wounds of racism and resolve some of her stereotypes and faulty assumptions regarding white professionals. She had to relearn that there were white persons who could be trusted to learn, grow, and become reliable allies. In addition, white senior staff members had to repeatedly grapple with their own assumptions and expectations regarding people of color. All staff had to learn that building and maintaining trust and respect requires a vigilant and regular practice of conocimiento, deep listening, and dialogue.

Upon reflection of my work with the advocacy center, I believe there were three key aspects of the consultation that influenced their success as a multicultural team and organization.

1. *Vision.* Organizations typically have a stated mission; however they become more powerful when they clarify their vision. Ideally, the staff of an organization must ask what type of society or world do we desire and how will our organization contribute to its advancement? I created this opportunity several times for the advocacy center. The staff knew that their organization was about service and justice, yet the commitment had not been translated into a short living statement that could inspire and guide the work. My responsibility was to make their vision conscious and explicit. Through the dialogues on vision the staff became mindful of their goals to unlearn racism, end oppression, and advance multicultural respect.

2. *Porvida Potential.* Too often, we limit our ability to facilitate the development of others because we fail to accept their inherent potential for growth and change. I entered this organization assuming their inherent goodness and ability for growth. This sense of optimism contributed to helping individuals, and the group become more conscious and effective in living their porvida potential—working and interacting with courage, respect, and love.

My porvida attitude helped me as the facilitator to forgive insensitivities and seek ways to support growth. Working with the advocacy center, I sought to create numerous opportunities where staff could express their idealism for doing their work. This sharing allowed them to inspire each other and become more courageous in speaking about justice and love. Although I encountered success within this organization, on other occasions working for other organizations, I must acknowledge that I was not the one to bring multicultural respect to blossom. In some occasions my role is only to leave the seeds of potential so that the next director or consultant may be more successful in developing a positive diversity consciousness within the organization.

3. *Healing.* Again, healing means to restore wellness and wholeness. Within the advocacy group there was need for healing, particularly to transform relationships of distrust into relationships of understanding and respect. Within every organization there are persons who have been injured by the "isms" perpetuated by our culture or society. They have felt the embarrassment, pain, or invalidation of direct racism or sexism. They have been made to feel less worthy than others. They need healing that requires expressing their personal hurt, being heard, forgiving others, requesting of others a commitment to change, and then deciding to move on. Similarly, those who have been perpetuators of racism, sexism, or homophobia also need healing. They need to connect with the inherent goodness of their spirit, recognize the origins of their prejudicial behavior, own their privilege, forgive themselves, and commit to learning to be more human.

Keeping healing in the forefront of my work with the advocacy group, I provided one-to-one and group opportunities for the management team and staff members to express their feelings and confusions related to working together. I provided them the opportunity to heal and learn from their experiences and then apply their learning to making improvements in their relationships or in the organization.

At the advocacy center, we eventually developed a culture in which the norm was sharing support, learning from each other, and encouraging each other's success. For those more involved in the direct service we explored ways to serve as agents for self-esteem building and empowerment. Throughout our various sessions, I wove in teaching on internalized oppression, what we sometimes call EL NO, and created opportunities to engage staff in examining how they sometimes contribute to devaluing others and how can they become a stronger voice that affirms and empowers others.

In conclusion, I believe the courage of the executive director and the commitment of the entire staff made the advocacy center actualize more of its full potential. However, I also know that my commitment and use of the Porvida Approach facilitated, encouraged, and supported their success. The outcome was a win-win-win situation—growth for the organization, its staff and clients, myself, and toward our greater vision of a better world.

## THE RELEVANCY OF THE PORVIDA APPROACH TO CONFLICT RESOLUTION

The vision of every professional educator or community service worker should be for a healthy society that works for all people. Whatever is the focus of work it should be done toward advancing this vision. Just as I have used the Porvida Approach to make counseling, facilitation, and organizational planning more porvida in outcomes, so it should be with the work of conflict resolution. Facilitating to resolve conflict should provide yet another opportunity for doing the education, community building, and cultural development toward advancing the better society. Within this context, I have several wisdom points to offer the conflict resolution community.

1. Make the intervention a pursuit of the greatest good. From the onset, the facilitator should communicate and then negotiate with interested parties a conflict resolution plan that acknowledges that the work will be done toward advancing the greatest common good—a win-win outcome for all parties and greater community we share. Within this context, the parties must be willing to engage in experiences, conversations, and learning moments that will serve to enhance mindfulness of vision, mutual understanding, trust building, and win-win resolutions.

2. Be mindful of the vision. Make the vision for the ideal organization, community, or society the context and standard for doing the conflict resolution work. Invite participants to begin their work by identifying their vision of the ideal organization or society. Particularly, seek to have them brainstorm the values of this ideal such as fairness, justice, respect, valuing

differences, and so on. Then, as the facilitator commit to and solicit their commitment to work together consistent with these values. Remind the group that we are here not only to address the needs of each other's interest group but to advance the vision of a better community for all. With this context set, use it as a reference by which to consider all aspects of the conflict resolution strategy. How can we pursue resolution of our conflict so as to advance our shared vision? Continually, challenge the group to consider the common good.

3. Draw upon spirit and intuition. The strategy may not be possible in all occasions, yet in some circumstances it is most appropriate. Within indigenous and many other cultural communities, there are traditional ways for beginning community gatherings to set the tone for optimal good will and creative problem solving. In our Native American and Latino communities we often begin with a sage burning ceremony and opening prayer. This ritual extends an invitation for ancestors and unborn children to be present as we engage in current problem solving so that the outcomes are also good for our children seven generations in our future. This type of opening helps establish an environment where participants are more open to listen to each other and also consider their heart and intuition. I have used this general strategy for diverse multicultural groups using rituals that honor their belief or nonbelief systems. Invariably the outcomes have been positive as all persons experience an invitation to draw upon their spirit and be their best—more open, considerate, and forgiving.

4. Build community. Continually integrate into the conflict resolution process the building of community and trust. To create resolution that respects each other we must have a basic familiarity of each other. Do this by encouraging conocimiento in which people discover each other's origins, realities, and aspirations. Through the use of strategic questions within dyads, small groups, and the full group experience have participants share so as to develop mutual understanding and trust. This will open participants to better consider each other's needs and realities.

5. Validate the realities of each group. We live in a society of much negativity and limited validation. By and large people typically do not believe their concerns or perspectives are being heard. For this reason, we must ensure that all perspectives are sufficiently expressed and heard. Integrate into

the conflict resolution process the opportunity for each party to provide a teaching experience of their concerns or perspective. Use a combination of full group presentations and small group conversations to ensure that each party has made their perspective or concerns understood.

6. Pursue multicultural respect. Make conflict resolution the work of human development and cultural evolution. Intentionally create environments that advance multicultural respect and understanding. Remind persons that we each bring our own uniqueness to the table. However, some of us by virtue of our class, cultural, ethnic, or sexual orientation experience also bring a community experience that needs acknowledgment and understanding. Therefore, create opportunities by which the different cultural groups can express their wants, needs, and value they bring. Provide for strategic multicultural conocimiento in which all persons are encouraged to share their cultural stories, learn about their differences, and develop relationships of increase understanding and trust. Also, engage groups in identifying the practices and values they desire to see within the community they share together so that the conflict resolution dialogues can serve as opportunities to practice these values. For example if the value is mutual respect, then the practice of our group dialogue should include active listening and courageous sharing, and so on.

7. Pursue collaborative problem-solving. Too often we view "conflict" as differences that lead to antagonism, confrontation, and irreconcilability. However, conflict can be a tool for optimizing tremendous win-win creativity. In doing the vision work, spirit welcoming, community building, affirmation, and shared teaching, we set the tone and begin the skill development for collaborative problem solving. Although all dialogue experiences up to this time have been toward developing resolution, now it is time to set up specific opportunities for participants to work on developing resolutions. Using dyads and small groups, have participants develop resolution options and then bring the groups together to present their best thinking and to identify resolutions that can be refined and accepted.

8. Document the good work. Ensure that the resolution process always includes a summary report to document all key presentations, dialogue points, and agreements. Once all parties leave its imperative to have a document that records all final agreements and key insights or understandings

that led to these resolutions. Ideally, this is the responsibility of the facilitator, the designated servant of the full group and the conflict resolution process.

CONCLUSION

A couple of years ago, I met several professionals working in the field of conflict resolution. In our exchange, they emphasized the relevancy of my work as an activist and a consultant to those within their field. Since that time I have assumed increase projects involving conflict resolution to directly experience the relevancy of the Porvida Approach to transform conflict into creative team problem solving, particularly among individuals, communities, or organizations committed to community service.

Again, experience affirmed that because individuals or groups share a general commitment to community service are they be able to effectively work with each other. Invariably there is the necessity to engage in conversation to make explicit their common vision and to develop relationships of mutual trust. The professional utilizing the Porvida Approach or proactive facilitation can help individuals and groups develop a culture and deeper relationships that empower them to optimize outcomes for the common good. These groups learn why and how to transform conflicts into opportunities for collaborative learning. They become groups to assist us in advancing the vision of a better society one conflict and resolution at a time.

I extend thanks to the colleagues who inspired me to offer this writing.

# 18 Mediating Filipino Culture

TED CORONEL

The mediation model developed and most often taught in the United States assumes universal truths. Yet the ideals stressed in mediation do not necessarily transcend cultural differences. Using Filipino culture as an example, I will analyze why mediation often becomes an artificial process for people of color.

Alternative models of mediation need to be developed and valued within the United States. As the mediation field continues toward a more unified and systematic discipline, these alternative models need to be honored. Today, many mediators proclaim themselves to be specialists in given fields, such as divorce or environmental mediation. Cultural competency involving different ethnicities should be a specialization as well. In cross-cultural conflicts, co-mediation with respective cultural mediators may be the ideal environment for producing true resolution for all of the involved disputants.

The mediation method taught and encouraged in the United States centers around, as John Paul Lederach labels it, a prescriptive approach to mediation.[1] Emphasis is placed on notions of universal truth and a single, all-encompassing way to resolve disputes. The process of acquiring the mediation skills follows the Eurocentric approach to education, in which the teacher has the knowledge that will be entrusted to the students. Cultural issues are explained and ultimately worked out within the given model. Instead of acknowledging differences in cultural philosophies regarding dispute resolution, the mediation model defines cultural differences merely as issues of which a mediator must have an awareness, but the model itself is not seen to need inherently to change.

## THE MEDIATION MODEL

When I was completing my basic mediation skills class, a requirement in order to be recognized as a legitimate mediator within the state of Washington, the program followed a prescriptive approach. The method taught was a single model of mediation, which the trainers suggested could feasibly deal with all sorts of disputes.

The definition I was taught was this: Mediation is a process in which an impartial third party helps two or more people in a dispute reach a mutually agreeable, voluntary, and informed settlement of their own making.

The mediator has the obligation to remain impartial. The mediator does not advocate for either side or evaluate the issues for the disputants. The mediator acts as "a guardian of the process," who guides the disputants through a systematic set of steps, ending with resolution of their conflict.

The mediation model, as it's taught by the Bellevue Neighborhood Mediation Program where I trained, involves eight steps:

1. Case development
2. Preliminary phase
3. Mediator opening statement
4. Client initial statement/mediator feedback
5. Agenda building
6. Negotiations
7. Caucus (optional)
8. Settlement agreement/closure

This model stresses a low-context, individualistic approach to dispute resolution. In *Art and Science of Negotiation,* Howard Raiffa explains how negotiators break down a problem into its component parts, evaluate the various negotiation options, and arrive at a resolution that maximizes the payoffs to both sides. Mediation in this conception centers on the problem as the focal point of the dispute.[2]

Using role-plays throughout the sessions, the instructor trained the class to use this model and emphasized what were or were not appropriate behaviors for a mediator. While being trained, I saw the model I was learning as a useful tool. I welcomed the concept of universal truths and, in the role-plays, used the mediation model as the process for dispute resolution.

I became comfortable and confident with the model and envisioned myself successfully translating the skills taught to real-life situations with real disputants.

However, I was aware of a contradiction: personally I did not feel that *I* would be inclined to use the same mediation model to resolve my own disputes. Initially, I rationalized my reluctance by defining my difficulties with the method as personal ones. My Filipino heritage, I assumed, had no relevance to why I would not use the model.

But subsequently, after further introspection, I realized that the success I envisioned in using the learned mediation model for dispute resolution relied on the disputants' being white. When I substituted people of color as the disputants, the process felt more uncomfortable. It was when, in my imagination, I replaced the disputants specifically with people of Filipino descent that I felt that the whole process was unnatural. Instead of seeing an enriching dispute resolution process, I saw myself regurgitating, step-by-step, a process that I knew I had to follow. My awkwardness stemmed from hoping that the Filipino disputants would not think of me as acting as unnaturally as I felt I was acting. The whole process felt out of character. We were a group of Filipinos, mediator and disputants, being told to forgo our natural characteristics and act in a way that we would not normally act. According to the basic mediation class and the prescribed model, however, the process should be *the* way to resolve disputes, regardless of ethnicity. In my Filipino vision, the whole process seemed altogether insincere.

## FILIPINO CULTURE

The growth of the Asian American population trails only Latinos in the United States. There are now more than ten million individuals who are Asian American. Filipinos constitute the second largest Asian American group, with a population of 1.9 million.[3] The Filipino community within the United States still has close ties with the Philippines. Most have family members remaining in the Philippines and are predominately first- or second-generation Filipino Americans. Filipino culture remains strong in Filipino Americans through their close ties with other Filipinos within their community and a continued connection with the Philippines.

Similar to other Asian cultures, Filipino negotiations center around a high-context style that stresses the value of relationships. Disputes cannot be detached from the relationships of the disputants involved. Instead, issues are seen through the prisms of relationships. A sense of community is more important than individual concerns. Within Filipino culture, *hiya* controls and motivates behavior within society. *Hiya,* as anthropologist Frank Lynch explains, is "the uncomfortable feeling that accompanies awareness of being, in a socially unacceptable position, or performing a socially unacceptable action."[4] It is, in essence, a sense of shame. To act in ways against the approval of the community would be considered to be acting without *hiya,* which results in withdrawal of acceptance within the group. In the barrios of the Philippines, community harmony, including all forms of crime control, is maintained by the entire community, which resolves disputes largely through a group consensus applying the value of *hiya.*[5] Filipino Americans and their sense of *hiya* make it difficult for mediation approach, which emphasizes individual issues to be useful in resolving disputes.

Filipino culture also has a different concept of a go-between. While a mediator is essentially a go-between, the notion of an involved third party differs greatly in Filipino culture. A go-between in Filipino culture plays a very active role in situations. Face-to-face situations are less common in Filipino culture because the ideas of *hiya* may come into play. Instead of losing face in society, Filipino culture uses a go-between to help resolve issues within individuals in the community. Lynch observed what he termed smooth interpersonal relations (SIR) among Filipinos, valuing the idea of a go-between in relationship-building.[6] Again, group harmony is more important than individual concerns.

Another aspect of Filipino culture that negatively affects Filipinos using the mediation process involves what is commonly termed "internalization of the oppressor." The Philippines was essentially a colony passed around for almost four hundred years. The Philippines was under the control of the United States from 1898 until the Japanese invaded the country during World War II. The United States "liberated" the Philippines from the Japanese and the United States "granted" the Philippines its independence in 1946. Most Filipinos hold the United States in high regard. The internalization of the oppressor causes victims of colonization to regard their own knowledge as worthless when compared to that of the colonizer.[7]

If a Filipino American is involved in a dispute with an Anglo American and the disputants decide to go through a mediation process where, because of the lack of mediators of color, chances are high that the mediator will also be Anglo American, the Filipino American would most likely not see himself or herself on equal ground with the other participants. Beyond Filipino culture's ideas regarding *hiya* and group harmony, a Filipino American involved in mediation may inherently believe that the other participants, mediator and disputant, are more in the right than he or she.

A FILIPINO MODEL OF MEDIATION

Instead of moving toward standardizing practices, the mediation field within the United States needs to honor cultural values that call for alternative models of mediation. The key to dispute resolution is flexibility. The current model of mediation is not flexible. For mediation to be applicable and acceptable for all citizens of the United States, the field needs alternative models that respect differing concepts of dispute resolution that other cultures may practice. Contrary to popular thought on mediation, cultural difference cannot be addressed within the mediation model currently practiced in the United States.

A model of mediation more accommodating to Filipino culture would look at the dispute through the prism of relationships. The dispute cannot be seen as a problem that can stand on its own. The win-win attitude of the current mediation model is not applicable in Filipino culture. Individual contentment is secondary to group cohesiveness for Filipinos. A Filipino model of mediation would stress community harmony over individual issue regarding the dispute. Relationship building is the key concept, not resolving the problem. True satisfaction cannot be derived if the problem is solved with both parties benefiting but the relationship between the disputants has ended.

A Filipino model of mediation would also have a more active mediator who could represent group harmony and cohesiveness. The mediator may suggest solutions, direct discussion and, in essence, be an advocate for both disputants. The mediator should act as the go-between as commonly defined in Filipino culture. The reluctance of Filipino Americans to air their grievances openly calls for a mediator who is more actively involved in the process.

Because of the more active role of the mediator in a Filipino model, the mediator needs to be a respected member of the community. Moreover, familiarity with the disputants, a concept that the current model of mediation frowns upon, would be encouraged in a Filipino model. The key concept in a Filipino model of mediation is to mend the relationship. A mediator who is familiar with the disputants can more actively assist in mending the relationship and remind the disputants of their responsibilities to the community.

SUMMARY

The idea of alternative models of mediation poses new challenges in the mediation field's movement toward standardizing practice. Alternative models of mediation, however, would not weaken the credibility of mediation. Instead, using a term popular in mediation today, these alternative models would help "enlarge the pie." It would make mediation more acceptable to all people living in the United States. Mediators who specialize in specific cultural models of mediation would broaden the appeal of mediation to all people within the United States. In essence, the acceptance of alternative models would help legitimize the field of mediation as an acceptable way of resolving disputes.

# 19 *Tres Culturas*

*A Case Study of School Peer Mediation*
*with Three Cultures in a Texas Middle School*

RAY LEAL

One must first trace one's journey to its beginning before evaluating that journey's success. My own "peacemaking" journey began in Isleta Pueblo where a wise clan mother spoke with me concerning American youth. I had recently switched teaching disciplines from political science to criminal justice. It was the early nineties and there had been a dramatic increase in juvenile crime. The clan mother remarked that "the children are the future and the violence must stop." She then asked me if I knew how to make peace. With no apparent answer forthcoming from me, she guided my future by advising me to learn how to make peace and to work with school children. Some weeks later I enrolled in secondary school peer mediation training conducted by the New Mexico Center for Dispute Resolution. The conversation at Isleta Pueblo led to my active involvement with the National Association for Mediation in Education (NAME) located at the University of Massachusetts. I would later receive more conflict resolution training from CDR Associates and the Harris County Dispute Resolution Center in Houston. As my career for the past twenty-five years has been devoted to higher education I naturally focused my efforts at my institution, St. Mary's University of San Antonio, Texas.[1]

In addition to receiving sage advice I also came to peacemaking naturally. Both of my parent's families were pioneers in the establishment of both Laredo and San Antonio, Texas. Originating from Spain and the Canary

255

Islands my family found itself in the evolution of Texas under Spanish, Mexican, Texan, and American governments. Over time my family adapted to successive migrations of various European groups. Through intermarriage with various groups the family came to possess Spanish, Irish, German, French, and Italian surnames. My family was and continues to be a rainbow of colors and a league of cultures. Through the process of transculturation[2] the Leal, Ramirez, Martin, Henry, Benavides, Bruni, and Leyendecker family became culturally diverse and tolerant. As my mother would caution me, "There are no bad or good people or races, only people with bad or good intentions."

Yet in spite of my diverse upbringing I was well aware of the conflicted history of Texas, a former slave state, and a place where war was waged by Texans and later Americans against the Mexican people. This confluence of three cultures *(tres culturas)* would come to shape race relations and the politics of the state well into the current century. There was and continues to be a natural tension among Anglos, African Americans, and Hispanics. Much of this tension has played itself out in state and federal courts, with many cases being filed by the NAACP and the Mexican American Legal Defense and Educational Fund (MALDEF) on behalf of African Americans and Hispanics. The intercultural conflict, litigation, and history of Texas form a living context for programs attempting peer mediation in Texas schools.

This article will deal with a successful case study of Smithson Valley Middle School (SVMS) located in Comal County close to New Braunfels, Texas, adjoining the Hill Country. The Hill Country is a region composed of twenty-five counties near the geographical center of Texas. Between 1840 and 1850 most settlers to the area were from Tennessee, Arkansas, and Missouri, but Hessians and Lower Saxons from Germany also populated this rural area prior to the Civil War.[3] By the 1870s the towns of New Braunfels, Fredericksburg, Comfort, Boerne, and Mason came to be known as the German Hill Country because of a strong German cultural imprint. The Germans also created a distinctive religious subculture composed of enclaves of Lutheran-Catholics, Methodists, and freethinkers.[4]

It was within this historical context that changing demographics in Texas would bring cross-cultural conflicts into the region's schools. The influx of Hispanic and African American students from urban areas into this previously isolated, rural German region would bring about a need for peer mediation. This case study will relate how a culturally relevant peer mediation training model[5] was used to assist in the training of students and teachers and in the implementation of a successful peer mediation program that effectively dealt with differences among three cultures of students—African American, Anglo, and Hispanic. More specifically, it will discuss the initiation of mediation training at the school, the training model used, the nature and types of disputes, implementation of the program in the school, and outcomes.

Smithson Valley Middle School is a suburban school close to both the German Hill Country and the San Antonio metropolitan area. In the eighties its student population was largely white, Anglo, Christian, and middle-class even though the population also included students from poor, rural families. Historically, the area was an agricultural area and the "cowboy" culture had a major impact on socialization. Historically, it was the Spanish who brought cows and horses to Texas. Many words such as "rodeo" and "lasso" are Spanish words used by the early "vaqueros" (cowboys). In spite of this common ground, the cultural diversity brought about by demographic changes in Texas schools would lead to cross-cultural conflicts. The juxtaposition and convergence of cultures sometimes creates conflict and tension as new behavior patterns are introduced into an institution such as a school. The minority population at SVMS was numerically small, but as juvenile gang violence expanded in San Antonio in the early nineties more African American and Mexican American students enrolled in the safer suburban school. Minority families concerned about this violence saw moving to a rural area with good schools as a way to protect their children from urban school violence.

The early nineties in Texas saw a dramatic rise in juvenile crime, and the state of Texas responded with a "zero tolerance" approach in its public schools. In keeping with the national trend across American education and in society, school administrators, much like law enforcement officials, decided that "get tough" discipline policies would keep students in line. However, much like the rhetoric of the War on Drugs little consideration was given to the benefits and costs of the new school policies.[6] Large expenditures on procurement of additional school police were made as Texas launched its new school discipline policies. Unfortunately, few evaluative studies were ever made of the outcomes of these new disciplinary policies. Some schools, however, began to take an interest in less harsh, and possibly more effective, conflict management strategies that might alleviate disciplinary problems on their campuses.

Smithson Valley Middle School was under the leadership of Dr. Patrick Hollis[7] who advocated collaborative leadership with his teachers. He was well aware that the demographic changes in Bexar and Comal Counties were reflected in the changing composition of the student body at SVMS. Compounding the normal issues affecting middle school students such as puberty and divorced parents to name a few, there were also urban versus rural, rich versus poor, and intercultural differences among a student body composed of white, Hispanic, and black students. These three cultures *(tres culturas)* would come into conflict over issues such ethnic pride, style of dress, music, language, as well as other issues. The interaction of these three groups found its way into the classrooms as disciplinary problems.

Classroom discipline became a major focus of faculty meetings. Several teachers had knowledge of the peer mediation training that had been conducted in other area middle schools by faculty and students of the criminal justice department of St. Mary's University.[8] The St. Mary's program involved training of university students for academic credit using the New Mexico Center for Dispute Resolution training model.[9] University students were then involved in the training of secondary school teachers and students. They were particularly effective because of their closeness in age to the students and their testimonials before the teachers. Additionally, the university mediator-trainers were a diverse group of Hispanics, blacks, and Anglos who, even though they were using a traditional North American model of mediation, brought cultural sensitivity to the trainings. They had also mediated intercultural disputes at other secondary schools in south Texas.

Dr. Hollis requested information from St. Mary's University, and I paid him a visit to provide him with an orientation regarding the possibility of peer mediation training at SVMS. I emphasized that it would be important to have a minimum of 70 percent of faculty and staff support the proposed training. Hollis mentioned that some teachers were skeptical that peer mediation would work in their school with students from three cultures, but he was strongly committed to fostering a more positive school climate that would effectively deal with student conflicts.

The training developed for SVMS by St. Mary's University trainers included several components that included cultural awareness and Texas history questionnaires, expectations of the teachers, modeling of appropriate intercultural interactions, communication and mediation skill training, field trips to the university, design and implementation of the peer mediation program, and follow-up by trainers. Given the past discrimination against Mexican Americans and African Americans in Texas, many secondary school texts have omitted these two groups in their coverage of Texas history. It was not surprising then to find that most teachers had little or no knowledge of the African Americans known as the "buffalo soldiers" of the Tenth Cavalry who provided protection for settlers in Texas from the Apaches and other hostile tribes.[10] It was, therefore, necessary to conduct a "cultural awareness" survey of participants to assess their own knowledge of these two cultures.

After the questionnaires were administered and evaluated it was clear that the training must begin with cultural awareness training as well as a brief historical account of the roles of the three cultures in Texas. The model developed for training included use of words and concepts important to these cultures. For example, the term *respeto* (respect) and its significance to Mexican Americans was discussed. Commonality among the three cultures was stressed particularly in discussing the "cowboys" of Texas. Teachers were made aware that the vaqueros, Anglo cowboys, and black cowboys all played a part in the formation of this distinctive Texas subculture. The history of slavery, the Mexican American War, and the Civil War were discussed in terms of their legacy for race relations in Texas. This model of cultural competency training was later presented at a national conference on peacemaking.[11] The results of this portion of the training liberated the teachers from viewing these three cultures from a "culture bound" perspective determined from an "old Texas" view full of stereotypes and discrimination to a "new Texas" view that represented the new realities of a multicultural state that required tolerance of cultural diversity. Several teachers commented that they could now understand the underlying historical causes of racial tensions in Texas.

The next phase of the training involved a demonstration of appropriate intercultural interactions by the trainers. Particular attention was paid to the concept of "ownership" or the notion that people other than Mexican Americans or African Americans are experts on those two cultures. It was emphasized that it is important to let members of the affected culture group be the discussion leaders on important values and traits of that group without interference from other culture groups. Characteristics and values of the middle student subculture were discussed and analyzed as well.

Next came the teaching of basic communications and mediation skills to the teachers. In 1995 the faculty and staff of SVMS numbered fifty-seven persons. The training was voluntary and forty persons completed the training provided by St. Mary's University. This constituted 70 percent of the faculty and staff completing the training that would have positive outcomes for SVMS and the trainees. Several teachers commented after this phase that they now understood that they must improve their listening skills. After this phase teachers were introduced to simulated mediations based on intercultural disputes. These role plays had been designed by the trainers from previous conversations with the principal and teachers regarding disputes at SVMS. The trainers' stories about their participation in successful mediations that dealt with intercultural disputes, combined with their own diverse cultural heritages, added to their effectiveness in the training. Moreover, they were all criminal justice undergraduate majors and had a good understanding of juveniles in our society. Their past trainings and mediations at middle schools in San Antonio proved to be invaluable as well.

One example of a simulated mediation scenario that mirrored real student disputes was a conflict over the value of Tejano versus country and western versus rap music and middle students' inability to tolerate each other's musical preferences, leading to more serious conflicts. Cultural insights contributed by the faculty and staff were also integrated into the training. For instance, Hollis mentioned that given the history of the region some parents would encourage their children to "duke it out" rather than back down, in keeping with the "cowboy" culture of Texas.[12] While teachers were taught communications and mediation skills based on the New Mexico Center for Dispute Resolution model, particular attention was paid to how language and body language are used by the three cultures in different ways, in order that teachers would learn not to impose the mainstream model of speaking and being on the other two cultures. The need to let nonmainstream students vent their emotions in a mediation setting and its importance in gaining the confidence of the disputants was discussed. Cultural preferences in the use of body language were demonstrated by Mexican American and African American student-mediators.

The last phase of the training for teachers involved an exercise in the design and implementation of a peer mediation program at SVMS by the teachers. After several brainstorming sessions the teachers felt ready to implement their new peer mediation program. The first step was the training of SVMS students by their teachers and St. Mary's University student-mediators in order to develop a cadre of trainers. The training closely mirrored that provided to the teachers except that the student training was more condensed and also involved a field trip to St. Mary's University for the teachers and students to promote bonding between them and ensure a successful peer mediation program.

The training led to a major change in the school climate and the interaction among the three cultures. From the teachers' perspective St. Mary's students provided them with the "know-how" and skills that made classroom management more effective. It also fostered greater cooperation among teachers and between the teachers and students. Students felt empowered to bring issues before the teachers and be heard. Student behavior improved campus-wide and students were now empowered to resolve conflicts in an acceptable manner. Disciplinary referrals of students by teachers to the vice principal were decreased by close to 40 percent.[13]

Hollis saw the most direct impact of the training on SVMS students. He emphasized three points in student behavior change. First, students felt empowered to make decisions and effect outcomes in their lives at school. They were now "in charge" of their lives and their school. Second, school climate changed for the better because it was now fashionable and accepted by peers to intervene in disputes and resolve conflicts. Additionally, students understood that it was important to resolve conflict because later in their careers they would be expected to work with and get along with their fellow employees. Third, students knew that their voice could be heard in any argument and conflict. Using the structure of peer mediation, the majority of issues could be resolved in an acceptable and peaceful manner.

The confidence expressed by teachers in SVMS students was highlighted during the national conference of the National Association of Secondary School Principals held in San Antonio. SVMS was chosen as a "demonstration school" for this conference, which meant a bus of principals and educators from all over the country would tour SVMS. It was decided in a faculty meeting that SVMS students would act as tour guides for the distinguished guests. Hollis recounted his thoughts about this initiative, "If you want to know the truth about a school, ask a kid." In the weeks following the tour of SVMS, students received letters from principals, superintendents, professors, and university chairpersons congratulating them on "their" school.

Hollis recounted one special moment at SVMS during his tenure as principal. He was standing in the hall when a sixth grader approached him and asked, "Are you the principal?" He replied that he was and she responded, "I love the way you run this school. It's the coolest place!" Hollis mentioned that this particular moment reminded him of why he had gone into the teaching profession. However, the success of SVMS was also noticed by the state of Texas. The Texas Association of Secondary School Principals (TASSP) chose Dr. Patrick Hollis as "principal of the year" in 2003. The governor of Texas also recognized SVMS as a "Safe School" for two years; this distinction was shared with less then one hundred other schools. The teachers trained by St. Mary's University were also successful in their careers. Five became principals and three became counselors in the district in the ensuing years. Although little research has been conducted on the topic, SVMS provides one example of the "multiplier effect" of effective training and successful peer mediation programs.

It is always the hope of any trainer that the training provided would also go beyond the school trained to other schools and the parents. However, in this case the district's central administration and the parents were the least affected. SVMS teachers provided teachers at the Smith Valley High School with training, but the support of the high school's leadership was not forthcoming. The central administration of Comal Independent School District tolerated the program at SVMS but was not interested in its expansion to the district's other schools. They also were unaware that Hollis had received the TASSP "principal of the year" award. Perhaps this lack of recognition was due to the administration being involved in litigation involving other schools in the district.

As dispute resolution grew out of the need to provide a user-friendly alternative to litigation, it is somewhat ironic that the Comal Independent School District found itself involved in litigation in the nineties.[14] This litigation was initiated in 1993 as a Section 42, 1983 Civil Rights Act, discrimination case by the parents of students enrolled in Canyon High School and Canyon Middle School. After four years of motions, countermotions, and negotiations and many hundreds of hours by attorneys, the case was settled out of court to the satisfaction of parents whose children had been subjected to racial discrimination in two of the district's schools. Unfortunately, racial tensions at one of the district's high school continue even today. In October 2004 during a football game between Smithson Valley High School and Judson High School of San Antonio, a Smithson Valley student admitted to tagging the Judson buses with racial slurs of "KKK" and "White Power."[15]

The impact on the SMVS parents was more mixed, according to Hollis. Some were impacted because their children brought home their newly acquired skills and began using them within a family context. Most parents approved of the SVMS peer mediation program and were enthused that their children were being trained in conflict resolution. However, other parents were unaffected or unaware of the program. In retrospect, efforts to involve parents in peer mediation programs need more effort and research.

Hollis was personally affected by the program in a variety of ways. First, he became aware of the large amount of conflict we must deal with on a daily basis. His newly acquired skills made him a more effective leader. Hollis and his teachers were able to mold SVMS into a highly successful school and go on to successful careers in secondary education. Second, through the intercultural competence and cohesion of the St. Mary's mediator-trainers he was able to see how three cultures could peacefully coexist in a school setting. Third, he continues to be a strong advocate for peer mediation in America's secondary schools, particularly in the aftermath of Littleton, Colorado, and other cases of school violence.

In retrospect I must list the training at Smithson Valley Middle School as among the most successful my students and I had ever conducted. It was personally gratifying that in spite of the conflicted history of Texas it was possible to teach African American, Anglo, and Hispanic students the art of peaceful coexistence and respect for each other's cultures in a middle school setting. As I learned from that clan mother in Isleta Pueblo, "the children are the future." So, it is with great satisfaction that I have witnessed my students teach younger students the way of peace in a world that seems determined to destroy itself. In the words of John Lennon, "All we are saying is give peace a chance!"

# 20 From Volunteerism to Vocation

*Challenges in Breaking into*
*Professional Mediation*

SELINA C. LOW

I can still recall getting introduced to mediation back in 1991. San Francisco Community Boards, one of the first community mediation centers in the nation, recruited me at an outreach table at the Visitacion Valley Community Center located on the south side of the city. They told me Community Boards was looking for volunteers to help people resolve conflicts peacefully in the neighborhoods. It seemed like the perfect opportunity. I was graduating from San Francisco State University and still exploring what to do in life. I knew I wanted to help people and contribute to making neighborhoods safe in my hometown, particularly in communities of color.

When we first moved to Visitacion Valley, my family and I were one of the few Chinese American families in a largely African American working class neighborhood. It offered a nice retreat from the hustle and bustle of the city with the sense of community and diversity. However, it also had all the problems of urban violence: assaults and robberies. I grew up amid crime. This was my impetus for volunteering with Community Boards, to provide a resource for people in my neighborhood and throughout San Francisco to address conflict in a peaceful way before it escalated into violence.

## EXPOSURE TO COMMUNITY BOARDS

Looking back, I believe I received some of the best training possible from Community Boards. The class of 1991 had an incredible pool of talented and diverse trainers. They taught me the four-phase process and about a powerful tool called active listening. I learned about acknowledging power imbalances and ways to try to equalize that difference. Additionally, I learned about working together as a team on mediation panels. The organization's philosophy of fairness and social justice was reflected in the way the trainers taught us to prepare a balanced agreement and to facilitate meetings in a respectful manner, keeping the clients at the forefront. We learned about working with parties from different cultural backgrounds.

Another special quality emanating from the trainers was their genuine concern for the trainees. The trainers not only conveyed the mediation process, but they impressed upon me the overall purpose of mediation—to empower others to resolve their own conflicts and to build peaceful, cohesive communities.

## ACTUALLY DOING IT! SUCCESSFULLY

Soon after the training, I was mediating disputes alongside two other mediators. I assisted people in improving their understanding of each other and in negotiating agreements to a range of situations that arose in neighborhoods. Next, I became a trainer, mostly because I enjoyed engaging with my trainer friends.

Community Boards became more than simply a place to volunteer. It became a home for community members. I looked forward to holiday parties and picnics where staff and volunteers came together to share in each other's lives and enjoy each other's company. We were a people diverse in race, nationality, age, sexual orientation, and other backgrounds, drawn together and to each other by our common interest in community and peaceful, collaborative conflict resolution. Because of my respect for the organization and connections to the people, I volunteered in other capacities such as outreach and event organizing.

About five years after my start with the organization, my volunteerism turned into a career at Community Boards. I did everything from case intake (responding to client calls), public relations and volunteer coordination, to marketing, training coordination, and training, giving me the opportunity to see firsthand the internal workings of a mediation organization.

## TRANSITION TO PROFESSION

In 2001, I attempted to do the work I loved professionally. Though I had heard it was difficult to make a living in mediation, I felt confident I could consult part-time. By this time, at the age of thirty-four, I had ten years of mediation experience and extensive experience as a trainer. Over the years, I had handled a wide range of disputes. Further, I had also gained experience as a facilitator for large community meetings involving contentious issues such as use of public space.

As a coach and trainer, I had expanded my knowledge of conflict resolution skills and mediation processes. I had been told by leaders in the field that my qualifications were excellent with my broad experiences as a practitioner and program staff person. Being a woman of color practitioner with training and knowledge of multiculturalism were additional assets because the field severely lacked diversity.

But transitioning into the professional world of mediation proved to be challenging and difficult. I soon discovered there seemed to be few, if any jobs for mediators. Also, there was no clear process to move in and up into mediator positions. This situation was a stark difference from the widespread opportunities for volunteer mediators. Paid opportunities seemed limited and narrowly advertised.

I also found networking with professional colleagues to be a culture shock. Once when I attended an event for professional mediators, I noticed an obvious difference between the constituency this organization drew and my first mediation program. The former seemed to consist of mostly white practitioners, seemingly in their forties and older. I immediately felt the lack of diversity. I also observed a great contrast in the culture—the manner in which people connected, who interacted with whom and how, and the way the meeting was run. People seemed less open and friendly to meeting new people. They seemed to be focused more on what people did than who people were. My perception was that people were interested only in people who looked like they could offer them business; otherwise a person was not worth taking the time to know.

At this event, I introduced myself to a practicing mediator who was an older white woman. I experienced her to be guarded and less conversational. Eventually, she told me she had been practicing mediation for about two years, getting contract work from some of the governmental agencies. When I shared that I was just getting started in mediation professionally and was applying to various programs, she immediately lost her rigid composure and became energized. She began to aggressively engage me. At that time, I felt she wanted to absorb every bit of information I had. She even took notes during our conversation! I was taken aback because initially, she was reluctant to share information, but she became enthusiastic about retrieving information I offered. This felt bad as I was used to networking being recip- rocal and colleagues being concerned for each other. In the larger scheme of things, I felt insulted that this woman, who was already earning an income from mediation, did not want to share resources with someone who was not making a living from the practice and yet, she was willing to extract resources from that same person.

RESISTANCE WITH PROGRAMS

I eventually found a helpful practicing attorney mediator. Taking her advice, I attempted to volunteer with other alternative dispute resolution (ADR) programs that offered greater visibility and possible paid mediations. I con- tacted other programs including nonprofit mediation organizations, govern- mental ADR programs, bar associations, county courts. I soon discovered trying to mediate for other ADR programs, whether as a volunteer or paid mediator, was a discouraging and disillusioning experience. Away from the oasis of Community Boards where seasoned mediators welcomed and en- couraged new generations of practitioners to promote nonviolent conflict resolution, I found entry into the professional world of mediation cold and competitive.

Many of the programs offered similar responses: We don't get very many mediations. I do not know when our next training will be held. We are not accepting new mediators. We are very busy. We do not use external mediators, only sometimes. The manner of delivery of such statements was brusque and unfriendly, poorly representing the spirit of mediation. Many of the organizations seemed impressed by the expanse and diversity of my knowledge and experience and yet these programs could not figure out how to utilize me despite their need to promote mediation and my offer of marketing/public relations expertise. And when asked if the addition of a woman-of-color mediator to their pool would be valuable, the coordinators acknowledged the shortage of diverse practitioners and admitted a problem existed.

Yet an unspoken resistance lingered. It seemed the coordinators, who were in positions to make change, either said they had no information on the demographics of their mediators or showed they were uncomfortable discussing the lack of racial and age diversity. I sensed a feeling of competitiveness, possessiveness, and fear of having to share opportunities and resources.

A NONATTORNEY MEDIATOR

Another discovery I made was that ADR programs seemed to be slanted toward attorney mediators. Many of the coordinators of the ADR programs I contacted were attorneys. Few coordinators specifically stated they only used attorneys, but even for those accepting nonattorney mediators, I found the application process and orientation to be tailored to those with a legal background. For example, many applications requested areas of specialization. I wondered, How many cases equaled a specialization? Could I check the box if I had ever mediated this type of case before? I believe this put applicants from a community mediation background at a disadvantage because he or she would be unlikely to have a specialization.

Also, the applications used legal terminology; for example, some specializations were listed as Intellectual Property, Probate. Most likely only attorneys would understand such language or have such experience. I was not certain what kind or how much experience made me eligible to indicate Personal Injury, Criminal, or Environmental, though I had experience with what sounded like these types of issues. What kinds of people handled

Bankruptcy, Malpractice, Patent/Trademark other than attorneys? I thought, Was it necessary to have this specific knowledge to effectively facilitate a mediation where the disputants would create their own agreements?

I found similar examples on the few governmental mediator jobs advertised. For example, candidates had to show experience of handling a great of number of cases with specialized legal knowledge, putting younger, nonattorney mediators at a disadvantage.

On another form, an applicant was rated by the number of mediations performed involving attorneys. Candidates from a community mediation background would be at a disadvantage because such programs often discouraged representation by attorneys.

Though ADR programs stated they accepted nonattorney mediators, I found an underlying preference for attorney mediators. In one case, I inquired with a coordinator of a local court program that was seeking mediators. I had heard about this opportunity through an attorney mediator of color who knew my background and felt confident I could do the work. After learning about my background, the coordinator did not seem impressed with my extensive experience in community mediation. He then discouraged me from applying to his program and suggested I apply to another court program, alluding to the fact he was not accepting any more applicants.

Some days later, I learned that a new mediator I had just trained through Community Boards, who was also a young attorney, had just been accepted onto the same court panel. These examples showed me how attorney mediators had an advantage in paid mediation opportunities.

I began to wonder why mediation experience or extensive knowledge of conflict resolution skills did not seem to be a more important criteria for acceptance onto panels. Also, I thought it disturbingly ironic that community mediation was not valued despite these programs' serving as the training and practice ground for many a professional mediator, attorney mediators included.

CONCLUSION

Over the past two years, I have found transitioning to professional mediation from community mediation to be a challenge. A clear vocational path for finding and securing mediator jobs is nonexistent. Qualifications for contract work as well as opportunities with other ADR panels offering greater exposure seem to be tailored toward older mediators and mediators with a legal background. The few jobs advertised seemed to be slanted toward attorney mediators.

What I believe is important for struggling individuals who seek to break into mediation is to be aware of the current barriers and to continue to believe in one's self and abilities. Gain support from colleagues who care about you and whose talents you respect. Do not horde information on opportunities but share ideas with other struggling mediators. Treating people with genuine love and support gets the same back. At the same time, develop relationships with those mediators who are gaining work. Diverse mediator teams are highly valuable, particularly in cross-gender, cross-cultural conflict.

Learn about qualifications that are required for the few mediator jobs and contract work available such as listed on government Web sites using mediators. Continue to enhance your abilities and become familiar with laws in your specialty areas. This endeavor can include taking law classes at your local community college. Make sure you collect and save any and all certificates for training and/or classes and document how many hours of training you have had. Document the number of cases done and track the type of cases they are. Share with people in all your circles—what you do and how you do it. People notice those who clearly articulate their unique work and model its principles through concern and respect for people.

Get involved with groups that shape mediator credentialing, best practices, and laws that govern the field. Encourage cultural competency and other mediator knowledge and experience to be recognized as qualifications than just legal knowledge. Ask the question, How is attorney training and knowledge a greater qualification for mediation work than nonattorney mediator training, orientation, and experience?

While it has been my perception that many professional mediation organizations alienate young mediators of color and nonattorney mediators, I would offer a suggestion for programs that truly desire to have a diverse membership: Get feedback from mediators of diverse races, ages, and work experience, and so on, to gain information on improving outreach, recruitment, and retention efforts. Then, integrate these ideas, including the creation of a welcoming culture that fosters a sense of sincere goodwill and appreciation for the person as well as the mediator.

I believe there should not be a "war" between attorney and nonattorney mediators or white mediators and mediators of color if we simply treat each other with the same values and principles we encourage of clients—goodwill, understanding, collaboration, and appreciation for diversity. As a colleague of mine said, "There is enough conflict to go around."

# 21 Is Reconciliation Possible?

*Lessons from Combating "Modern Racism"*

VALERIE BATTS

REFLECTIONS ON WAR AT THE DAWNING
OF THE TWENTY-FIRST CENTURY

Transformation in the world context involves a multifaceted process of generating a different conceptualization of possibilities for how humans will live together in a global community where "war" no longer means the same thing as it meant historically.* The "theater of war" concept, developed at least five hundred years ago when Europeans designated "battlefields" as the acceptable arena for conflict, was one thing. The "battlefield" in the twenty-first century, however, is quite another thing. We have seen, particularly in the wake of September 11, that the battlefield is now the *entire globe!* Today's global arena for war means at a fundamental level each citizen of each country will need to come to view war in the twenty-first century in a new way. We can start this process in the United States. One way is to acknowledge and rethink the origins and current impacts of intragroup tensions within our own country.

As I witnessed the events of September 11, my own response as a U.S. citizen was complex. On the one hand, I was horrified and deeply saddened

*This chapter originally appeared in Waging Reconciliation: God's Mission in a Time of Globalization and Crisis (New York: Church Publishing Inc., 2002), 35–75, and is reprinted by permission of the publisher.

as I realized how many people were dying. Then I got scared as I thought about my brother-in-law and his family who live and work in Manhattan and my cousins who work in Washington, D.C., near the Pentagon.

Next came a vivid memory from October 1969. After what was called a "riot" in my newly desegregated public high school in eastern North Carolina, National Guard Troops were called into my school and placed in each classroom for many months. This fact seems especially ludicrous to me now in light of the violence our nation and the world have witnessed since 1969 and most recently in the months following September 11. Yet the posting of the National Guard in my school represented a "worse case scenario" that most whites in our community had anticipated for years. Such folk believed that if blacks and whites did not stay in their respective places, with whites clearly on top, we would end up with racial violence. Blacks were feared as the aggressors yet, ironically, none of the National Guard—the only people who had guns—as I recall were black.

It was always clear to me that as an African American young adult who spoke out against injustice, I could be a target for the National Guard and other government officials if I was not careful. I also knew at some level, that my brother, my friends, or I could be a random target because of the color of our skin, even if we were not speaking out against injustice. Such "racial profiling," as it is now called, was one of many "laws of the land" that we had to deal with growing up black in the 1950s United States South.

Looking back on my life in the segregated South, I realize that among the buffers from the intense racism and white supremacy of the time was the tiny black Episcopal Church in which I was coming of age. In church I met the first white person I could trust, Father Jack Spong, who was then and continues to be a challenger for justice in the faith community and beyond. My father was for many years a senior warden in the parish and took his job seriously. Even in the Christian tradition, commitment to justice and equality is often obscured by the politics of our economic and social history of oppression or liberalism so much so that it is hard to see our call to humility in the modern day. As a result I also grew up knowing how oppressive Christianity can be.

As the sixties progressed, and I became increasingly politically conscious, it became clear to me that the United States government defined political activism that attempted to change governmental policy toward groups as "a threat to national security" at least and as "terrorism" at worst. Many of my friends and I lived with much pain and anger at being part of a country that professed "freedom of speech" yet was a country where we saw repeated injustice and *knew* that harm was inevitable if we "got out of line."

Interestingly, when I recently talked with a divinity student colleague about conflicts after September 11, her response was very different. She grew up as a middle class, white, U.S. citizen in rural Maine. She was raised to believe that "America" was a free and open society and that anyone who worked hard could get ahead. As a teen, she participated and led many social events for soldiers who came through her town on their way to and from military missions to protect our soil from the "evils of communism." She did not even fully know, for example, that segregation continued in the South of the United States until the late 1960s and had no understanding about its continuing impact. As the student has become aware of injustices both within our society and across the world, it has been an often painful and wrenching process to reconcile her earlier views with what she sees around her. A future religious leader, she is trying hard to find ways to contribute her ongoing learning to her community in ways that can be heard and utilized for community transformation and reconciliation.

## ASSUMPTIONS AND DEFINITIONS

Reconciliation is, at its core, a process of transformation for both sides in a conflict. The same transformation is also critical to an effective multicultural strategy of change. In our work on antiracism and multiculturalism at Visions, Inc., we define multiculturalism as the process of recognizing, understanding, and appreciating one's own culture as well as the culture of others. Multiculturalism stresses learning to appreciate the impact of differences in social location based on such variables as race, gender, class, age, sexual orientation, religion, physical ability, and language. This learning process is dynamic; as we begin to see the impact of differences, our sense of ourselves, others, and the world shifts. We impact others and others impact us differently. There is an interactive process occurring, potentially at four levels: the personal, interpersonal, institutional, and cultural (Figure 1).

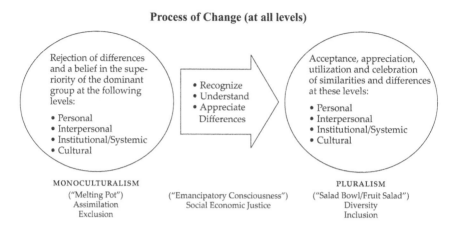

Figure 1. Assumptions and definitions of the multicultural process of change. Designed by Valerie A. Batts, Ph.D.; John Capitman, Ph.D.; and Joycelyn Landrum-Brown, Ph.D. © VISIONS, Inc. Reproduced with permission.

Several social activists in recent history have described how this multicultural reconciliation process plays out in oppressed/oppressor contexts. Diane J. Goodman, in *Promoting Diversity and Social Justice: Educating People from Privileged Groups,* refers to the dynamic as the "intertwined fate of the oppressor and the oppressed."[1] She quotes from the work and experience of several critical leaders in this field.

According to Paulo Freire, humanization is the vocation of human beings: "As oppressors dehumanize others and violate their (the oppressed's) rights, they themselves also become dehumanized." Freire further states, "Dehumanization, which marks not only those whose humanity has been stolen, but also (though in a different way) those who have stolen it, is a *distortion* of becoming more fully human."[2] Nelson Mandela, in his book *Long Walk to Freedom,* adds:

> I knew as well as I knew anything that the oppressor must be liberated just as surely as the oppressed. A man who takes away another man's freedom is a prisoner of hatred, locked behind the bars of prejudice and narrow-mindedness. I am not truly free if I am taking away someone else's freedom, just as surely as I am not free when my freedom is taken away from me. The oppressed and the oppressor alike are robbed of their humanity.[3]

Martin Luther King Jr. also noted this connection: "I can never be what I ought to be until you are what you ought to be, and you can never be what you might be until I am what I ought to be."[4]

True reconciliation can happen, then, only when all parties understand each other in ways that lead to behaving differently. For those with historic and current social, economic, and political power, that is, United States citizens of European ancestry, White Australians, White South Africans, and many others of European descent, reconciliation requires acknowledging the historic and continuing impact of racial privilege as well as working with the "targets" of this power imbalance in order to effect reconciliation at the personal, interpersonal, institutional, and cultural levels.

Racism, however, is not the only form of oppression in need of reconciliation. My colleagues and I at Visions, since 1984, have used in our anti-oppression work a framework for understanding the multiplicity of ways in which dysfunctional power imbalances can occur in the United States and in the wider world (Table 1).

Although forms of oppression vary, we have found the model and the process of change outlined in the remainder of this chapter to be useful in identifying and challenging power imbalances and thereby leading to a process of transformation and reconciliation. I invite you to "try on" our model of combating "modern racisms" as one framework or strategies necessary for "waging reconciliation."

## A MODEL FOR COMBATING "MODERN RACISM"

The national debate continues regarding whether or not affirmative action is still a necessary and effective strategy for attempting to correct historic power imbalances between the races. This debate is another example of the complex and insidious ways in which racism and racial prejudice in this country continue to inhibit the effective creation of a society in which true equal access to opportunity exists for every citizen.[5] In my graduate school work at Duke University in Durham, North Carolina, in the late 1970s, I worked with researchers who were demonstrating that such debates are actually covert or "symbolic" ways of expressing deeply ingrained biases that are typically unrecognized as such.[6] In the remainder of this paper, I

TABLE I

DYSFUNCTIONAL POWER IMBALANCES

| Types of Oppression | Variable | Nontarget Groups | Target Groups |
|---|---|---|---|
| Racism | Race/color | White | People of color (African, Asian, Native, Latino/a Americans) |
| Sexism | Gender | Men | Women |
| Classism | Socioeconomic class | Middle, upper class | Poor, working class |
| Elitism | Education level | Formally educated | Informally educated |
| | Place in hierarchy | Managers, exempt, faculty | Clerical, nonexempt, students |
| Religious oppression | Religion | Christians, Protestants | Muslims/Catholics, others |
| Anti-Semitism | Religion | Christians | Jews |
| Militarism | Military status | WWI and WWII, Korean, Gulf War veterans | Vietnam veterans |
| Ageism | Age | Young adults | Elders (40+ by law) |
| Adultism | Age | Adults | Children |
| Heterosexism | Sexual orientation | Heterosexuals | Gay, lesbian, bisexual, transgender |
| Ableism | Physical or mental ability | Temporarily able-bodied | Physically or mentally challenged |
| Xenophobia | Immigrant status | U.S. born | Immigrant |
| Linquistic oppression | Language | English | English as a second language, non-English |

Source: VISIONS, Inc., 2000. Reprinted with permission.

will describe my process of coming to understand this subtle or "modern" form of racism. I will also offer a model for identifying and changing modern racist behaviors. This model has evolved from consultation and training services offered to individuals and groups from the public and private sector since 1984.[7]

The model begins by describing *personal, interpersonal, institutional,* and *cultural* expressions of modern racism. Examples of white behavior are given, followed by a discussion of the impact of modern racism on blacks and other target group populations.[8] A description of target group responses is offered. Relationships between these expressions in blacks[9] and other people of color and whites are analyzed. The model concludes by reviewing the change process I have developed with many colleagues. Our interventions strive to eliminate guilt and blame and to encourage acceptance of responsibility and understanding of personal and systemic dysfunctional consequences of practicing modern racism and internalized oppression.

## MY LEARNING CONTEXT

As briefly alluded to above, I was born in the segregated South of the United States in the early 1950s. My parents were educators and were involved in efforts to ensure quality education for black children. My father was the principal of the first black middle school in our community. This school was built under the doctrine of "separate but equal" in the mid-1960s. I remember numerous "battles" that he, my mother, and their friends and neighbors fought to keep bringing adequate resources into our community. I remember our struggles to integrate public facilities. I remember both the fear and the determination within our community to bring about equal access. I remember when the struggle began to change from economic and social parity to integration.

I completed my junior year of high school in the last year of the existence of the segregated Booker T. Washington High School. My last year of high school was completed at the forcibly desegregated Rocky Mount Senior High School. Upon reflection, I believe my interest in addressing the subtle forms of racism began then. As a student activist, I was involved in several efforts to expose unstated assumptions and to encourage honest acknowledgment and dialogue about racial prejudice. Something kept telling me, "If we do not examine people's hearts, this desegregation process will not work."

Upon entering college in 1970, I became part of the largest class of black students to enter the University of North Carolina at Chapel Hill up to that time. There were approximately two hundred of us. There were about two hundred other black students already on campus. Given a student body of over twenty thousand, we were a small and largely invisible group. Part of how we survived this "foreign" experience was by forming a black support group, the Black Student Movement. Even when taking age into account, the "culture shock" I experienced during those first years at UNC was as great as any I have experienced while traveling across the United States and internationally as an adult.

Chapel Hill, North Carolina, was and still is a liberal Southern community. Howard Lee was mayor during those years, making him among the first black mayors since reconstruction. Hubert Humphrey won the presidential election in Orange County, North Carolina. It was the only county in the state that Ronald Reagan did not carry. The late Richard Epps was elected student body president and made national headlines as the "first black student body president" of a major Southern university.

At the same time, other black students and I were still battling assumptions of inferiority and continual pressures to assimilate to white cultural norms. Such efforts typically occurred as "off the mark" attempts to help us by whites or were expressed by them in the ways that we were unseen or our cultural expressions were misunderstood or minimized. The absence of role models or symbols of our worth and value also contributed to the perpetuation of assumptions of inferiority. As black students we developed many "survival strategies," (manipulating guilty whites, playing the clown, and working extra hard, etc.) some of which ultimately proved detrimental to us. The seeds were being sown for the life's work I was to move on to.

After leaving Chapel Hill, I decided to teach in a predominantly black Southern medical school. It was an important reimmersion experience.[10] I reconnected with the richness and security of black culture. I also began to see how the "survival strategies" that I had seen among us as students existed also among black people in predominantly and historically black environments. I began to ponder the impact of racism on blacks and how it can affect us even when we are the majority group in an educational system. I also began to notice how black students responded differently to black and white teachers.

I left this work in 1977 and went back to graduate school, this time at Duke University. The social psychology literature was beginning to assert that racism was all but gone in the United States. Public opinion polls were showing increased acceptance of blacks in all walks of life.[11] Three years later, the federal government took the position that we as a country had solved the racial problem and made efforts, for example, to dismantle the voting rights act. Some analysts suggest that social science as a discipline participated in this process of denial.[12] Current examples of such participation are still alive and well.[13]

The stance that racism had all but been eliminated in our country was quite problematic for me. It discounted both my experience as well as what I saw around me. In talking with others, I discovered that it was troubling to many blacks and whites who realized that it is not possible to change over three hundred years of history in a mere twenty to thirty years, even under the best of circumstances.[14] I was not alone in seeing continued resistance to integration of public institutions and facilities and to equal opportunity efforts to change the status quo and bring blacks and other people of color into positions of power and influence. This resistance became a symbol of a modern form of racism.

Fortunately, there were social psychologists at Duke working to challenge the notion that racism had declined significantly in the then thirteen years since the passage of the Civil Rights Act of 1964. Their work provided a theoretical framework for conceptualizing the experience I had been having throughout my journey into "desegregated America." The differentiation of racism into "old fashioned" and "modern" forms was very useful.

The view that blacks are inherently inferior to whites has been referred to as "old-fashioned" racism.[15] Its corollary, of course, is the myth of white superiority. Until 1954, racism was the law of the land. Old-fashioned racism involved behaviors, practices, and attitudes that overtly defined blacks as inferior and whites as superior. Blacks were thus entitled to fewer of society's benefits and resources. Behaviors, such as whites expecting blacks to defer to them in department stores, or practices of separate entrances to these stores, with blacks coming through small back entrances, are examples of the old forms. Laws prohibiting contact between blacks and whites, ranging from separate school systems to segregated seating on buses, are also examples. Lynchings, cross burnings, and Ku Klux Klan (KKK) activities are extreme forms. Even the paternalistic treatment by whites toward their black nannies is a kind of old-fashioned racism. The nanny is loved and valued as long as she understands her subservient role. She is expected to be seen and not heard around adults, to appreciate the family leftovers, to take her meals in the kitchen with the children, as well as to be called by her first name by them.

These forms of racism all have in common the overt acceptance of blacks as less than equal and whites as better than blacks. The civil rights movement that reached its zenith in 1965 in this century with the passage of the Civil Rights Act made many of these behaviors illegal for the first time. Although antilynching laws had been passed earlier, they were more stringently enforced as a consequence of public response to the new ruling. As overtly racist behavior in the public arena became illegal, it also became unpopular even in personal, private settings.[16] Although KKK activities did not stop entirely, legal sanctions were brought against many of its members.[17] Student groups who protested white supremacist activities on our nation's campuses were supported rather than the supremacists' rights to freedom of speech. It appeared that our country's three hundred year legacy of subjugation of brown peoples was beginning to abate.

At the same time this explicit resistance to old-fashioned expressions of negative racial attitudes, we still saw painful struggles across the country as black people attempted to attain parity in the public and private sector. We saw this more subtle type of resistance justified on nonracial grounds.

EXPRESSIONS OF RACISM

Modern racism has been defined as "the expression in terms of abstract ideological symbols and symbolic behaviors of the feeling that blacks are violating cherished values and making illegitimate demands for changes in the racial status quo."[18] It is, further, the attribution of nonrace-related reasons for behaviors that continue to deny equal access to opportunity to blacks and other targets of systemic oppression.[19] It is still based on the assumptions, the underlying beliefs, that blacks are inferior and whites are superior. The negative affect that accompanies these beliefs does not change just because of changes in law and practice. Rather the affect has to be submerged given the changes in what is viewed as legal and acceptable in the society.

What happens, then, when whites are in a position of having negative affective responses to blacks or other people of color? Given the lack of appropriateness of old-fashioned racist behaviors, it is likely that the affect will be expressed in subtle and covert ways.[20] The impact of the expression of this subtle or modern racism is as detrimental to change in our society as old-fashioned racism. The expression of such behaviors continues to result in blacks and other people of color being targeted to receive fewer of the benefits of being a citizen in the United States. The impact also perpetuates the "invisible knapsack of privilege" that whites are more likely to experience and take for granted.[21] Illustrations include explanations of white flight in response to school desegregation such as "It's not the blacks, it's the buses"; beliefs that affirmative action is "reverse discrimination"; acceptance of "the doctrine of color blindness"; or minimization by whites of the systemic causes and impacts of continued disparate treatment that whites and people of color receive in the United States.

Behavioral strategies used in the struggles to change old-fashioned racism typically included cultural exchange activities as well as confrontational training seminars or workshops. The cultural exchanges often heighten awareness of differences but without continued contact did not create substantive change in attitudes or behavior. Confrontational change workshops often left participants feeling blamed or attacked. Other participants came away having a sense of what it feels like to be oppressed but feeling guilty and powerless.

When I left Duke University and started working as a professional psychologist, I began to conduct workshops to challenge modern racism.[22] Participants have come from across the United States and from a variety of settings: educational settings, including public and private schools, universities and community colleges, mental health agencies, psychotherapy practices, hospitals, religious groups, community groups, arts groups, affirmative

action organizations, legal services, corporations, state and local governments, and long-term care settings. Ongoing consultation relationships with
several organizations from the public and private sector have also provided
information on how modern racism occurs and on strategies for change.[23]

Modern racism can be expressed at the *personal, interpersonal, institutional,* or *cultural* levels. In its typical expression these levels interact.[24]
Following is an example drawn from one of our workshops that illustrates
how each level operates and a definition of each level.

### AN EXAMPLE OF THE MULTIPLE LEVELS

A female workshop participant who grew up in Louisville, Kentucky, was
a teacher in a northern public school system. She was trying to understand
why the black and Latino students in her classes perceived her as a racist
when she felt she treated everybody the same. If anything, she admitted, she
tried harder to make things fair and equitable for them. In her tone of voice
was the message, "After all, I feel sorry for all the injustices these children
face and for the poor conditions surrounding their lives. I'm trying to help
them. Why don't they value my efforts?"

The schoolteacher was genuine in her desire to help, yet exploration of
her behavior led her to realize that outside of her awareness, she was operating on a personal assumption that black and Latino students are inferior due
to their upbringing in nonmainstream (that is, less adequate) communities.
She behaved toward them in interpersonal situations as if they were helpless
and less capable. This form of racism is different from old-fashioned racism
in that the woman's genuine desire was to correct for past inequities, not
to perpetuate them. The consequence, however, was the same. The students
were still being treated like second-class citizens and thus were being set
up to either accept the inferior helpless point of view or to reject the white
person or the educational system she represented.

An exploration of this woman's racial learning was revealing. She was
born in a northern city in the late forties. As a young child, she liked to ride
at the back of the bus when she and her family members went downtown
on Saturdays. Her family moved to Louisville when she was nine. This was
before buses had been desegregated in that town. The woman remembered

vividly the first Saturday that she and her mother took the bus in her new hometown. She got on the bus and eagerly started to walk toward the back as she had always done. Her mother called out to her to stop and sit at a seat near the front. As nine years olds are prone to do, she resisted, saying, "No, come on, let's go to the back." Her mom grabbed her arm nervously and said, "Sit down." She pulled her down. The woman remembers feeling confused and puzzled. She noticed with interest her mother's discomfort but said no more.

They reached their destination, went shopping, and then returned to the bus for the ride back home. The young girl again got on first and decided to try to go to the back. She was hoping her mother's previous behavior was just a fluke. Just as she said, "Look Mom, there are seats at the very back, let's hurry," her mother grabbed her and shook her, saying, "If I ever catch you going to the back of the bus again, I'll spank you." Her mother was shaking with apparent fear and rage. The woman remembers being shocked, then scared. She looked around the bus and noticed for the first time that all the people at the front of the bus were white and that all of the people at the back were black.

The woman immediately flashed on other things she had heard from her family about colored people and said to herself, "Oh, I am supposed to stay away from these people." She remembers feeling sad and scared on the ride home. She was finally learning her place as a white person. She remembers that all through public school she stayed in her place and kept to her own kind although she never quite believed it was right. She went to college during the sixties and became an active supporter of the Civil Rights Movement. She decided to go into teaching partly as a result of taking a sociology course in which she learned about the problems facing disadvantaged minorities. She remembers being filled with guilt during college about the ways blacks had been treated. She was ashamed of her family and angry with them. She genuinely wanted to make things better for black people.

This woman tried hard from the time of her college years "not to see color." As she started teaching black and Latino students, she dismissed subtle nagging sensations of guilt, disgust, or fear. She convinced herself that "people are just people" and turned any remaining negative affect into pity for the "victims" of systemic oppression. She stayed away from whites who expressed overtly negative racial attitudes and tried hard to be fair and honest and to get her students of color to perform just like white students.

As will be outlined in detail later, this woman's personal and interpersonal responses actually set up the perpetuation of dysfunctional interracial behavior even though that was not her intention. Further, she was employed by a school system that had a majority of black and Latino students, but 80 percent of the school personnel were white. Few of these white staff members had contact with people of color in their personal or professional lives, except for students. The school system saw its role as helping to prepare students to succeed in the United States of America, as defined by white, male, Protestant, middle class, middle-age, heterosexual, physically able norms.

The school's culture reflected the values of this "normative" group as well. Most black and Latino students felt isolated and alienated in the environment. In addition to experiencing interpersonal racism from school personnel like the workshop participant, they also were experiencing racism in its institutional and cultural expressions. There were no bilingual education programs. The administration could not see the usefulness of such activities because their job was to teach these children standard English. When Latino students spoke to each other in Spanish, they were often reprimanded. Black English was viewed as substandard even though many of the black children communicated clearly that they were, in fact, bilingual as well. They spoke Black English at breaks and at home, yet knew how to speak and write the way they were being trained to do at school. In both cases, the students were comfortable with their two cultures; school personnel were not.

Similarly, most of the textbooks stressed "American" (that is, United States) and European culture. Except on special occasions, typically because of student or parent interest, little attention was focused on African, African American, or the variety of Latino cultures. Faculty and administrators felt the students would not be adequately prepared for the "real world" if they spent a lot of time focusing on such "frills" as jazz, salsa, life in Brazil or Cuba, or issues in South Africa. For the students of color, these were very important issues. No attempts to use these interests to teach basic skills were being considered. Again, the assumption of those in charge about how learning should occur, both in terms of process and content, did not allow for inclusion of cultural differences.

In summary, a definition of each level of racism is offered below:

- *Personal.* At this level, racism is prejudice or bias. It is the maintenance of conscious or unconscious attitudes and feelings that whites are superior and that blacks or other people of color are inferior or that these groups' differences are not acceptable in some way. Personal level racism includes cognitive or affective misinformation or both.[25] The misinformation may be learned directly, as through overt messages, or indirectly as through observation.

- *Interpersonal.* Behaviors based on conscious or unconscious biased assumptions about self and other are interpersonal manifestations of racism. It is often through uncomfortable or tense cross-cultural interactions that individuals discover subtle racist behaviors within themselves or others.[26]

- *Institutional.* An examination of power relationships reveals institutional racism. The question to be asked is, to what extent do the intended and unintended consequences of policies, practices, laws, styles, rules, and procedures function to the advantage of the dominant group and to the disadvantage of people of color? To the extent that whites in this society have the political, economic, educational, social, and historical power and access to institutionalize prejudices (that is, the myths of white superiority and black inferiority) against blacks and other people of color, whites are in a position to practice or maintain institutional racism.[27]

- *Cultural.* The ability to define European American and Western cultural preferences as "right and beautiful" is the consequence of having institutional power and access in this country. When the standards of appropriate action, thought, and expression of a particular group are perceived either overtly or subtlety as negative or less than, cultural racism has occurred. Conformity to the dominant culture is then viewed as "normal" when in fact the myth of the inherent superiority of the group setting the standards is operating. If such is the case, it is likely that a given individual will need to change his or her behavior to fit those of the dominant group just to be accepted as competent, attractive, or talented.[28]

MODERN RACISM

As illustrated in the example above, modern racism is often not malicious by intent. Understanding the expressions or levels just outlined helps in clarifying how the consequence of particular behaviors can result in racism regardless of motivation. The schoolteacher, for instance, was supportive of institutional changes that would bring in more black and Latino teachers. Yet, her personal and cultural biases and preferences made it hard for her to accept a prospective Latino language teacher who in English classes taught Spanish to English speakers and English to Spanish speakers, and then had them spend some time dialoguing in the nonnative and then the native languages in each class. The white teacher found herself agreeing with the administration that while this idea perhaps had some merit, it was not efficient and it was redundant with what the students learned in Spanish foreign language classes.

Following is a description of suggested ways that modern racism occurs. It is useful to consider that the behaviors outlined can manifest themselves at each of the four levels defined above. It is also the case that currently racism is likely to manifest itself in subtle forms. This is not to discount, of course, the increase in overt old-fashioned racist behavior that has continued to escalate across the United States since 1985.[29] These reactions might be thought of as the backlash from a decade or so of denial in our country that racial problems do continue to exist.[30] Modern racism theory attempts to explain the impact of the growing silence on racial issues in society from approximately 1975 to 1985 as well as the current controversy or tendency to explain racism away or to be reluctant to see it.

Institutional gains made between 1954 and 1965 were clear and obvious. As civil rights issues became more substantive, however, and therefore more of a challenge to the power brokers, the character of racism began to change. Derrick Bell notes:

> Rather than eliminate racial discrimination, civil rights laws have only driven it underground, where it flourishes even more effectively. While employers, landlords, and other merchants can no longer rely on rules that blatantly discriminate against minorities, they can erect barriers that although they make no mention of race, have the same exclusionary effect. The discrimination that was out in the open during the Jim Crow era could at least be seen, condemned, and fought as a moral issue. Today, statistics, complaints, even secretly filmed instances of discrimination that are

televised nationwide ... upset few people because, evidently, no amount of hard evidence will shake the nation's conviction that the system is fair for all.[31]

Let us take the issue of education, for example. The first battle for equality was to allow blacks entry into previously all-white schools. The struggle for this civil right was arduous but resulted in a clearly definable outcome: blacks going to schools with whites. Once this goal was accomplished, whites quickly wanted to move to the position that the issue was resolved.[32] But ensuring equity requires more than having blacks in schools with whites.[33] The larger questions were not yet addressed, such as how many blacks and other people of color help control the curriculum that all children receive; what relevant materials will be used that reflect and affirm diverse cultures as equal or important and that expose the myth of white and Western superiority; where schools will be located; and how much money will be spent on children's education.[34]

The other reality is that whites, as a group, never really accepted open enrollment. Instead, white flight was clearly the option taken by the majority, while blacks and other target groups remained in schools that they no longer controlled. This phenomenon became more entrenched as bankers, realtors, and developers engaged in housing and lending discrimination while the federal government failed to enforce housing discrimination law. It was a much more silent strategy than the anti-integration mobs of the late 1950s and early 1960s. Yet its power to negatively impact the educational experience of much of the country's youth has yet to be fully realized.

Stated differently, our society's actions by its shift toward a belief that racism has ended, discounted the unavoidable impact of more than three hundred fifty years of history. It did not allow individuals and institutions to alter structures, materials, attitudes, and, in many cases, behavior to fully create equity in a multicultural sense. Rather, it forced whites and people of color to struggle in new ways to attempt to handle the remains of these centuries of oppression. Legislative changes were made but the hearts and minds of people remained the same.[35] John Dovidio and Samuel Gaertner assert that this difficulty in acknowledging racism was made even more difficult in such a climate because of a deeply held U.S. value on "doing the right thing."[36] If racism is now "wrong," how can we admit that we still struggle with it?

The following list of behaviors or manifestations of modern racism for the dominant or nontarget groups are offered from my colleagues and my experiences to help explain this struggle.[37] The accompanying examples come from our work in educational settings.

1. *Dysfunctional rescuing.* This form of modern racism is characterized by helping people of color based on an assumption that they cannot help themselves; setting them up to fail; being patronizing or condescending; helping people of color in such a way that it limits their ability to help themselves. This "help that does not help" is often motivated out of guilt or shame. It may be conscious or unconscious and is often embedded in the "culture of niceness or politeness" thus making its limiting aspects hard to discern.

Examples of dysfunctional rescuing are:

A white teacher "gives" a black student who is making a "B+" an "A" instead of challenging her. The student is active in the black student association and is obviously quite bright. The teacher feels vaguely guilty about societal injustices and worries that the student might see him as racist. The teacher is not active in campus efforts to change institutional racism and believes that if he just "does right by blacks," everything will be okay.

A white department head brings a thirty-year-old black female into a previously all-white male biology department. He feels good about insisting that she be chosen and denies the importance of the reluctance of his colleagues. All of these faculty have been at the institution for at least ten years and have failed to support the hiring of any target group members. The department chair fails to recognize the potential setup for failure involved in bringing target groups into a hostile environment without a plan for impacting the culture. "Tokenism" is another name for this process of "doing what's right" without preparing the existing organization for this change.

2. *Blaming the victim.* In this form, racism is expressed by attributing the results of systemic oppression to the target group; ignoring the real impact of racism on the lives of blacks or other people of color; blaming people

of color for their current economic situation; or setting target group members up to fail and then blaming them.[38] To provide structural and status changes but to give inadequate support, that is, time, training, or mentoring, for the development of positive and constructive outcomes, is one illustration. The nontarget accepts little or no responsibility for current inequities and puts all the responsibility on target group members for negative outcomes.

Examples of blaming the victim include:

A black student is labeled as having misplaced priorities because of her work on black issues on her campus; she is considered bright but too busy being angry to study. She was not accepted into a student leaders campus honorary society because her concerns were viewed as "too narrow."

A Latina female becomes depressed and exhibits paranoid symptoms in a faculty meeting after being the lone Latina and female faculty person for a year in a previously all-white male department where she is largely avoided or patronized. The chairman recommends she get psychiatric treatment.

3. *Avoidance of contact.* Modern racism may also be manifested by not having social or professional contact with people of color; making no effort to learn about life in communities of color; living in all-white communities; or exercising the choice that whites most often have of not being involved in the lives of people of color.

Examples of the avoidance of contact are:

A white university administrator who lives in an all-white neighborhood says, "I just don't have the opportunity to meet black people."

A white supervisor is a very pleasant person but does not confront a situation when two black male employees engage in conflict. The supervisor, however, would confront the situation if the employees were white.

4. *Denial of cultural differences.* In this expression, modern racism means minimizing obvious physical or behavioral differences between people as well as differences in preferences that may be rooted in culture; discounting the influence of African culture and of the African American or Asian American experience; or being color-blind in a way that masks discomfort with differences.

Examples of the denial of cultural differences include:

A white faculty member describing the only black faculty member he works with and trying hard to avoid saying that the faculty member is black.

A white administrator says with much exasperation, when being given information about racial differences in retention of blacks in his university, "What does race have to do with it? Aren't people just people? Skin color doesn't matter, we are all just people."

5. *Denial of the political significance of differences.* Finally, modern racism may be manifested by not understanding or denying the differential impacts of social, political, economic, historical, and psychological realities on the lives of people of color and whites, minimizing the influence of such variables on all our lives and institutions. This modern racism may be accompanied by an attitude that cultural differences are just interesting or fun. Such a stance results in an unwillingness to acknowledge the multiplicity of ways in which the impacts of the myth of white superiority continue. The stance also minimizes white privilege as well as the insidious nature of the prevalence of the mentality and practice of "West is best" by those in positions of power and control in key aspects of life in the United States and most of the world as the beginning of the twenty-first century. This type of modern racism is firmly entrenched and is perhaps the most binding. Unraveling the hold of a dominant Western perspective will take a massive rethinking of many of our ways of being and doing in the United States, especially in light of September 11.

Examples of the denial of the political significance of differences are:

A white middle-level manager came to a workshop very upset about the affirmative action plan his company has implemented. He was convinced that affirmative action was reverse discrimination and said, "We don't need affirmative action here. We hire blacks." Blacks comprised 10 percent of the management positions (up 8 percent in two years because of the plan) and 90 percent of the custodial positions.

A white faculty member dismissed Jesse Jackson's campaign for president as minimally important at best, for after all, Jackson had no governmental experience. When students pointed out the number of voters Jackson had registered and the large number of popular votes he had obtained, the faculty member said, "That's not really important; what's important is that he is not a qualified applicant."

INTERNALIZED OPPRESSION

As discussed in the definition of institutional racism above, African Americans and other targets of racism are in a reactive posture. This is not to minimize in any way the personal, economic, and political power that target group members have available to them. It is intended to challenge targets and nontargets to think seriously about the extremely detrimental impact of maintaining a society where institutional power is distributed predominantly to one group.

It is difficult for those who suffer at the hands of oppression not to buy into, at some level, the misinformation that society has perpetuated about victim status.[39] Internalized oppression is the incorporation of negative or limiting messages regarding our way of being and responding in the world by targets of systemic oppression. We define our uniqueness as inferior or different in an unhealthy or un-useful manner. As the character of racism changes, so does the reaction of people of color to it. Most forms of internalized oppression had their origins in situations when their manifestation was necessary for physical or psychological survival.[40] Such behaviors are most likely to occur initially as survival responses in institutions or in situations where the target person perceives a threat. Five expressions of internalized oppression have been identified.[41]

1. *System beating.* This expression of internalized oppression involves attempting to get over on, or around the system; manipulating others or the system through guilt, psychological games, or illicit activities; acting out anger; or playing dumb, clowning, being invisible. The strategy involves an awareness that one is an outsider; on the belief that the target group member cannot succeed by being direct and/or by being herself or himself. The target group person feels a need to "take care" of whites' feelings or to hide parts of oneself for fear of being misunderstood or viewed unfavorably because of his or her "difference." It may also take the form of using anger or hostility to manipulate whites.

Examples of system beating are:

A black student manages to go through four years of college with a reading deficit. He is a star basketball player and learns through the grapevine how to take courses where he can "get over" and receive a passing grade.

A Latino teacher in an "upscale" independent school does not speak out, for fear of being disliked, when faculty and staff condemn Latino yard workers for speaking Spanish and using English poorly.

A black hospital employee intimidates all of her white superiors such that she just comes and goes to work as she pleases and does as little work as possible. Any negative feedback is defined by this employee as racism on the part of her bosses.

2. *Blaming the system.* This manifestation is characterized by deflecting responsibility for one's actions; putting all the blame on the other or the system for one's problems; or refusing to learn about and acknowledge mental, emotional, and stress-related issues as real. This expression results in an externalizing and blaming of others that in effect gives away the target group members' ability to effect change. It sometimes masks a sense of hopelessness in the target group's ability to visualize or implement a more desirable system.

Examples of blaming the system include:

A black student, who is not studying, blames his teacher and the "system" for his bad grades. He is unwilling to accept what role his lack of preparation may have in his failure to succeed.

A Latina employee applies for a job for which she is not qualified, and says it is the system's fault when she does not get hired. She is unwilling to take advantage of opportunities to get the appropriate training and "blames" it on the fact that her English is too poor.

3. *Antiwhite avoidance of contact.* This form of internalized oppression includes avoiding contact with whites; distrusting all whites (obsessive concern and suspicion); being overly sensitive to rejection; rejecting people of color who are perceived as "not black enough" or "not Chinese enough," and so on; escaping (through fantasy, dreams, drugs, alcohol, sex, food, withdrawal). Such a stance is fueled by a rage that can be self-destructive to the person who carries it. The utility of anger is to stop injustice and to insist on and create equity; when it becomes internalized it can hamper the autonomy of the target group person.

Examples of antiwhite avoidance of contact are:

A Chinese employee who refuses to talk to a white supervisor about a job-related problem because he says the supervisor will not understand. He does not admit that he is really uncomfortable talking to whites. He therefore limits his own chances for a positive change in his situation.

A black who calls another black an "Uncle Tom" because the latter is working hard to get a promotion and because he is light-skinned. This perpetuation of "colorism" and of a denial of the impressive "profound work ethic" among black people is self-limiting.

4. *Denial of cultural heritage.* In this expression, internalized oppression means distrusting one's own group, accepting that one's group is inferior, giving deference to whites, ejecting or devaluing one's cultural heritage, valuing and overemphasizing white standards of beauty, valuing and accepting whites as the highest authority and white standards as superior. Such a stance colludes with the myths of "white superiority and inferiority of people of color."

Examples of denial of cultural heritage include:

A Latino patient who does not want a Latino nurse or doctor because the patient thinks they are not as well qualified as a white nurse or doctor.

A black employee who does not associate much with blacks, who is uncomfortable considering her African heritage, and who, when with whites, aggressively expresses negative opinions of blacks as a group.

5. *Lack of understanding or minimization of the political significance of racial oppression.* Internalized oppression can also be manifested by being passive and unassertive; feeling powerless (learned helplessness), misdirecting anger to persons with less power, having difficulty expressing anger, avoiding conflicts at all costs, turning anger inward resulting in high blood pressure, strokes, ulcers; buying copiously (symbolic status striving; conspicuous consumption of goods—clothes, cars, and so on); in-group fighting, displaying sexist or other "ism" behaviors, for example, heterosexism, classism, and so on, taking advantage of the lack of information or feelings of powerlessness of other people of color. This stance involves failure to examine the pervasive nature of racism and the multiplicity of ways in which target group members are set up to collude with its perpetuation. It can also result in an unwillingness to accept that the historical legacy of racial oppression has not been corrected systematically and its effects continue to impact most aspects of life.

Examples of a lack of understanding or minimization of the political significance of racial oppression are:

A black first-level manager is unwilling to apply for a promotion because he does not think he will get it. He is sure that the organization will not promote a person of color simply because there are none presently. He has the necessary skills but does not believe he can be successful. He does not understand how to seek out and organize support to promote systemic change.

An Asian supervisor always does what the white manager wants and is harder on the employees of color whom he supervises. He believes that the white supervisor cannot be and should not be successfully confronted but feels powerful as he "pushes" his supervisees of color.

One can see that the five modern racisms have their corollary or parallel in the five internalized oppressions. Table 2 shows their relationship to each other.

## HOW MODERN RACISM AND INTERNALIZED OPPRESSION INTERACT

Challenging modern racism and internalized oppression begins as individuals give up the need to deny that "isms" still exist. Rather, they start to look for manifestations of oppression in the personal, interpersonal, institutional, and cultural contexts. Modern racism and internalized oppression are often played out in a complementary fashion. Given a white who practices

TABLE 2

BEHAVIORAL MANIFESTATIONS OF MODERN RACISM
AND INTERNALIZED OPPRESSION

| Modern Racism | Internalized Oppression |
|---|---|
| 1. Dysfunctional rescuing | 1. System beating |
| 2. Blaming the victim | 2. Blaming the system |
| 3. Avoidance of contact | 3. Antiwhite avoidance of contact |
| 4. Denial of differences | 4. Denial of cultural heritage |
| 5. Denial of the political significance of differences | 5. Lack of understanding of the political significance of differences |

dysfunctional rescuing, for example, many people of color will resort to system beating rather than confront the behavior, if they perceive it to be the safest choice, or if they have no permission to be assertive with whites. Such actions reinforce the dysfunctional behavior on both parts and keep the system intact.

People of color, who for a variety of reasons have adopted a "don't trust whites" stance, will often be misunderstood by whites who practice avoidance of contact. The white person will take the person of color's avoidance of contact stance personally and will often use it as justification of further avoidance. Such whites discount the realities of racism for blacks or other people of color and do not seek information about their experiences. They are also likely to perceive blacks or Latinos, for instance, who are in a pro-black or pro-Latino posture as antiwhite when the individuals are not.

At the institutional level, most welfare laws of the late 1960s were written from a dysfunctional rescuing position. Recipients, typically children and their mothers, were set up to fail and are now being blamed for their plight. Monetary benefits were inadequate, the process for attaining help was dehumanizing, and the incentives for getting training or for working were not available.[42] Those welfare recipients who attempted to beat the system used blame to justify their actions while avoiding any responsibility for changing their conditions.

Using the system when there are no other feasible options is "survival behavior" and not reactive internalized oppression. Indeed, a critical question to be asked as individuals are teasing out "the dance" between modern racism and internalized oppression is, When is a given target group members' "difficult behavior" reflective of a survival strategy? In the face of overt or covert racism, internalized oppression behaviors can be the key to psychological or physical survival. It is very important that such behaviors, which are reactive to racism, not be used to blame people of color or other target group members for their adaptations to oppression.

PROCESS OF CHANGE

As has been illustrated, many examples of modern racism have been generated from our training and consultation efforts since 1984. Participants in these efforts typically share a common goal: learning how to incorporate an appreciation of cultural diversity and multicultural strategies in their work or organizational settings. They want to be able to create or enhance this appreciation both interpersonally and structurally. There is an apparent debate among change agents in this field regarding the focus or outcome of such strategies. There is considerable discussion regarding the questions, Are we providing diversity work, antiracism work, or are we promoting multiculturalism? Where does antibias work fit into this discussion?

Such a debate can become distracting to the effort. It is our assumption that we are essentially looking at all of these issues in any successful change effort.[43] Diversity speaks to the need to change numbers and, in many cases, perspective. It addresses who is in a given organization and what ideas, images, processes, and so on are included in the group's work. Cultural diversity speaks specifically to the inclusion of such aspects from a cultural instead of, or in addition to, an individual perspective. Antibias efforts are also aimed at ensuring that multicultural work looks at all forms of bias or discrimination. We believe that successful antiracist, multicultural work has to include this focus.

Antiracism efforts speak to the need to explicitly address historic and current power imbalances. Addressing these imbalances successfully will include attention to how they play out with respect to all power discrepancies. Women of color, for example, are targets of racism and sexism. To address sexism successfully, one must address racism. To address heterosexism successfully, as another case in point, racism must be addressed as well since there is differential access for lesbians and gay men of color. In both instances, nontargets experience costs in addition to privileges as men and as heterosexuals. And the list goes on. It is not possible to successfully address racism in any lasting manner without raising these other aspects. The issue for change agents will be, Where do we begin, not Will we consider all of these parameters?

We see multiculturalism as the process through which change occurs. Multicultural strategies are designed to increase the ability of individuals and groups to recognize, understand, and appreciate differences as well as similarities. This three-step process occurs most often in stages and involves first recognizing and unlearning one's biases. For most of us in the United States, our worldview incorporated negative perceptions or other dysfunctional adaptations to people who were different from the accepted norm. This norm, unfortunately, for most U.S. citizens from both nontarget and target groups, involved an evaluation of how close one fits to being white, male, young to middle aged (twenty-five to forty-five), heterosexual, United States–born and American English speaking, Protestant, middle class, and physically able.

The second step of a multicultural change process involves seeing and thinking about the content of cultural group differences. Reclaiming one's ethnic background is part of this process, as is giving up dysfunctional ethnocentrism. The goal is coming to experience that being equal does not mean being the same and that valuing diversity means being willing to accept the validity of ways of being other than one's own. As a third step this belief begins to be applied personally and systemically. It includes explicit attention to power sharing, redistribution of resources, and redefinition of "what is right and beautiful" at all levels. As the implementation of this worldview starts to occur, appreciation becomes the process. Participants start to embrace the value, philosophy, and practice that any system, institution, program, or curriculum is enhanced by the acknowledgment and usage of cultural differences as a critical factor.

Personal and interpersonal change involves, then, acknowledging and valuing one's own cultural background and recognizing the particular dynamics found within different cultural groups. This process includes working through cognitive and affective misinformation about other cultural groups as well as about one's own group. It is facilitated by regular contact with persons from and information about different groups as well as with ongoing contact with members of one's own group as mentors. Willingness to try on new behaviors, to make mistakes, and to disagree are necessary parts of the process.

It is important to stress that unlearning modern racism and internalized oppression in all of its expressions is a *process*. Part of the reason that the character of racism shifted for most people in the United States rather than changed is because there was such an urgent need to fix the problem.[44] The goal in changing racism is to stay open when behaviors or practices arise that are, in their consequences, regardless of their intent, discriminatory. It also means examining fully the multitude of ways in which our society currently still functions economically, socially, politically, and culturally to the advantage of whites and to the disadvantage of people of color. As long as such institutional and cultural racism continues to exist, modern racism behaviors or practices will continue to emerge even among well-intentioned people.

Changing institutional and cultural racism involves a commitment by all members of an organization to examine norms, values, and policies. Overt power discrepancies must be changed. More subtle reward systems that reinforce status quo behaviors must give way to systems that include diversity and multiculturalism at every point. Institutions typically have to start by acknowledging the fear among those who control the current structure of either losing that control or of doing the wrong thing (that is, being called a racist or making things worse by focusing on differences). These fears often manifest as anger, backlash, and need to control how change occurs or as guilt, shame, or the experiencing of target group authority figures as not experienced or competent enough. There is a need to acknowledge and work through those fears at all levels of the organization.[45]

Training in racism awareness and multiculturalism is crucial to removing fear and other barriers. Such training helps organization members appreciate what they will gain as individuals and as an organization by fully embracing multiculturalism. Training should occur within and across different levels of the organizational hierarchy and within and between different cultural groups.[46] It is crucial to a long-term successful intervention that all individuals come to see that some of the work in dismantling oppression entails working within one's own group; that is, whites need to learn to challenge and support other whites, and people of color need space for continual self-definition and within-group problem solving and agenda setting. Successful group coalitions at this point in our history entail the ability to coalesce and to separate.

Review of organizational structures, processes, norms, and values by multicultural teams is a crucial next step. Individuals working within a structure to create change will need to develop allies. Involvement of team members as facilitators, trainers, and institutional change agents with high visibility helps employees see that the organization's commitment is real and is ongoing. The team members should set up methods of communicating their process and important outcomes. Problem spots within the organization need to be highlighted and changed. Areas that are acknowledging differences and working well should be celebrated.[47]

Unlearning racism in all its expressions is offered as a model for understanding how oppression works in any target or nontarget relationship.[48] It is crucial that individuals realize how each person is sometimes in both positions. Multiculturalism, then, involves committing to the process of altering the variety of ways in which individuals and groups establish one-up/one-down dynamics. To paraphrase James Baldwin's comments in an open letter to Angela Davis, if they come for you tonight, they will be back for me in the morning.[49]

## A FINAL WORD AND A CALL

I believe the Episcopal Church's House of Bishops, as well as religious and spiritual leaders from around the world and in all traditions, have a critical role to play in developing an effective psychology and spirituality necessary to create a peaceful world discourse. The above model for combating modern racism and its many manifestations is offered as one way that religious leaders can become effective change agents for a reconciled human community. Many within the world's religious traditions have boldly or quietly done such in the past. Now is our time to do the same. If not now, when? If not us, who?

Another of the prophetic words of Martin Luther King Jr., written about the United States in the 1960s, are bringing me both comfort as well as fear at what will happen if we do not provide such leadership at this time.

> I refuse to accept the cynical notion that nation after nation must spiral down a militaristic stairway into the hell of thermonuclear destruction. I believe that unarmed truth and unconditional love will have the final word in reality.[50]

Although Dr. King no longer lives with us to inspire us, his message lives on. As bishops and religious leaders dedicated to "waging reconciliation" we must "keep on keeping on" following King's prophetic words:

> Darkness cannot drive out darkness; only light can do that. Hate cannot drive out hate; only love can do that. Hate multiplies hate, violence multiplies violence, and toughness multiplies toughness in a descending spiral of destruction. . . . The chain reaction of evil—Hate begetting hate, wars producing more wars—must be broken, or we shall be plunged into the darkness of annihilation.[51]

# 22 What Is Justice in Conflict Resolution Practice?

S.Y. BOWLAND

> We call it ubuntu, botho. It means the essence of being human.
> You know when it is there and when it is absent. It speaks about
> humanness, gentleness, hospitality, putting yourself out on the
> behalf of others, being vulnerable. It recognizes that my humanity
> is bound up in yours, for we can only be human together.
> —Archbishop Desmond Tutu

This quotation from Archbishop Desmond Tutu speaks to the environment we must create for the resolution of conflict.[1] I use his explanation of *ubuntu* when I define justice, both as a feeling, an outcome and an experience. It is especially important to me when facilitating conflicts involving Black people. Historically and consciously, as an African American woman and when working in the Black community, I experience justice as a spiritual presence, not often described much beyond spirituality but known in greater depth by those who know. There is a saying, "If you know you know, and if you don't you don't." Maybe experience closes the gap from not knowing to knowing.

I imagine the pursuit of justice in conflict resolution as a mutual effort by all parties that addresses the heart of the pain and injury sustained, a spiritual journey for some and a matter about society for others. Justice is a term many of us feel well informed about; we know justice when we see it and when we experience it. Most of us have been well trained by society to seek justice and to think we understand it because we have all contributed to its definition and application. Yet, how many of us have been trained to understand, capture, and use the presence of justice when we feel it? This process is what I call spiritual justice. Most of us have learned about justice from television, radio, and other media images. Still others of us have learned about it from studying the law and reading the canons. These images, writings, and trainings frame our thoughts, ideas, and hearts. For those of us who have studied the law we know about justice through case law studies, precedent, and jurisprudence. But such methods have excluded a great number of peoples, cultures, and classes. In my community this exclusion is known as the politics of knowledge. Knowledge is created, maintained, and resourced by those who have the power to maintain the status quo.

The growth of the conflict resolution field has lead to a greater exploration by scholars and practitioners of the importance and presence of spirituality in mediation and other conflict resolution processes. Contained in this essay you will find my thoughts on the many ways justice has its space in conflict resolution and can contribute to a more peaceful existence for all.

The legal system uses the term justice when a crime against a person or society has occurred and the parties or society demand justice. We also hear about justice when people feel they have been wronged or injured and they seek resolution to their conflict. These references to justice usually involve some punishment as an outcome as well as a reward for the injured party and society. Both reward and punishment occur at the same time as different ends of a spectrum, leaving little room for the qualities Archbishop Tutu describes to be present in the room on a spiritual level. How would conflict resolution look different using the model of *ubuntu, botho* as a way of assuring the presence of justice in the process? This essay is a story of how I work to incorporate spiritual justice in conflict resolution processes.

I believe justice must be present in the room to solve any problem among people, communities, and cultures. The extent to which conflict resolution practitioners can contribute to an environment fostering justice depends greatly on their training and experience. Developing the energy and essence of spiritual justice in conflict resolution processes is a must, especially for communities of color.

The spirit Archbishop Tutu describes offers a cultural context for people who have an individual or collective experience of bias or prejudice, and it aids in the discovery and elimination of "isms." The practice of being human together must be alive in any arena designed for problem solving. But many Black people have told me that they do not feel any such spirit in conflict resolution processes they experience, especially when facilitations happen through the courts.

Personally, I most experience the presence of justice through feelings. As a facilitator for the parties engaged in the process, I feel justice as a sense of comfort coupled with the strength to risk taking a journey on a road to fulfillment. In my experience, those of us from oppressed backgrounds and environments of domination have a special radar that scans and picks up potential and existing threats to our human dignity. It scans memories of past experiences and present sources of protection. Like a button that is always on, or a record that plays constantly, our radar searches for examples of behaviors that may be injurious or may be beneficial. White people I have spoke with on this topic suggest to me that they experience this process as a test, and guess what? who likes a test you are not prepared for? Yet for the person who has been oppressed, it is a necessary test to establish whether justice is present or absent.

What follows are my responses to interview questions posed by Beth Roy and Mary Adams Trujillo, followed by practical suggestions for mediators and my closing reflections.

Q. What does justice mean?

A. What does justice mean? Based on my experience as a practitioner, I think that we have several parallel interpretations of the meaning of justice, different meanings for different people depending upon circumstances. "Just us" is an expression comedian Richard Pryor used when telling a joke. Here is how I remember hearing it as a young lady: "How can Black people go to court looking for Justice when all you would see in the jails is 'just us?'"

I've been thinking about justice for a long time, all my conscious life. I can remember being a young person growing up in Harlem and seeing how things were different and seeing how different people lived different ways. To make it clearer, it always seemed that black people had it harder than non-black people. I was always curious about why things appeared as they did. Where I lived in Harlem was near Columbia University. So, you could walk down one street and see Columbia University, this famous school. And then you could go in the opposite direction for two or three blocks and see the projects. And you'd be like, how did this happen and is this fair? Or how is this clear? How is this possible? Of course, the majority of people accessing Columbia University were white and the majority of us in the projects were poor to working class black and Hispanic families.

Living accommodations were not the only place where I could see the race and class divide. I could see it at school—most of the teachers were white. You could also see it on the streets. Who waited for the bus and where? Who walked to the train station? Who walked home form the train and bus stations? Just us. Yes, from the living accommodations to the most basic parts of family life we could feel and experience what seemed like little justice. It was a feeling, like the white communities were better protected, better nourished and better than us. In our family life we experienced the absence of justice when we missed the many loved ones who were incarcerated for crimes they may and may not have committed.

It was not uncommon between me and my classmates to have a loved one in prison. No one talked about it because of the shame associated with it, like "Maybe I am bad, too."

However, it was a great day when the loved one got out. I remember my Aunt Alice fixing a big dinner for everyone so we could welcome the loved one back home. This was a form of restorative justice and reconciliation. I can recall the words during or after dinner, "We are all here to show love and support for ——. He's not going to get into any more trouble, isn't that right?" The expressions of support would go around the table. Then the acclamations of assistance would follow. So in essence a plan for success was created and Aunt Alice would work to be the peacekeeper to keep the agreements in place. Thank you, Aunt Alice!

And yes, the squeaky wheel gets the oil, because we were always putting out fires, so little attention was given to those of us who wanted to work and think differently about our life experiences and the "isms" we experienced. Where were the role models? So, yes, there was a feeling of who's got my back? The double consciousness of "Am I bad, too, if my relatives are bad?" is an underlying concern affecting the minds greatly of young ones.

I had all of those thoughts when you asked me what does justice mean. In terms of conflict resolution, I would say the meaning of justice is held by those stakeholders in the conflict, and the role of the practitioner is to get as clear an understanding of one's definition as possible, so as to be most effective in facilitating the dialogue for resolution.

To me, justice means that when I see you and you see me, we see each other and we see dignity and respect for each other. And that we won't do anything to hurt or injure each other and that we understand that you have to have forgiveness and that we had to work through problem solving together. It doesn't mean that I've got to punish you, or shame you or me.

But I think that when justice gets played out in different types of structures—a workplace, or family, or personally—and if it is based on some sort of retaliation because of something you've done that has hurt or injured someone, the outcome seems ineffective for any community.

When most people I talk to or work with say "justice" they automatically want to say "fairness" and "equity." But I don't really see fairness and equity as variables that make up justice. I think if we put the human person or the human spirit at the center of justice we get a whole different outcome than if we talk about fairness or equity. Because who decides fairness? Who decides equity? But if we put the human spirit or the human person at the center of the discussion, then we get to decide what we need at that moment, and we don't have to follow a pattern or practice that's predesigned to say, "Well, that's right," or "That's wrong."

Q. How do you think the historical or social experience of African Americans in particular supports or informs notions of justice?

A. I think it has done so in many ways, on personal, social, and political and levels, and it has been very expensive for us. I can speak to the way that it happened in my community. The concept of justice was packed very heavily with experiences where there was clearly a lack of treating people with basic human dignity.

When I was young, concepts of justice were shown through TV news coverage and other media messages. At the same time, I think justice was informed by how we watched families come together. We saw how families worked, and we could see how different patterns or effects happened. There was a belief that justice is present with opportunities; so if you could have an opportunity and you came with your skills and if you succeeded, then I think there was a feeling that there was some sense of justice that was present. You might wonder how could such a complicated concept of what was right and fair and wrong and good be addressed in such a simple form as TV. Here's how: Blacks seldom were seen in positive roles, were always highlighted—and often still are highlighted—in a negative fashion in news stories or simple family shows. What was *not* done has as much impact as what *was* done, year after year after year. That negative impact, coupled with poverty, ill treatment in the law and known unfairness to black communities, yes . . .

Justice is not a law; maybe it should be. It is used in the legal system to define right and wrong. Instead, I see justice as a thread through all parts of life. Justice is really about being—what we see and the way we behave. It's not a thing that is outside of me; it's a thing that's in me.

But the way that it is applied to systems and structures is a thing outside of a person. So right at the very core is a basic fundamental value we miss, most importantly, the opportunity to provide forgiveness, healing and reparations, and to create wholeness.

Justice is a way of being. It's in everything we do. Yes, the notion of justice offered to the world from the black perspective, in my opinion, is that justice provides an opportunity for a lived experience that is unlike any we have had. To embrace the belief and experience that I am my sister's keeper is the way I relate to the *ubunto, botho* concept. That what happens to her, also happens to me and if I hold this notion, I am likely to do no harm to her or she to me. At most we will live longer and happier lives for it. We will seek opportunities always to be harmless to one another and to ourselves. This idea suggests a presence of love and support for one another. I rarely have a memory of punishment in my memory bank as a way of solving a problem among caring individuals.

**Q.** We often speak of justice as either restorative and retributive. Could you give some examples that would illustrate the presence of both forms?

**A.** Okay, I'll give you an example, first of restorative justice operating. I can remember doing a juvenile mediation, where the young children were there because of a fight. During the mediation process they apologized to each other. They were comfortable with each other and they decided to move forward, even though there had been some harm or some injury done. It was really unbelievable the way that they wanted to forgive each other and go forward, and have a pleasant future together, even though they had had a difficult past. They experienced the movement from betrayal to knowledge to understanding and then they forgave each other. It was a gift to watch and facilitate this outcome. As you might imagine, these children were very hurt and that is why they had the fight, to try to ease some of their pain. They needed more examples of how to do this in a more dignified way, and so did the adults.

But the adults in the room didn't want to let it go. They articulated a desire for punishment, that something had to be done. I tried to reframe their responses by asking, "What are the securities that you would need to see put in place to ensure that you have some sense of safety for the children? Can we hear the young people articulate how they might look out for each other? I hear the young people saying that they forgive each other." I facilitated a space in the mediation for the children to create the way they wanted their future to be together. I appreciated watching that happen. To me, that was justice becoming present in the room.

I don't want to give the impression that fairness and equity, equality are not justice. I'm not saying that. There is a social justice, an economic justice, a spiritual justice, political justice, personal justice and many more that appear in the mediation process. What I'm saying is that some people say justice is present if all of us are treated fairly or that justice is present if all of us are treated equally. But even there we have some judgment about who decides what's fair and who decides what is equitable. It's the parties in the moment who have the experience, and they need to decide what justice is or how justice works. If we incorporate the belief that there is a sense of human dignity between us, and I'm not going to do anything to harm you and you're not going to do anything to harm me, we have a better opportunity to get at justice and peacefulness as coexisting efforts.

Q. In your example, for you the children had obtained a state of being just, but the adults wouldn't leave it there; they wanted punishment. So would you say two very different forms of justice, both retributive and restorative, were entangled in that process?

**A.** Right. In this case, the children then fell into—well, going against their elders. And that made it really difficult. And then what does the child do? Even with my reframing, looking at the issue as safety or security, the adults didn't want to let it go. The children had to take a stand on their own and be leaders for their parents. As a facilitator I had the responsibility to address the question of self determination—who gets to decide?—and this I did. The children had to decide and figure out how they could return to their communities and work together. The children had to articulate their plan to their parents, so the parents would know how to support their efforts or offer alternative suggestions if necessary. The children have a community they too are responsible to and for, but unless we create the space for all of us to learn and be informed, this is important information we miss to help support their safety.

**Q.** How did you do all that?

**A.** I did a couple of things. I did a caucus because I wanted to find out exactly what was the source of the adults' pain—that they couldn't give the children the opportunity to return to their lives with forgiveness. I asked, "Can't we at least give them that opportunity, to return?" One parent was very concerned about what could happen. We went through it again, "What are the security methods or the safety methods that we can put in place?"

Normally what I do—particularly in cases where there have been fights—is ask each child in front of the other one, "Can this person be safe in front of you? Can this person return to your community, school without fear of danger?"

"Would you tell me now, if you think there is a danger? And if a danger develops later will you tell the other child or your parent or other adult? And what does that safety look like? And when it's not safe, what could happen?"

"What could you do to be an advocate or a leader for safety or for peace in your community?"

Then they would both communicate with each other what those answers would be. And then I would ask, "Do you believe what he or she just said? Do you feel you could return and feel safe?" Once they can answer, "Yes!" then I feel we have some resolution. We've addressed the very specific act of what brought them here. And we've addressed a larger contextual part about returning to a safe community. We've also addressed just in case something happens, what are the plans that we have in place? Sometimes if it's a school situation versus a community situation those things change.

In this case, after talking to one parent, I brought the other parent in, so the parents could talk. Because it was clear that the issue wasn't really about the children, it was about the parents. That makes things sort of complicated because the process is really for the children. In this particular case both gender and race were dynamics, because it was a black parent and it was a white parent.

As the parents talked, they found out they had a common past. Wow, that was an experience to watch unfold too! [Laughs] They found out they knew some of the same people. And then they went back and did some memory stuff. Going back brought up some memories, and it became clear to me that one of the reasons that one of the parties wasn't letting go was because of the racial dynamic—the daddy really wanted to be sure that there was some punishment in place for this little black boy that he believed violated his little girl. And it wasn't about putting his hands on her; it was about something else.

This is the retributive aspect of justice, that the father insisted on punishment. After the white parent left, the black parent did express to me that he thought that it was a kind of racial involvement because it was a small town they had both come from. I asked why didn't he bring up the race question, and he gave a very usual reply: "I just want to get out of here." Thus, court alternative dispute resolution processes still bring with them the fear of mistreatment and unfairness for some people, and especially for many Black people.

Restorative justice, however, is a process where the participants learn more about how to engage understandings of dignity, feelings, empathy, healing when someone has been injured or harmed.

For me, though, once the little boy and the little girl had smiled and felt like they understood what had happened that day and what caused the problem, and it was clear that it wasn't going to happen again—you just knew that little boy wasn't going to get in no more trouble no more for anything! He realized that he probably was more or less a scapegoat, because he wound up being the one that got singled out, though he probably wasn't operating alone. That happens in a lot of juvenile mediations; there are usually responsible parties who are not at the table, particularly when the mediations are at school. The administration and the teachers are not usually there. Somebody's usually missing, especially if it is not clear who threw the first punch.

Q. What are some specific principles that guide your mediations? How do you figure out what's going on and what you need to do?

A. I'll comment on a few particular things I do—how I try to create an environment that invites justice. These things might be a little different depending on the type of mediation: juvenile, workplace, domestic.

After I do the preliminaries, the introductions and the opening statements, I always want to put people at ease. You know, saying, "It's a serious matter that brings you here, but I want you to feel comfortable while you're here so we can talk openly and address all the needs that come up." Once I think that people can take a deep breath, I reassure them that I'm going to ask basic kinds of questions, such as, "Tell me why you are here, and what you would like to have happen." A basic principle is creating an environment that is comfortable, where I feel that all the parties present can talk.

In matters that involve discrimination, I indicate from the very beginning that I am skilled in facilitating dialogues on race matters and complaints of discrimination. Some practitioners may think that's not being neutral, but I don't think there can be any kind of honest communication if race is an issue and people don't feel confident the facilitator can handle it.

Here's another matter that's part of my issue around the dynamic of neutrality: I'm going to have feelings. I want to be conscious of my feelings. I don't want to be in a mediation being oblivious to the dynamics of what is going on and not having any feelings, okay?

The issue is what I do next. When I have a feeling, an intuition, for example, I had better test it to see whether what I think is accurate or not accurate. The feedback I get from the parties will help me to determine if I am helping them in the process or getting in their way during the process. Thus, this information is useful to me as a conflict resolution practitioner and it provides me the space to move the process along in a supportive fashion.

**Q.** So you use intuition as a skill in your mediation?

**A.** Yes, absolutely. There is often something in the training that recognizes the importance of intuition, but intuition is also different on a cultural level. One of the sources of knowledge that enables me to figure out what's happening is body language, for instance, or mannerisms. If you listen very carefully to the parties' opening statements you can begin to read—that's another phrase I use: read—what's going on in a particular family dynamic or in a workplace dynamic that allows you to be as effective as you can as a mediator. What is different about my intuition is that is cultured with a knowledge and experience around race, class, gender, and humanity. I can openly express and articulate with some clarity how I can see or feel the presence of the dynamic of oppression for the parties.

At the heart of the experience of discrimination is a sense of the loss of dignity and humanity. Clearly, there is a need for restorative justice principles and the relentless pursuit of social justice, in mediation and in life.

I end with some ideas about how to best implement Archbishop Tutu's concept of *ubuntu* in order to bring spiritual justice into our work of mediation. Here are suggestions that include a mixture of knowledge, skills, and ability:

1. Know the community you are seeking to engage. The knowledge must include personal experience, too. If you don't have that experience, partner with someone who does.

2. Build a relationship with the community you seek to engage. The relationship should be built beyond just the purpose of mediation.

3. If you do not know, ask. If you cannot ask, get help and research. If you still do not know, withdraw from the mediation.

4. Engage an awareness of human dignity concepts from that community.

5. Get an understanding of that culture's worldview.

6. Work to get the experiences you need from the people who have the knowledge.

7. Participate in an ongoing learning community on the topic under consideration.

8. Familiarize yourself with an understanding of restorative justice principles, in particular the meaning and application of forgiveness, restoration, dignity, respect, humanity, oppression, and self determination.

9. Employ "collective consciousness" when you feel you cannot do the intervention alone. This is the art of drawing on a collective strength derived from the energy of working with others to eliminate oppression.

10. Develop your skills in presentation and facilitation of guiding questions and reframing in dialogues on race and other ways people are discriminated against. Begin by letting the parties know that you are skilled at facilitating dialogue or complaints based on race or whatever "ism" applies.

11. Familiarize yourself with civil rights law, its purpose, meaning, and application for protected classes, and its uses and historical content.

12. Understand yourself and the baggage you bring to your conflict resolution practice; learn the art of being a self-reflective practitioner.

13. Understand and apply values, knowledge, skills, abilities, and cultural competencies in your ADR practice.

14. Contact PRASI as a supportive writing, coaching, and mentoring multicultural community network of practitioners of color.

15. Keep a journal and track your new learnings to share with others.

16. Take a race-focused facilitation training class.

To me, the concept of justice is associated with a magnificent presence of power in multiple dimensions. Justice brings with it power in the sense of spirit, of emotion, of economics, of healing and opportunity. In any conflict resolution process, these multiple sources of power are fully determined by the parties who are involved and by the influence of society, culture, and gender. The conflict resolution practitioner has the duty to facilitate the space for the parties to have free expression of their intentions and interpretations of justice, so that the parties can create the justice they need and continue in their healing process—and beyond. We still need more ways to engage community healing when an injury is addressed only on an interpersonal level in a mediation or other conflict resolution process.

I imagine that being so consumed with the presence of justice as a way of life or a way of being is what attracts me to the quote by Archbishop Desmond Tutu. The quote brings such clarity to me of what we must do to work toward peace and justice. If we experience the presence of humanity, then we must always see in others what they have the opportunity to see in us. Justice holds the power of forgiveness and the power of healing. Justice is a journey, on a road one travels both alone and often times with others.

NOTES

BIBLIOGRAPHY

INDEX

# Notes

I. WILDERNESS: SCARED OF THE SACRED

1. Robert F. Berkhofer Jr., *The White Man's Indian: Images of the American Indian from Columbus to the Present* (New York: Vintage Books, 1979), 120–21.

2. "Just as the wilderness is the background against which medieval society is delineated, so wildness in the widest sense is the background of God's lucid order of creation. Man in his unreconstructed state, faraway nations, and savage creatures at home thus came to share the same essential quality." Richard Bernheimer, *Wild Men in the Middle Ages: A Study in Art, Sentiment, and Demonology* (Cambridge: Harvard Univ. Press, 1952), 19–20.

3. "The whole of creation possessed meaning only in terms of God's purpose, and each event, trivial or great, displayed His secret will.

"When conceived of as the tale of a chosen people, the history of New Englanders naturally reminded the pious of the trials of the Israelites of old. Like the Old Testament Jews the Puritans fled a corrupt Egypt, in their case Anglican England, for the promised land, and like those ancient Israelites they too landed in the desert or wilderness, often spoken of as "howling" or "savage" and usually inhabited by Satan's agents. . . .

"The journey into the wilderness became as much a controlling metaphor for the story of the Puritans collectively as the spiritual pilgrimage formed the basis of the personal narrative, and the struggle between Puritans and Indians represented externally what the conflict between conscience and sin did internally.

"[In the Puritans' view], Indian character and lifestyle in general showed Native Americans to be in the clutches of Satan, for their souls in the wilderness were as unregenerate as their lands were uncultivated." Berkhofer, 81–83.

4. Wallace Stegner, *Wolf Willow: A History, a Story and a Memory of the Last Plains Frontier* (repr., New York: Penguin Books, 1990), 86.

5. Donald Worster, *Under Western Skies: Nature and History in the American West* (New York: Oxford Univ. Press, 1992), 37.

6. Todd Wilkinson, "Call of the Wild," *Denver Post Magazine*, May 21, 1995, 12.

7. Redwood National Park pamphlet, Northern California, 1994. Minnie Reeves was a Chilula woman who lived to be more than one hundred years old.

8. Robert Lipsyte, "R.I.P., Tonto," *Esquire*, Feb. 1994, 39–45.

9. Berkhofer, 21.

10. Mathew King, *Noble Red Man: Lakota Wisdomkeeper Mathew King*, ed. Harvey Arden, (Hillsboro, Ore.: Beyond Words, 1994), 65.

11. William H. Koetke, *The Final Empire: The Collapse of Civilization and the Seed of the Future* (Arrow Point Press, 1993), 914. Generally speaking, a climax ecosystem is one that contains maximum biodiversity and production. For instance, an old-growth forest under this definition is a climax system, and a forest that has been clear-cut or that is managed for only one commercially profitable tree species would be a disturbance system. If a clear-cut forest or managed forest were left alone for a considerable length of time, a succeeding series of smaller plant species would begin to grow in the clear spaces, each preparing the way for larger, more complex plant communities, leading once again to the climax system.

12. Peter Nabokov, ed., *Native American Testimony: A Chronicle of Indian-White Relations from Prophecy to the Present, 1492–1992* (repr., New York: Penguin Books, 1991), 397–99.

13. When my wife and I lived in Fresno, California, we and a few other urban Indians put on a powwow each April. Little rain falls in the San Joaquin Valley from April through October, so we should have been perfectly safe in setting a powwow date far in advance, with a fair degree of certainty that we would not be rained out. However, every year we got rained on. It took us some years before we finally realized that the man we always asked to bless the grounds, chief of one of the local rancherias, came from a long line of medicine men well known locally for their ability to bring rain. Well, we could not ask him to stop singing for rain, nor could we *not* ask him back, so we just decided to put up with the rain.

14. Richard T. Sherman, *Lakota Ecology Stewardship Model* (Kyle, S.D.: Oglala Lakota (Sioux) Parks and Recreation Authority, Dec. 1994), A2.

15. Ibid., A15.

16. For general discussion, see, for example, Gregory Cajete, *Native Science: Natural Laws of Interdependence* (Santa Fe: Clear Light, 1999); Thomas C. Blackburn and Kat Anderson, eds., *Before the Wilderness: Environmental Management by Native Californians* (Menlo Park, Calif.: Ballena Press, 1993); Paul E. Minnis and Wayne J. Elisens, eds., *Biodiversity and Native America* (Norman: Univ. of Oklahoma Press, 2001).

17. "Europeans portrayed their own continent in terms of intellectual, cultural, military, and political superiority, for Europa was usually pictured wearing a crown, armed with guns, holding orb and scepter, and handling or surrounded by scientific instruments, pallets, books, and Christian symbols. While Asia was richly dressed, rarely did she possess superior signs of power, learning, or religion. America and Africa appeared naked, and the former usually wore a feathered headdress and carried a bow and arrow. Europe, in brief, represented civilization and Christianity and learning confronting nature in America." Berkhofer, 24.

18. Gary Snyder, *The Practice of the Wild: Essays by Gary Snyder* (San Francisco: North Point Press, 1990).

19. See, generally, Philip Deloria, *Playing Indian* (Yale Univ. Press, 1999); Shari Huhndorf, *Going Native, Going Native: Figuring the Indian in Modern American Culture* (Ithaca, N.Y.: Cornell Univ. Press, 2001).

20. Look at what has happened since the U.S. Forest Service began using Smokey the Bear in its antifire public relations campaign. Millions of acres of forests have degraded, become diseased, or changed character, and millions of dollars are spent each year fighting fires that now burn too hot when they finally do burn.

21. Lipsyte, 41.

22. So also says Aldo Leopold, in *A Sand County Almanac, With Essays on Conservation from Round River,* (New York: Sierra Club/Ballantine, 1970), 262: "Almost equally serious as an obstacle to a land ethic is the attitude of the farmer for whom the land is still an adversary." Also, at 264: "To the laborer in the sweat of his labor, the raw stuff on his anvil is an adversary to be conquered. So was wilderness an adversary to the pioneer." Oren Lyons agreed, in Lipsyte, 41: "'This was once all ours,' he says, watching the wind ruffle the water. 'We lived with the lake, with the land, as part of it. The white man's religion talks about mastering the earth.'"

23. Leopold, 269.

24. Richard Simonelli, an editor for *Winds of Change,* says Europeans have a conquering mentality that stems from the questions "Who am I?" and "What am I?" The overlying shadow of scientists' quests for knowledge is those basic questions, which allow them to go out and conquer whatever they need in a search for knowledge.

3. BEYOND MEDIATION—RECONCILING AN INTERCULTURAL
WORLD: A NEW ROLE FOR CONFLICT RESOLUTION

1. "An Emerging American Progressive Ideology for the Year 2000." *Social Policy,* Spring, 1987, 26.

4. THE SHIRT ON MY BACK: THE DAILY CONTINUUM OF VIOLENCE

1. This history of a shirt was inspired by and adapted from the 1985 song "Are My Hands Clean?" written by Bernice Johnson Reagon and performed by Sweet Honey in the Rock, the stunning acapella African American women's group.

2. Evelyn Nieves, "Prosperity's Losers: A Special Report; Homeless Defy Cities' Drives to Move Them." *New York Times,* 7 Dec. 1999.

3. Pierre Bourdieu, Philippe Bourgois, Michel Foucault, Beth Roy, and Nancy Scheper-Hughes, prime among others, have created these terms and powerfully influenced my views here.

5. THE RAPE OF BLACK GIRLS

1. Elizabeth A. Stanko, "'I Second That Emotion': Reflections on Feminism, Emotionality, and Research on Sexual Violence," in *Researching Sexual Violence Against Women: Methodological and Personal Perspectives,* ed. Martin D. Schwartz (Thousand Oaks, Calif.: Sage, 1997).

2. Susan Hippensteele, "Activist Research and Social Narratives: Dialectics of Power, Privilege, and Institutional Change," in *Researching Sexual Violence Against Women: Methodological and Personal Perspectives,* ed. Martin D. Schwartz (Thousand Oaks, Calif.: Sage, 1997).

3. Ibid., 87.

4. Bessel A. van der Kolk, Alexander C. McFarlane, Lars Weisaeth, eds., *Traumatic Stress: The Effects of Overwhelming Experience on Mind, Body, and Society* (New York: Guilford Press, 1996), xi.

5. Maria Yellow Horse Brave Heart-Jordan, "The Return to the Sacred Path: Healing from Historical Trauma and Historical Unresolved Grief among the Lakota" (Ph.D. diss., Smith College School for Social Work, 1995).

6. I put "slave" in quotation marks because the language denotes dehumanization. Africans were enslaved, not slaves; that is, the condition did not usurp their humanity. To speak of the "slaves" from Africa supports the notion of freed "slaves," yet this distinction does not in anyway discount the incredible brutality and terrorism leveled against enslaved Africans to keep them in line.

7. Lori Robinson, *I Will Survive: The African-American Guide to Healing from Sexual Assault and Abuse* (Emeryville, Calif.: Seal Press, 2002), xxii.

8. Deborah Gray White, *Ar'n't I Woman? Female Slaves in the Plantations South,* (New York: W. W. Norton and Company, 1985), 164.

9. Cited in Jennifer Wriggins, "Rape, Racism, and the Law," *Harvard Women's Law Journal* 6 (1983): 103, 118.

10. Joy DeGruy Leary, *Post Traumatic Slave Syndrome: America's Legacy of Enduring Injury and Healing* (Milwaukie, Ore.: Uptone Press, 2005).

11. Among other works, see Judith Herman, *Trauma and Recovery: The Aftermath of Violence—From Domestic Abuse to Political Terror* (New York: Basic Books, 1997).

6. APPELLATE RECOURSE TO THE SUPERNATURAL: *KITHITU* AMONG THE AKAMBA

1. See Gerhard Lindblom, *The Akamba in British East Africa: An Ethnological Monograph,* 2nd ed. (Upsala: Appelberg, 1920); C. B. Hobley, *Ethnology of Akamba and Other East African Tribes* (Cambridge: Cambridge Univ. Press, 1910); Kivuto Ndeti, *Elements of Akamba Life* (Nairobi: East African Publishing House, 1972); and John Middleton, *The Kikuyu and Kamba of Kenya* (London: International African Institute, 1965).

2. A family in Kikamba (the language of the community) would be expressed in terms of "*mbaa*," which literally translates as "those of." It would be the extended patriarchal lineage of a grand or great grandparent.

3. Several close families (distant relatives) would form a clan.

4. Normally referred to as *nzama.*

5. Compare with the Kikuyu community in Jomo Kenyatta's *Facing Mount Kenya* (Nairobi: Kenway, 1978).

6. Information from Mr. Joseph Mutisya, an elder currently engaged in dispute resolution at Mtito Andei Chief's office.

7. Compensation for the killing of a man would be between eleven and thirteen cows plus one bull; loss of an eye, one bull and a goat; loss of a leg, five cows; for theft, punishment would be aimed at compensation save for habitual thieves who would be chased away or executed, etc. For more discussion on this, see generally, D. J. Penwill, *Kamba Customary Law* (Nairobi: Kenya Literature Bureau, 1951).

8. Peter Gulliver, *Disputes and Negotiations: A Cross Cultural Perspective* (New York: Academic Press, 1979), 2.

9. Lindblom, 169–70, points out that because of its destructive power, the *kithitu* is never kept in a village or near cultivated land but out in the wilds where no person can stumble on it, and further that on no account may it be touched with naked hands. Protective oil has to be applied to "neutralize" the powers believed to dwell in it.

10. Largest ethnic group in Kenya, neighbors of the Akamba.

11. Note the similarity in language with the Akamba.

12. Witchcraft, spirits, etc.

13. O. K. Mutungi, *The Legal Aspects of Witchcraft in East Africa With Particular Reference to Kenya* (Nairobi: East Africa Literature Bureau, 1977), 64–66, mentions a type that was used to resolve land disputes where disputants were known, another that was used when an alleged wrongdoer was unidentified, and a third where the guilt of a person was determined in a crowd. With due respect, it would appear that his third classification falls under ordeals rather than *kithitu.*

14. Native Tribunal Appeal Case 68 of 1949.

15. Lindblom, 59–60.

16. The colonial authorities in Kenya had established Native Tribunals to deal with disputes in the administrative regions.

17. Causing death of another accidentally or otherwise was penalized by compensation referred to as blood price. For details, see Penwill, generally.

18. Emile Durkheim, *The Elementary Forms of the Religious Life* (London: George Allen and Unwin, 1976).

19. Hans-Georg Soeffner, *The Order of Rituals: The Interpretation of Everyday Life* (New Brunswick, N.J.: Transaction, 1997).

20. Ibid., 73.

21. Lindblom, 122.

22. A group of young male adults who would sometimes execute decisions by elders.

23. Witchcraft Act (Chapter 67, Laws of Kenya, 1962).

24. In 1968, the Resident Magistrate for Machakos and Kitui Districts promulgated a formal procedure for administering *kithitu.*

25. A. F. Thomas, "Oaths, Ordeals and the Kenya Courts: A Policy Analysis," *Human Organisation* 33, no. 1 (1974): 60.

26. Lindblom, 75.

27. High Court of Kenya, Civil Appeal No. 149 of 1967, quoted in Soeffner, 63.

28. For example, the Roman Catholic Church programs for Oceania and Africa.

29. Additional readings of interest are Dirk Berg-Schlosser, *Tradition and Change in Kenya: A Comparative Analysis of Seven Major Ethnic Groups* (Munich: Ferdinand Schöningh, 1984); John S. Mbiti, *African Religions and Philosophy* (London: Heinemann, 1969); Michael Palmer and Simon Roberts, *Dispute Processes: ADR and the Primary Forms of Decision Making* (London: Butterworths; Charlottesville, Va.: Lexis Law Publishing, 1998).

7. WHY RESEARCH MATTERS: THE RECIPROCAL NATURE OF KNOWLEDGE

1. Clifford Geertz, *The Interpretation of Cultures: Selected Essays* (1973; reprint, New York, Basic Books, 2000), 9.

2. Renato Resoldo, *Culture and Truth: The Remaking of Social Analysis* (Boston: Beacon Press, 1993).

3. Dwight Conquergood, "Rethinking Ethnography: Towards a Critical Cultural Politics," *Communication Monographs* 58 (1991): 179–204.

4. Homi K. Bhabha, *The Location of Culture* (London: Routledge, 1994), 236.

5. Thomas E. Harris and John C. Sherblom, *Small Group and Team Communication* (Boston: Allyn and Bacon, 2002).

8. WHITHER NEUTRALITY? MEDIATION IN THE TWENTY-FIRST CENTURY

1. Jerold S. Auerbach, *Justice Without Law?* (Oxford: Oxford Univ. Press, 1983); Ronald M. Pipkin and Janet Rifkin, "The Social Organization in Alternative Dispute Resolution: Implications for Professionalization of Mediation," *Justice System Journal* 9 (1984): 202–27.

2. Stephen Goldberg, Eric Greene, and Frank Sander, eds., *Dispute Resolution* (Boston: Little, Brown, 1985); W. Burger, "Isn't There a Better Way?" *American Bar Association Journal* 68 (1982): 274–77.

3. N. A. Welsh, "The Thinning Vision of Self-Determination in Court-Connected Mediation: The Inevitable Price of Institutionalization?" *Harvard Negotiation Law Review* 6 (2001): 1–96.

4. Robert A. Baruch Bush and Joseph P. Folger, *The Promise of Mediation: Responding to Conflict through Empowerment and Recognition* (San Francisco: Jossey-Bass, 1994).

5. Albie Davis, "The Logic Behind the Magic of Mediation," *Negotiation Journal* 5, no. 1 (1989): 23.

6. Kathryn Girard, Janet Rifkin, and Annette Townley, *Peaceful Persuasion: A Guide to Creating Mediation Dispute Resolution Programs on College Campuses* (Amherst: Univ. of Massachusetts, 1985); Ray Shonholtz, "Neighborhood Justice Systems: Work, Structure and Guiding Principles," *Mediation Quarterly* 5 (1984): 3–30.

7. See for instance, Laurence Boulle and Hwee Hwee The, *Mediation: Principles, Process, Practice* (Singapore: Butterworths Asia, 2000); "Authorized Practice of Mediation," Association for Conflict Resolution, American Arbitration Association, and American Bar Association Section of Dispute Resolution (2004).

8. Deborah Kolb and Associates, *When Talk Works: Profiles of Mediators* (San Francisco: Jossey-Bass, 1994).

9. Janet Rifkin, Jonathan Millen, and Sara Cobb, "Toward a New Discourse for Mediation: A Critique of Neutrality," *Mediation Quarterly* 9, no. 2 (Winter 1991): 151–65.

10. Bernard Meyer, *Beyond Neutrality: Confronting the Crisis in Conflict Resolution* (San Francisco: Jossey Bass, 2005); Rifkin, Millen, and Cobb; Leah Wing, *Mediation and Social Justice* (Amherst: Univ. of Massachusetts, 2002).

11. Walter R. Borg and Meredith Damien Gail, *Educational Research: An Introduction* (New York: Longman, 1989).

12. And this is rather ironic, given that the mediation field is simultaneously committed to the belief that there can be more than one reality: that each disputant's story of a conflict should be accepted and valued by a mediator; that mediators are in search of the stories of each person's truth as opposed to hearing each side of "a" truth to be discovered.

13. See Mari Matsuda's explanation and critique of liberalism in "Looking to the Bottom: Critical Legal Studies and Reparations," in *Critical Race Theory: Key Writings that Formed the Movement,* ed. K. Crenshaw, N. Gotanda, G. Peller, and K. Thomas (New York: New Press, 1995), 63–79.

14. Trina Grillo, "The Mediation Alternative: Process Dangers for Women," *Yale Law Journal* 100 (1991): 1545–1610; Christine B. Harrington, *Shadow Justice: The Ideology and Institutionalization of Alternatives to Court* (Westport, Conn.: Greenwood, 1985).

15. Richard Delgado, Chris Dunn, Pamela Brown, Helena Lee, and David Hubbert, "Fairness and Formality: Minimizing the Risk of Prejudice in Alternative Dispute Resolution," *Wisconsin Law Review* 6 (1985): 1359–1404.

16. Bush and Folger; Goldberg, Greene, and Sander.

17. See "Model Standards for Mediators," passed by the Association for Conflict Resolution, the American Arbitration Association, and the American Bar Association Section of Dispute Resolution. http://www.acrnet.org.

18. Davis, 23.

19. Lee Anne Bell, "Theoretical Foundations for Social Justice Education," in *Teaching for Diversity and Social Justice,* ed. Maurianne Adams, Lee Anne Bell, and Pat Griffin (New York: Routledge, 1997), 3–15; John Rawls, *A Theory of Justice* (Cambridge, Mass.: Harvard Univ. Press, 1971).

20. This is the case internationally, along national and hemispheric lines as well; however, for this article I have concentrated on the United States.

21. M. Baker, V. French, Mary Adams Trujillo, and Leah Wing, "Impact on Diverse Populations: How CRE Has Not Addressed the Needs of Diverse Populations," in *Does It Work? The Case for Conflict Resolution Education in Our Nation's Schools,* ed. Tricia S. Jones and Daniel Kmitta (Washington, D.C.: CREnet, 2000), 61–78; M. A. Chesler, "Alternative Dispute Resolution and Social Justice," unpublished manuscript, 1991; Christopher Cooper, "Mediation in Black and White: Unequal Distribution of Empowerment by Police," in *Not Guilty: Twelve Black Men Speak out on Law, Justice, and Life,* ed. Jabari Asim (New York: Amistad, HarperCollins, 2001), 125–41; John Forester, *The Deliberative Practitioner: Encouraging Participatory Planning Processes* (Cambridge, Mass.: MIT Press, 1999); Wing.

22. The following is a working definition of social justice: the conditions in which each person, group, and community has access to the resources they need for connection, health, safety, and prosperity; in which each has agency for the determination of their future and a sense of interdependency, caring, and responsibility for others; this is viewed as an enduring process and goal for society (Lee Anne Bell; Rawls).

23. A master narrative, or grand narrative, is a leading mainstream cultural story a nation tells itself and others about the society (Richard Delgado and Jean Stefancic, eds., *Critical White Studies: Looking Behind the Mirror* [Philadelphia: Temple Univ. Press, 1997], 220–26). Neutrality is a valued concept within the U.S. master narrative, made evident by its centrality to society's leading institutions: the law and courts as well as even its informal (and increasingly institutionalized) alternative dispute resolution forums such as mediation.

24. Cooper, 125–41; Michele Hermann, "New Mexico Research Examines Impact of Gender and Ethnicity in Mediation," in *The Conflict and Culture Reader,* ed. Pat K. Chew (New York: New York Univ. Press, 2001); Wing.

25. Baker et al., 61–78; Hermann.

26. Wing.

27. Maurianne Adams, Lee Anne Bell, and Pat Griffin, eds., *Teaching for Diversity and Social Justice* (New York: Routledge, 1997). Delgado et al., 1359–1404; Barbara J. Flagg, "The Transparency Phenomenon, Race-Neutral Decision Making and Discriminatory Intent," in *Critical White Studies: Looking Behind the Mirror,* ed. Richard Delgado and Jean Stefancic (Philadelphia: Temple Univ. Press, 1997), 220–26; Matsuda, 63–79.

28. Baker et al., 61–78.

29. Rifkin, Millen, and Cobb; Nadim R. Rouhana and Susan H. Korper, "Case Analysis: Dealing with the Dilemmas Posed by Power Asymmetry in Intergroup Conflict," *Negotiation Journal,* Oct. 1996, 353–66; Wing.

30. Rifkin, Millen, and Cobb, 151–65.

31. S. Cobb and J. Rifkin, "Practice and Paradox," in *Narrative Mediation: A New Approach to Conflict Resolution*, ed. J. Winslade and G. Monk (San Francisco: Jossey-Bass, 2000), 35–65; Wing.

32. Cobb and Rifkin.

33. Rifkin, Millen, and Cobb, 151–65.

34. Sara Cobb, "A Narrative Perspective on Mediation: Toward the Materialization of the 'Storytelling' Metaphor," in *New Directions in Mediation: Communication Research and Perspectives*, ed. Joseph P. Folger and Tricia S. Jones (Thousand Oaks, Calif.: Sage, 1994), 48–63; Cobb and Rifkin, 35–65; J. Winslade and G. Monk, *Narrative Mediation: A New Approach to Conflict Resolution* (San Francisco: Jossey-Bass Publisher, 2000).

35. Cobb and Rifkin, 35–65; Wing; Winslade and Monk.

36. Thomas Ross, "The Richmond Narratives," in *Critical Race Theory: The Cutting Edge*, ed. Richard Delgado and Jean Stefancic (Philadelphia: Temple Univ. Press, 1995), 38–47.

37. A counternarrative is a story that is not representative or resonant with the hegemonic cultural story of a society.

38. I use the terms "Latina," "White," and "African American" to refer to those involved in the mediation. These are not offered as equivalent categories but rather to reflect the terms of self-identification that each participant in the study used to describe her or himself in relation to others. Yet, I recognize that there is the possibility that some might have used different terms had Spanish been the language of conversation in the mediation and the interviews (C. R. Venator-Santiago, personal communication, 2002).

39. Racialization, as defined here, is the process and structures by which an individual and/or group is categorized by associating them with others seen as belonging to the same socially constructed racial group. When this process results in sustaining inequality and injustice for a group or individual based on such groupings (Stephen Small, "The Contours of Racialization: Structures, Representations and Resistance in the United States," in *Race, Identity, and Citizenship: A Reader*, ed. Rodolfo D. Torres, Louis F. Miron, and Jonathan Xavier Inda [Malden, Mass.: Blackwell, 1999], 47–64), I refer to it as *negative racialization*. Common markers for racialization are ancestry, phenotype, hair texture, facial features, eye color, heritage, and national origin (S. Dale McLemore, Harriet D. Romo and Susan Gonzalez Baker, *Racial and Ethnic Relations in America* [Boston: Allyn and Bacon, 2001]), Alex M. Saragoza, Concepcion R. Juarez, Abel Valenzuela Jr., and Oscar Gonzalez, "Who Counts? Title VII and the Hispanic Classification," in *The Latino Condition: A Critical Reader*, ed. Richard Delgado and Jean Stefancic (New York: NYU Press, 1998), 44–51; Tzvetan Todorov, "Race and Racism," in *Theories of Race and Racism*, ed. Les Back and John Solomos (London: Routledge, 2000), 64–70.

40. I am using the descriptor White Anglo to refer to someone who is categorized in the United States as White, not Hispanic, and an English speaker (Anglophone).

41. Lee Ann Bell, 3–15; Richard Delgado and Jean Stefancic, *Critical Race Theory: An Introduction* (New York: NYU Press, 2001).

42. The thematic of race in the master narrative argues that racism emerges only from intentional desire to cause harm. This manifests, then, in the legislation and interpretation of civil rights laws. Though there are exceptions to the requirement of proving intentionality, they are, as stated, exceptions.

43. Flagg, 220–26.

44. Crenshaw et al., *Critical Race Theory*, 14.

45. Delgado and Stefancic, *Critical Race Theory*, 22.

46. Hermann, 91.

47. Baker et al.; Sharon Bailey, "Diverse Traditions," *Newsletter of the National Conference on Peacemaking and Conflict Resolution* (2001).

48. Baker et al., 61–78; Cooper, 125–41; Pipkin and Rifkin, 202–27.

49. Baker et al., 61–78.

50. Paolo Freire, *Pedagogy of the Oppressed* (New York: Herder and Herder, 1972; reprint, New York: Continuum, 1989); D. Marya, personal communication (1997).

51. See the works of D. Bailey, "Life in the Intersection: Race/Ethnic Relations and Conflict Resolution," *The Fourth R* 78 (1997): 18–19; Cobb and Rifkin, 35–65; Cooper, 125–41; Rifkin, Millen, and Cobb; Lawrence Susskind and Jeffrey Cruikshank, *Breaking the Impasse: Consensual Approaches to Resolving Public Disputes* (New York: Basic Books, 1987).

52. Pipkin and Rifkin, 202–27.

9. RACE, (IN)JUSTICE, AND CONFLICT RESOLUTION: INJUSTICE IN THE AFRICAN AMERICAN COMMUNITY, EFFECTS ON COMMUNITY, AND THE RELEVANCE OF CONFLICT RESOLUTION

1. See Ben Hammer, "Black, White Performance Gap Widens, Study Finds," *Black Issues in Higher Education,* Nov. 6, 2003; "News and Views: A Comprehensive Guide to Black Student College Graduation Rates," *Journal of Blacks in Higher Education,* Apr. 30, 1999.

2. Jean M. Gerard and Cheryl Buehler, "Multiple Risk Factors in the Family Environment and Youth Problem Behaviors," *Journal of Marriage and the Family,* May 1999.

3. "African Americans Hurt as Manufacturing Jobs Disappear," *Chicago Defender,* July 14, 2003.

4. Edney Hazel-Trice, "The State of Black America; National Urban League's Annual Report Shows Stark Disparities Between Blacks and Whites; Officials Say Many of the Earlier Gains Are in Danger of Being Erased," *Sacramento Observer,* Apr. 13, 2005.

5. Surgeon General's Office, *Youth Violence: A Report of the Surgeon General,* December 2001. http://www.surgeongeneral.gov/library/youthviolence/chapter4/sec1.html.

6. "Facts About Single Parent Families," in *Parents Without Partners International.* http://www.parentswithoutpartners.org/Support1.htm.

7. Laurence Steinberg, "Youth Violence: Do Parents and Families Make a Difference?" *National Institute of Justice Journal,* no. 243 (Apr. 2000). http://www.ncjrs.gov/pdffiles1/jr000243f.pdf.

8. Jennifer Roback Morse, "Parents or Prisons." *Policy Review* 120 (Aug.–Sept. 2003). http://www.hoover.org/publications/policyreview/3448276.html.

9. Tennessee Department of Correction, "Impact of Incarceration on Children," presented at the 2003 Tennessee Correctional Association Conference, Nashville, Tenn. http://www.tennessee.gov/correction/pdf/tcapresentation.pdf.

10. Heidi Burgess and Guy Burgess, "Transformative Approaches to Conflict," 1997, Univ. of Colorado Conflict Research Consortium. http://www.colorado.edu/conflict/transform.

11. Sara Kristine Trenary, "Rethinking Neutrality: Race and ADR," *Dispute Resolution Journal*, Aug. 1999. http://findarticles.com/p/articles/mi_qa3923/is_/ai_n8873055.

12. John Paul Lederach, *The Little Book of Conflict Transformation* (Intercourse, Penn.: Good Books, 2003), 27.

13. Trenary.

14. David Turner and Elias Cheboud, "Advocacy and Conflict Resolution in Social Work: Can They Really Promote Justice? An Anti-Oppressive Approach," paper presented to International Joint Conference of Schools of Social Work and International Federation of Social Workers, Montreal, Quebec, Canada, July 2000. www.aforts.com/colloques_ouvrages/colloques/actes/interventions/turner_david.doc.

15. Trenary.

16. Turner and Cheboud, 1.

17. Michelle LeBaron, "Mediation and Multicultural Reality," *Peace and Conflict Studies*, June 1998, 41–56.

18. Ibid.

19. Cynthia R. Mabry, "African Americans Are Not Carbon Copies of White Americans: The Role of African American Culture in Mediation of Family Disputes," *Ohio State Journal on Dispute Resolution* 13 (1998): 405, 420–35.

20. Laura Ward Branca, "Culture Is to People Like Water Is to Fish," *Community Mediator*, Summer 2004.

21. LeBaron.

22. Mark Davidheiser, "Mediation and Multiculturalism: Domestic and International Challenges." http://www.beyondintractability.org/essay/mediation_multiculturalism/?nid=1190.

23. Paolo Freire, *Pedagogy of the Oppressed* (New York: Herder and Herder, 1972; reprint, New York: Continuum, 1989).

24. Alliance of African/African American Peacemakers, "A Call to Action—A Call for Unity." www.gmu.edu/departments/NCPCR/AAAP.html.

10. EXPERIENCE FROM THE ENVIRONMENTAL DISPUTE RESOLUTION FIELD: ADJUSTING THE PROCESS FOR MAXIMUM INCLUSION OF INTERESTS AND KNOWLEDGE

1. While the word *pueblo* in Spanish means "village," Native American Pueblos are sovereign entities. Out of respect for their uniqueness, the author and editors have chosen to defy grammatical conventions and capitalize all uses of the word.

11. 'IKE HO'OPONOPONO: THE JOURNEY

1. Mary Kawena Puku'i, E. Haertig, and C. Lee, *Nana I Ke Kumu: Look to the Source* (Honolulu: Queen Lili'uokalani Children's Center, 1972), 62.

2. For one example, see J. Kamhis, "Healing with Hawaiian Ho'oponopono," *Aloha Magazine* 15, no. 4 (1992): 45–49.

3. See N. Andrade, R. Johnson, J. Edman, G. Danko, L. Nahulu, G. Makini, N. Yuen, J. Waldron, A. Yates, and J. McDermott, "Non-traditional and Traditional Treatment of Hawaiian and Non-Hawaiian Adolescents," *Hawai'i Medical Journal* 53 (1994): 344–47. Also, N. Moku'au, "Responding to Pacific Islanders: Culturally Competent Perspectives for Substance Abuse Prevention," Center for Substance Abuse Prevention Cultural Competence Series 8, Special Collaborative Edition. Washington, D.C.: Department of Health and Human Sciences publication no. SMA 98-3195, 1998.

4. For a vivid picture of such problems, see K. H. Au and A. Kawakami, "Research Currents: Talk Story and Learning to Read," *Language Arts* 62, no. 4 (1985): 406–11; J. Daniels, M. D'Andrea, and R. Heck, "Moral Development and Hawaiian Youths: Does Gender Make a Difference? *Journal of Counseling and Development* 74 (1995): 90–92; Hawai'i Department of Health, *The Hawai'i Youth Risk Behavior Survey of Statewide Highlights of Middle and High Schools* (Department of Health, 1999); Moku'au; D. J. Reschly, "Minority Students in Gifted and Special Education," Presentation to the White House Commission on Excellence in Special Education, 2002.

5. D. P. Nishihara, "Culture, Counseling, and Ho'oponopono: An Ancient Model in a Modern Context," *Personnel and Guidance Journal* 56, no. 9 (1978): 562–66.

6. Hawai'i Department of Health.

7. Letter from U.S. Department of Education, Office of Special Education and Rehabilitative Services, to Patricia Hamamoto, superintendent of education, Hawai'i Department of Education, and Bruck S. Anderson, director, Hawai'i Department of Health, dated June 5, 2002. http://www.ed.gov/policy/speced/guid/idea/monitor/hi-final-report.pdf.

8. Reschly's argument is supported by many others in the field, such as Nishihara; A. Nape'a/u, video taped and transcribed interview on July 7, 2000; R. Stodden, "Native Hawaiian Youth Offender Successful Re-entry Project Grant Proposal with Hilo Board of Education," unpublished grant proposal, 1999; L. Venuti, "A School without Walls," *Kamehameha Journal of Education* 5, 1994, 47–50.

9. Mary Aiu, *Eliminating Health Disparities: Conversations with Pacific Islanders* (Scotts Valley, Calif.: ETR Publishing, 2004), 17.

10. Kawena Puku'i, Haertig, and Lee.

11. E. V. Shook, *Ho'oponopono* (Honolulu: Univ. of Hawai'i Program for Cultural Studies, 1985).

12. Deborah Meier, *The Power of Their Ideas* (Boston: Beacon Press, 1995).

13. W. W. K. Au, "What the Tour Guide Didn't Tell Me: Tourism, Colonialism, and Resistance in Hawai'i," in *Rethinking Our Classrooms,* vol. 2, ed. B. Bigelow (Milwaukee: Rethinking Schools, 1999).

14. W. A. Adams, *The Honolulu Advertiser,* Nov. 24, 2003, E3.

12. REFLECTIONS ON "AFRICAN AMERICANS IN MEDIATION
LITERATURE: A NEGLECTED POPULATION"

1. Cherise D. Hairston, "African Americans in Mediation Literature: A Neglected Population," *Mediation Quarterly,* now *Conflict Resolution Quarterly* 16, no. 4 (1999).

2. Bernard Mayer, *Beyond Neutrality: Confronting the Crisis in Conflict Resolution* (San Francisco: Jossey-Bass, 2004), 170.

3. L. Hurdle-Price, "Building an Organization Committed to Diversity: Is ACR Singing a New Tune, or Is This The Same Old Song?" *ACResolution* 3, no. 1 (2003): 4.

4. B. Major and C.P. Eccleston, "Stigma and Social Exclusion," in *The Social Psychology of Inclusion and Exclusion,* ed. Dominic Abrams, Michael A. Hogg, and Jose Marques (New York: Psychology Press, 2005), 63–87; Iris Marion Young, *Inclusion and Democracy* (New York: Oxford Univ. Press, 2000).

5. Cornel West, *Prophetic Thought in Postmodern Times,* (Monroe, Maine: Common Courage Press, 1993), 5.

6. Marvin Johnson, "Diversity Resistance." August 2001. http:www.mediate.com/pfriendly.cfm?id=708.

7. Kevin Avruch, "Type I and Type II Errors in Culturally Sensitive Conflict Resolution Practice," *Conflict Resolution Quarterly* 20, no. 3 (2003): 360.

8. Lewis R. Gordon, *Existentia Africana: Understanding Africana Existential Thought* (New York: Routledge, 2000), 61.

9. Lena Dominelli, *Anti-Oppressive Social Work Theory and Practice* (New York: Palgrave Macmillan, 2002), 8.

10. Hairston, 369.

11. Ibid., 357.

12. Ibid., 358.

13. Gerardo R. López and Laurence Parker, "Conclusion," in *Interrogating Racism in Qualitative Research Methodology,* ed. Gerardo R. López and Laurence Parker (New York: Peter Lang Pub Inc, 2003), 210.

14. David B. Lipsky and Ariel Avgar, "Commentary: Research on Employment Dispute Resolution: Toward a New Paradigm," *Conflict Resolution Quarterly* 22, no. 1–2 (2004): 183.

15. Linda Baron, "Commentary: The Case for the Field of Community Mediation," *Conflict Resolution Quarterly* 22, no. 1–2 (2004): 135–44; Lisa B. Bingham, "Employment Dispute

Resolution: The Case of Mediation," *Conflict Resolution Quarterly* 22, no. 1–2 (2004): 164; Joan B. Kelly, "Family Mediation Research: Is There Empirical Support for the Field?" *Conflict Resolution Quarterly* 22, no. 1–2 (2004): 6; Tricia S. Jones, "Conflict Resolution Education: The Field, the Findings, and the Future," *Conflict Resolution Quarterly* 22, no. 1–2 (2004): 258; Donald T. Saposnek, "Commentary: The Future and the History of Family Mediation Research," *Conflict Resolution Quarterly* 22, no. 1–2 (2004): 46.

16. Howard H. Irvin, Michael Benjamin, and Jose San-Pedro, "Family Mediation and Cultural Diversity: Mediating with Latino Families," *Mediation Quarterly* 16, no. 4 (1999): 326.

17. Christy Cumberland Walker, "The Myth of a Colorblind Society and the Need for Minority Dispute Resolution Organizations," *Family Mediation News,* Winter 2003, 14.

18. Mayer, 172.

### 14. POWER, CULTURE, CONFLICT

1. Carolyn Schrock-Shenk, ed., *Mediation and Facilitation Training Manual: Foundations and Skills for Constructive Conflict Transformation* (Akron, Penn.: Mennonite Conciliation Service, 2000).

2. Juliana Birkhoff, "Mediators' Perspectives on Power: A Window into a Profession?" Ph.D. diss., George Mason Univ., 2000.

3. Laura Nader, "Controlling Processes in the Practice of Law: Hierarchy and Pacification in the Movement to Re-Form Dispute Ideology" in *Ohio State Journal on Dispute Resolution* 9, no. 1 (1993): 1–25.

4. Hermann. Also, see the final report filed by Michele Hermann and her colleagues: "The MetroCourt Project Final Report" (January 1993).

5. Which is not to deny that some people also advocate nonviolence as an expression of deep-seated beliefs and spiritual values.

6. Beth Roy, *Some Trouble With Cows: Making Sense of Social Conflict,* (Berkeley: Univ. of California Press, 1994).

### 15. OUTSIDE INTERESTS, INSIDE NEEDS: TENSIONS IN CONFLICT RESOLUTION WORKSHOP PRACTICES BASED ON SRI LANKAN EXPERIENCE

1. The Sri Lankan NGO Thirupthiya was formed out of the British NGO Quaker Peace and Service–Sri Lanka and was a continuation of the field staff, work, and work style of QPS Sri Lanka.

2. Another area of concern is that facilitators often include shorthand in their agendas, such as "mapping of conflict," "photo language," "nature meditation," "cycle of violence," "river of life," and "ABC triangle." These terms are generally unfamiliar to the participants and explained with only one or two sentences. When the agenda is presented for approval participants tend to passively accept it rather than ask questions that clarify what these terms mean.

3. Held in the Central Province of Sri Lanka in August 2001 for leaders and activists of Sri Lankan NGOs.

4. This is concluded a myth on the basis that, (1) nearly one-third of the population of the Eastern province of Sri Lanka are Sinhalese (living in areas and pockets of Sinhala concentration), and (2) the known cases of individual Sinhalese living in communities of predominantly Tamil. However, what was not addressed is also the reality that (1) Sinhalese as a community had to leave the predominantly Tamil areas of the East when the war started in 1990, an incident for which there is a history, (2) there are hardly any Sinhalese living in the areas controlled by the LTTE, and (3) civilians in the Sinhala border villages in the East, which are either colonies or ancient villages, occasionally get attacked by the LTTE with the justification of them being planted within the territory of Tamil homeland by various regimes of the Southern Government. Hence the conclusion that the above statement is a myth does not imply that a Sinhalese can live anywhere in the East freely, without fear. This conclusion also does not imply that Tamils and Muslims can live anywhere in the East freely, without fear.

5. This is an exercise in which stereotypes towards Westerners and Sri Lankans are discussed prior to the discussion of stereotypes held by Sinhalese and Tamils toward each other. However, by not proceeding further with the discussion, the reality of disparities in wealth distribution and the differences in living standards of the rich and poor countries of the world are underestimated.

6. This is taken as a stereotype held by Westerners toward Sri Lankans. However, having a relaxed approach toward the flow of time is sometimes (mis)interpreted as laziness, but can also be identified as a cultural trait for a majority of Sri Lankans, who live away from major cities.

## 17. THE PORVIDA APPROACH: FOR MULTICULTURAL RESPECT AND ORGANIZATIONAL SUCCESS

1. Paolo Freire, *Pedagogy of the Oppressed* (New York: Herder and Herder, 1972; reprint, New York: Continuum, 1989).

2. Roberto Vargas and Samuel C. Martinez, *Razalogia: Community Learning for a New Society* (Oakland, Calif.: Razagentes Associates, 1984).

3. Roberto Vargas and Frances F. Korten, *Movement Building for Transformative Change* (Bainbridge Island, Wash.: Positive Futures Network, 2006).

## 18. MEDIATING FILIPINO CULTURE

1. John Paul Lederach, *Preparing for Peace: Conflict Transformation Across Cultures* (New York: Syracuse Univ. Press, 1995).

2. Howard Raiffa, *The Art and Science of Negotiation* (Cambridge: Belknap Press, 2005).

3. Frank H. Wu, *Yellow: Race in America Beyond Black and White* (New York: Basic Books, 2003).

4. Frank Lynch, *Readings on Philippine Values* (Quezan City: Ateneo de Manilla Univ. Press, 1973), 12, quoted in Alfredo Roces and Grace Roces, *Culture Shock! Philippines: A Survival Guide to Customs and Etiquette* (Singapore: Marshall Cavendish Corporation, 2007).

5. Ibid.

6. Ibid.

7. Frantz Fanon, *The Wretched of the Earth* (New York: Grove Press, 1965).

19. *TRES CULTURAS:* A CASE STUDY OF SCHOOL PEER MEDIATION
WITH THREE CULTURES IN A TEXAS MIDDLE SCHOOL

1. See Ray Leal, "From Collegiality to Confrontation: Faculty to Faculty Conflicts," in *Conflict Management in Higher Education*, ed. S. A. Holton (San Francisco: Jossey-Bass, 1995).

2. R. Torres-Raines, "Transculturation: A Faculty Development Model on the Texas-Mexico Border" (College Station, Tex.: Alpha Kappa Delta Sympsium, 1998).

3. Terry G. Jordan, "The Texan Appalachia," *Annals of the Association of American Geographers* 60 (Sept. 1970).

4. Terry G. Jordan, "Perceptual Regions in Texas," *Geographical Review* 68 (July 1978).

5. Ray Leal, "Building Your Own Campus Mediation Program: Different Models of College and University Programs," presentation at the Ninth Annual National Association for Mediation in Education conference, Amherst, Mass., 1994.

6. Ray Leal, "Conflicting Views of Discipline in San Antonio Schools," *Education and Urban Society* 27, no. 1 (1994): 35–44.

7. Hollis had received a doctorate in psychology prior to becoming the principal of SVMS.

8. Ray Leal, "The Next Generation of College and University Campus Mediation Programs," presentation before the annual conference of the Society of Professionals in Dispute Resolution, San Antonio, 1993.

9. New Mexico Center for Dispute Resolution, *Student Mediation in Secondary Schools: Training and Implementation Guide*, Albuquerque, 1995.

10. Tom Willard, *Buffalo Soldiers* (New York: Forge, 1997).

11. Ray Leal, "La Onda: Strategies for Hispanic Healing," annual conference of the National Conference on Peacemaking and Conflict Resolution, Phoenix, 1999.

12. Interview with Dr. Patrick Hollis, San Antonio, 2004.

13. Dr. Hollis in his 2004 interview made it clear that the amount of serious criminal activity perpetrated by the 2 percent of the student body who had made a life choice of criminality did not decrease, and peer mediation could not work with this population. More serious sanctions such as suspension, expulsion, and criminal charges were used on this student population.

14. *Terpening et al v. Comal I.S.D. et al*, 93-CV-423, U.S. District Court, Western District of Texas (San Antonio), 1993.

15. See Lisa Marie Gomez, "Racial Slurs Also Reported on Field," *San Antonio Express-News*, Oct. 2004.

21. IS RECONCILIATION POSSIBLE? LESSONS FROM COMBATING "MODERN RACISM"

1. Diane J. Goodman, *Promoting Diversity and Social Justice: Educating People from Privileged Groups* (Thousand Oaks, Calif.: Sage, 2001), 122.

2. Paolo Freire, *Pedagogy of the Oppressed* (New York: Herder and Herder, 1972; reprint, New York: Continuum, 1989).

3. Nelson Mandela, *Long Walk to Freedom: The Autobiography of Nelson Mandela* (New York: Little, Brown, 1994), 544.

4. Martin Luther King Jr., *Strength to Love* (Philadelphia: Fortress Press, 1981), 7.

5. Cardell K. Jacobson, "Resistance to Affirmative Action: Self-interest or Racism?," *Journal of Conflict Resolution* 29 (1985), 306–29; Thomas F. Pettigrew, "Modern Racism in the United States," *Revue Internationale de Psychologie Sociale* 2, no. 3 (1989): 291–303.

6. John F. Dovidio and Samuel L. Gaertner, eds., *Prejudice, Discrimination, and Racism* (Orlando: Academic Press, 1986).

7. This model was originally published as Valerie Batts, *Modern Racism: New Melody for the Same Old Tunes* (Cambridge: Episcopal Divinity School Occasional Papers, 1998). A form of the paper was distributed to the bishops as background reading in preparation for their meeting of September 2001.

8. Target group is a term used to describe blacks (that is, Africans from across the Diaspora) and other people of color as well as other groups who have been historically and currently "targeted" within U.S. society as "less than" or different in an inferior way from the dominant population. The statistical odds for successful outcomes are less for members of a target group. Nontarget groups, by contrast, are more likely to operate from a view that their "way" is better and to receive unearned privilege and increased life chances such as longer mortality, employment, access to credit and higher incomes. See Figure 2.

9. I assume in this paper, as has been my experience, that the dynamic of how racism manifests in United States regarding black-white relationships is the paradigm for understanding the myth of superiority based on color. I see that the dynamic plays out among Africans across the Diaspora as well as among indigenous people worldwide, people of color from Spanish-speaking countries, and Asians from all parts of Asia and the Pacific rim. When I use the term "black" I encourage readers to think inclusively and to note how the example I am sharing or the theoretical point I am making fits or does not fit for their target group experience.

10. Janet E. Helms, *Black and White Racial Identity: Theory, Research, and Practice* (New York: Greenwood Press, 1990); William E. Cross, *Shades of Black* (Philadelphia: Temple Univ. Press, 1991).

11. John McConahay, Beatrice Hardee, and Valerie Batts, "Has Racism Declined in America?," *Journal of Conflict Resolution* 2, no. 4 (1981): 563–79.

12. Phyllis A. Katz and Dalmas A. Taylor, Introduction to *Eliminating Racism: Profiles in Controversy* (New York: Plenum Press, 1988).

13. Jared Taylor, *Paved with Good Intentions: The Failure of Race Relations in Contemporary America* (New York: Carroll and Graf, 1992).

14. Joe R. Feagin and Hernan Vera, *White Racism: The Basics* (New York: Routledge, 1995); Richard B. Ropers and Dan J. Pence, *American Prejudice* (New York: Insight Books, 1995).

15. John McConahay and James Hough, "Symbolic Racism," *Journal of Social Issues* 32, no. 2 (1976): 23–45.

16. Dovidio and Gaertner.

17. Anne Braden, "Lessons from a History of Struggle," *Southern Exposure* 8, no. 2 (1980): 56–61.

18. McConahay and Hough, 38.

19. Valerie Batts, "Modern Racism: A T. A. Perspective," *Transactional Analysis Journal* 12, no. 3 (1983): 207–9; John Hope Franklin, "A Continuing Climate of Racism," *Duke University: A Magazine for Alumni and Friends* 71, no. 2 (1984): 12–16; Pettigrew.

20. John Capitman, "Symbolic Racism Theory Criteria for Individual Differences Measures of Prejudice and the Validity of the Feeling Thermometer" (Ph.D. diss., Duke Univ., 1980); Dovidio and Gaertner; Janel K. Swim, Kathryn J. Aikin, Wayne S. Hall, and Barbara A. Hunter, "Sexism and Racism: Old-fashioned and Modern Prejudices," *Journal of Personality and Social Psychology* 68, no. 2 (1995): 199–214.

21. Peggy McIntosh, "White Privilege and Male Privilege: A Personal Account of Coming to See Correspondences through Work in Women Studies" (working paper no. 189, Stone Center, Wellesley College, 1988).

22. Valerie Batts, "An Experiential Workshop: Introduction to Multiculturalism," in *Toward Ethnic Diversification in Psychology Education and Training*, ed. George Stricker and Elizabeth Davis-Russell (Washington, D.C.: American Psychological Association, 1990), 9–16.

23. Valerie Batts, "An Overview of Strategies for Creating a Multicultural Workforce," *Consulting Psychology Bulletin* (Winter 1990), 3–6.

24. James M. Jones, *Prejudice and Racism* (Reading, Mass.: Addison-Wesley Co., 1972).

25. Pierre L. van den Berghe, *Race and Racism: A Comparative Perspective* (New York: John Wiley and Sons, 1967); Batts, "Modern Racism."

26. Ropers and Pence.

27. Martha Minow, *Making All the Difference: Inclusion, Exclusion, and American Law* (Ithaca, N.Y.: Cornell Univ. Press, 1990); Claud Anderson, *Black Labor, White Wealth* (Edgewood: Duncan and Duncan, 1994); Melvin L. Oliver and Thomas M. Shapiro, *Black Wealth/White Wealth* (New York: Routledge, 1995).

28. James Jones, "Racism in Black and White: A Bicultural Model of Reaction and Evolution," in *Eliminating Racism: Profiles in Controversy*, ed. Phyllis A. Katz and Dalmas A. Taylor

(New York: Plenum Press, 1988), 117–35; Asa G. Hilliard, *The Maroon Within Us* (Baltimore: Black Classic Press, 1995).

29. Katz and Taylor; Pettigrew; Swim et al.; Jean T. Griffin, "Racism and Humiliation in the African American Community," *Journal of Primary Prevention* 12, no. 2 (1991): 149–67.

30. Andrew Hacker, *Two Nations: Black and White, Separate, Hostile, Unequal* (New York: Oxford Univ. Press, 1992).

31. Derrick Bell, *Confronting Authority: Reflections of an Ardent Protester* (Boston: Beacon Press, 1994), 149–50.

32. Joseph Katz, "White Faculty Struggling with the Effects of Racism," in *Teaching Minority Students,* ed. James H. Cones, John Ford Noonan, and Denise Janha (San Francisco: Jossey-Bass, 1983).

33. Joyce E. King, "Dysconscious Racism: Ideology, Identify, and the Miseducation of Teachers," *Journal of Negro Education* 60, no. 2 (1991): 133–45.

34. Norman Miller and Marilynn Brewer, "Categorizing Effect on In Group and Out Group Perception," in *Prejudice, Discrimination, and Racism,* ed. John F. Dovidio and Samuel L. Gaertner (Orlando: Academic Press, 1986), 209–29; Mwalimu J. Shujaa, ed., *Too Much Schooling, Too Little Education: A Paradox of Black Life in White Societies* (Trenton, N.J.: Africa World Press, 1994).

35. Patricia J. Williams, *The Rooster's Egg* (Cambridge, Mass.: Harvard Univ. Press, 1995).

36. Dovidio and Gaertner.

37. Mary Sonn and Valerie Batts, "Strategies for Changing Personal Attitudes of White Racism" (paper delivered at the Annual Convention of the American Psychological Association, Los Angeles, 1985).

38. William Ryan, *Blaming the Victim* (New York: Vintage Books, 1976).

39. Hilliard.

40. Derrick Bell; Na'im Akbar, *Chains and Images of Psychological Slavery* (Jersey City: New Mind Productions, 1984); Suzanne Lipsky, *Internalized Racism* (Seattle: Rational Island, 1978); Fahkry Davids, "Frantz Fanon: The Struggle for Inner Freedom, Part 2," *Free Associations* 6, no. 18 (1996): 205–34.

41. Joyce Brown and Valerie Batts, "Helping Blacks Cope with and Overcome the Personal Effects of Racism" (paper delivered at the Annual Convention of the American Psychological Association, Los Angeles, 1985).

42. Ryan, *Blaming the Victim*; William Ryan, *Equality* (New York: Pantheon Books, 1981); Anderson; Oliver and Shapiro.

43. Mark A. Chester and James Crowfoot, "Racism in Higher Education I: An Organizational Analysis" (Center for Research on Social Organization, Univ. of Michigan, Ann Arbor, working paper no. 412, 1989); Mark A. Chester and James Crowfoot, "Racism in Higher Education II: Challenging Racism and Promoting Multiculturalism in Higher Education

Organizations" (Center for Research on Social Organization, Univ. of Michigan, Ann Arbor, working paper no. 558, 1997).

44. Pettigrew; Minow.

45. James H. Cones, Denise Janha, and John Ford Noonan, "Exploring Racial Assumptions with Faculty," in *Teaching Minority Students,* ed. James H. Cones, John Ford Noonan, and Denise Janha (San Francisco: Jossey-Bass, 1983), 73–79; Mark Silver, "Reflections on Diversity: A White Man's Perspective," *Diversity Factor,* Summer 1995, 34–39; Janet E. Helms, *Affirmative Action: Who Benefits?* (Washington, D.C.: American Psychological Association, 1996).

46. Margaret D. Pusch, ed., *Multicultural Education* (Chicago: Intercultural Network, 1981); Gerald Jackson, "The Implementation of an Intraracial Awareness Coaching Program," *Corporate Headquarters,* Winter 1987, 9–30; Joyce King, "Dysconscious Racism"; Natalie Porter, "Empowering Supervisees to Empower Others: A Culturally Responsive Supervision Model," *Hispanic Journal of Behavioral Sciences* 16, no. 1 (1994): 43–56.

47. David Thomas and Robin Ely, "Making Differences Matter: A New Paradigm for Managing Diversity," *Harvard Business Review,* Sept.–Oct. 1996), 79–90.

48. Ricky Sherover-Marcuse, "Towards a Perspective on Unlearning Racism: Twelve Working Assumptions," *Issues in Cooperation and Power* 7 (Fall 1981): 14–15; Batts, "An Experiential Workshop"; Linda A. Camino, "Confronting Intolerance and Promoting Multiculturalism: Frameworks and Strategies for Adults, Youth, and Communities" (paper prepared for the Sun Prairie Research Project, Univ. of Wisconsin, 1994).

49. "An Open Letter to My Sister Angela Y. Davis," by James Baldwin, in Angela Y. Davis and others, *If They Come in the Morning: Voices of Resistance* (New York: Third Press, 1971).

50. Martin Luther King Jr., *The Words of Martin Luther King Jr.* (New York: Newmarket Press, 1983), 91.

51. King, *Strength to Love.*

22. WHAT IS JUSTICE IN CONFLICT RESOLUTION PRACTICE?

1. From "God Grew Tired of Us," a film directed by Christopher Quinn and Tommy Walker. http://www.spiritualityandpractice.com/teachers/teachers.php?id=239&g=1.

# Bibliography

Adams, W. A. "Then There Were None." *Honolulu Advertiser,* Nov. 24, 2003, E3.

Adams, Maurianne, Lee Anne Bell, and Pat Griffin, eds. *Teaching for Diversity and Social Justice.* New York: Routledge, 1997.

Aiu, Mary. *Eliminating Health Disparities: Conversations with Pacific Islanders.* Scotts Valley, Calif.: ETR Publishing, 2004.

Akbar, Na'im. *Chains and Images of Psychological Slavery.* Jersey City, N.J.: New Mind Productions, 1984.

Alliance of African/African American Peacemakers. "A Call to Action—A Call for Unity." 1998–99. http://www.gmu.edu/departments/NCPCR/AAAP.html.

"An Emerging American Progressive Ideology for the Year 2000." *Social Policy,* Spring 1987, 26.

Anderson, Claud. *Black Labor, White Wealth.* Edgewood, Md.: Duncan and Duncan, 1994.

Andrade, N., R. Johnson, J. Edman, G. Danko, L. Nahulu, G. Makini, N. Yuen, J. Waldron, A. Yates, and J. McDermott. "Non-traditional and Traditional Treatment of Hawaiian and Non-Hawaiian Adolescents." *Hawai'i Medical Journal* 53 (1994): 344–47.

Au, K. H., and A. Kawakami. "Research Currents: Talk Story and Learning to Read." *Language Arts* 62, no. 4 (1985): 406–11.

Au, W. W. K. "What the Tour Guide Didn't Tell Me: Tourism, Colonialism, and Resistance in Hawai'i." In *Rethinking Our Classrooms,* vol. 2, ed. B. Bigelow. Milwaukee: Rethinking Schools, 1999.

Auerbach, Jerold S. *Justice Without Law?* Oxford: Oxford Univ. Press, 1983.

Avruch, Kevin. "Type I and Type II Errors in Culturally Sensitive Conflict Resolution Practice." *Conflict Resolution Quarterly* 20, no. 3 (2003): 360.

Bailey, D. "Life in the Intersection: Race/Ethnic Relations and Conflict Resolution." *The Fourth R* 78 (1997): 18–19.

Bailey, Sharon. "Diverse Traditions." *Newsletter of the National Conference on Peacemaking and Conflict Resolution,* 2001.

Bailey, Steve. "A Chance to Lead." *Boston Globe,* Jan. 26, 2005.

Baker, M., V. French, Mary Adams Trujillo, and Leah Wing. "Impact on Diverse Populations: How CRE Has Not Addressed the Needs of Diverse Populations." In *Does It Work? The Case for Conflict Resolution Education in Our Nation's Schools,* ed. Tricia S. Jones and Daniel Kmitta. Washington, D.C.: CREnet, 2000.

Baron, Linda. "Commentary: The Case for the Field of Community Mediation." *Conflict Resolution Quarterly* 22, no. 1–2 (2004): 135–44.

Batts, Valerie. "An Experiential Workshop: Introduction to Multiculturalism." In *Toward Ethnic Diversification in Psychology Education and Training,* ed. George Stricker and Elizabeth Davis-Russell, 9–16. Washington, D.C.: American Psychological Association, 1990.

———. "An Overview of Strategies for Creating a Multicultural Workforce." *Consulting Psychology Bulletin,* Winter 1990, 3–6.

———. "Modern Racism: A T. A. Perspective." *Transactional Analysis Journal* 12, no. 3 (1983): 207–9.

———. *Modern Racism: New Melody for the Same Old Tunes.* Cambridge, Mass.: Episcopal Divinity School Occasional Papers, 1998.

Bell, Derrick. *Confronting Authority: Reflections of an Ardent Protester.* Boston: Beacon Press, 1994.

Bell, Lee Anne. "Theoretical Foundations for Social Justice Education." In *Teaching for Diversity and Social Justice,* ed. Maurianne Adams, Lee Anne Bell, and Pat Griffin. New York: Routledge, 1997.

Berg-Schlosser, Dirk. *Tradition and Change in Kenya: A Comparative Analysis of Seven Major Ethnic Groups.* Munich: Ferdinand Schöningh, 1984.

Berkhofer, Robert F., Jr. *The White Man's Indian: Images of the American Indian from Columbus to the Present.* New York: Vintage Books, 1979.

Bernheimer, Richard. *Wild Men in the Middle Ages: A Study in Art, Sentiment, and Demonology.* Cambridge, Mass.: Harvard Univ. Press, 1952.

Bhabha, Homi K. *The Location of Culture.* London: Routledge, 1994.

Bingham, Lisa B. "Employment Dispute Resolution: The Case of Mediation." *Conflict Resolution Quarterly* 22, no. 1–2 (2004): 145–74.

Birkhoff, Juliana. "Mediators' Perspectives on Power: A Window into a Profession?" Ph.D. diss., George Mason Univ., 2000.

Blackburn, Thomas C., and Kat Anderson, eds. *Before the Wilderness: Environmental Management by Native Californians.* Menlo Park, Calif.: Ballena Press, 1993.

Borg, Walter R., and Meredith Damien Gail. *Educational Research: An Introduction.* New York: Longman, 1989.

Boulle, Laurence, and Hwee Hwee Teh. *Mediation: Principles, Process, Practice.* Singapore: Butterworths Asia, 2000.

Braden, Anne. "Lessons from a History of Struggle." *Southern Exposure* 8, no. 2 (1980): 56–61.

Branca, Laura Ward. "Culture Is to People Like Water Is to Fish." *Community Mediator,* Summer 2004.

Brave Heart-Jordan, Maria Yellow Horse. "The Return to the Sacred Path: Healing from Historical Trauma and Historical Unresolved Grief among the Lakota." Ph.D. diss., Smith College School for Social Work, 1995.

Brown, Joyce, and Valerie Batts. "Helping Blacks Cope with and Overcome the Personal Effects of Racism." Paper delivered at the Annual Convention of the American Psychological Association, Los Angeles, 1985.

Burger, W. "Isn't There a Better Way?" *American Bar Association Journal* 68 (1982): 274–77.

Bush, Robert A. Baruch, and Joseph P. Folger. *The Promise of Mediation: Responding to Conflict through Empowerment and Recognition.* San Francisco: Jossey-Bass, 1994.

Cajete, Gregory. *Native Science: Natural Laws of Interdependence.* Santa Fe: Clear Light, 1999.

Camino, Linda A. "Confronting Intolerance and Promoting Multiculturalism: Frameworks and Strategies for Adults, Youth, and Communities." Paper prepared for the Sun Prairie Research Project, Univ. of Wisconsin, 1994.

Capitman, John. "Symbolic Racism Theory Criteria for Individual Differences Measures of Prejudice and the Validity of the Feeling Thermometer." Ph.D. diss., Duke Univ., 1980.

Chester, Mark A., and James Crowfoot. "Racism in Higher Education I: An Organizational Analysis." Center for Research on Social Organization, Univ. of Michigan, Ann Arbor, working paper no. 412, 1989.

———. "Racism in Higher Education II: Challenging Racism and Promoting Multiculturalism in Higher Education Organizations." Center for Research on Social Organization, Univ. of Michigan, Ann Arbor, working paper no. 558, 1997.

Cobb, Sara. "A Narrative Perspective on Mediation: Toward the Materialization of the 'Storytelling' Metaphor." In *New Directions in Mediation: Communication Research and Perspectives,* ed. Joseph P. Folger and Tricia S. Jones, 48–63. Thousand Oaks, Calif.: Sage, 1994.

Cobb, Sara, and Janet Rifkin. "Practice and Paradox." In *Narrative Mediation: A New Approach to Conflict Resolution,* ed. J. Winslade and G. Monk, 35–65. San Francisco: Jossey-Bass, 2000.

Cones, James H., Denise Janha, and John Ford Noonan. "Exploring Racial Assumptions with Faculty." In *Teaching Minority Students,* ed. James H. Cones, John Ford Noonan, and Denise Janha. San Francisco: Jossey-Bass, 1983.

Conquergood, Dwight. "Rethinking Ethnography: Towards a Critical Cultural Politics." *Communication Monographs* 58 (1991): 179–204.

Cooper, Christopher. "Mediation in Black and White: Unequal Distribution of Empowerment by Police." In *Not Guilty: Twelve Black Men Speak Out on Law, Justice, and Life,* ed. Jabari Asim. New York: Amistad, 2001.

Crenshaw, K., N. Gotanda, G. Peller, and K. Thomas. *Critical Race Theory: Key Writings that Formed the Movement.* New York: New Press, 1995.

Cross, William E. *Shades of Black.* Philadelphia: Temple Univ. Press, 1991.

Daniels, J., M. D'Andrea, and R. Heck., "Moral Development and Hawaiian Youths: Does Gender Make a Difference?" *Journal of Counseling and Development* 74 (1995): 90–92.

Davidheiser, Mark. "Mediation and Multiculturalism: Domestic and International Challenges." http://www.beyondintractability.org/essay/mediation_multiculturalism/?nid=1294.

Davids, Fahkry. "Frantz Fanon: The Struggle for Inner Freedom, Part 2." *Free Associations* 6, no. 18 (1996): 205–34.

Davis, Albie. "The Logic Behind the Magic of Mediation." *Negotiation Journal* 5, no. 1, (1989): 23.

Davis, Angela Y., and others. *If They Come in the Morning: Voices of Resistance.* New York: Third Press, 1971.

Delgado, Richard, Chris Dunn, Pamela Brown, Helena Lee, and David Hubbert. "Fairness and Formality: Minimizing the Risk of Prejudice in Alternative Dispute Resolution." *Wisconsin Law Review* 6 (1985): 1359–1404.

Delgado, Richard, and Jean Stefancic, eds. *Critical White Studies: Looking Behind the Mirror.* Philadelphia: Temple Univ. Press, 1997.

———. *Critical Race Theory: An Introduction.* New York: NYU Press, 2001.

Deloria, Philip. *Playing Indian.* New Haven: Yale Univ. Press, 1999.

Dominelli, Lena. *Anti-Oppressive Social Work Theory and Practice.* New York: Palgrave Macmillan, 2002.

Dovidio, John F., and Samuel L. Gaertner, eds. *Prejudice, Discrimination, and Racism.* Orlando: Academic Press, 1986.

Durkheim, Emile. *The Elementary Forms of the Religious Life*. London: George Allen and Unwin, 1976.

Fanon, Frantz. *The Wretched of the Earth*. New York: Grove Press, 1965.

Feagin, Joe R., and Hernan Vera. *White Racism: The Basics*. New York: Routledge, 1995.

Flagg, Barbara J. "The Transparency Phenomenon, Race-Neutral Decision Making and Discriminatory Intent." In *Critical White Studies: Looking Behind the Mirror*, ed. Richard Delgado and Jean Stefancic. Philadelphia: Temple Univ. Press, 1997.

Forester, John. *The Deliberative Practitioner: Encouraging Participatory Planning Processes*. Cambridge, Mass.: MIT Press, 1999.

Franklin, John Hope. "A Continuing Climate of Racism." *Duke University: A Magazine for Alumni and Friends* 71, no. 2 (1984): 12–16.

Freire, Paolo. *Pedagogy of the Oppressed*. New York: Herder and Herder, 1972. Reprint, New York: Continuum, 1989.

Geertz, Clifford. *The Interpretation of Cultures: Selected Essays*. 1973. Reprint, New York: Basic Books, 2000.

Gerard, Jean M., and Cheryl Buehler. "Multiple Risk Factors in the Family Environment and Youth Problem Behaviors." *Journal of Marriage and the Family,* May 1999.

Girard, Kathryn, Janet Rifkin, and Annette Townley. *Peaceful Persuasion: A Guide to Creating Mediation Dispute Resolution Programs on College Campuses*. Amherst: Univ. of Massachusetts, 1985.

Goldberg, Stephen, Eric Greene, and Frank Sander, eds. *Dispute Resolution*. Boston: Little, Brown, 1985.

Gomez, Lisa Marie. "Racial Slurs Also Reported on Field." *San Antonio Express-News,* Oct. 2004.

Goodman, Diane J. *Promoting Diversity and Social Justice: Educating People from Privileged Groups*. Thousand Oaks, Calif.: Sage, 2001.

Gordon, Lewis R. *Existentia Africana: Understanding Africana Existential Thought*. New York: Routledge, 2000.

Griffin, Jean T. "Racism and Humiliation in the African American Community." *Journal of Primary Prevention* 12, no. 2 (1991): 149–67.

Grillo, Trina. "The Mediation Alternative: Process Dangers for Women." *Yale Law Journal,* 1991, 1545–1610.

Gulliver, Peter. *Disputes and Negotiations: A Cross Cultural Perspective*. New York: Academic Press, 1979.

Hacker, Andrew. *Two Nations: Black and White, Separate, Hostile, Unequal.* New York: Oxford Univ. Press, 1992.

Hairston, Cherise. "African Americans in Mediation Literature: A Neglected Population." *Mediation Quarterly* (now *Conflict Resolution Quarterly*) 16, no. 4, 1999.

Hammer, Ben. "Black, White Performance Gap Widens, Study Finds." *Black Issues in Higher Education,* Nov. 6, 2003.

Harrington, Christine B. *Shadow Justice: The Ideology and Institutionalization of Alternatives to Court.* Westport, Conn.: Greenwood, 1985.

Harris, Thomas E., and John C. Sherblom. *Small Group and Team Communication.* Boston: Allyn and Bacon, 2002.

Hawai'i Department of Health. *The Hawai'i Youth Risk Behavior Survey of Statewide Highlights of Middle and High Schools.* Department of Health, 1999.

Hazel-Trice, Edney. "The State of Black America; National Urban League's Annual Report Shows Stark Disparities Between Blacks and Whites; Officials Say Many of the Earlier Gains Are in Danger of Being Erased." *Sacramento Observer,* Apr. 13, 2005.

Helms, Janet E. *Affirmative Action: Who Benefits?* Washington, D.C.: American Psychological Association, 1996.

———. *Black and White Racial Identity: Theory, Research, and Practice.* New York: Greenwood Press, 1990.

Herman, Judith. *Trauma and Recovery: The Aftermath of Violence—From Domestic Abuse to Political Terror.* New York: Basic Books, 1997.

Hermann, Michele. "New Mexico Research Examines Impact of Gender and Ethnicity in Mediation." In *The Conflict and Culture Reader,* ed. Pat K. Chew. New York: New York Univ. Press, 2001.

Hilliard, Asa G. *The Maroon Within Us.* Baltimore: Black Classic Press, 1995.

Hippensteele, Susan. "Activist Research and Social Narratives: Dialectics of Power, Privilege, and Institutional Change." In *Researching Sexual Violence Against Women: Methodological and Personal Perspectives,* ed. Martin D. Schwartz. Thousand Oaks, Calif.: Sage, 1997.

Hobley, C. B. *Ethnology of Akamba and Other East African Tribes.* Cambridge: Cambridge Univ. Press, 1910.

Huhndorf, Shari. *Going Native, Going Native: Figuring the Indian in Modern American Culture.* Ithaca, N.Y.: Cornell Univ. Press, 2001.

Hurdle-Price, Lynne. "Building an Organization Committed to Diversity: Is ACR Singing a New Tune, or Is This The Same Old Song?" *ACResolution* 3, no. 1 (2003): 4.

Irvin, Howard H., Michael Benjamin, and Jose San-Pedro. "Family Mediation and Cultural Diversity: Mediating with Latino Families." *Mediation Quarterly* 16, no. 4 (1999): 325–39.

Jackson, Gerald. "The Implementation of an Intraracial Awareness Coaching Program." *Corporate Headquarters,* Winter 1987, 9–30.

Jacobson, Cardell K. "Resistance to Affirmative Action: Self-interest or Racism?" *Journal of Conflict Resolution* 29 (1985): 306–29

Johnson, Marvin E. "Diversity Resistance." http://www.mediate.com/pfriendly.cfm ?id=708.

Jones, James M. "Racism in Black and White: A Bicultural Model of Reaction and Evolution." *In Eliminating Racism: Profiles in Controversy,* ed. Phyllis A. Katz and Dalmas A. Taylor. New York: Plenum Press, 1988.

———. *Prejudice and Racism.* Reading, Mass.: Addison-Wesley, 1972.

Jones, Tricia S. "Conflict Resolution Education: The Field, the Findings, and the Future." *Conflict Resolution Quarterly* 22, no. 1–2 (2004): 233–68.

Jordan, Terry G. "Perceptual Regions in Texas." In *Geographical Review* 68 (July 1978).

———. "The Texan Appalachia." In *Annals of the Association of American Geographers* 60 (Sept. 1970).

Kamhis, Jacob. "Healing with Hawaiian Ho'oponopono." *Aloha Magazine* 15, no. 4 (1992): 45–49.

Katz, Joseph. "White Faculty Struggling with the Effects of Racism." In *Teaching Minority Students,* ed. James H. Cones, John Ford Noonan, and Denise Janha. San Francisco: Jossey-Bass, 1983.

Katz, Phyllis A., and Dalmas A. Taylor. Introduction to *Eliminating Racism: Profiles in Controversy.* New York: Plenum Press, 1988.

Kawena Puku'i, Mary, E. Haertig, and C. Lee. *Nana I Ke Kumu: Look to the Source.* Honolulu: Queen Lili'uokalani Children's Center, 1972.

Kelly, Joan B. "Family Mediation Research: Is There Empirical Support for the Field?" *Conflict Resolution Quarterly* 22, no. 1–2 (2004): 3–36.

Kenyatta, Jomo. *Facing Mount Kenya.* Nairobi: Kenway, 1978.

King, Joyce E. "Dysconscious Racism: Ideology, Identity, and the Miseducation of Teachers." *Journal of Negro Education* 60, no. 2 (1991): 133–45.

King, Martin Luther Jr. *The Words of Martin Luther King Jr.* New York: Newmarket Press, 1983.

———. *Strength to Love.* Philadelphia: Fortress Press, 1981.

King, Mathew. *Noble Red Man: Lakota Wisdomkeeper Mathew King,* ed. Harvey Arden. Hillsboro, Ore.: Beyond Words, 1994.

Koetke, William H. *The Final Empire: The Collapse of Civilization and the Seed of the Future.* Portland, Ore.: Arrow Point Press, 1993.

Kolb, Deborah, and Associates. *When Talk Works: Profiles of Mediators.* San Francisco: Jossey-Bass, 1994.

Leal, Ray. "Building Your Own Campus Mediation Program: Different Models of College and University Programs." Presentation at the Ninth Annual National Association for Mediation in Education conference, Amherst, Mass., 1994.

———. "Conflicting Views of Discipline in San Antonio Schools." *Education and Urban Society* 27, no. 1 (1994): 35–44.

———. "From Collegiality to Confrontation: Faculty to Faculty Conflicts." In *Conflict Management in Higher Education,* ed. S. A. Holton. San Francisco: Jossey-Bass, 1995.

———. "La Onda: Strategies for Hispanic Healing." Phoenix: National Conference on Peacemaking and Conflict Resolution, 1999.

———. "The Next Generation of College and University Campus Mediation Programs." San Antonio: Presentation before the annual conference of the Society of Professionals in Dispute Resolution, 1993.

Leary, Joy DeGruy. *Post Traumatic Slave Syndrome: America's Legacy of Enduring Injury and Healing.* Milwaukie, Ore.: Uptone Press, 2005.

LeBaron, Michelle. "Mediation and Multicultural Reality." *Peace and Conflict Studies,* June 1998, 41–56.

Lederach, John Paul. *Preparing for Peace: Conflict Transformation Across Cultures.* New York: Syracuse Univ. Press, 1995.

———. *The Little Book of Conflict Transformation.* Intercourse, Penn.: Good Books, 2003.

Leopold, Aldo. *A Sand County Almanac, With Essays on Conservation from Round River.* New York: Sierra Club/Ballantine, 1970.

Lindblom, Gerhard. *The Akamba in British East Africa: An Ethnological Monograph,* 2nd ed. Upsala: Appelberg, 1920.

Lipsky, David B., and Ariel Avgar. "Commentary: Research on Employment Dispute Resolution: Toward a New Paradigm." *Conflict Resolution Quarterly* 22, no. 1–2 (2004): 175–89.

Lipsky, Suzanne. *Internalized Racism*. Seattle: Rational Island, 1978.

Lipsyte, Robert. "R.I.P., Tonto." *Esquire,* Feb. 1994, 39–45.

López, Gerardo R., and Laurence Parker. "Conclusion." In *Interrogating Racism in Qualitative Research Methodology,* ed. Gerardo R. López and Laurence Parker. New York: Peter Lang, 2003.

Mabry, Cynthia R. "African Americans Are Not Carbon Copies of White Americans: The Role of African American Culture in Mediation of Family Disputes." *Ohio State Journal on Dispute Resolution* 13 (1997–98): 405, 420–35.

Major, B., and C. P. Eccleston, "Stigma and Social Exclusion." In *The Social Psychology of Inclusion and Exclusion,* ed. Dominic Abrams, Michael A. Hogg, and Jose Marques. New York: Psychology Press, 2005.

Mandela, Nelson. *Long Walk to Freedom: The Autobiography of Nelson Mandela.* New York: Little, Brown, 1994.

Matsuda, Mari. "Looking to the Bottom: Critical Legal Studies and Reparations." In *Critical Race Theory: Key Writings that Formed the Movement,* ed. K. Crenshaw, N. Gotanda, G. Peller, and K. Thomas. New York: New Press, 1995.

Mayer, Bernard. *Beyond Neutrality: Confronting the Crisis in Conflict Resolution.* San Francisco: Jossey-Bass, 2004.

Mbiti, John S. *African Religions and Philosophy.* London: Heinemann, 1969.

McConahay, John, Beatrice Hardee, and Valerie Batts. "Has Racism Declined in America?" *Journal of Conflict Resolution* 2, no. 4 (1981): 563–79.

McConahay, John, and James Hough. "Symbolic Racism." *Journal of Social Issues* 32, no. 2 (1976): 23–45.

McIntosh, Peggy. "White Privilege and Male Privilege: A Personal Account of Coming to See Correspondences through Work in Women Studies." Working paper no. 189, Stone Center, Wellesley College, 1988.

McLemore, S. Dale, Harriett D. Romo, and Susan Gonzalez Baker. *Racial and Ethnic Relations in America.* Boston: Allyn and Bacon, 2001.

Meier, Deborah. *The Power of Their Ideas.* Boston: Beacon Press, 1995.

Meyer, Bernard. *Beyond Neutrality: Confronting the Crisis in Conflict Resolution.* San Francisco: Jossey-Bass, 2005.

Middleton, John. *The Kikuyu and Kamba of Kenya.* London: International African Institute, 1965.

Miller, Norman, and Marilynn Brewer. "Categorizing Effect on In Group and Out Group Perception." In *Prejudice, Discrimination, and Racism,* ed. John F. Dovidio and Samuel L. Gaertner. Orlando: Academic Press, 1986.

Minnis, Paul E., and Wayne J. Elisens, eds. *Biodiversity and Native America*. Norman: Univ. of Oklahoma Press, 2001.

Minow, Martha. *Making All the Difference: Inclusion, Exclusion, and American Law*. Ithaca, N.Y.: Cornell Univ. Press, 1990.

Moku'au, N. "Responding to Pacific Islanders: Culturally Competent Perspectives for Substance Abuse Prevention." Center for Substance Abuse Prevention Cultural Competence Series 8, Special Collaborative Edition. Washington, D.C.: Department of Health and Human Sciences publication no. SMA 98-3195, 1998.

Morse, Jennifer Roback. "Parents or Prisons." *Policy Review* 120 (Aug.–Sept. 2003). http://www.hoover.org/publications/policyreview/3448276.html.

Mutungi, O. K. *The Legal Aspects of Witchcraft in East Africa With Particular Reference to Kenya*. Nairobi: East Africa Literature Bureau, 1977.

Myers, Linda James. *Understanding an Afrocentric World View: Introduction to an Optimal Psychology*. Dubuque, Iowa: Kendall/Hunt, 1988.

Nabokov, Peter, ed. *Native American Testimony: A Chronicle of Indian-White Relations from Prophecy to the Present, 1492–1992*. Reprint, New York: Penguin Books, 1991.

Nader, Laura. "Controlling Processes in the Practice of Law: Hierarchy and Pacification in the Movement to Re-Form Dispute Ideology." In *Ohio State Journal on Dispute Resolution* 9, no. 1 (1993): 1–25.

Ndeti, Kivuto. *Elements of Akamba Life*. Nairobi: East African Publishing House, 1972.

New Mexico Center for Dispute Resolution. *Student Mediation in Secondary Schools: Training and Implementation Guide*. Albuquerque, 1995.

"News and Views: A Comprehensive Guide to Black Student College Graduation Rates." *Journal of Blacks in Higher Education,* Apr. 30, 1999.

Nieves, Evelyn. "Prosperity's Losers: A Special Report; Homeless Defy Cities' Drives to Move Them." *New York Times,* 7 Dec. 1999.

Nishihara, D. P. "Culture, Counseling, and Ho'oponopono: An Ancient Model in a Modern Context." *Personnel and Guidance Journal* 56, no. 9 (1978): 562–66.

Oliver, Melvin L., and Thomas M. Shapiro. *Black Wealth/White Wealth*. New York: Routledge, 1995.

Palmer, Michael, and Simon Roberts. *Dispute Processes: ADR and the Primary Forms of Decision Making*. London: Butterworths; Charlottesville, Va.: Lexis Law Publishing, 1998.

Parents Without Partners. "Facts About Single Parent Families." www.parentswithout partners.org.

Penwill, D. J. *Kamba Customary Law.* Nairobi: Kenya Literature Bureau, 1951.

Pettigrew, Thomas F. "Modern Racism in the United States." *Revue Internationale de Psychologie Sociale* 2, no. 3 (1989): 291–303.

Pipkin, Ronald M., and Janet Rifkin. "The Social Organization in Alternative Dispute Resolution: Implications for Professionalization of Mediation." *Justice System Journal* 9 (1984): 202–27.

Porter, Natalie. "Empowering Supervisees to Empower Others: A Culturally Responsive Supervision Model." *Hispanic Journal of Behavioral Sciences* 16, no. 1 (1994): 43–56.

Puku'i, Mary Kawena, E. Haertig, and C. Lee. *Nana I Ke Kumu: Look to the Source.* Honolulu: Queen Lili'uokalani Children's Center, 1972.

Pusch, Margaret D., ed. *Multicultural Education.* Chicago: Intercultural Network, 1981.

Raiffa, Howard. *The Art and Science of Negotiation.* Cambridge: Belknap Press, 2005.

Raines, Franklin. "40 Acres and a Mortgage." *Sojourners,* Sept.–Oct. 2002.

Rawls, John. *A Theory of Justice.* Cambridge, Mass.: Harvard Univ. Press, 1971.

Reschly, J. "Minority Students in Gifted and Special Education." Presentation to the White House Commission on Excellence in Special Education, 2002.

Resoldo, Renato. *Culture and Truth: The Remaking of Social Analysis.* Boston: Beacon Press, 1993.

Rifkin, Janet, Jonathan Millen, and Sara Cobb. "Toward a New Discourse for Mediation: A Critique of Neutrality." *Mediation Quarterly* 9, no. 2 (Winter 1991): 151–65.

Robinson, Lori. *I Will Survive: The African-American Guide to Healing from Sexual Assault and Abuse.* Emeryville, Calif.: Seal Press, 2002.

Roces, Alfredo, and Grace Roces. *Culture Shock! Philippines: A Survival Guide to Customs and Etiquette.* Singapore: Marshall Cavendish Corporation, 2007.

Ropers, Richard B., and Dan J. Pence. *American Prejudice.* New York: Insight Books, 1995.

Ross, Thomas. "The Richmond Narratives." In *Critical Race Theory: The Cutting Edge,* ed. Richard Delgado and Jean Stefancic. Philadelphia: Temple Univ. Press, 1995.

Rouhana, Nadim N., and Susan H. Korper. "Case Analysis: Dealing with the Dilemmas Posed by Power Asymmetry in Intergroup Conflict." *Negotiation Journal,* Oct. 1996, 353–66.

Roy, Beth. *Some Trouble With Cows: Making Sense of Social Conflict.* Berkeley: Univ. of California Press, 1994.

Ryan, William. *Blaming the Victim.* New York: Vintage Books, 1976.

———. *Equality.* New York: Pantheon Books, 1981.

Saposnek, Donald T. "Commentary: The Future and the History of Family Mediation Research." *Conflict Resolution Quarterly* 22, no. 1–2 (2004): 37–54.

Saragoza, Alex M., Concepcion R. Juarez, Abel Valenzuela Jr., and Oscar Gonzalez. "Who Counts? Title VII and the Hispanic Classification." In *The Latino Condition: A Critical Reader,* ed. Richard Delgado and Jean Stefancic. New York: NYU Press, 1998.

Schrock-Shenk, Carolyn, ed. *Mediation and Facilitation Training Manual: Foundations and Skills for Constructive Conflict Transformation.* Akron, Penn.: Mennonite Conciliation Service, 2000.

Sherman, Richard T. *Lakota Ecology Stewardship Model.* Kyle, S.D.: Oglala Lakota (Sioux) Parks and Recreation Authority, Dec. 1994.

Sherover-Marcuse, Ricky. "Towards a Perspective on Unlearning Racism: Twelve Working Assumptions." *Issues in Cooperation and Power* 7 (Fall 1981): 14–15.

Shonholtz, Ray. "Neighborhood Justice Systems: Work, Structure and Guiding Principles." *Mediation Quarterly* 5 (1984): 3–30.

Shook, E. V. *Ho'oponopono.* Honolulu: Univ. of Hawai'i Program for Cultural Studies, 1985.

Shujaa, Mwalimu J., ed. *Too Much Schooling, Too Little Education: A Paradox of Black Life in White Societies.* Trenton, N.J.: Africa World Press, 1994.

Silver, Mark. "Reflections on Diversity: A White Man's Perspective." *Diversity Factor,* Summer 1995, 34–39.

Small, Stephen. "The Contours of Racialization: Structures, Representations and Resistance in the United States." In *Race, Identity, and Citizenship: A Reader,* ed. Rodolfo D. Torres, Louis F. Miron, and Jonathan Xavier Inda. Malden, Mass.: Blackwell, 1999.

Snyder, Gary. *The Practice of the Wild: Essays by Gary Snyder.* San Francisco: North Point Press, 1990.

Soeffner, Hans-Georg. *The Order of Rituals: The Interpretation of Everyday Life.* New Brunswick, N.J.: Transaction, 1997.

Sonn, Mary, and Valerie Batts. "Strategies for Changing Personal Attitudes of White Racism." Paper delivered at the Annual Convention of the American Psychological Association, Los Angeles, 1985.

Standing Bear, Luther. *Land of the Spotted Eagle.* Lincoln: Univ. of Nebraska Press, 1933. Reprint, 1978.

Stanko, Elizabeth A. "'I Second That Emotion': Reflections on Feminism, Emotionality, and Research on Sexual Violence." In *Researching Sexual Violence Against Women: Methodological and Personal Perspectives,* ed. Martin D. Schwartz. Thousand Oaks, Calif.: Sage, 1997.

Stegner, Wallace. *Wolf Willow: A History, a Story and a Memory of the Last Plains Frontier.* Reprint, New York: Penguin Books, 1990.

Steinberg, Laurence. "Youth Violence: Do Parents and Families Make a Difference?" *National Institute of Justice Journal,* no. 243 (Apr. 2000). http://www.ncjrs.gov/pdffiles1/jr000243f.pdf.

Stodden, R. "Native Hawaiian Youth Offender Successful Re-entry Project Grant Proposal with Hilo Board of Education." 1999.

Surgeon General's Office. *Youth Violence: A Report of the Surgeon General.* December 2001. http://www.surgeongeneral.gov/library/youthviolence/chapter4/sec1.html.

Susskind, Lawrence, and Jeffrey Cruikshank. *Breaking the Impasse: Consensual Approaches to Resolving Public Disputes.* New York: Basic Books, 1987.

Swim, Janel K., Kathryn J. Aikin, Wayne S. Hall, and Barbara A. Hunter. "Sexism and Racism: Old-fashioned and Modern Prejudices." *Journal of Personality and Social Psychology* 68, no. 2 (1995): 199–214.

Taylor, Jared. *Paved with Good Intentions: The Failure of Race Relations in Contemporary America.* New York: Carroll and Graf, 1992.

Thomas, A. F. "Oaths, Ordeals and the Kenya Courts: A Policy Analysis." *Human Organisation* 33, no. 1 (1974): 60.

Thomas, David, and Robin Ely: "Making Differences Matter: A New Paradigm for Managing Diversity." *Harvard Business Review,* Sept.–Oct. 1996, 79–90.

Todorov, Tzvetan. "Race and Racism." In *Theories of Race and Racism,* ed. Les Back and John Solomos. London: Routledge, 2000.

Torres-Raines, R. "Transculturation: A Faculty Development Model on the Texas-Mexico Border." College Station, Tex.: Alpha Kappa Delta Symposium, 1998.

Trenary, Sara Kristine. "Rethinking Neutrality: Race and ADR." *Dispute Resolution Journal,* Aug. 1999. http://findarticles.com/p/articles/mi_qa3923/is_/ai_n8873055.

Turner, David, and Elias Cheboud. "Advocacy and Conflict Resolution in Social Work: Can They Really Promote Justice? An Anti-Oppressive Approach." Univ.

of Victoria, British Columbia, July 2000. www.aforts.com/colloques_ouvrages/colloques/actes/interventions/turner_david.doc.

van den Berghe, Pierre L. *Race and Racism: A Comparative Perspective.* New York: John Wiley and Sons, 1967.

van der Kolk, Bessel A., Alexander C. McFarlane, and Lars Weisaeth, eds. *Traumatic Stress: The Effects of Overwhelming Experience on Mind, Body, and Society.* New York: Guilford Press, 1996.

Vargas, Roberto, and Frances F. Korten. *Movement Building for Transformative Change.* Bainbridge Island, Wash.: Positive Futures Network, 2006.

Vargas, Roberto, and Samuel C. Martinez. *Razalogia: Community Learning for a New Society.* Oakland, Calif.: Razagentes Associates, 1984.

Venuti, Len Tai. "A School without Walls." *Kamehameha Journal of Education* 5 (1994): 47–50.

Walker, Christy Cumberland. "The Myth of a Colorblind Society and the Need for Minority Dispute Resolution Organizations." *Family Mediation News,* Winter 2003.

Welsh, N. A. "The Thinning Vision of Self-Determination in Court-Connected Mediation: The Inevitable Price of Institutionalization?" *Harvard Negotiation Law Review* 6 (2001): 1–96.

West, Cornel. *Prophetic Thought in Postmodern Times.* Monroe, Maine: Common Courage Press, 1993.

White, Deborah Gray. *Ar'n't I Woman? Female Slaves in the Plantations South.* New York: W. W. Norton and Company, 1985.

Wilkinson, Todd. "Call of the Wild." *Denver Post Magazine,* May 21, 1995.

Willard, Tom. *Buffalo Soldiers.* New York: Forge, 1997.

Williams, Patricia J. *The Rooster's Egg.* Cambridge, Mass.: Harvard Univ. Press, 1995.

Wing, Leah. *Mediation and Social Justice.* Amherst: Univ. of Massachusetts, 2002.

Winslade, J., and G. Monk. *Narrative Mediation: A New Approach to Conflict Resolution.* San Francisco: Jossey-Bass Publisher, 2000.

Worster, Donald. *Under Western Skies: Nature and History in the American West.* New York: Oxford Univ. Press, 1992.

Wriggins, Jennifer. "Rape, Racism, and the Law." *Harvard Women's Law Journal* 6 (1983).

Wu, Frank H. *Yellow: Race in America Beyond Black and White.* New York: Basic Books, 2003.

Young, Iris Marion. *Inclusion and Democracy.* New York: Oxford Univ. Press, 2000.

# Index

Italic page numbers indicate figures and tables.